ISBN: 9781407722443

Published by:
HardPress Publishing
8345 NW 66TH ST #2561
MIAMI FL 33166-2626

Email: info@hardpress.net
Web: http://www.hardpress.net

ENGLAND AND ROME.

LONDON :
GILBERT AND RIVINGTON, PRINTERS,
ST. JOHN'S SQUARE.

ENGLAND AND ROME.

A DISCUSSION

OF THE

PRINCIPAL DOCTRINES AND PASSAGES OF HISTORY

IN COMMON DEBATE

BETWEEN THE

MEMBERS OF THE TWO COMMUNIONS.

BY

W. E. SCUDAMORE, M.A.

RECTOR OF DITCHINGHAM,

AND LATE FELLOW OF ST. JOHN'S COLLEGE, CAMBRIDGE.

LONDON:

RIVINGTONS, WATERLOO PLACE.

DEIGHTON, CAMBRIDGE.   J. H. PARKER, OXFORD.

1855.

ADVERTISEMENT.

THE present work originated in a reply to some "Letters on Roman Catholic Principles," published in a country journal nearly two years ago. The arguments which these advanced were neither new nor forcible; but as they derived a degree of persuasiveness from the candid and kind tone of the writer, it was thought desirable that they should receive an answer: and, at the instance of friends, I was induced, somewhat reluctantly, to undertake the task. The result was, that a series of letters appeared in the columns of the same journal, which are the groundwork of the several dissertations now offered to the reader.

The epistolary form of composition is attended by so many disadvantages, that it may be a question whether it would not have been better to abandon it in preparing for the press an edition otherwise much altered, and greatly enlarged. I have, nevertheless, determined to retain it, in the hope that it may tend to mitigate the prejudice, which most readers, perhaps, are apt to entertain against a work of this nature, by reminding them that the controversy was not of the author's seeking, but arose from an attack, not the less dangerous, because unavowed, upon the Church to which he owes the twofold duty of a son and servant. It will be seen, however, that no greater use has been made of the original correspondence, than serves to put the several subjects handled in a clear light, and in a form convenient for discussion. The volume is, therefore, complete in itself, and virtually has no dependence on any preceding publication.

The method attempted, explicitly for the most part, and in effect every where, has been to state each question with as much fulness and precision as seemed requisite, and then to support the representation given by authorities which must be allowed by all to be decisive upon the point at issue. The appeal, therefore, is not to holy Scrip-

ture as understood by ourselves, or to the principles of natural reason, from the use of which we
are in a great measure debarred by difference of
opinion as to the meaning of the one and the
proper application of the other; but to the Fathers
and Schoolmen, to mediæval divines, and recent
historians in the communion of Rome, and where
the doctrines of the Church of England are in
question, to her own formularies, and the consen-
tient teaching of her Reformers.

There is one portion of the work, which, while it
goes beyond the literal promise of the title-page,
may also, at first sight, appear occupied with a
matter of comparatively little moment. The greater
part of Letter IX. (which may be considered altogether in the light of an appendix, or supple-
mental chapter) is devoted to an examination of
M. Rohrbacher's defence of certain Popes who
lived in the earlier half of the tenth century. If
my remarks upon this subject had merely affected
the character of a particular book, I should not
have thought it necessary to repeat them in the
elaborate form which they have assumed upon
revision. But interests far higher are involved.

False doctrine is supported by an appeal to falsified history. It is, therefore, a plain duty, in those to whom the means of knowing the truth have been given, to lose no opportunity that may be offered for its vindication.

To provide against possible inaccuracy in the citation of Books, Chapters, &c. in the Notes, the volume and page are generally given too. The editions used are described by their date and place of publication, when first quoted.

CONTENTS.

PART II. Pp. 136—170.

PART IV. Pp. 213—228.

LETTER VII. Pp. 290—320.

THE DOCTRINE OF PERSECUTION.

LETTER VIII.

DEVELOPMENT OF DOCTRINE. THEORY.— EXAMPLES.

PART I. Pp. 321—340.

.

SECT. IV. FURTHER EVIDENCE OF THE CORRUPT STATE OF THE
CHURCH IN THE TENTH CENTURY.

Testimonies of Atto of Vercelli and Rathierus of Verona.

CONCLUSION.

LETTER I.

I. ON THE INFALLIBILITY OF THE CHURCH. II. THE EARLY CHURCH OUR WITNESS TO THE CANON OF HOLY SCRIPTURE. III. THE EARLY CHURCH A SURE AND SUFFICIENT INTERPRETER OF THE BIBLE. IV. THE ENGLISH REFORMATION A RETURN TO THE DOCTRINES OF ANTIQUITY. V. THE MODERN ROMAN TEST OF DOCTRINE NOT APPLICABLE, IF IGNORANCE AND IMMORALITY CAN BECOME GENERAL IN THE CHURCH. VI. TESTIMONIES TO THE CORRUPT STATE OF WESTERN CHRISTENDOM FROM THE TWELFTH TO THE SIXTEENTH CENTURY.

MY DEAR SIR,

You will recognise in the following pages an enlarged edition of the reply which I thought it my duty to offer to your Letters on Roman Catholic Principles. It is presented to the public a second time, at the request of some valued members of the Church of England, to whose opinion in this matter I owe especial deference. You will observe that it has undergone some alteration, as well as enlargement, in the course of revision; but there is only one change in which you are more interested than the rest of my readers. In this reprint I have departed from the formality prescribed by custom to those who make a public journal the medium of their controversy, and venture to address myself to you directly, as to one

B

LETTER
I.

of whom, in spite of serious differences, I have learned to think with much esteem. The kindly spirit which pervades your Letters will both account to others for my desire to meet you thus face to face, and lead you, I persuade myself, to grant, without reluctance, the privilege of a friend to a respectful, though uncompromising, antagonist.

The public discussion of religious questions is rarely attended with much advantage. It is too apt to engender feelings which cloud the spiritual perception and are not compatible with the genuine love, or disinterested pursuit of truth. Nor does the mischief rest with the excited disputants. All those, and they are many, who are disposed to judge religion by the failings of its professors, are thus confirmed in their indifference or scepticism. There are times, however, when the reasons on which a general rule is founded will sanction our neglect of it; and such an occasion, unless I quite misread your tone and language, was furnished by the "Letters of a Saxon Catholic." Impressed with this belief, I readily entered upon the task which others proposed to me, and endeavoured to point out, as well on your own account, as for the truth's sake, some of the many and serious mistakes of fact and principle into which you had unconsciously fallen. I have had no reason to regret the step; at least, no evil can have ensued from a dis-

cussion which both, as I believe and trust, endeavoured to conduct in mutual charity, and in the
fear of God. The task which I attempted then in
haste and superficially I now resume at leisure,
and hope to prosecute at greater length. As we
proceed, you will, I dare say, occasionally find me
protesting against the errors which you hold, or the
means too often used by others to enforce or to defend them, in language which you may think severe
to harshness. Should it prove so, I intreat you not
for that reason to suppose that I am accusing *you* of
aught unworthy, or that I doubt the feelings and
intentions with which you entered upon this controversy. A re-examination of your arguments may
possibly have deepened my conviction of the
unsoundness of your cause, but has not affected
my estimate of yourself personally, or lessened
my anxiety to do you justice.

I. The question which first presents itself for
reconsideration respects the infallibility of the
Universal Church.

This is not, as you seem to think, a doctrine
peculiar to your communion, nor need we go to
Pope or Council for licence or encouragement to
hold it. Christ has Himself promised that "the
gates of hell shall not prevail against it," and in
that promise has sealed the charter of its infallibility. He has thus guaranteed its preservation
from all such error, in practice or in doctrine, as

would make it cease to be *His* Church. Observe, however, that He has not promised the same immunity from less destructive evils. In some things, therefore, the Universal Church may err. Nor has He promised a necessary continuance to any particular branch of it. For aught that we are told, one part after another may fall to ruin, and lose even the name of a Christian community. We only know that the Church of Christ, whether composed of many members or of few, cannot entirely fail; and from this we infer that no truth or ordinance which is essential to its existence will ever be wholly lost, or utterly corrupted. In this sense we thankfully acknowledge that the Church is infallible. The promise must be fulfilled; but then it may be fulfilled without recourse to your hypothesis; and we observe further, that both Scripture and analogy would lead us to expect a very different accomplishment. These give some reason to apprehend that when the Lord returns to judgement, the spring of living water in His Church, though still unfailing, will yield but little, and to few; that, as with Israel our solemn type, a "remnant" only will be found of all our tribes. "When the Son of man cometh, shall He find faith upon the earth?" Yet whether those fearful words of His will really be fulfilled as I suggest; and if so, where that remnant will be found; whether it will be the spiritual offspring of the present Greek, or

Roman, or English communion, or will be gathered, as His faithful ones are now gathered, from amidst them all, these are, and must remain, among those "secret things which belong unto the Lord our God." One thing alone is certain, that the promise was not to any single branch, as to the English or the Roman, but to the Universal Church, wrapped up, as it then was, in the Apostles, our common fathers in the faith.

From this *indefectibility* of the Church, however, the modern Roman Catholic,—on no authority, with no necessity,—but rather against the whole tenor of Scripture, and the belief of the first ages, and to the great and manifest injury of all Christendom,—infers its claim to an entire and absolute inerrancy in faith and morals; and then, with a still greater daring, proceeds to arrogate the exclusive possession of these high privileges to his own favourite communion. One consequence of this crime against truth and right is very grievous. Like every other sin which man commits, it is made to work out the most awful part of its own punishment. The presumed safeguard from error becomes, in the result, its chief support and source of strength. For to maintain the inerrancy of the Church is to claim a Divine sanction for whatever the Church has taught, and thus, by denying the necessity, to preclude the hope, of reformation. At the same time, by fostering a careless reliance on the received opinions of the day as a sufficient and safe rule of faith and duty, it facilitates the progress, and prepares a way for the ultimate authorization, of every new superstition or false theory in morals that may arise.

II. But you proceed to argue that we receive the Bible at the hands of the Church; and that, unless the latter be infallible, the genuineness of the book to which she bears witness is not capable of proof.

Here again the Church of England can go with you some way, and only desires to take another road when you part company with truth. We do, indeed, receive the Bible from the Church; but not, as you suppose, from the Church of the nineteenth century; much less from any single portion of it. The Christian body was in existence and duly organized before the New Testament was written, and therefore witnessed the gradual accumulation of its inspired contents. As each Gospel or Epistle was put into circulation, it came into the custody of the Church, and by the Church has been transmitted down to us. Upon the testimony of the Church, then, *that is to say, of the Apostolic and primitive Church*, which had means, denied to us, of tracing each book to its reputed author, we believe the Scriptures now in our hands to be the Word of God, the genuine and unadulterated production of inspired men. This fact was established many centuries ago; and the evidence of it remains in the histories, the treatises, and sermons of an innumerable host of early Christian writers. The testimony of the *modern* Church of Rome to the canon of holy Scripture is therefore quite superfluous and unnecessary. It can add nothing to the certainty of its inspired authorship; —nor would this fact lose one tittle of the real evidence on which it rests, if that Church were to be swept out of existence to-morrow.

You say, however:—

"It is because *I know* that the Church is holy that *I am equally assured* that the Bible is so."

But let me ask whence you have learnt that the present Church is holy? If from your personal observation and reflection, the inference is a mere exercise of private judgement, and utterly without weight upon your own principles. You will hardly avow that you believe it because the Church herself asserts it? If you refer me to holy Scripture, I reply that such testimony cannot be pleaded until the authority of Scripture has been established;— the very thing for which you send me to the present Church. We are to credit the Scriptures because the Church bids us, and to believe the Church because the same Scriptures witness to her! Who does not see that even thus you are making your Church " bear witness to herself?"—or who can miss the inference :—" Her witness is not true?"

III. Another argument intended to show the necessity of an unerring Church, you state as follows :—

"The Bible stands in need of the Church because it does not *explain* itself."

It is true that the Church has not only preserved for us the uncorrupted Bible, but has also assisted us to the right interpretation of it. But then it is *the early undivided Church*, and not the present Church of Rome, to which we owe this benefit also. The primitive Christians, though scattered throughout the world, held every where the same great doctrines, received immediately, or through a few faithful hands, from the same inspired teachers. Now we are able to ascertain from writings of the period what this universal belief of the primitive Church was, and thus determine, by a method *morally infallible*, the real teaching of the Bible on every dogma then deemed an article of faith. It was on this principle that the Church of England reformed herself three hundred years ago. The revival of letters in Europe had led many to suspect that additions both in doctrine and discipline had been made to the ancient system of the Church during the dark ages. Since antiquity was pleaded for all, and the testimony of Scripture for some, at least, of the suspected innovations, the only practicable method of deciding the important question was evidently by an appeal to the belief and practice of the early Christians. From their ample remains, therefore, did our leading Reformers, who by the good providence of God were men of judgement and personal humility as well as learning, endeavour to ascertain, in the first place, whether the inspired writers of the New Testament had taught their immediate disciples to understand it as the Church of Rome then understood it; and secondly, whether they had insisted on any ordinances or doctrines, as necessary to salvation, to which no allusion is apparent in their extant writings [1].

[1] That no such doctrine or ordinance was only orally delivered by the Apostles might be safely inferred from the fact, that the early Fathers never taught any thing as necessary in belief or practice for which they did not claim the express testimony of Scripture; but it so happens, most providentially, that they have also very frequently asserted its complete sufficiency for this purpose. Thus Clemens Alexandrinus (Strom. vii. Opp. p. 757. Colon. 1688):—" We look not for the testimony that is from men; but we confirm that which is questioned by the voice of God, which is the surest of all demonstrations,—or rather is the only demonstration." Tertullian (Adv. Hermog. c. xxii. Opp. tom. ii. p. 84. Ed. Semler, Halæ Magdeb. 1828):—" I reverence the fulness of Scripture . . . Let the shop of Hermogenes show that it is written. If it is not written, let him fear the evil appointed for those who add or take away." S. Cyril of Jerusalem (Catech. iv. c. xii. p. 56. Oxon. 1703):—" Nothing whatever ought to be delivered concerning the Divine and holy mysteries of the faith without the Divine Scriptures. . . . Do not even believe me telling you these things, unless you receive the proof of what I declare from the Divine Scriptures." His namesake of Alexandria (Glaph. in Gen. l. ii. Opp. tom. i. p. 29. Lutet. Par. 1638):—" How shall we receive and class among truths that which the Divine Scripture hath not said?" S. Augustine (c. Litt. Petillian. l. iii. c. 7. Opp. tom. ix. col. 477. Paris, 1836—1838), in allusion to Gal. i. 8:—" Whether concerning Christ, or His Church, or any thing else that pertains to the faith, and our life—(I will not say, Although

The result of the investigation was decidedly against Rome, and therefore, so soon as it pleased God to grant the means and opportunity, the corrupt novelties to which she clung were ejected, we trust for ever, from the reformed offices and formularies of the Church of England.

IV. As it is of no little importance that we should clearly understand the leading principles of the Reformation in our own country, I subjoin some testimonies that will establish beyond contradiction the truth of the foregoing statement.

1. In the Preface to the Book of Common Prayer put forth in 1549, we are invited to "search out by the ancient Fathers," "the first original and ground of the Common Prayers in the Church, commonly called Divine Service," and are told that for "many years passed the godly and decent order

---

we, as we are in no way to be compared to him who said, Although we; but I will by all means say, as he added)—If an angel from heaven were to preach to you any thing beside that which ye have received in the Scriptures of the Law and of the Gospel, let him be anathema." Many passages to the same effect may be seen in Ussher's Answer to a Jesuit, ch. ii., Of Traditions; or in Beveridge on the Articles, Art. VI. Roman statements are as follows: Bellarmine (Controv., De Verbo Dei, lib. iv. c. iii. tom. i. p. 45. Colon. 1628):—"We assert that all necessary doctrine is not expressly contained in the Scriptures, whether it be of the faith or of morals." Dens (Theolog. Mor. et Dogm. de Virt. N. 67, tom. ii. p. 109. Dubl. 1832):—"Are divine traditions to be admitted beside Sacred Writ? Our heretics deny it chiefly on this ground, that all the truths of the faith are contained in Sacred Writ. Against this *error* the Catholic faith teaches, &c." Other quotations to the like purport will be given in Letter VIII. P. I.

of *the ancient Fathers* (with regard to the lessons from Scripture) had been altered, broken, and neglected." After a description of these corruptions, the improvements introduced into the reformed book are thus explained:—

" These inconveniences therefore considered, here is set forth such an order whereby the same shall be redressed. . . . . So that here you have an order for prayer, (as touching the reading of holy Scripture,) *much agreeable to the mind and purpose of the old Fathers*, and a great deal more profitable and commodious than that which *of late* was used."

2. A similar appeal to antiquity occurs in the preface to our Ordinal which appeared in 1552:—

" It is evident unto all men, *diligently reading holy Scripture, and ancient authors, that from the Apostles' time* there hath been these orders of ministers in Christ's Church, Bishops, Priests, and Deacons, &c."

3. In the first year of Queen Elizabeth, A. D. 1558, the principle received the formal and complete sanction of the civil government. A statute then enacted to provide for the adjudication of causes spiritual, imposed the following restrictions on the powers of the court which it created:—

" Provided always . . . . that such person or persons . . . . shall not in any wise have authority or power to order, determine, or adjudge any matter or cause to be heresy, but only such as have heretofore been determined, ordered, or adjudged to be heresy, by the authority of the Canonical Scriptures, or by the first four General

Councils, or any of them, or by any other General Council, wherein the same was declared heresy by the express and plain words of the said Canonical Scriptures [2]."

The authority of the four Councils to which such unrestricted confidence is given was recognised in a similar manner by the Convocation of 1640, Can. IV.[3] The last of them was held at Chalcedon, A. D. 451.

4. In the year 1571, the Church passed in Convocation a decree, of which the following extract is part :—

"Preachers shall above all things be careful never to teach any thing in their sermons which they would have religiously held and believed by the people, but that which is agreeable to the doctrine of the Old and New Testament, and which the Catholic Fathers and ancient Bishops have gathered from the said doctrine [4]."

5. The Convocation of 1604 appeals in several of its canons to the practice of the "primitive Church." The motive of this will be apparent from the following statement which occurs in one of them :—

"So far was it from the purpose of the Church of England to forsake and reject the Churches of Italy, France, Spain, Germany, or any such like Churches, in all things which they held and practised, that as the Apology of the Church of England confesseth, it doth with reverence retain those ceremonies which do neither

[2] 1 Eliz. c. 1. § 36.
[3] Cardwell's Synodalia, vol. i. p. 399.
[4] Cardw., u. s., p. 126.

endamage the Church of God, nor offend the minds of sober men; and only departed from them in those particular points wherein they were *fallen both from themselves in their ancient integrity, and from the* Apostolic Churches, which were their first founders [5]."

To the authority of the Church and of the Statute Law we may add the testimony of our Reformers, as it stands on record in their acknowledged writings.

6. Let us hear Cranmer:—

"Touching my doctrine of the Sacrament, and any other my doctrine of what kind soever it be, I protest that it was never my mind to write, speak, or understand, any thing contrary to the most holy Word of God, *or else against the holy Catholic Church of Christ*, but purely and simply to *imitate and teach* those things only which I had learned of the Sacred Scripture, and of the holy Catholic Church of Christ *from the beginning*, and also *according to the exposition of the most holy and learned Fathers and Martyrs of the Church. . . . .* And I profess and openly confess, that in all my doctrine and preaching both of the Sacrament and of other my doctrine whatsoever it be, not only I mean and judge those things, *as the Catholic Church and the most holy Fathers of old with one accord have meant and judged*, but also I would gladly use the same words that they used, and not use any other words, but to set my hand to all and singular their speeches, phrases, ways, and forms of speech, which they do use in their treatises on the Sacrament, and to keep still their interpretation [6]."

[5] Cardw., u. s., p. 262.

[6] Appeal from the Pope to the next General Council, Feb. 14, 1556. Works, vol. iv. p. 127. Oxf. 1833.

7. Equally decided is the language of Ridley:—

"In that the Church of God is in doubt, I use herein the wise council of Vincentius Lirinensis, whom I am sure you will allow, who giving precepts how the Catholic Church may be in all schisms and heresies known, writeth in this manner: 'when,' saith he, 'one part is corrupted with heresies, then prefer the whole world before that one part; but if the greatest part be infected, then prefer antiquity.' In like sort now, when I perceive the greatest part of Christianity to be infected with the poison of the See of Rome, *I repair to the usage of the primitive Church* [7]."

8. The Apology of the Church of England by Bishop Jewel was published in 1562, with the consent and approbation of the upper house of Convocation [8], and though many have regretted the temper which it occasionally displays, has from the first been considered by all to represent fairly the grounds and method of the English Reformation. These then it states as follows:—

"We, as I have said, in respect of the changes of religion have done nothing rashly or without precedent, nothing except slowly and with great deliberation; nor should we ever have brought ourselves to do it, if the manifest and undoubted will of God, revealed to us in holy Scripture, and regard to our own salvation, had not conspired to force us. For although we have departed from that Church which *they* call Catholic, and they lead persons incapable of judging to mislike us on that account, nevertheless it is enough for us, and it ought to be

[7] Life by Gloucester Ridley, Book viii. p. 613. 1763.
[8] Collier, P. ii. B. vi. p. 479.

enough for a prudent and pious man, and one whose thoughts are on eternal life, that we have departed from that Church which may err, which Christ who cannot err foretold so long before should err, and which with our own eyes we clearly saw had departed from the holy Fathers, from the Apostles, from Christ Himself, and from the primitive and Catholic Church. But *we have approached as nearly as we could, to the Church of the Apostles, and of the ancient Catholic Bishops and Fathers,* which we know was yet a pure, and as Tertullian says, an uncorrupted virgin, undefiled as yet by any idolatry, or grave and public error. Nor have we ordered our doctrine alone, but also the Sacraments and Forms of Public Prayer, by the pattern of their rites and institutes. And as we know that Christ Himself and all godly men, for the most part, have done, we have restored religion, shamefully neglected and depraved by them, to its original condition and pristine state. For we consider that the restoration of religion was to be sought in the same quarter from which it had its beginning ; for this maxim, says the very ancient Father Tertullian, is effectual against all heresies :—*that whatever was first is true ; whatever is later is corrupt*[9]."

It cannot be necessary to adduce further evidence. We have heard, from their own lips, as it were, a clear and ample statement of the views and principles of the chief actors in the English Reformation; and we have learnt from public documents of national authority how they were enabled to embody them in the laws and ordinances of

[9] In Enchirid. Theol., vol. i. p. 322.

the Church.   But all conspire to tell us, distinctly
and emphatically, that the religious movement
which those men conducted was, in the strictest
sense, in purpose and effect, an appeal from the
corrupt Latin Church of the sixteenth century to
the Church Catholic, and to that Church in its best
period of purity and knowledge.

V. As the advocates of Rome are not likely to
condemn very strongly a course of proceeding
which their Church has herself affected to adopt,
I will now leave it, without further comment, to
approve itself to the good sense of the impartial
reader.   It may, however, receive an useful illustration from a contrast with that mode of self-
defence to which they are reduced in these days
of critical learning and more general intelligence.
That the new theory may have the advantage of a
friendly expositor, you shall yourself inform us to
what, or to whom, you and your friends appeal as
your unerring guide in faith and practice :—

" Thousands upon thousands of every nation make up
the Roman Catholic Church, and it is the testimony of
all these thousands perfectly agreeing which interprets
for each individual Catholic the sense of Scripture."

It is obvious that such an appeal is, after all, not
much better than a tortuous and covert mode of
consulting one's own views and feeling.   The person who is thus content to rest his faith on the
opinions of the majority is himself an unit among

those "thousands upon thousands," trained with them from infancy in the same habits and sentiments, breathing continually the same atmosphere of superstition or religion, and passively, if not actively, contributing by influence and example to cement the general allegiance to that great mass of truth, or error, which is the common possession and mutual bond of all. Not one among those thousands has a better reason to give for the faith that is in him, than you who thus appeal to their collective testimony. Each believes only because others believe. When the belief arose; how it arose; who first suggested it; on what grounds it was received; whether it is taught in Scripture, or acknowledged by the primitive Church; these and many other questions of first importance to those who are inquiring if it be *true*, are quite beside the scope and object of this modern test. *The people hold it*,—as they once held a doctrine of Jupiter and Venus,—and *therefore* it is true. But why so, if the equally received faith in Jupiter was false and blasphemous? If indeed the *only possible* fulfilment of Christ's promise to His Church included and implied this inerrancy of the popular belief, I would admit it without scruple, and suppose that its apparent absurdity was due to the imperfection of my own intellect. But it is certain that the words of Christ are capable of another and far more probable interpretation, and that they have been

c

otherwise explained from the beginning. Submission to this new rule of faith is a betrayal of our reason quite as gratuitous as it is absurd.

To make numbers the criterion of truth is indeed to contradict the surest maxims of the wise, and the experience of every age. "To follow a multitude" is, proverbially, to "do evil." The faithful have ever been, not the unthinking crowd, but an obscure, perhaps despised "remnant;" the "broad way," trodden by the many, is not the path in which we are taught to expect truth and safety. Why should the members of the Roman Communion be an exception to this universal law? Is there aught in their circumstances, or in their general character, which would lead us to infer that God is revealing Himself to mankind in their belief and practice? Reflect one moment on the acknowledged state of learning and morality among those "thousands upon thousands" to whose authority we are referred. Can any one really believe that the teaching of the Spirit is to be gathered from the masses of debased Italy, of cruel and licentious Austria, or sceptical and profligate France? Can it indeed be seriously maintained and thought that doctrines, unknown to the Church for many ages, must necessarily be true, because they are now unanimously believed among the ignorant Spaniards and Portuguese, and their still more degenerate cousins in South America.

Yet such is at present the palmary argument of Roman controversialists; and so, I fear, they are too often *compelled* to reason, or risk the utter shipwreck of their faith.   Conscious of the novelty of certain doctrines of their Church, and ignorant of that solid ground on which they might stand by our side, they see that for them there is no medium between boundless credulity and total unbelief.   Hence that resolved defiance of conviction and disregard of facts which astonishes us so often in men who are not otherwise either unreasonable or dishonest.   Hence the courage, akin to desperation, with which they avow consequences that an inexperienced opponent would have supposed that they must—beyond all question—have overlooked.   You are not yourself, permit me to remark, without your share of this strange hardihood. Too intelligent not to know, and too honest to deny the degraded state of Roman Christendom, you venture notwithstanding to question its effect on the religious belief of the corrupt multitude :—

"I do not find the wickedness of the greater number of Catholics any thing at all surprising, ... but I do find it surprising that all these numbers should so agree in their testimony, &c.   This indeed I find wonderful, and only the more wonderful on account of such general wickedness; for this shows the weakness of the witnesses, while their agreement shows the force of truth."

c 2

What, then? Is there no meaning in that saying of our Lord; "If any man is willing to do the will of my Father, *he* shall know of the doctrine whether it be of God [1]?" or have we never heard of those, who having "consented to iniquity," are by a most righteous judgment allowed to "believe lying [2]?"

There is no fact connected with the moral and spiritual nature of man more certain than the instinctive repugnance of the habitual sinner to the pure doctrines of the Gospel. The truth of God has no home in a heart forsaken of His Spirit; or to keep nearer the surface, how can the sinner really cling to a faith by which he is at every turn condemned? He is soon driven to take refuge in indifference or unbelief, or in one of those many perversions of the truth, by which its obligations are evacuated or eluded. The zealous attachment of an unholy multitude to a particular scheme of doctrine or mode of worship is, therefore, in reality its strongest condemnation. If it were of God, they would not, because they could not, love it. If then a religion with an acknowledged basis of truth is found to attract and retain the impenitent and reckless, the inference is unavoidable:—it has accommodated itself to their corrupt tastes and depraved imaginations, and their attachment is not to the original truth, but to the subsequently incorporated

[1] John vii. 17.   [2] 2 Thess. ii. 10, 11, Rheims Version.

error[3]. Thus when Roman Catholic writers ex- LETTER
patiate on that fervent devotion to the Blessed

[3] An apt illustration occurs in Dr. Newman's Lectures on Certain Difficulties, &c. Lond. 1850 :—" In a Catholic country the ideas of heaven and hell, Christ and the evil spirit, saints, angels, souls in purgatory, the grace of the blessed sacrament, the sacrifice of the mass, absolution, indulgences, the virtue of relics, of holy images, of holy water, and of other holy things, are facts, by good and bad, by young and old, by rich and poor, to be taken for granted. They are facts brought home to them by faith; substantially the same to all, though coloured by their respective minds, according as they are religious or not, and according to the degree of their religion. . . . . It is the spectacle of a supernatural faith acting upon the multitudinous mind of a nation; of a divine principle dwelling in the myriads of characters, good, bad, and intermediate, into which the old stock of Adam grafted into Christ has developed. . . . . A bad Catholic does not deny hell, for it is to him an incontestable fact, brought home to him by that supernatural faith with which he assents to the Divine Word speaking through Holy Church; he is not angry with others for holding it, for it is no private decision of their own. His thoughts take a different turn; he looks up to our Blessed Lady; he knows by supernatural faith her power and her goodness; he turns the truth to his own purpose, his own bad purpose, and he makes her his patroness and protectress against the penalty of sins which he does not mean to abandon. Hence the strange stories of highwaymen and brigands devout to the Madonna. And their wishes leading to the belief, they begin to circulate stories of her much desired compassion towards impenitent offenders; and these circumstances fostered by the circumstances of the day and confused with others similar, but not impossible, for a time are in repute. Thus the Blessed Virgin has been reported to deliver the reprobate from hell and to transfer them to purgatory; and absolutely to secure from perdition all who are devout to her, repentance not being contemplated as the means. Or men have thought by means of some sacred relic to be secured from death in their perilous and guilty expeditions. . . . Once more, listen to the stories, songs, and ballads of the populace; their rude and boisterous merriment still runs upon the great invisible subjects which possess their imagination. Their ideas of whatever sort, good, bad, or indifferent, rise out of the next world. Hence if they would have plays, the subjects are sacred; if they would have games and sports,

Virgin so often exhibited by robbers and assassins and women living by their sin, they are unwittingly urging a fatal argument against the practice of their Church. The thought at once occurs to every serious and unsophisticated mind :—" What fellowship hath righteousness with unrighteousness? and what communion hath light with darkness? and what concord hath Christ with Belial?" If the Roman worship of departed saints be from *below*, the result is consistent, and what might have been expected; if from *above*, it has reversed a law of our moral nature, which reason, experience, and the written Word join in declaring to be irreversible.

VI. At times, however, you appear not quite forgetful of this sacred principle, and even to feel a little embarrassment when it happens to cross your path. For though compelled to own the

these fall, as it were, into procession, and are formed upon the model of sacred rites and sacred persons. If they sing and jest, the Madonna, the Bambino, or St. Peter, or some other saint is introduced, not from irreverence, but because those are the ideas which absorb them. . . . . Let a Catholic mob be as profligate in conduct as an English, still it cannot withstand, it cannot disown, it can but worship the crucifix; it is the external representation of a fact of which one and all are conscious to themselves and to each other. And hence, I say, in their fairs and places of amusement, in the booths, upon the stalls, upon the doors of wine-shops, will be paintings of the Blessed Virgin or St. Michael, or the souls in purgatory, or some such subject. Innocence, guilt, and what is between the two, all range themselves under the same banner; for even the resorts of sin will be made doubly frightful by the blasphemous introduction of some sainted patron."—Lect. ix. pp. 228—234.

"general wickedness" prevailing among those "thousands upon thousands" of every nation whose testimony you receive as the voice of the Church, and therefore regard as an oracle of heavenly truth, yet, with a startling inconsistency, you elsewhere affirm that "the Church is not and never was corrupt;" and argue that, therefore, "it never did, and never could corrupt the Bible." How you propose to reconcile this bold assertion with the foregoing confession, I find it quite impossible to conjecture. As such language, however, and the mistake which it betrays are only too common in these days, I beg to refer you, by way of example, to the history of the tenth century, as related by Cardinal Baronius, or to the Epistles of the poet Petrarch[4]; to the Tract of Nicholas de Clemangis "On the *Corrupt* State of the Church[5];" to the Report of the Papal Commissioners appointed by Paul III. to advise on "the removal of abuses[6];" to the Hundred Grievances of the German Nation, presented to Adrian VI. by the diet of Nuremberg[7]; or to any other document of undoubted authority in the collection of Orthwin a Graes, or in Brown's Appendix to that book, describing the general immorality

[4] Those which refer to this subject have been extracted by Goldastus, tom. ii. pp. 1345—65.

[5] Orthuin. Grat. Append. p. 555.

[6] Ibid. p. 231. Among them were Cardinals Pole, Contarini, Sadolet, and Caraffa, afterwards Paul IV.

[7] Orthuin. Grat. p. 354. An abstract of them is given by Dupin, Cent. xvi. l. i. c. xv. Eng. tr. vol. iii. p. 184. Dubl. 1721.

and superstition of western Christendom from the twelfth to the sixteenth century. There can be but one result with any upright mind.

I will produce at once, however, a few testimonies to which exception is impossible, as they are from persons whose training and position would tend to blind them to the full extent of the evil, and lead them to speak of it with moderation and reserve.

1. The following extract from S. Bernard describes the state of the Church in the twelfth century:—

" All Christians—and nearly all men—' seek their own, not the things which are Jesus Christ's.' The very duties of the ecclesiastical dignity have passed into a matter of filthy lucre, and into a work of darkness; not the salvation of souls, but the luxury of riches is their object. For this they receive the tonsure; for this they frequent the churches, celebrate masses, sing psalms. For bishoprics, archdeaconries, abbacies, and other dignities there is in the present day a shameless struggling, that the revenues of the churches may be squandered in superfluities and vanities [8]."

2. The state of things which immediately preceded the great movement in Germany is thus described by Cardinal Bellarmine:—

" For my part, I am of opinion that the sophisms, heresies, defections of so many people and kingdoms from the true faith, in a word, all the calamities, wars, tumults, seditions of these most unhappy times have had their rise from no other cause than these;—that the pastors and the

[8] Serm. vi. in Ps. *Qui habitat.* Opp. tom. ii. p. 61. Par. 1667.

other priests of the Lord sought Christ, not for Christ's sake, but that they might eat of his loaves. For some years before the Lutheran and Calvinian heresy arose, there was hardly any,—as those who lived then bear witness,—there was, I say, almost no severity in the ecclesiastical courts, no discipline in morals, no instruction in sacred literature, no reverence in divine things; there was almost, in fine, no religion. That highly honourable condition of the clergy and the sacred order had come to nought; the priests were a laughing-stock to every worthless knave; they were despised by the people, and laboured under deep and lasting infamy[9]."

3. Of cotemporary testimonies to the deep corruption of the Church in the century that produced the Reformation, I shall produce first that of an Austrian Bishop who wrote in the year 1519 :—

" As of old in the Roman empire, so now in the Roman court, is there an infamous gulf in which riches are swallowed up. Avarice has increased. The law has perished from the priest, the vision from the prophets, counsel from the aged. The keys of the Church are abused and in bondage to simony and ambition[1]. . . . . Rome is now the gulf and mammon of hell, where the devil, the captain of all covetousness, dwells, selling the patrimony of Christ, which He purchased by His passion; who instructs us that we should freely give what we have freely received. It has now become a proverb, The court of Rome seeks

---

[9] Concio 28: *De Evang. quinque panum.* Opp. tom. v. col. 296. Colon. 1617.

[1] Joh. Chemensis, Onus Ecclesiæ, c. xix. § viii. fol. xxxv. Colon. 1531. Respecting the author, see Placcius, Theatr. Anonym. tom. i. p. 144. Hamb. 1708.

not the sheep without its wool. It hears those who give ; it shuts the gate to those who do not give. Against the exorbitant abuse of dispensations the Emperor Sigismund uttered this reproach in the Council of Constance :— ' We read that Christ gave to Peter the power of remitting sins only, not of committing them,' &c.[2] . . . . I fear that we have now come to that declaration of the Apostle, I know that after my departure ravening wolves shall enter in among you (that is, among the Bishops), not sparing the flock. For where is there a good man and one approved in work and doctrine chosen for a bishop ? —not a boy, not a carnal person, and ignorant of spiritual things ? . . . . . Who, alas ! of the bishops now-a-days preaches or takes care for the souls committed to him ? Unskilled in divine things, they love worldly wisdom ; attending rather to offices of finance than to the work of Christ. They adorn their bodies with gold, their souls with mud. It is a matter for shame with them to exercise their spiritual functions ;—their glory to indulge in buffoonery. . . . Contrary to the canons, they keep about them panders, flatterers, buffoons, who occupy themselves with vanities, instead of learned men and of good repute. . . . Sometimes they get together unprincipled divines and crafty lawyers, who, for their covetousness, bend the laws as they please, like wax ; who say what pleases them, and keep back what displeases[3]. . . . Nothing so provokes God to wrath, or gives men occasion to sin, as the licentiousness of those set over them,—in whom at the present day is fulfilled that of the prophet : ' See what the elders of the house of Israel are doing in the darkness,' &c. . . . In Germany there are few with cure

[2] § xiii. fol. xxxvi.   [3] c. xx. §§ ii. iii.

of souls who are not rotting in the foul sin of concubinage [4]."

His account of the religious orders of both sexes is still more sad; while his lamentations over the general ignorance and wickedness remind the reader of St. Paul's description of the spiritual and moral condition of the heathen world.

4. Let us now listen to the confession of Pope Adrian VI., as contained in the instructions with which he furnished his nuncio at the diet of Nuremberg in 1522:—

" We know that in this holy see there have been for some years past many abominable things, abuses in spiritual matters, strainings of authority, and that all things, in short, have gone wrong. Nor is it strange if the disease has descended from the head to the members, from the supreme pontiff to the other prelates below him. We all (that is, the prelates of the Church) have gone astray, every one his own way; nor has there been now for a long time one who has done good, no not one. . . . Touching our part in which matter, you will promise that we will use our best endeavour that this court, from which, peradventure, all this evil has proceeded, be first reformed; that as corruption has flowed hence to all below, so also from the same the health and reformation of all may flow [5]."

5. The next witness whom I shall cite is Cardi-

[4] c. xx. § vi.
[5] In Richer. Hist. Conc. Gen. l. iv. p. ii. c. v. Orthuin. Grat. t. i. p. 345. Ed. Brown. Rainald. ad an. 1522, t. xx. p. 365. Colon. 1694.

nal Campeggio, a name well known in England in connexion with the divorce of Henry VIII. and Catharine of Arragon. In a constitution for the removal of abuses published by him in 1524, as the Pope's nuncio in Germany, he states in the following terms the result of the deliberations of a council held at Ratisbonne in the preceding year:—

"It was no less the opinion of the assembly, that this most wicked heresy, (the Lutheran,) which approves itself to the rude people, through that liberty of which it gives them a false persuasion, under the pretence of evangelical charity, has in a great measure owed its rise, partly to the abandoned lives of the clergy, partly to the abuse (no longer to be dissembled) of sacred sanctions and ecclesiastical constitutions;—and, therefore, that it would be of no little moment towards the extirpation of the sect of these Lutheran heretics and their followers, that the clergy should, by the infliction of due censure, be brought back to habits of good living, and courses suitable to them, and that the abuses which offend the laity be abolished[6]."

6. Twenty-eight years later, the same confession and complaint was repeated by the Cardinal of Lorraine before the great Council of Trent:—

"The hand of the Lord hath touched us, O my fathers, and brethren. The corrupt morals of all classes, the entire ruin of Church discipline,—these things have provoked against us the just judgement of God in his wrath. . . . Whom shall we accuse, my brother bishops?

[6] In Orthuin. Grat. t. i. p. 423.

Whom shall we declare the cause of so great an evil? I remember your wishes, nor have I forgotten your universal judgement on this matter:—it behoves me to say this, not without inward shame, and great sorrow for my past life. On *our* account, my brethren, has this tempest arisen. Wherefore cast us into the sea! What shall I add more? You have the confession of the accused: punish them, as seemeth good. Now let judgement begin with the house of God, and let those who have been vessels of the Lord be cleansed. Let us take heed to ourselves, and to the whole flock. Let us cease to do evil and learn to do well," &c.[7]

7. This may be regarded as the confession of the Church in France. The following is the cotemporary statement of a distinguished inhabitant of the neighbouring province of Luxemburg:—

"Not that I would here praise or defend the abuses and vices, the base, disgraceful, and libidinous mode of life under which that See (of Rome) especially, and, indeed, the whole estate of the Catholic Church in general, has, for some centuries, for the most part, grievously and inordinately laboured, and still labours. . . . Wallowing in filth and wickedness in the sanctuary of the Lord, they (the clergy) have polluted Him by the most foul and most grievous abuses. . . . In the halls of the princes and prelates of the Church, you cannot see many doctors of theology, religious, or others of better conduct and of piety, and studious of Christian and holy living, who are careful to see that the offices of the Church are admi-

[7] Instruction et Missives . . . . concernant le Concile de Trente, p. 204. S. l. 1613.

nistered in a holy and catholic manner, that the health of souls is cared for, and that the sheep intrusted to them find the food of life; but you may see many drunkards, bullies, whoremongers, buffoons, flatterers, worthless persons, blasphemers, unclean, impious, &c.; also a multitude of horses for pride, and empty, idle ostentation. . . . . Of God and divine things, &c., there is generally never any mention, except, perchance, in pretence, and with superficial feeling, word-deep. Nay, if there happen to be one here, who, in simplicity and humility, sets himself to live like a Christian in all chaste and holy conversation, he is immediately set down by all as a hypocrite, a senseless animal, &c. Let any one tell me that it is not so, and I will endure to be convicted of falsehood [8]."

8. If we turn to the distant country of Poland, we find the evils of the day referred to the same causes, by a synod of bishops convoked by Lipomani the papal legate, at Lowicz, in the year 1556:—

" We say, then, that the first cause of the introduction of heresy into this kingdom was the negligence of the pastors and prelates of the Flock of Christ; among whom, as the Apostolic See holds the chief place, so we fear that it is, (may it forgive us!) to some extent, also the cause of this evil, principally for four reasons."

[8] Nicholas Mameranus in Schelhorn. Amœn. Hist. Eccles. tom. i. p. 378. Francof. 1737. He quotes to the same purpose from three of his cotemporaries: Isidore Clarius, Bishop of Foligno, the editor of the Latin Bible, who speaks of Italy in particular; Lindanus, Bishop of Ruremonde in the Netherlands, and afterwards of Ghent; and Rueward Tapper, an eminent theologian of Louvaine. Mameranus wrote in 1552. He was a firm adherent of the Church of Rome.

The reasons given are :—neglect to send a legate to arrange matters,—the delays and interruptions of the Council of Trent,—the mischievous privileges granted to kings, &c., by the Pope,—the avarice displayed by the court of Rome in dealing with ecclesiastical benefices.—Leaving the Pope, they then proceed as follows :—

" In the second place, is the negligence of the right reverend our bishops, which is altogether the source of great calamity. For though they rejoice in a triple authority, episcopal, senatorial, and temporal, certain, alas ! seem to have made a good use of none of them, &c. . . . But, since we have said so many things of the negligence of the right reverend lords the bishops, are they only to be blamed in this respect? Nay ; others without number besides. We all, I say, observed that there is, both in the ecclesiastical state, and every religious order, a great debasement of morals. For we see all places filled with luxury, pomp, avarice, lusts, idleness, and carelessness, and, what in priests seems worse than all, ignorance of God's law," &c.[9]

[9] Respons. Prælat. in Conc. Lovitiensi, in Mansi Suppl. tom. v. col. 709. Contrast with the above representations of unexceptionable authority the delusive declamation of Dr. Newman in the following passage. It follows an account, in his peculiar vein, of the conversion of the Anglo-Saxons :—" Such was the religion of the noble English ; they knew not heresy ; and, as time went on, the work did but sink deeper and deeper into their nature—into their social structure and their political institutions ; it grew with their growth, and strengthened with their strength, till a sight was seen—one of the most beautiful which ever has been given to man to see—what was great in the natural order, made greater by its elevation into the supernatural. The two seemed as if made for each other ; that natural temperament and that gift of grace ; what was heroic, or generous,

If statements such as these do not describe a corrupt and unholy condition of the Church of Rome at the several periods to which they refer, there is neither meaning nor use in language.

I am, &c.

or magnanimous in nature, found its corresponding place, or office, in the divine kingdom. Angels in heaven rejoiced to see the divinely wrought piety and sanctity of penitent sinners; apostles, popes, and bishops, taken to glory, threw their crowns in transport at the foot of the throne, as saints, and confessors, and martyrs came forth before their wondering eyes out of a horde of heathen robbers; guardian spirits no longer sighed over the disparity which had so fearfully intervened between themselves and the souls given them in charge. It did indeed become a peculiar, special people, with a character and genius of its own; I will say a bold thing—in its staidness, sagacity, and simplicity, more like the mind that rules, through all time, the princely line of Roman pontiffs, than perhaps any other Christian people whom the world has seen. And so things went on for many centuries." From *Christ on the Waters*, a Sermon preached at Birmingham, Oct. 27, 1850, and published by Burns, London. Has Dr. Newman really and honestly dreamt himself into this mediæval Utopianism, or may we suppose that he favoured this view in 1850, as he had favoured the opposite in 1840, because it was (in his own words, *Essay on Development, Advert.* p. ix) "necessary for his position?"

LETTER II.

MY DEAR SIR,

I AM about to offer some remarks on certain statements made by you with regard to the books of holy Scripture received by our respective Churches. Speaking of "the Protestant version," by which I presume that you mean the version for which the Church of England is in a certain sense responsible, you say among other things :—

"It does not contain the whole Bible, such as the Apostles left to the Church. Catholics will be glad to receive Catholic Bibles ; but they will not accept as such the Protestant mutilated copy."

Of your own authorised version you speak as follows :—

D

"I most distinctly deny that our Roman Catholic Bibles contain one single book more or less than was received by the Apostles and the early Church."

I. Before I bring these representations to the test of actual facts, I will endeavour to explain briefly the real state of the case. The English version of the Bible consists of three parts, the Old Testament, the New Testament, and the Apocrypha. We believe in the full inspiration of the two former, and regard them as of complete authority, in every question of faith or morals. The Apocryphal books, however, are not by us, and were not, either by the Jews or primitive Christians, esteemed of equal authority with the other Scriptures. Although we read them, as did they, "for example of life and instruction of manners," we "do not apply them to establish any doctrine." Such is the declaration of the Church of England in the Sixth Article of Religion. The Church of Rome, however, has in this, as in many other things, deliberately departed from the original rule of the whole Christian world. For by a decree of the Council of Trent passed in the year 1546, it has placed in the Canon all the Scriptures in our version except the two Books of Esdras and the Prayer of Manasses, and declared that it "receives and venerates them all with an equal affection of piety and reverence [1]."

[1] Sess. iv. Dec. de Can. Script.

It appears then that the Church of England, so far from having a "mutilated" Bible, retains the *whole* Bible of the early Church, and at the same time preserves the primitive distinction between the Canonical and the Apocryphal Scriptures. While, on the other hand, the Church of Rome has for the last three centuries had a Bible which is at once *altered* and *mutilated.;—altered*, because she has added to the original Canon of Scripture of the first class so many books of the inferior class; and *mutilated* (on *her own* principles), because, with a strange inconsistency, she has stopped short in her presumptuous course, and not ventured to add them all. For there is ample evidence to show, that certain of the omitted books were treated by the ancients with quite as much respect as some of those now canonized. In fact, the rejection of the First Book of Esdras and the Third of Maccabees is acknowledged by Bellarmine to present a considerable "difficulty;" the latter being mentioned in one of the pseudo-apostolical canons, the other being cited by SS. Clemens Alexandrinus, Cyprian, Athanasius, Augustine, and another early writer whose name is lost[2].

The testimonies which I am about to allege in support of the representation here given are only a portion of a vast mass of evidence still extant and available. They are, nevertheless, to my mind,

[2] De Verbo Dei, l. i. c. xx. Disput. tom. i. p. 18.

so clear, so ample and conclusive, that I am constrained to believe that you had not given the subject that impartial investigation which it required, before you unfortunately committed yourself to the statements which I have quoted from your letters. I cannot but hope that after an attentive consideration of the simple facts of the case, you will be ready to acknowledge how strangely you have been deceived.

II. As the question between us respects the Books of the Old Testament, it is our duty to ascertain first what was the doctrine of the ancient people of God upon this subject; for they "received the lively oracles to give unto us." Their testimony presents itself in a convenient form in the following statement published by Josephus, their historian, for the information of the heathen world :—

" We have only twenty-two books which contain the records of all the past times, which are justly believed to be divine; and of them, five belong to Moses, which contain his laws and the traditions of the origin of mankind till his death. This interval of time was little short of three thousand years; but as to the time from the death of Moses till the reign of Artaxerxes, king of Persia, who reigned after Xerxes, the prophets who were after Moses, wrote down what was done in their time in thirteen books. The remaining four books contain hymns to God, and precepts for the conduct of human life. It is true, our history hath been written since Artaxerxes very particularly, but hath not been esteemed of the like authority with the former by our forefathers, because there hath not been an exact succession of prophets since that time; and how firmly we have given credit to these books of our own nation, is evident by what we do; for during so many ages as have already passed, no one has been so bold as either to add any thing to them, to take any thing from them, or to make any change in them; but it is become natural to all Jews, immediately and from their very birth, to esteem these books to contain divine doctrines, and to persist in them, and if occasion be, willingly to die for them [3]."

We are here expressly told that the Jewish Canon contained no historical books of later date than the reign of Artaxerxes Longimanus, that is, none later than those of Ezra and Nehemiah; and the reason assigned for the inferior authority of later history, namely, the withdrawal of prophetical inspiration, tells with still greater force against the canonicity of the didactic books of Wisdom and Ecclesiasticus. These are also excluded by the number given by Josephus, of those which contain " precepts for the conduct of human life." The Jewish Canon, then, consisted of those books only which were originally written in Hebrew, or Chaldee, which are still acknowledged by the Jews, and found in their Bibles.

III. I believe however that you will agree with

[3] C. Apion. l. i. c. 8. Works, vol. ii. p. 521. Whiston's Tr., ed. 1825.

me thus far, for the fact is acknowledged by all the better controversialists of your Church. Indeed you say with them :—

"I receive the Bible from the hands of the Christian Church, and not from the Jews of Palestine."

But let me ask you on what grounds, and by what authority, the Christian Church presumed to alter, as you say it did, the Canon of the Old Testament? Have you any trace of a revelation vouchsafed to prophet, apostle, or evangelist, by which it became known that the Church of the Jews had erred in this particular? Among the references to Books of the Old Testament found in the New, the *Index Testimoniorum* at the end of the Vulgate does not give one to any portion of the Apocrypha. Who, then, among the early Christians, would wittingly have ventured to enlarge the Canon which was received by Christ Himself and His Apostles, as certainly as by the whole people of God for several centuries before them? The first Christians were all Jews, and could bring with them into the Church no other Scriptures than they themselves acknowledged. Gentile converts, and especially those who lived in distant countries, would necessarily receive their knowledge of the Books of the Old Testament from their Hebrew instructors: and by this means the ancient Jewish Canon became, as a matter of course, the recognised rule of the whole Christian Church.

Although such a result was to all appearance inevitable, it will be well to show by positive testimony that it did actually take place. As the task before me, however, is somewhat tedious, you will perhaps allow Bellarmine to answer for some of those persons whose views we wish to ascertain. An incidental observation of that author, much to our purpose, thus happily presents itself:—

" Many of the ancients, as Melito, Epiphanius, Hilary, Jerome, Ruffinus, in setting forth the Canon of the Old Testament, avowedly followed the Hebrews, and not the Greeks [4]."

It was not every Father who had occasion to touch upon this question; but it would have been easy for Bellarmine to have added many names to his brief list. I shall endeavour in some measure to supply the deficiency.—

1. Perhaps few things show more strikingly how universal was this regard to the Jewish canon than the example of Tertullian, who—under a strong fanatical impulse, if not already separated from the Church,—asserted the divine authority of the Book of Enoch. Before he could do this, he was obliged to persuade himself it had been anciently received by the Jews, and rejected by them at a later period only on account of the express testimony which it bore to Christ [5].

[4] U. s. p. 19.
[5] De Hab. Mul. c. iii. tom. iii. p. 32.

2. The testimony of Origen is very express:—

" You must know that the Books of the Old Testament are two-and-twenty, *as the Hebrews inform us ;*—which is the number of the letters in their alphabet [6]."

As this statement of Origen is quoted by Eusebius, and inserted by SS. Basil and Gregory of Nazianzum in their selection from the commentaries of Origen, we may add their names to the number of those who have avowedly adopted the Jewish Canon [7]. Eusebius has also quoted with approbation the passage from Josephus which I have already given [8].

3. Similarly S. Athanasius:—

" The Books of the Old Testament are, altogether, twenty-two in number; for so many, as I have heard, are the letters of the Alphabet with the Hebrews said to be [9]."

4. S. Cyril, bishop of Jerusalem, is a voucher, not for himself only, but for the Apostles too, and the whole primitive Church:—

" Read the Divine Scriptures, the twenty-two books of the Old Testament, which have been translated by the seventy-two interpreters."

He then gives a history of this translation of the Hebrew Canon, and adds:—

[6] In Euseb. Hist. Eccl. l. vi. c. xxv. p. 183. Paris, 1678.
[7] Philocal. c. iii. p. 24. Cantab. 1676.
[8] L. iii. c. x. p. 68.
[9] Ep. Fest. xxxix. Opp. tom. ii. p. 38. Colon. 1686. Similarly the author of the Synopsis Sacræ Scripturæ inter Opp. Athan. tom. ii. p. 58.

" Read the twenty-two Books of these interpreters, and have nothing to do with apocryphal writings. Diligently study them only, which we read with confidence in Church. The Apostles and the ancient Bishops, the rulers of the Church, who delivered them to us, were wiser than thou. Do not thou, then, a son of the Church, tamper with what is established [1]."

4. S. Chrysostom :—

" *All* the sacred books of the Old Testament were composed originally in the language of the Hebrews ;—and in this all would agree with us [2]."

" He inspired the blessed Moses ; He engraved the tables. . . . After that He sent Prophets. . . . War came on. . . . The books were burnt. Again He inspired another excellent man, I mean Ezra, to publish them, and caused them to be put together out of remnants. And after this, He provided that they should be translated by the Seventy. They translated them. Christ came. He receives them. The Apostles disperse them to all mankind [3]."

5. S. Augustine :—

" Scriptures not in the Canon of the Jews cannot be urged with such force against gainsayers [4]."

6. I shall conclude with the very direct testimony of a Syrian writer of the sixth century, the value of which is much enhanced by the fact that the work from which it is taken was translated into

---

[1] Catech. iv. cc. xx. xxii. pp. 64, 65.
[2] Hom. iv. in Gen. § 4. Opp. tom. iv. p. 32. Paris, 1835.
[3] Hom. viii. in Ep. ad Hebr. § 4. tom. xii. p. 127.
[4] De Civ. Dei, lib. xvii. c. 20. § 1. tom. vii. p. 2. col. 766.

Latin by an African Bishop of the same age. It is in the form of a dialogue between a scholar and his master :—

"*S.* Why have these books (just before named) not a place among the Canonical Scriptures?"

"*M. Because* among the Hebrews also they were received with this distinction, as Jerome and others bear witness [5]."

You see then that Bellarmine did not exaggerate when he said *many :* rather he should have said *all.*

To have deliberately preferred a Greek version to the Hebrew original, and a Greek collection of Scriptures to a Canon authenticated by the consent of the people of God for several centuries, would obviously have been an extreme absurdity; but it would also have been fraught with mischief to the cause of Christ. A very powerful argument would have been lost, if the supreme authority of the Hebrew Bible had been forgotten, or ignored. The Christian teacher could have appealed no longer to an enemy to warrant the authenticity of those Scriptures by which he was condemned. With what confidence could he have said with Justin Martyr?—

"That the books peculiar to our religion are to this day preserved among the Jews, is the result of a Divine

[5] Junilius de Partibus Div. Leg. Bibl. Patrum, Galland, tom. xii. p. 80. Ven. 1778.

Providence exerted in our behalf. For, that we may not, by bringing them out of the Church, give to men who seek to slander us room for the pretence of forgery, we think good to produce them out of the Synagogue of the Jews," &c.[6]

Or with S. Augustine?—

" Lest men, hard to be convinced, should say, . . . that with the Gospel we have preached we have forged prophets, by whom what we preach might appear to have been foretold, we convince them by the fact that all those Scriptures in which Christ was foretold are in the hands of the Jews; the Jews have all those identical Scriptures. We produce our books out of the hands of enemies, to confound other enemies . . . . The Jew bears the book from which the Christian is to derive his belief," &c.[7]

IV. The uniformity with which the early Fathers adhered to this principle is the more remarkable from the mistakes into which some of them fell in its application. Junilius, for example, and his Syrian authority imagined that the Books of Job, Chronicles, and Ezra were placed by the Jews in the same class with Judith and the Maccabees, and consequently themselves assigned to them no higher rank. Such errors, which were the germ of the Tridentine corruption of the Canon, must be attributed in some measure to the general infelicity of the time, to the comparative scarcity of books,

---

[6] Cohort. ad Græc. c. 13. Opp. tom. i. p. 48. Jenæ, 1842.
[7] Enarr. in Ps. lvi. § 9. Opp. tom. iv. P. i. col. 760.

and the difficulty and delays which attended the quest of information among the Apostolic Churches of the East: but they arose principally, there can be no doubt, from the universal ignorance of Hebrew among the Christians of Gentile origin. They were unhappily dependent on translations of the Bible, which gave them no certain means of distinguishing between the ancient canonical Books, and those writings of less authority, and, for the most part, without a Hebrew original, which were often appended to them. When they were aware that any doubt existed, they sought information, as you will see, where common sense told them to seek it, in the practice and traditions of the native Churches of Palestine. Having acknowledged, therefore, the mistakes of a few writers, with respect to one or two Books,—I now affirm it as undeniable, that, although the primitive Church, or at least a great part of it, did, *in a certain sense*, as the Jews had done before, and as the Church of England does now, *receive* every Book in the present Roman Canon, and some that are not in it too,—yet it did not receive all with equal honour, and ascribe to all the same authority; but distributed them, as the Jewish Church had done, and as we do, into distinct classes; one containing the strictly canonical Books, the other, those called by us apocryphal, but termed also, in early times, ecclesiastical or deutero-canonical. Some of the

evidence on which this assertion rests, I will at
once bring before you.

1. About the middle of the second century, only sixty years or so after the death of the last Apostle, Melito, Bishop of Sardis, travelled into Palestine for the express purpose of investigating the Canon of the Old Testament. He afterwards made a selection from the Scriptures whose character he had thus ascertained, and, in an epistle prefixed to it, described the course that he had taken, and the result of his inquiries. From this epistle, which Eusebius has preserved, we learn that the Church in Palestine, the mother of all other Churches, re-ceived and communicated to others the same Canon of Old Testament Scripture, which we of the Church of England acknowledge and possess. He does not mention any part of the Apocrypha[8].

2. Less than a century after the death of this witness, Origen occupied the catechetical chair at Alexandria, the place where most of the Apo-cryphal Books of the Jews are believed to have been written. Yet, in his copy of the Canon, not one of them is mentioned. On the contrary, at the end of it he remarks:—

" The Book of Maccabees does not belong to these[9]."

[8] Euseb. Hist Eccl. l. iv. c. xxvi. p. 120.   An apparent difference from our Canon is the omission of the names of Nehemiah and Esther; upon which see note 2, p. 47.

[9] Euseb. u. s. l. vi. c. xxv. p. 184. Niceph. Hist. Eccl. l. v. c. xvi. tom. i. p. 364. Par. 1630. The book of the Minor Prophets is omitted

3. Probably after about the same interval from the time of Origen, a Council of thirty-two Bishops, assembled at Laodicea, decreed that "Psalms composed by private persons and Books not in the Canon were not to be used in Church; but only the Canonical Books of the Old and New Testament." The Canon of the Old Testament subjoined to this decree agrees with that of Melito and Origen [1].

In the middle and towards the end of the fourth century, flourished S. Athanasius, Bishop of Alexandria, Cyril of Jerusalem, Hilarius of Poictiers, Epiphanius of Constantia in Cyprus, Gregory of Nazianzum, and Ruffinus an Italian Presbyter, whose several and independent declarations, proceeding from every part of ancient Christendom, bear united testimony to the exclusive authority of the old Hebrew Canon.

4. Of these, S. Athanasius tells us that he was induced to publish a correct Canon, because there was reason to fear lest some, deceived by a resemblance of name, should mistake the forgeries of heretics for the genuine Word of God. At the end of the usual list he says:—

in both these transcripts, but restored by Ruffinus in his translation of Eusebius.

[1] Cann. lix. lx. Conc. Mansi. tom. ii. col. 574. Bevereg. Pandect. tom. i. p. 480. Oxon. 1672. The date of this Council is uncertain. The most probable opinion places it in 365. See Bever. Annot. annexed to tom. ii. p. 193.

" These are the fountains of salvation, so that whoever thirsts is satisfied with the oracles in these. The doctrine of godliness is preached in these alone. Let no one add to them ; let no one take from them . . . . But for the sake of greater accuracy I am obliged to add that there are other books also, which are not reckoned in the Canon, but have been appointed by the Fathers to be read by those who have lately joined the Church, and desire to be instructed in religion ; to wit, the Wisdom of Solomon, the Wisdom of Sirach, Esther, Judith, and Tobias," &c.[2]

[2] Ex Epist. Fest. xxxix. tom. ii. p. 39. In another writing (Synops. Sacr. Script. Ibid. p. 58) ascribed to Athanasius by Baronius, Bellarmine, Dupin, &c., though probably none of his, the Book of Esther is, in the same manner, expressly rejected. The truth seems to be that some of the ancients, ignorant of Hebrew and so unable to separate the genuine text from the spurious matter evidently mixed up with it, were led to regard the whole as of doubtful authenticity. In the Synopsis, tom. ii. p. 109, is an abstract of the rejected book in which we find particulars taken from both. The first verse also is given : " In the second year of the reign of Artaxerxes the great, on the first day of the month Nisan," &c. (p. 58) ; that is, the book began with the dream of Mordecai, now in Vulg. c. xi. v. 2. We are thus enabled to identify it as the original of the Latin version in common use before that of S. Jerome, who says (in loco) :—" This which is neither in the Hebrew nor in any of the interpreters, was the beginning of the Vulgate edition." When he made his version he removed all the parts which he found without Hebrew original to the end of the book, and distinguished them from the genuine Esther by an obelus carefully placed by the side of every line. About the half of these spurious additions are found inserted at two several places in the Greek version of the Seventy. It is singular that only two years before Sixtus V. published the present standard Roman Bible, which is founded on the version of S. Jerome, he authorised (in 1588) a Latin version of the LXX. compiled from the remains of earlier translations (which had originated with himself when Cardinal), in which the Book of Esther appears *interpolated*, and not, as in the later version, with several unconnected pieces *added* at the end.

5. S. Cyril of Jerusalem gives a Canon of Holy Scripture from which he excludes every book in dispute between us and Rome. As he has quoted some of these writings it would, if he had done no more, have been sufficiently clear that the omission was intentional, and made with a full knowledge of their peculiar character. The inference however is superfluous; for he expressly adds:—

"Let all the rest be placed without in a second class [3]."

Melito, Gregory Nazianzen, and others simply omit the name of Esther from their Canon. It by no means follows from this that they excluded the book which the Jews (with us) received. In the Synopsis above quoted we are told:—"Some of the ancients have said that Esther was put into the Canon by the Hebrews; and that Ruth was reckoned as one book with Judges, and similarly Esther with some other," p. 59. Ezra and Nehemiah generally went under the common name of Ezra; and it is antecedently probable that Esther would be often united with them, both because Ezra was supposed by many to have been its author, and because the actions recorded in it fall chronologically between the sixth and seventh chapters of his history. The probability is made almost a certainty by the following circumstance. In the so-called Apostolical Constitutions (l. ii. c. lvi. Coteler. tom. i. p. 262. Antv. 1698) we have a list of the books appointed to be *read in Churches* :—"The Books of Moses and Joshua, of Judges and Kings, those of Chronicles, and those of the Return (from Babylon), the books of Job," &c. Now in one of the Canons attributed by the author of these Constitutions to the Apostles, with which, therefore, we must believe him to agree, we find enumerated among the books "to be had in reverence and considered holy by all the clergy and laity," after the Books of Chronicles, " Ezra, two books; Esther, one;" &c. (Can. ult.; Bever. Cod. Eccl. Prim. tom. i. p. lix. Oxon. 1848.) It is evident then that, under the common name of the Books of the Return, the Constitutions indicate the three several Books of Ezra, Nehemiah, and Esther.

[3] Catech. iv. c. xxii. p. 65. He quotes Ecclus. Cat. vi. c. iii. p. 80,

6. They are equally omitted in a list of the Canonical Scriptures found in the writings of S. Hilary, who informs us, however, that some persons thought fit to add to the Old Testament the Books of Tobias and Judith [4].

7. S. Epiphanius speaks of the Books of Wisdom and Ecclesiasticus as "profitable and useful," but tells us that they are not classed with the other Scriptures, not having been kept by the Jews in the ark of the Covenant. His Canon contains none of the Apocrypha [5].

8. S. Gregory Nazianzen concludes a metrical catalogue of the Sacred Books, from which the Apocrypha are similarly excluded, with these words : —

"Thou hast them all : any beside these are not among the genuine [6]."

9. Ruffinus after enumerating those Scriptures "which are believed, according to the tradition of the Fathers, to have been inspired by the Holy Ghost, and delivered to the Church of Christ,"

&c.; Wisdom, Cat. ix. c. ii. p. 115, &c.; The Song of the Three Children, ibid., &c.

[4] Prol. in Psal. § 15. Opp. tom. ii. p. 145. Wirceb. 1785.

[5] De Mens. et Pond. § iv. Opp. tom. ii. p. 162. ed. Petav. Par. 1622. Sim. Adv. Hær. l. i. tom. vi. § vi. Opp. tom. i. p. 19.

[6] Carm. xxxiii. Opp. tom. ii. p. 98. Colon. 1690. In p. 194 is a similar list in a poem often attributed to S. Amphilochius of Iconium, but ascribed by Billius (Scholia, col. 1477), Dupin (cent. iv. in S. Amphil. vol. i. p. 265), and Oudin (De Scriptor. Eccl. Sæc. ix. de Opp. S. Amph. tom. ii. col. 223), to Gregory.

precisely as they stand in our Sixth Article, observes:——

"These are the Scriptures which the Fathers placed
in the Canon from which they would have the principles of
our faith asserted and maintained. It ought to be known
however that there are other books also which our forefathers did not call *Canonical* but *Ecclesiastical*."

Of the latter class he names the Books of Wisdom and Ecclesiasticus, Tobias, Judith, and the
Maccabees [7].

10. By far the most important witness of this
period is S. Jerome. This very industrious writer
spent the last thirty-four years of his life at Beth-
lehem, where in 405, he completed a Latin version
of the Hebrew Scriptures. From a preface to his
translation of the Books of Samuel and Kings,
wherein he enumerates the Books which he has
translated, we learn that his Canon of the Old
Testament differed in no respect from ours. He
expressly tells his readers that "all beside those
(which he has named) are to be placed among the
Apocrypha," and adds that the Books of Wisdom
and Ecclesiasticus, Judith, Tobias, and the Shepherd, "are therefore not in the Canon [8]." In a
preface to the Books of Solomon, he says of Wisdom and Ecclesiasticus:——

[7] De Symb. Apost. cc. 37, 38. Opp. Hieron. tom. v. p. 141. Par.
1706.

[8] Opp. tom. i. col. 322. *This* Preface he styles Prologus Galeatus.

"As the Church reads Judith, Tobit, and the Mac- cabees, but does not admit them among the Canonical Scriptures, so let her read these two volumes to edify the people, not to establish the authority of her doctrines [9]."

Elsewhere, he expressly rejects Baruch [1], the History of Susanna, the Song of the Three Children, and the "fables" of Bel and the Dragon [2]. He afterwards, at the request of some friends, translated, or rather paraphrased, the Books of Tobit and Judith [3],—but with no change of mind as to their authority.

11. In Africa, at the end of the fourth century, the term *canonical* was applied to the Books of Wisdom and Ecclesiasticus, Tobias, Judith, and the Maccabees, as well as to the Scriptures of the old Hebrew Canon; in short, to all the Books from which lessons were read in churches [4]. It is evi-

[9] Ibid. col. 1419.
[1] Prol. in Hierem. ibid. col. 554.
[2] Præf. in Dan. tom. i. col. 990.
[3] Præf. in Tob. ibid. col. 1158. Præf. in Judith. col. 1170. It is strange that the Church of Rome, while raising these Books to the same rank with those in the Hebrew Canon, should practically have shown so little respect for them as to retain the loose and *imperfect* paraphrase of S. Jerome, rather than provide an accurate version for the instruction of her people.
[4] The Council of Carthage, A.D. 397, adopted the decrees of the smaller synod held at Hippo in 393 (Mansi, tom. iii. coll. 849, 893). Among these was one enjoining that "nothing but the Canonical Scriptures be read in Church under the name of the Divine Scriptures." A list of the Canonical Scriptures follows, in which are enumerated five Books of Solomon, Tobit, Judith, and the two Books of Maccabees.—Hippo, can. xxxviii. Mansi, u. s. col. 896: Carth. can. xlvii. Ibid. col. 891) ; Cod. Afr. can. xxiv. col. 726.

dent, however, from the language of S. Augustine, who was present at the two Councils, the records of which have made us acquainted with this fact, that the African Fathers did not thereby intend to put them on an equality with Moses and the Prophets. Thus he excludes them and the other Apocryphal Books from that position, by asserting the withdrawal of the prophetical gift after the return from Babylon:—

During the whole of that time, from the period when they returned from Babylon, after Malachi, Haggai, and Zechariah, who prophesied then, and Ezra, they had no prophets until the advent of our Saviour [5]."

He says, accordingly, of the Book of Maccabees:—

"This Scripture, which is called the Book of Maccabees, the Jews do not regard as they do the Law, and the Prophets, and the Psalms; to which the Lord Himself bears testimony as to his own witnesses. (Luke xxiv. 44.) . . . but it has been received by the Church not without profit, if it be read or heard with sobriety [6]."

When some had blamed him for quoting the Book of Wisdom in the course of an argument on doctrine, he did not in reply maintain its authority in questions of that nature, but remarked simply:—

"As if, even without the testimony of this Book, the thing which I wished to teach from it were not clear of itself [7]."

[5] De Civ. Dei, u. s., c. xxiv. col. 771.
[6] Contra Gaudent. l. i. § 38. tom. ix. P. ii. col. 1006.
[7] De Prædest. Sanct. § 26. tom. x. P. i. col. 1369.

Adding however :—

" A sentence of the Book of Wisdom ought not to have been rejected, which has been thought fit to be read in the Church of Christ, from the place of the readers, through so long a period of years [8]."

Of another he says :—

" The Book of Ecclesiasticus . . . says that Samuel prophesied even when dead. But if objection is made to this Book out of the Hebrew Canon, (because it is not in it,) what shall we say of Moses, who . . . in the Gospel is said to have appeared to the living [9] ?"

12. In the year 691, a Council of two hundred and eleven eastern Bishops, assembled at Constantinople, expressly adopted and confirmed all the Canons of the ancient Synod of Laodicea [1];—a fact which shows that, even so late as the close of the seventh century, not one of the Apocryphal Books had yet obtained a footing in the Canon of the Universal Church.

V. I trust, my dear Sir, that whatever you may have thought previously, you are now at least convinced that the Church of Rome has placed in the first class of holy Scripture Books to which the Universal Church for many ages, and therefore the Apostles, its first teachers, assigned a very different rank. I now proceed to show that, although so early as the end of the fourth, or beginning of the

---

[8] § 27. col. 1370.

[9] De Cura pro Mortuis, c. xviii. tom. vi. P. i. col. 883.

[1] Can. Trull. ii. Mansi, tom. xi. col. 940. ·

fifth century, one or more of those Books began to be cited by some of the Latins without any express intimation of their inferior authority, the distinction between them and the Canonical Scriptures was nevertheless, until the fourth session of Trent, repeatedly set forth and approved by the best writers in communion with Rome.

1. A quotation from the First Book of Maccabees is introduced, with the following apologetic remark, by Pope Gregory the Great, who died A.D. 600 :—

" Concerning which matter, we do not act irregularly, if we produce a testimony out of Books, which, though not canonical, were yet published for the edification of the Church[2]."

2. The Venerable Bede, who died in 730, mentions incidentally that the Old Testament consisted of twenty-four Books[3], while, in another place, he has the following decisive passage with regard to the Book of Maccabees :—

" Thus far the Divine Scripture contains the series of historical events. But those things which took place among the Jews after these are furnished from the Book of Maccabees and the writings of Josephus and Africanus[4]."

3. In the middle of the ninth century flourished Anastasius, librarian to the Pope, and Abbot of a

[2] Mor. lib. xix. c. xiii. in Job. xxix. Opp. tom. i. col. 567.   Par. 1675.
[3] In Apoc. c. iv. Opp. tom. v. col. 771.   Colon. 1612.
[4] De Ætat. Mundi, A.M. 3496, tom. ii. p. 108.

monastery at Rome.   To an Ecclesiastical History which he compiled from various Greek ·authors, this writer has annexed an appendix borrowed from a Patriarch of Constantinople in the preceding century, and containing, with several other catalogues of historical interest, a general Canon of the Scriptures, of every degree of authority.   From this document then we may learn with certainty what were the Books received by the Church of Rome in the time of the translator.   But here we find the Book of Maccabees, of Wisdom, Ecclesiasticus, Judith, Susanna, and Tobit noted as writings "to which objection is made, and which are not received by the Church [5]."

4. In the earlier half of the twelfth century, we find that Peter the Venerable, Abbot of Clugny, a personal friend of S. Bernard and of the Pope Eugenius, observed and taught the same distinction :—

"There remain, after these authentic Books of Holy Scripture, six others which are not to be dismissed in silence,—those of Wisdom, of Jesus the son of Sirach, Tobit, Judith, and the two Books of Maccabees, which although they have not been able to attain to the high rank of the foregoing, yet, on account of their laudable and very necessary doctrine, have deserved to be adopted by the Church [6]."

[5] Hist. Eccles. p. 189.   Par. 1649.

[6] Biblioth. Cluniac. col. 1143 ; by Marrier and Quercetanus.   Par. 1614.

5. In the thirteenth century lived Hugo de S. Charo, frequently called Hugh the Cardinal, to whom we owe the origin of our concordances of holy Scripture. In a Preface to his commentary on the Book of Joshua, this writer expressly says, that the Books of Ecclesiasticus and Wisdom, the Books of Maccabees, Judith, and Tobias, are "Apocryphal, and not reckoned in the Canon [7]."

6. These writings are similarly excluded from the Canon of De Lyra, the most celebrated commentator of the fourteenth century:—

"Having with God's help, written on all the Canonical Scriptures, ... I intend, relying on the same help, to write on the others which are not in the Canon, to wit, the Books of Wisdom, Ecclesiasticus, Judith, Tobit, and the Maccabees [8]."

He also cites and explains S. Jerome's account of their authority and value.

7. From the many witnesses of the fifteenth century, I select Antoninus, Bishop of Florence, who was canonized in 1523 by Adrian VI. This author, with the same reference to S. Jerome, declares that the six Books just named are "incompetent to decide disputed points," and suggests that "they perhaps have the same kind of authority

[7] Opp. tom. i. fol. 178, fa. 1. Ven. 1600. His opinion of them is comprised in the following couplet:—

"Hi quia sunt dubii, sub canone non numerantur;
Sed quia vera canunt, Ecclesia suscipit illos."

[8] Opp. tom. ii. fol. 283, fa. 1. Argent. 1501.

as the sayings of holy doctors approved by the Church [9]."

It is a remarkable fact that the very century in which the Council of Trent destroyed the primitive distinction between the Apocrypha and the Canon supplies testimonies in its favour as weighty as any to be found in the remains of the eight hundred years preceding. Of these I shall lay before the reader some of the more important.

8. From the ninth century downward, a Commentary on Scripture, known as the Ordinary Gloss, had been in great use among the Christians of the Latin tongue. It was a collection of expository notes gathered from approved writers and enlarged from time to time by many different hands. Its paramount reputation may be inferred from the title, namely, that of "authority," under which it was often cited. In the years 1501–2 an edition of the Bible with this Gloss and other annotations was published at Bâle, in the preface to which we read as follows:—

"Since there are many who from not bestowing much pains on holy Scriptures suppose that all the Books in the Bible are to be reverenced and religiously regarded with an *equal* veneration [the very words of the decree of Trent], not knowing how to distinguish between the Canonical Books and the Non-canonical, which the He-

[9] Sum. Theol. P. iii. tit. xviii. c. vi. § ii. Opp. tom. ii. Bas. 1511.

brews reckon among the Apocrypha .... we have therefore in this work distinguished and distinctly enumerated,
first, the Canonical Books, and afterwards the Non-
canonical, between which there is the same difference, as
between certainty and doubt. For the Canonical were
written under the dictation of the Holy Spirit; but when
or by whom the Non-canonical or Apocryphal were put
forth is not known. Nevertheless because they are very
good and useful, and nothing is found in them contrary
to the Canonical, therefore the Church reads and permits
them [1]."

9. In the year 1522 appeared the famous compilation of Francis Ximenes, known as the Com-
plutensian Polyglott, on which the Cardinal and
seven others had been engaged for no less than
seventeen years. The work was dedicated to
Leo X., and published with his express and formal
sanction [2]. In it the Books of Wisdom, Ecclesiasticus, Judith, Tobit, and Maccabees, with the
additions to Esther and Daniel are excluded from
the Canon, and the reader is informed that "the
Church receives them rather for the edification
of the people than for the confirmation of her
doctrines [3]."

10. The great Cardinal Caietan, whose death
took place only twelve years before the present
Roman Canon was settled by the Council of Trent,

---

[1] Bibl. cum Gloss. Ordin. et Expos. N. de Lyra. fol. 2, fa. 1.
[2] Prefixed to the first volume.   [3] Tom. ii. Prol. 2.

concludes his annotations on the Book of Esther
with these words :—

" Here, then, we end our commentaries on the historical Books of the Old Testament. For the rest, namely, Judith, Tobias, and the Books of the Maccabees, are accounted extra-canonical by the blessed Jerome, and are placed among the Apocrypha with the Books of Wisdom and Ecclesiasticus [4]."

In an epistle dedicatory addressed to the Pope, he enlarges on the obligation which "the whole Latin Church" owes to S. Jerome, for the care with which he distinguished these Books from the true Canon,—"thus saving us from being reproached by the Jews with forging for ourselves Books, or parts of Books, of the ancient Canon, which they are entirely without [5]."

11. In several versions of the Bible, published by members of the Church of Rome, within the quarter of a century immediately preceding the fourth session of Trent, the ancient distinction was carefully observed, and the grounds of it explained [6];

[4] Comment. in *Omnes Authenticos* V. T. Libros, fol. 481, fa. 2. Paris, 1546.

[5] Ibid. prefixed. This dedication is suppressed in the collected edition of his Commentaries, Lyons, 1639. A much longer series of testimonies, patristic and mediæval, than has been here given, may be seen in Bishop Cosin's Scholastical History of the Canon, cc. iii.—xviii.

[6] See the Latin version of Pagninus, Lugd. 1528, fol. 305, fa. 1, reprinted at Cologne in 1541; also the Prologue to the French version of Jaques Le Fèvre (Stapulensis), printed by Martin L'Empereur at Antwerp in 1530, reprinted in 1534 and 1541; and the

while every edition of the ordinary version during the same period, so far as I can learn, was accompanied by the well-known prefaces of S. Jerome [7]. Nay, strange to relate, these prefaces, so explicit and decisive against the equal authority of the Apocrypha and the Canon, continued to appear long after the decision of Trent [8]; and, stranger still, in some instances, they are accompanied by the decree of the Council [9].

Italian of Brucioli, Venice, 1532, (observe particularly the note prefixed to the Book of Baruch, fol. 274, fa. 2); republished, Ven. 1538, with some Apocryphal additions, and again with a commentary, Ven. 1540. The Prologues of Jerome appear with the new version published at Paris in 1545 by R. Stephens in parallel columns with the Vulgate, and accompanied by the notes of Vatablus. The decree of Trent is dated April 8, 1546. The curious title-page to the second edition (Ven. 1538) of Brucioli's version shows that the additions to Daniel and Esther (now in the Canon of Rome) were so far from being generally received in his day, that they were hardly known :— " The Bible containing the sacred books of the O. T. . . . to which are added two Books of Esdras, and some more chapters of Daniel and Esther *lately discovered*, as also the Third Book of Maccabees," &c.

[7] I find them, for example, in the Parisian of R. Stephens, 1528, 1532; and of John Benedict, 1541; in those of Lyons, 1519, 1522, 1526, 1536; of Antwerp, 1534, 1540; and in that of Cologne, 1529.

[8] I have observed them, e. g. in the edition of Malermi's old version published at Venice in 1541; in the Paris editions of Benedict, 1549, 1564, and of Stephens, 1545, 1555, and 1557; in that of Lyons, 1583, which had an express sanction from Rome (see last page); in the Antwerp, 1565, published by permission of Philip II.; in the Frankfort of 1566. The decisive Prologus Galeatus, which has been quoted in p. 50, is given without the other prefaces in the Venetian of 1557, with the Scholia of Isidorus Clarius, fol. 92. f. 2.

[9] E. g. the decree appears with all the Prefaces in the Roman edition of 1624; in the Antwerp of 1599 (see the end of the volume); in the Parisian of 1652 by Vitre (see end), of 1629 and 1729, Sumpt. Soc. (Interpr. Dupl.; altera vetus, altera nova; cum notis Vatabli,

I think, my dear Sir, that you have now ample LETTER
means of judging the character of the statement II.
SECT. V.
which you have quoted from Dr. Dixon:—

"The Canon (i.e. as we must understand it, the Canon
adopted at Trent) was clearly determined by the unanimous consent of the eastern and western Churches,
centuries upon centuries before the Council of Trent[1]."

This assertion is calculated to try severely the
courtesy, as well as charity, of an opponent.

VI. It does not satisfy this person to claim SECT. VI.
the universal consent of the western Church; he
has the confidence to appropriate that of the eastern

&c.); in the Lyons of 1676 (see the end), and of 1727, by Andreas
Laurens. (For the decree, see P. i. opposite Gen. i.; for the Prefaces, P. v. p. 203, after the last book of Esdras). In the Antwerp
collection of versions, 1616, we have the Decree accompanied by the
Epistle to Paulinus and the Prologus Galeatus. In the edition
authorised by Sixtus V. in 1590, the Prefaces were all omitted; but
two years later, in the revision of Clem. VIII., it was intimated that
the "Holy See did not condemn those who had inserted the Prefaces
of S. Jerome, &c., in other editions." I am unable to say how far
this practice prevails now; but an incidental remark of Liebermann
would lead one to infer that it is general:—"S. Jerome, in the Prologus Galeatus, which has been prefixed to the Vulgate, &c." Instit.
Theol. l. i. c. i. tom. i. p. 81. Mogunt. 1853. It should be added that
the notes by which S. Jerome has distinguished the parts of Esther
which are found only in the Greek, or the old Latin version, and
were not acknowledged by the Jews, are given in all those editions
which insert his Prefaces.

[1] From "General Introduction to the Sacred Scriptures, by the
Most Rev. Dr. Dixon, late Scripture Professor at Maynooth. Vol. i.
Diss. i. p. 33." Similarly Liebermann:—"The Council (of Trent) did
not put forth this solemn decree to reconcile differences among Catholics, or to confirm still anxious and doubting minds;—there was only
one Canon of all the Churches, and that settled;—but to establish the
ancient and general doctrine of the whole Church against the inno-
vators." l. ii. p. ii. c. i. art. ii. p. 403.

too. And you have believed him ! For you declare,
I find, that upon this subject of the Canon, "as
upon nearly every other point, the Greeks agree
with you ;"—whereas, there is not in all history a
shadow of foundation for the assertion. It is noto-
riously the very opposite of the truth. The Greeks
never shared in that uncertainty, with regard to some
of the Apocryphal Books, which certainly prevailed
largely in the western Church for centuries before
the Reformation; and their doctrine with respect
to them is at the present time the same that it ever
was. This will be sufficiently proved by a short
extract from the "Longer Catechism of the Orthodox, Catholic, Eastern Church, examined and
approved by the most holy Governing Synod of
Russia," and therefore a document of undeniable
authority. After an enumeration of the Scriptures
of the Old Testament, (agreeing, name for name,
with that in the Sixth Article,) we have the following questions and answers on the Apocrypha :—

"*Q.* Why is there no notice taken in this enumeration
of the Books of the Old Testament of the Book of the
Wisdom of the son of Sirach, and of certain others ?

A. Because they do not exist in the Hebrew.

Q. How are we to regard these last-named Books?

A. Athanasius the Great says, that they have been appointed by the Fathers to be read by proselytes, who are
preparing for admission into the Church [2]."

---

[2] Longer Catechism, translated in Blackmore's Doctrine of the
Russian Church, p. 38.

VII. The professed object of your first letter is to explain, for our general benefit, the "real sentiments of Roman Catholics concerning the Bible and the Church." I beg that you will not suppose me to accuse you of dealing insincerely with the public, if I express my regret, that in the performance of your self-imposed task, you have not confined yourself to the authorised statements of your Church. You will perceive, upon reflection, that we cannot permit your word to vouch for more than your own opinion. In fact, the well-known policy of Rome, and the constant language of her favourite writers, are so inconsistent with the spirit and substance of your remarks, that I am constrained to ascribe to you a share in the very strange ignorance on this subject which prevails so largely among the Roman Catholics of England. I cannot, for example, imagine you to be aware of the condemnation of the following propositions, pronounced by Clement XI. so late as the beginning of the last century :—

"The reading of holy Scripture is for all." "The obscurity of the holy Word of God is no reason why the laity should dispense with reading it." "Christians ought to keep the Lord's day holy by reading pious books, and, above all, the holy Scriptures: it is ruinous to wish to keep a Christian from such reading." "To forbid to Christians the reading of holy Scripture, particularly of the Gospel, is to forbid the use of light to the sons of light[3]."

[3] Bullar. Clem. XI. Ann. 1713. Props. 80—82, 85.

These pious sentiments, with many others as little open to real objection, were declared by the Pope, and through him by the Church of Rome, to be "scandalous, pernicious, impious, blasphemous, suspected of heresy, savouring of heresy, favourable to heretics, heresies, and schisms, &c.;"—and yet I must think that those English and French members of that Church, who speak and write of holy Scripture in the tone which I am happy to observe in your letters, do in their hearts approve of them [4].

Another conviction is forced on my mind by your remarks. You evidently are not aware, that the Bible, as a book, is utterly unknown to the mass of the people in countries where the Church of Rome is dominant [5].

As little can you know that you and your brethren in England are indirectly indebted to us, whom you are taught to regard as heretics, for the

[4] See further remarks on this subject in Letter ix. Sect. ii.

[5] Take for example the state of things at Rome itself:—"As to the holy Scriptures, the only thing portable which assumes the name is a sort of Catechism of Bible history; and the smallest allowed edition of the Scripture text itself in the Italian language with which I am acquainted is Martini's, in upwards of twenty volumes. Even this, accompanied as it is with notes, and sanctioned by the licence of all the authorities, is nevertheless practically denied to general use. . . . . I am credibly informed by Romanists themselves, the moment any one betrays an inquiring disposition, as the result of reading the Bible, he is recommended to discontinue reading it; and if he needs further admonition, he is denied admission to the confessional," &c. —Voice from Rome. Burns, 1842, p. 8. The number of volumes in the edition mentioned is thirty-one, the Old Testament occupying twenty-two.

advantage which you enjoy in this respect over the less fortunate subjects of Rome in other countries. The case stands thus. Pius IV., in 1564, by the Fourth Rule of the Index of Prohibited Books, forbade the reading of holy Scripture in the vulgar tongue, without a special licence in writing from the Bishop or Inquisitor. The ground of the prohibition was set forth as follows :—

" It is manifest from experience that, if the holy Bible in the vulgar tongue be every where permitted indiscriminately, more harm than good arises therefrom, owing to men's rashness [6]."

Now, how comes it to pass, that, in spite of this universal law,—a law based, as you see, upon reasons which are at least as true now as they were in the days of Pius,—the English Roman Catholic has really enjoyed that degree of liberty of which you boast? The question shall be answered out of Dens, an authority to whom you will not, I am sure, except :—

" According to Steyart, the law has been received, and hitherto observed (with some variety, according to the nature of the countries) in by far the greatest part of the Catholic world; yea, in the whole purely Catholic part of the world. *Only where* Catholics have to live among heretics, has greater licence been allowed [7]."

Again, you say, " Catholics will be glad to receive

---

[6] Reg. Ind., printed after the Conc. Trident. Can.
[7] Theol. de Virt. N. 64. tom. ii. p. 103.

F

Catholic Bibles." I do not dispute your statement; but I should be very glad to see you test the fact by an experiment. Devote yourself, and all that you have, to procure for your poorer brethren, in all parts of your communion, a plentiful and accessible supply of the holy Scriptures in their own tongue. Make it a part of your task, also, to promote the devout and intelligent study of the sacred volume among the influential and educated laity. It is a work worthy of your best energies, and of sacrifices as great as ever man made. You will deserve, and if you succeed, you will in time receive, the general gratitude of the whole Christian world;—but, in the meanwhile, how much encouragement do you expect from those whose previous sanction it will be necessary to obtain? I do not say that you will in no case receive any. Where 'heretics' abound, and men must see the Bible in some shape or other, you may, upon the principle stated by Dens, be permitted to disseminate a cheap and convenient version, provided always that it be accompanied by notes, "precluding every possible danger of abuse [8]." This liberty, however, you will still enjoy, in a good measure, at the discretion of the local superiors of your people. But elsewhere, though annotated versions in the vulgar tongue have been warmly approved in general terms by two Popes,—one of them, perhaps for that chiefly, styled the Protestant

[8] Pius VI. to Martini, Ep. prefixed to Version.

Pope,—your attempt will meet, I fear, with little countenance or support. Of this you will be satisfied when you consider that, with all the means at the disposal of the Popes, they have not themselves thought proper to provide versions for general use, but have left the work to the casual piety of their more zealous, or less politic, subjects. It may perhaps be pleaded that there has been one exception to this neglect, in the attempt of Sixtus V. to introduce an Italian version among the people of that tongue, but the attempt, if it were made [9], serves only by its failure to show how irreconcilable is the free use of holy Scripture with the peculiar interests of the Church of Rome. The following is the account of its reception given by the biographer of this Pope :—

" Sixtus had already begun to have the Vulgate printed the year before this, which, though it afforded subject for

---

[9] I say this because the authority of Leti is not great. There is no reason, however, to doubt his accuracy in this respect. He says himself :—" Writers are found who, to excuse this Pontiff from a charge (though an unjust one), which the good Catholics, and especially the Spaniards, have brought against him, have given themselves licence to assert that Sixtus had never any thought of having such a work printed ; which is a strange oversight indeed, as it is proved not only by the authentic relations of many cotemporary writers, but by the visible evidence of many copies which are to be seen in divers libraries, as in that of the Grand Duke of Tuscany, the Medicæan of S. Lorenzo, the Ambrosian of Milan, and so many others ; not to speak of two copies found in the library at Geneva [where Leti resided many years] of the same Roman impression as the rest."—Vita di Sisto V., P. iii. l. iv. vol. iii. p. 386. Amsterdam, 1693.

many to talk about, yet did not give rise to so much noise as that of the present year (1589), in which he determined to have the Bible printed in the Italian tongue, —which was done at the press established by him ; and Sixtus ordered its publication by a very ample Bull ; which truly gave occasion to much talk ;—and some of the Cardinals spoke about it to the Pope, who made a jest of their scruples, going so far as to answer to certain Cardinals and to the (Spanish) Ambassador Olivarez, who spoke to him of it as a scandalous thing, and agreeable to the sentiments of the heretics,—' I have had it made for you who do not understand the Latin.' The more scrupulous Cardinals wrote about it to the Catholic King, that he might be pleased to provide for this by his zeal and through his authority, seeing that he was more interested than any other, in respect of the kingdom of Naples, and of Sicily, and the duchy of Milan, where, if such a Bible were read by all the commonalty, the novelty could not but unsettle the consciences of those people, since it was a law of the heretics to read the holy Scripture in the vulgar tongue [1]."

The Pope is said to have persevered, though the King of Spain warmly supported the remonstrances of his ambassador; but from some cause or other, probably in consequence of his death, which took place in the autumn of the ensuing year, his well-meant project was not attended by any permanent result.

VIII. Let us suppose, however, that Rome, conquered by opinion, has at length granted a reluctant

[1] Vita, u. s., p. 384.

sanction to the strange enterprise of her too zealous
son.   Another difficulty appears.   Your aim is to
distribute " Catholic Bibles ;" but what is a " Catholic Bible ?" Forgive me, if my language should cause
you pain : you cannot learn the truth without it.—
We will conceive you, then, presiding at a board of
interpretation, surrounded by translators such as
have too frequently come forward in your communion to minister an adulterated food to the
spiritual cravings of the people.   They assume,
and that honestly enough, that the Bible must at
all events agree in meaning with the established
doctrine of their Church ; but then this harmony is
not always quite so apparent as could be wished ;—
nay, there are some cases in which it perversely
happens that these two authorities seem at direct
variance with each other.   What then is to be done ?
If we may judge from the past, there will be
neither lack of resources, nor scruple in applying
them [2].   To some of your advisers, a skilful selection
of marginal notes will approve itself as the best
vehicle of the true Roman sense; another will
suggest the more effectual method of mistranslation ;
while a third party will insist on the advantages of

[2] Let not the reader suppose that these frauds have been observed
and condemned only by writers not in the communion of Rome.   To
give an example to the contrary ;—Father Simon honestly ascribes the
peculiarities of Véron's French version to this motive :—" As he was
a professor of controversies, he hath adapted some passages to his
own notions."—Crit. Hist. of Versions, N. T., vol. ii. c. xxxi. p. 236.

a still bolder practice, and advocate a little judicious interpolation. But a few days ago I held in my hand a Roman Catholic version of the New Testament in French, from which I culled some choice specimens of the use of these two last-named admirable expedients. Here are a few by way of sample :—

S. Matt. iii. 2. Do penance[3]; for the kingdom of heaven is at hand.

S. Luke ii. 41. His father and mother went every year in pilgrimage[4] to Jerusalem.

S. Luke iv. 8. Thou shalt worship the Lord thy God, and Him only shalt thou serve with latria[5].

Acts xiii. 2. As they offered to the Lord the sacrifice of the mass and fasted.

In the heading of this chapter we also read, "The sacrifice of the mass."

Eng. Tr. 1692. Véron was appointed missionary to the Protestants by Louis XIV. He died in 1649.

[3] This is very common where the Greek text has μετανοεῖν, which cannot possibly mean 'to do penance;' e. g. Luke x. 13; xiii. 3. 5. Acts ii. 38, &c. The English Roman Catholic version has the same mistranslation in all these places and many others. Its source is in the phrase *pœnitentiam agere*, used in the Vulgate, but the French version has "do penance" (faites pénitence) in one place at least (Acts iii. 19) where the Vulgate has *pœnitemini*.

[4] Similarly S. Paul, 2 Cor. viii. 19, is made to speak of "the companion of his pilgrimage;" and the Greek ξένος is frequently represented by 'pilgrim' (pélérin); as Matt. xxv. 35, &c.; Luke xxiv. 18.

[5] Roman Catholic divines hold that saints and angels may be adored with *dulia*, while *latria*, the highest kind of worship, is reserved for God. The effect of the interpolation is therefore to destroy the prohibition of saint-worship implied in the text.

1 Cor. iii. 15. If any man's work burn, he shall bear
the loss ; but he himself shall be saved, yet so as by the fire of purgatory.

1 Cor. vii. 10. But to those who are joined together by the Sacrament [6] of marriage, I give commandment, &c.

1 Tim. iv. 1. But the Spirit saith clearly that in the last times some shall separate themselves from the Roman faith.

Heb. xi. 30. By faith the walls of Jericho fell down after a procession of seven days round them.

1 John v. 17. There is a sin which is not mortal, but venial [7].

I am sure, my dear Sir, that this is not the way in which you would prepare a " Catholic Bible." Nor do I believe that the later divines of France, whatever their faults may be, or have been, would have lent countenance to a fraud so impious and shocking. At the same time, they cannot be acquitted of all participation in the sin of their

---

[6] This also occurs more than once, as 2 Cor. vi. 14 ; 1 Tim. iv. 3.

[7] A complete account of the version from which these extracts are made may be seen in Bishop Kidder's " Reflections on a French Testament," 1690, and the Memoir prefixed by Archdeacon Cotton to his reprint of it, published by Cochran, London, 1828. Nine copies at least exist in England ; two in the British Museum ; two in Dublin, viz. one in Trinity College, the other in Archbishop Marsh's Library ; one at Lambeth ; two at Oxford, viz. one in the Bodleian, the other at Christ Church ; one in the Chapter Library at Durham ; and one in the private collection of the Duke of Devonshire. Its title is as follows :—" Le Nouveau Testament de Nôtre Seigneur Jésus Christ. Traduit de Latin en François par les Théologiens de Louvain. A Bordeaux, &c., 1686." It appeared the year after the revocation of the edict of Nantes, and was designed to aid the effect of the persecution in the conversion of the Huguenots.

fathers.   Their great Bible in Latin and French[8], with notes and dissertations from Calmet, &c., contains many instances of mistranslation and interpolation, evidently originating in a motive similar to that which influenced the editors of the New Testament from which I have quoted.   It is true that the additions to the sacred text are in this edition printed in Italics, and therefore, if they had been confined to mere verbal elucidations of the necessary meaning of the original, no objection could have been made.   But there are some cases, unfortunately, in which a passage of uncertain meaning is by this means restricted to a particular sense,—and that, one which it will hardly bear,— and others, in which the version is thus made a vehicle for the insinuation of doctrines, or points of discipline, to which no reference can be discerned in the original.   The following texts will serve for example :—

Acts i. 15.   In those days Peter, *in quality of head of the Church*, rose up in the midst of the brethren.

Acts ii. 46.   They went every day to the temple, in the unity of the same spirit ; they persevered in prayer, and, breaking the bread *of the holy Eucharist* in the houses *of the faithful*, they partook of *this divine* food with joy and singleness of heart.

1 Tim. iii. 11, 12.   Let their wives likewise, (i. e. the

[8] Sainte Bible, en Latin et en Français, avec des Notes, &c., tirées du Commentaire de Calmet, de l'Abbé de Vence, &c.   I have used the fourth edition.   Paris, 1820—1824.

wives of the deacons,) *if they are married*, be honest, &c. Let them take for deacons, *when they shall be obliged to take married men for that purpose*, those who shall have married but one wife.

S. James v. 14, 15. Is any one sick among you? Let him send for the priests of the Church, and let them pray over him, anointing him with oil in the name of the Lord. And the prayer of faith, *joined to the holy unction*, shall save the sick: the Lord shall comfort him; and if he has sins, they shall be remitted to him. *Nevertheless, wait not to purify yourself from them by this remedy; but have recourse to the confession which Jesus Christ has established in His Church*[9].

I think, my dear Sir, that you will now find it less difficult to understand why we are unable to accept your honest English feeling upon this, and certain other subjects, as a true representation of the principles of your Church, or of your co-religionists in general.

I am, &c.

[9] This method of Italicised interpolation · was first adopted by Godeau, Bishop of Vence, who in 1668 published what he called a "pure and exact" version of the N. T. Its avowed plan was to "add certain words in a parenthesis and in Italics" where the text was obscure, or the connexion not very apparent. According to Father Simon his intention was entirely good; but from carelessness or some other cause "he often extended or limited the sense by this means *without* including his additions in a parenthesis, or distinguishing them by an Italic letter."—Crit. Hist., u. s., c. xxxiv. p. 262.

LETTER III.

LETTER
III.

MY DEAR SIR,

I OBSERVE with regret that you have fallen into the error, not uncommon among Roman Catholics, of supposing that the Queen of England is entitled by law to exercise over the Church in her realms a spiritual supremacy in all respects similar to that which you concede to the Bishop of Rome over your own communion. It is not my intention to dwell at any length upon your mistake, or upon any of the inferences to which it has led you; but I think it desirable that you and your readers should have the means of correcting an opinion as mischievous in its tendency as it is derogatory to the Church of your native land. I propose, therefore, in the present Letter, to inquire into the real nature and extent of the Royal Supremacy in

matters ecclesiastical, as established both by the LETTER
laws of the country and of the Church. III.

I. The mind of the Church is thus declared in SECT. I.
the Thirty-seventh Article of Religion :—

" Where we attribute to the Queen's Majesty the chief
government, by which title we understand the minds of
some slanderous folks to be offended, we give not to our
Princes the ministering either of God's Word or of the
Sacraments, the which thing the *Injunctions* also lately
set forth by Elizabeth our Queen do most plainly testify;
but that only prerogative, which we see to have been given
always to all godly Princes in holy Scriptures by God
Himself ; that is, that they should rule all estates and
degrees committed to their charge by God, whether they
be ecclesiastical or temporal, and restrain with the civil
sword the stubborn and evil-doers."

A similar reference to the Injunctions here mentioned occurs in the Statute, 5 Eliz. c. i. s. 14; by
which it was provided that the oath of supremacy
expressed in 1 Eliz. c. i. should be " taken and expounded in such form as set forth in an *Admonition*
annexed to the Queen's Majesty's *Injunctions*," &c.

The document to which the Article and the
Statute thus concur in sending us,—"*An Admonition
to simple men deceived by malicious*,"—was designed
to warn the ignorant against the notion of its being
implied in the oath above mentioned, that " the
Kings or Queens of this realm, possessors of the
crown, may challenge authority and power of ministry

of Divine service in the Church," &c.; "for certainly," it proceeds to explain,—

"Her Majesty neither doth nor ever will challenge any other authority than that was challenged and lately used by King Henry VIII. and King Edward VI., which is, *and was of ancient time,* due to the imperial crown of this realm[1]; that is, under God, to have the sovereignty and rule over all manner of persons born within these her realms, dominions, and countries, of what estate, either ecclesiastical or temporal, soever they be, so as no other foreign power shall or ought to have any supremacy over them[2]."

In the first year of William and Mary, the oath of supremacy was abolished; so that since that time the royal authority in ecclesiastical matters has rested solely on the declaration of the Church itself as just quoted, supported by that general sanction which the Articles have at various times obtained from the civil magistrate. These were accepted by the Queen in 1562, and by Parliament nine years after, and are also recognised by the last Act of Uniformity[3].

II. It is evident, then, that the only authority in things spiritual which has been entrusted by the law to the sovereigns of this country does not differ intrinsically from that which was exercised by their

---

[1] This ground was taken by Henry and his councillors from the first. See Gardiner, De Verâ Obedientiâ, foll. 17, 18. Argent. 1536.

[2] Wilkins' Conc. vol. iv. p. 188.

[3] 13 & 14 Car. II. c. iv. See Cardwell, Synodalia, vol. i. p. 74.

ancestors before the Reformation.   A similar authority, in fact, was once acknowledged to belong
to all Christian princes within their dominions, and
whether claimed or not, must still in effect be exercised, even by sovereigns in strict communion
with the Church of Rome.   I would earnestly
advise those who really wish to do justice to the
Church of England in this matter, to peruse, for
example, the collection of documents relating to
the Council of Trent, published by the French
government in 1613[4].   They will find there, in
the influence exercised in that Council by the Kings
of France and Spain, and in the rigid control which
they retained over the Bishops whom they sent to
it, a complete counterpart to English despotism at
the same period.   Or, in the *Epitome of Austrian
Ecclesiastical Law,* published by a Roman Catholic
statesman, the Count dal Pozzo, with a view to
suggest to the English government the best mode
of dealing with Irish discontent, they may see the
principles on which those sovereigns acted embodied by another nation in an elaborate and formal
system of written law.   I will make a few extracts
from this work on " the rights of sovereigns with
respect to religious matters :"—

   " The sovereign, in his capacity of defender of the
Christian religion, has undoubtedly the right, and has,

---

[4] Instructions et Missives des Roys Très-Chrestiens, &c., concernant le Concile de Trente.

at the same time, the duty, of providing that the citizens shall be instructed in the true principles of the Christian doctrine : he is obliged to watch over the prayers of the ministers of religion,—the catechism of children in the schools,—the instruction of young candidates for holy orders,—and consequently, also, the teaching of divinity. He has then occasionally both the power and the duty of enacting laws on all these matters suitable to the nature of the case."

" It likewise lies within the competence of the sovereign as the protector of the Church, to inculcate, by every means in his power, the due observance of the canons of the Church.   His principal task is to remove all abuses, because they prevent the efficacy of religion in diffusing a benevolent influence over the State.

" The rulers of Austria, duly renowned for their piety, have issued numerous laws and regulations on various points of ecclesiastical discipline ; such as, the conditions to be accomplished by candidates for holy orders ; the collation of benefices ; the order of performing the external Divine service ; the suppression of certain corrupt practices surreptitiously introduced into the ceremonies of worship, &c. . . . . The accidental rites of religion, as, for example, the great number of holidays, processions, pilgrimages, and nocturnal assemblies, may prove, in one way or another, prejudicial to the State.   It is, therefore, a privilege inherent in the sovereign, by his rights of *examination* and *prevention*, to reduce these arbitrary rites, under a certain regulation, as often as he judges them to be detrimental to the public welfare. . . . . It belongs to it to prescribe under what conditions the marriage contract can be validly established ; and all questions upon the validity of this contract, and on its consequences,

should be solved by the civil courts alone. These principles are laid down in the imperial constitution of 16th
January, 1783. . . . . It rarely happens that controversies
on disputed dogmas of the different persuasions are
attended with any advantage, while they are frequently
dangerous to the public tranquillity. It belongs, therefore, to the sovereign, considered either as protector of
the Church, or as defender of the State, to interpose in
order to put an end to such disputes. . . . . Religion abstractedly considered formed no part of the social com-
pact. . . . . It is, therefore, a right of the sovereign to allow
all his subjects, of different persuasions, the free exercise
of their religions, whenever it appears to him that the tenets
and ceremonies of any religious form whatsoever are not
repugnant to the welfare of the State. . . . Again, with respect to *ecclesiastical persons*, it seems clear and reasonable
that the sovereign, by his rights of *inspection* and *protection*, should possess the power of restricting their numbers, if they should increase in a manner injurious to the
State ; that he should settle the necessary qualities and
conditions of candidates for holy orders, their claims to
obtain benefices and ecclesiastical employments, with the
view that no improper or inefficient ministers should be
admitted to the sacred functions. Besides, the great
influence which the clergy possess over the people is a
further inducement to the head of the State to devote
his attention to this important task, and to exercise his
right of *prevention*. In short, he has full jurisdiction to
compel the ministers of the Church to perform their
duties, even by the most rigorous means. . . . . The same
rights appertain to the sovereign with respect to the
religious orders, &c. . . . . It is a matter of the utmost
importance to the State, that the honours and offices of

the Church should be conferred exclusively on persons from whose influence the State has nothing to dread. From this principle arises the right which the sovereign has, and ought to have, of choice among the candidates for ecclesiastical honours and offices; of excluding those about whom he entertains just apprehensions that their influence may be injurious to the State," &c.[5]

On these principles, or such as these, did the author from whom I quote advise and even urge the English nation to legislate, in the event of his Roman Catholic brethren in this kingdom obtaining the privileges for which they were contending :—

"Let the king (of England) be invested by Act of Parliament with all the rights and prerogatives which other kings or heads of governments exercise elsewhere without opposition; let sound and wise regulations upon ecclesiastical matters be introduced, and let them be faithfully observed[6]."

His mode of stating the result will surprise many :—

"At the same time that the Pope will always be considered as the head of Catholicism as to the spiritual jurisdiction and dogmatic matters, the King of England may, by the authority of Acts of Parliament, assume with great propriety, and without any inconsistency, the functions of the *head* of Catholicism as to the external policy of this persuasion[7]." "They will see the King

[5] Catholicism in Austria, pp. 120—128. London, 1827.
[6] Dissertation, &c., appended to Catholicism in Austria, p. 209.
[7] Pref. p. xvi.

of England as much the *head* of the Catholic Church as he possibly can be (salvâ substantiâ), almost as much so as he is of the Protestant Church, because his situation will be precisely that of the Emperors of Austria, Russia, &c.[8] "

It appears then that this able foreigner could see no difference in principle between the Royal Supremacy in England and in Austria, and deemed it both expedient and just that the supremacy exercised over the Church in this country by sovereigns attached to its communion should be extended over the ecclesiastical affairs of their Roman Catholic subjects. Nay, it is evident, if he proposed the Austrian law as a strict model for our proceedings, that he would invest the civil ruler with a power of continual and minute interference in spiritual matters from which the Church of England is altogether free.

We see also, that according to this writer, the Emperor of Russia, a prince not in communion with Rome, is nevertheless in such a position that, adopting a phrase common in England though certainly improper, he does not scruple to speak of him as the *head* of the Roman Catholic Church in his dominions. I will illustrate this by another extract:—

"The Empress of Russia, Catherine II., in the years 1782 and 1795, only by ukases, founded Catholic Epis-

---

[8] Dissertation, &c. p. 207.

G

copal Sees, reserving to herself the right of nomination; ordered, that Catholic prelates should receive no mandates but from her and the senate; forbade the publication of any document from the court of Rome before the government had declared that it contained nothing contrary to the laws of the State; and threatened with the severest penalties such Catholic priests as should attempt, under any pretence whatever, to convert Russian subjects belonging to other communions. The Pope did not oppose the Empress, but conferred the canonical institution upon the Bishops nominated by her. A similar practice obtains in the present day, not only in Russia, but also in that part of Poland which was re-united to the Russian empire in 1815 [9]."

I shall offer no comment on the propriety or wisdom of these arrangements, whether proposed or in existence. I refer to them, because they will enable you and your friends to understand somewhat better the relation subsisting between the Church and State in England; and will therefore mitigate, if they do not altogether remove, your prejudice against it [1]. With such facts before him,

---

[9] Dissertation, &c. p. 194.

[1] "Kings have a supreme power immediately from God, and inferior to God alone in things temporal. But by things temporal I understand not only those things which are merely temporal, but even spiritual things, especially material, so far as they are necessary for the preservation of peace in the temporal state, or oppose to it a necessary hindrance; for from that point of view things spiritual exceed the limits of the spiritual and enter the rank of things temporal. And according to this explanation may be defended in a sound and catholic sense the proposition that kings are supreme lords in things spiritual, as they take on them the nature of things

a serious and truthful Roman Catholic will feel it best to maintain silence on the question of the Royal Supremacy; or, if he is obliged to deal with the subject, will certainly avoid the tone of triumph and derision too common with ill-informed and disingenuous disputants.

III. I cannot quit this subject without entering my protest against the language in which you have expressed your view of the Royal Supremacy. You speak repeatedly, and with some apparent satisfaction of our chief ruler as "the Supreme Head" of the Church of England. I am sure you cannot be aware that neither the Church nor the law of the land acknowledge this title; and that its employment is highly offensive to every well-instructed and thoughtful Churchman. The tyrant Henry put forward a claim to be so called, simply and absolutely; but Convocation refused to humour him so far, and he was obliged to content himself with the style of "Supreme Head, *quantum per Christi legem*

---

temporal, in the same manner as in the temporal."—Catholico-Romanus Pacificus, § xiii. p. 161. Oxon. 1678. The author of this book was a learned Benedictine, named John Barnes. His fate was melancholy. "For his sober work," says Dr. Basire, "that good Irenæus, though of blameless life and unspotted reputation, was seized in the middle of Paris, stripped of his habit, and in a barbarous manner tied like a beast to a horse, and being thus carried away with the utmost speed, first into Flanders, then to Rome, was there thrust into the dungeon of the Inquisition, and afterwards into a prison for lunatics."—Pref. (from Basire's Liberty of the Britannic Church. Eng. Trans. p. 40, note.) He had promised the public a work on the Primacy, which may have accelerated his fate.

licet [2]." The grounds on which he was permitted to assume the title when thus modified will surprise you greatly, and, if I am not much mistaken, constrain you to confess that the Church of England is not justly charged with Erastianism for that act of her Convocation.   They were thus stated by Bishop Gardiner:—

"I certainly do not see why it should offend any one that the prince is called the head of the English Church, more than that he is called the head of the kingdom of England. . . . Since the Church of England is at this day composed of the same persons, as are signified under the word kingdom, of whom the prince is the head when they are termed the kingdom of England, shall he not be the head of the same persons when they are called the Church of England? . . . Beyond doubt, if he be the head of the people, and that by the ordinance of God, which no one denies, even then when both people and prince are widely separated from God by unbelief, how much more now when coming, by the power of God, to the same profession of faith, they have by that means formed a Church, ought he to retain the name of head [3]?"

To the objection that "Christ only is the Head of the Church," he replies:—

"We all confess it. . . . But wherein Christ, the Mediator of God and man, Himself God and man, is the Head of the Church, *that* Church admits of no qualification, since it is not the English alone, but the French also, and Spanish, and Roman too, being confined to no place. . . .

[2] Collier's Eccl. Hist. P. ii. b. i. p. 62.
[3] De Ver. Obed. foll. 9, 11.

Therefore let this be beyond controversy, as a thing, strife about which—not to say disputation—would be impious. And that this may be put aside, and no ground left for misrepresentation,. to the word 'head' is added 'on earth,' and to the word 'Church' is added 'of England⁴.' "

That the warmest *English* partisans of Rome at this period were able to see that the title, however objectionable, was not absolutely and entirely irreconcilable with their own theory of the Papal Supremacy, is evident from the fact that it was employed by Queen Mary nearly a year after her accession, and probably up to the time of her marriage. We have the express testimony of a French Bishop, then at the court of England, to this important fact:—

" To assure them (the English nobles, &c.) the more of their possession (of the Church property in their hands), and to make them regard the coming of this prince (Philip) with more favour and patience, she has not been ashamed to take again that blasphemous title which she had dropped three months ago,—causing herself now, and for the last six days, to be called *Supreme Head* of the Church of England and Ireland⁵."

⁴ De Ver. Obed. foll. 16, 17.
⁵ Noailles, Ambassades en Angleterre, par Vertot, v. iii. p. 175. A Leyde, 1763. The despatch bears date April 23, 1554. The title which Noailles terms blasphemous was used in his own country about half a century later. In one of the documents published by royal authority in 1609, under the name of "Traictéz des Droicts et Libertéz de l'Eglise Gallicane," we are told that the Bishops of the time of Clovis "esteemed the King assisted by his Council of State, and not

From another Roman Catholic writer we learn that she only ceased to exact the oath of supremacy from clergymen on their promotion at the time to which the above extract refers [6].

How Cranmer understood it may be collected from the general tenor of his answers to the commissioners on his trial;—though the explanation which he gave has probably suffered from the carelessness or malice of a hostile reporter:—

"*Dr. Martin.* Who say you then is the supreme head? *Cranmer.* Christ. *M.* But whom hath Christ left here on earth his vicar and head of the Church? *Cr.* Nobody. *M.* Oh, why told you not King Henry this, when you made him supreme head? and now nobody is! This is treason against his own person, as you then made him. *Cr.* I mean not but every king in his own realm and dominion is supreme head, and so was he supreme head of the Church of Christ in England [7]. *M.* Is this always true, and was it ever so in Christ's Church? *Cr.* It was so. *M.* Then what say you by Nero? *Cr.* He was the mightiest prince of the earth after Christ was ascended.

the Pope, the head on earth, after God, of the Church in his kingdom," p. 175.   Dupin honestly allows that this and several similar propositions in the same volume "may have a good sense." Dissert. Histor. D. vii. c. iii. § viii. p. 582. *Paris*, 1686.

[6] Sarpi, Hist. Conc. Trid. l. v. ann. 1554, p. 312.   Aug. Trinob. 1620.

[7] So Gardiner, De Ver. Obed. fol. 18, fa. 2:—"Princes have in fact always been heads of the Church, even then when they were only called its defenders, if to be the heads of the Church is to be over the whole body, and to enjoin to its several members what might be for the good of the whole, sometimes to relax and indulge, and so to regulate and govern each that the glory of God and the profession of the faith be daily increased."

M. Was he head of Christ's Church? *Cr.* Nero was Peter's head. *M.* I ask whether Nero was head of the Church, or no? If he were not, it is false that you said before that all princes be, and ever were, heads of the Church within their realms. *Cr.* Nay, it is true; for Nero was head of the Church, that is, in worldly respects of the temporal bodies of men of whom the Church consisteth; for so he beheaded Peter and the Apostles [8]."

The same questions were put to Rogers the Protomartyr by Gardiner, who had himself been the most forward advocate of the new title, and with the same result. His own account of his examination has been preserved :—

"*Rogers.* I know none other head but Christ of the Catholic Church, &c. . . . *L. Chancellor.* Why didst thou then acknowledge King Henry the Eighth to be the supreme head of the Church, if Christ be the only Head? *R.* I never granted him to have any supremacy in spiritual things, as are the forgiveness of sins, giving of the Holy Ghost, authority to be a judge above the Word of God. *L. Ch.* Yea, said he, and Tunstal, Bishop of Durham, and N., Bishop of Worcester, if thou hadst said so in his days, (and they nodded the head at me with a laughter,) thou hadst not been alive now. *R.* Which thing I denied, and would have told them how he was said and meant to be supreme head.—But they looked and laughed one upon another, and made such a business, that I was constrained to let it pass.—There lieth also no great weight thereupon, for *all the world knoweth what the meaning was* [9]."

It is evident, then, that the true doctrine of the supremacy was not forgotten or denied by those

---

[8] Fox, b. xi. vol. iii. p. 550. Ed. 1684. [9] Ibid. p. 99.

who allowed the king to assume the title which he so much coveted. But the very facts which prove this, prove also the extreme danger of the concession. They show that ignorant and designing men could give it an interpretation entirely foreign to its original meaning; and thus make it in the hands of an unscrupulous and powerful prince, an engine for the subversion of all truth and order in the Church. There can be little doubt that it led mainly to those misconceptions against which the *Admonition* already quoted was expressly directed. It is probable, however, that the profanity of the title was the chief cause of its abrogation. This took place on the accession of Elizabeth, when the oath of supremacy was so altered as to declare her simply " the supreme governor in this realm, . . . as well in all spiritual or ecclesiastical things or causes, as temporal." The feeling of the Queen herself upon this subject is clearly described in some contemporary letters of Bishop Jewel :—

" The Queen is not willing to be styled in speech or in writing the *head* of the English Church; for she says forcibly that that dignity has been given to Christ alone, and is not suitable for any mortal :—moreover, that those titles have been so foully defiled by Antichrist, that they cannot be piously employed by any one for the future [1]."

SECT. IV.   IV. It is true that inconsiderate members of the

[1] Ep. xiv. ad Bulling. May 22, 1559. Zurich Letters. First Series. Camb. 1842. Sim. Ep. ix. ad Pet. Mart. :—" The Queen does not choose to be called the head of the Church,—which certainly does not displease me."

Church of England sometimes speak of the sovereign as its "head," or even as its "supreme head;" and we have therefore little right to blame the Roman Catholic who, like yourself and the Count dal Pozzo, may fall into the same error. But we must and do protest against the justice and propriety of taunts and arguments, the imaginary grounds of which have been derived from this mistake. Or, if it be thought right to judge the Church of England by the loose expressions of her ignorant or thoughtless children, let Rome be weighed in the same balance : or rather,—for we can afford to ask less than justice for ourselves,— against the vulgar error upon our side, set the well-weighed judgement of the grave divines and learned canonists of Rome. That inaccurate expression of the Royal Supremacy on which we are commenting, can never, in the mind of the most prejudiced, compete with the absurdity and impiety of such propositions as the following, deliberately uttered and maintained for the exaltation of the Bishop of Rome. They have been collected by a celebrated writer of your communion, who condemns them as strongly as, I trust, you will yourself:—

"In those things which the Pope wills, his will is to him instead of reason . . . . nor is there any one to say to him, Why doest thou so[2]?"

[2] Gloss. in verba *Veri Dei vicem*, Corp. Jur. Can. Decret. Greg. IX. l. i. tit. vii. cap. iii. in Tentativa Theologica, a Treatise on Episcopal

" The Church is the slave born of the Roman Pontiff[3]."

" Thou art our shepherd, our physician, our pilot, our husbandman; thou, in fine, art a second God on the earth[4]."

" The sight of thy Divine Majesty, by whose flashing splendour weak eyes are blinded[5]."

" The power of the Pope is infinite, in that 'the Lord is great, and so is his power, and of the greatness thereof there is no end[6].' "

" As no one can appeal to himself, so no one can appeal from the Pope to God, for the sentence and the court of God and the Pope are one and the same[7]."

The following is the dedication of a work written against the famous Declaration of the Gallican Clergy:—

" To the Best, the Greatest, and Chief Pontiff, Innocent XI., Christ's Vicar, Lord of the city and of the world, sole janitor of heaven, earth, and hell, and infallible oracle of the faith, Nicholas Cevoli humbly dedicates, consecrates, presents," &c.[8]

Take another instance from the Decrees of Gratian, a collection of early decisions on which the Canon Law of Rome is founded:—

" It is clearly enough shown that the Pope, who, it is certain, was styled a God by that pious Prince Constan-

Rights, &c. by Father A. Pereira, Priest and Doctor of Lisbon, p. 130. Engl. Tr. by Mr. Landon. Lond. 1847.

[3] Card. Cajetan. De Comp. Pap. et Conc. Ibid.

[4] Marcelius, Archbishop of Corfu, in an oration to Julius II. in the fifth Lateran Council, Sess. iv. A.D. 1512. Pereira, p. 181.

[5] Pucci, in the same Council, Sess. x. Ibid.

[6] Aug. Triumph. de Ancon. in Summâ Theol. Ibid.

[7] Id., u. s.   [8] Pereira, ibid.

tine, ... can neither be bound nor loosed in any degree by the secular power; and that God cannot be judged by men is manifest[9]."

This extraordinary argument is ascribed to Pope Nicholas I. The statement respecting Constantine is, of course, a fiction; but if you have cast your eyes over these blasphemies, you will not be surprised, though you may be grieved, to learn that in many editions of the Canon Law the Bishop of Rome is roundly and directly styled "Our Lord God the Pope[1]."

These sentiments and expressions of Popes, canonists, and divines have never been rejected or

[9] Gratian, P. i. dist. xcvi. c. vii. *Satis evidenter.* More than a hundred examples of extravagance, similar to those in the text, are collected in the *Gravamina adversus Syn. Trident. Restit.* P. ii. caus. viii. *Ob Tyrannidem Papæ,* p. 201. Argent. 1565.

[1] In the gloss on the Extrav. of John XXII. tit. xiv. c. iv. "It is quite certain that the Popes have never reproved or rejected this title, for the passage in the gloss referred to appears in the edition of the Canon Law published at Rome in 1580, by Gregory XIII., and the *Index Expurgatorius* of Pius V., which orders the erasure of other passages, yet leaves this one."—Pereira, p. 180. "So it is in two editions published at Lyons in 1584 and 1606; and in those of Paris published in 1585, 1601, 1612."—Id. p. 130. It also occurs in those of Lyons in 1526, 1556, 1559, 1572, and those of Paris in 1522, 1561. See note to the Epistle prefixed by Calfhill to his Answer to Martiall's Treatise of the Cross, p. 6. Parker Society's edit. Gregory XIII., in the Bull appended to his edition, speaks of it in these terms:—"We decree, sanction, and ordain that it shall not be permitted to any one . . . . to add to or take from, to alter or transpose, or to add any interpretations to, the books of Canon Law as *revised, corrected, and expurgated* by our command," &c. This Bull appears in the subsequent editions, and also in the editions of the Corpus Juris Can. without the glosses.

condemned, and only in one instance,—namely, in this last and perhaps worst case,—silently, and after a long time, withdrawn by the authorities of the Church of Rome. Surely then, before Roman Catholics endeavour to persuade us that their Church is not responsible for them, they should at least cease to taunt the Church of England with the title of Supreme Head, sometimes ignorantly ascribed to our chief magistrate—a title admitted but for a short period, and then only with a saving qualification, and which now for three hundred years has been repudiated and abolished.

V. Pursuing the imaginary parallel between the Papal Supremacy and the Royal authority in England, you next come to the conclusion that "we must ascribe to the Queen the power of *defining doctrine* when disputed;" and you gravely refer us to the famous Gorham case as an example of its exercise. I should hope that ere this you have without my aid discovered the groundless nature of this opinion ; but as I have reason to believe that it is largely entertained by Roman Catholics both here and abroad, I must entreat your patience while I show briefly its true character and value. If you will take the trouble to refer to the judgement delivered in the case in question, you will at once see that the judges expressly and pointedly disclaimed doing the very thing which you assert that they did. You say

that they " defined doctrine." *They* tell us that
they merely decided a question of fact : —

" The question which we have to decide is not whether
they (*i. e.* the opinions of Mr. Gorham) are theologically
sound or unsound, *but* . . . whether these opinions are contrary or repugnant to the doctrines which the Church of
England by its articles, formularies, and rubrics requires
to be held by its ministers," &c.

In the course of the trial, the defective constitution of this tribunal as a court of appeal in matters
ecclesiastical betrayed itself in a remarkable manner.
It soon became evident that the judges did not at
all understand the closeness and precision with
which the terms of theological science are used by
good divines, and that they had even, in some instances, quite failed to apprehend their proper
meaning[2]. The result was, that they attributed to

---

[2] " Ecclesiastical discipline, together with theology, representing
organized and historic systems, are full of technical terms, which are
to be learned only like the technical terms of other sciences or arts ;
and lawyers have no greater inborn or spontaneous knowledge of
these terms than they have of the differential calculus. Neither have
they, in virtue of their being lawyers, the theological habit of mind,
without which these technical terms are in many cases ill to be
apprehended. We may frequently observe that when they get into
people's mouths, they are, because misunderstood, only instruments
of delusion to those who use and those who hear them. For example,
many men, and even a judge or two, will talk about an *opus operatum*,
meaning thereby a perfunctory or ceremonial act—a sense, I need
not say, wholly different from the true one. In short, Right Rev.
Sir, to lay aside circumlocution, and utter outright the word which
solicits me, there is great fear lest judges, dragged *pro re natâ* into

certain formularies of the Church a vagueness and uncertainty from which they are entirely free, and, at the same time, ascribed to Mr. Gorham opinions comparatively harmless, and certainly very unlike those for which he was rejected by his Bishop. To give countenance to their decision, they brought forward some passages from various divines, the accuracy and genuineness of which they, most unfortunately, had taken upon trust [3]. Moreover, contrary to the usual practice in cases of appeal, they omitted to notice the grounds on which the judgement of the court below was based, and to give their reasons for dissenting from it. Such errors and irregularity, however, do not alter or affect the *nature and essence* of the jurisdiction which they exercised in the name of the sovereign. The Queen on that occasion put forth substantially no other authority than that "supreme power over all persons, and in all causes," which she occasionally exercises over Roman Catholics and other classes of Dissenters, when her aid is invoked for the settlement of their internal differences. Thus in the matter of the famous Hewley Trust her judges were called upon to "consider the particular religious creed and faith" of various dissenting bodies

theology, should, and of course to the detriment of somebody or other, talk nonsense."—Mr. Gladstone's Letter to the Bishop of Aberdeen, p. 8. London, Murray, 1852.

[3] See Letters to a Seceder by the present writer, L. viii. p. 91.

"as compared with that of Lady Hewley[4]," and, in pursuance of this obligation, the Vice-Chancellor of England "delivered from the bench something very like a dogmatic treatise, and concluded with a judgement that alienated dissenting endowments from purposes to which they had hitherto been applied on grounds avowedly dogmatic[5]." To convince you that Roman Catholics are subject to an authority of the same kind, whatever the form under which it may be exercised, I beg to refer you to the report of a case tried at Galway, on the 27th day of August, 1850, the event of which turned upon the question whether certain parties had observed the prescribed discipline of the Church of Rome. The titular Bishop of the diocese deposed to the rules of that discipline :—

" The Council of Trent does not require more than one year between the admission and profession of a nun ; but the rules of the Convent of Mercy require two. In some instances the Church dispenses with the usual time," &c.

In both these cases then, as clearly as in that of Mr. Gorham, the representatives of Her Majesty were called upon to decide whether certain parties before them had or had not conformed to the internal principles of the religious body to which they belonged. If then such exercise of her Supremacy

[4] Speech of the Lord Chancellor in the House of Lords, May 3, 1844.
[5] Mr. Gladstone's Letter, u. s., p. 7.

be held a stain upon the Church of England, it is equally a note against Protestant Dissent and against Rome.

VI. Before we proceed to consider the account which you have given us of the Papal Supremacy, I must beg you to observe that your statements do not always exhibit the acknowledged doctrine of your Church, or even of the majority in it. And yet you must allow that nothing which has not either the expressed sanction of Rome, or general opinion in its favour, ought to be called a " Roman Catholic Principle." There is danger, therefore, lest you should, unintentionally of course, mislead some of your readers by the indiscriminate application of that term to all the opinions which you have put forth. For this reason, I think it necessary to point out the extreme inaccuracy of the following representation :—

" Roman Catholics do not believe the Pope to be inspired, or impeccable, or personally infallible, or arbitrarily absolute."

' There is only one particular in this statement which can be allowed to pass without challenge. I freely acknowledge that Roman Catholics do not believe the Pope to be "impeccable," and should very much doubt whether their adversaries had ever given occasion for the denial by supposing it of them. The case is different with respect to his "inspiration." I believe that this is explicitly held by very many of his subjects, and implicitly by nearly all the rest. Indeed, I do not see how those who believe him to be infallible can avoid supposing him "inspired." Whence can inerrancy in doctrine proceed, but from the Spirit of truth, given to lead the Church into all truth? His inspiration is on this ground maintained by doctors of great weight and name. Thus Dens:—

"The Chief Pontiff defining *ex cathedrâ* matters relating to faith or morals is infallible; which infallibility proceeds from the special assistance of the Holy Ghost [6]."

And Liguori:—

" It belongs to the Providence of the Holy Spirit that the Pope shall never act or decree aught rashly or imprudently in matters so important [7]."

Nor is it right to assert universally that Roman Catholics do not believe the Pope to be " personally infallible;" by which I presume you to mean that they do not believe it impossible for him to hold heretical opinions in private, though assured that he

[6] Theol. Mor. et Dogm. De Eccl. n. 96, de Infall. S. Pont.; tom. ii. p. 159.

[7] Dissert. de Pont. Auct. § i.; tom. i. p. 146. Antv. 1821. The Church of Rome, as represented by the Papal system, has thoroughly identified herself with the teaching of Liguori. "The Congregation of Rites allowed the cause of his beatification to be brought forward in 1796, and on the 14th of May, 1802, decided that it might be safely proceeded with, the Cardinal-reporter having declared that the theologians, who had examined his manuscript and printed works, had found nothing censurable in them." Life, by Dr. Wiseman, p. 54. This decision of the theologians was confirmed by Pius VII., May 18, 1803. Dublin Calendar, 1845, p. 167.

H

would be restrained from declaring them *ex ca-thedrá*. For, however absurd it may seem, and contrary to the facts of history, many Roman Catholics do certainly contend that his infallibility is not limited to his decrees or actions as he is the head of the Church. Thus, Dens has a chapter to prove, that " the Pope cannot be a heretic even in his private capacity [8]."

Again;—the Pope, you tell us, is not regarded by those whom he rules as " arbitrarily absolute."

We know that in practice he is much controlled in the government of the Church by the College of Cardinals; but this is a mere accident. They do not pretend to any divine right to advise or influence him, and Popes may act, and have acted, in entire independence of them. Thus, the system of nepotism was abolished by a Bull of Innocent XII. against the earnest remonstrances of the Cardinals [9]. The very title which is given to one class of. Papal briefs, as proceeding *motu proprio*, from the uninfluenced will of the Supreme Pontiff, ascribes an arbitrary power to him who issues them. In fact, the present teachers of the Church of Rome re-

---

[8] De Eccles. n. 97, p. 162. Bossuet says truly enough that the assertors of Papal infallibility *must* hold this extravagant opinion, if they would avoid inextricable difficulties. App. ad Defens. Declar. Cler. Gall. l. iii. c. x. p. 101 ; Amstel. 1745.

[9] Etat du Siège de Rome, tom. 2, p. 84, in Bowers' Popes, Inn. XII. ; vol. vii. p. 681. Dubl. 1768.

cognise *in theory* no obstacle to his will, and no restraint upon his power. "The Pope has a plenitude of power in the Church," is their maxim adopted from Aquinas. This power is explained to be both "directive and co-active," and to extend over "all the faithful, even Bishops and Patriarchs," who are "bound to obey him in all things which concern the Christian religion, faith, morals, rites, Church discipline, &c.[1]" Hence it belongs to him *alone*, by virtue of his primacy, to "convoke general Councils, to preside over and confirm them," and from his sanction and confirmation the decrees of such Councils derive all the authority which they possess. This, we are told, was heretofore the general belief, except in France[2]: and it is notorious that now even France can no longer be named as an exception.

I am aware that a very different account of the powers and privileges of the Papacy is sometimes offered to the English public, and in most cases, I am willing to hope, with no intention to deceive. But we have seen enough to warn us that in this controversy the opinion of an individual must not be taken for the doctrine of the communion. This will appear still more clearly as we proceed. In-

[1] Dens, De Eccles. n. 94, p. 155.
[2] Id. n. 95, p. 156. The reader will perhaps remember that the Theology of Dens is a work in great use and esteem among the Roman Catholic Clergy of Ireland. See Parliamentary Debates, July 16, 1835. 3rd Ser. vol. 29, col. 605, &c.

deed, there are some statements in your letters, which, even in the present day, are more safely published in an English than in a Roman journal. Forgive me, therefore, if, in conclusion, I suggest the necessity of greater caution, and an enlarged knowledge of the real doctrines of our Church, lest you should appear to be taking an unfair advantage of your privileges as an inhabitant of this favoured land. It is a point of honesty, which I am sure you would not willingly neglect, to represent Rome as Rome would have herself represented. Besides, you may find that even an Englishman is not always safe. I would fain see you spared the humiliating predicament of the late Bishop Baines [3]. May you never have cause with him to frame the painful wish, that your country may yet protect you against your Church!

I am, &c.

[3] See Life of Bishop Baines in the Catholic Magazine, Nos. lxvi. —lxix., 1850; or Letters to a Seceder, p. 173.

LETTER IV.

PART I.

MY DEAR SIR,

I PROPOSE, in the present letter, to examine with some care the several arguments which you have alleged in support of the Papal Supremacy.

In common with most living members of your communion you have been taught to suppose that the pretensions which you uphold are sanctioned by holy Scripture:—

" The reason why Roman Catholics acknowledge the Pope to be chief Bishop is as follows:—We believe that there is no truth more clearly shown in holy Writ than that our blessed Lord did Himself confer a spiritual supremacy on S. Peter."

The passages in which, following Bellarmine and many others, you imagine this doctrine to be contained are S. John xxi. 15—17; S. Luke xxii. 31, 32; and S. Matt. xvi. 18, 19.

It is not necessary that I should argue at any length upon the meaning of these texts; because the Church of Rome has herself provided a test by which we may determine the correctness of the inference you desire to draw from them. By the Creed of Pope Pius IV. the Roman Catholic is bound to "receive and interpret holy Scripture *only* according to the *unanimous consent* of the Fathers [1]." Our plan, therefore, must be to inquire whether the passages alleged were understood with one consent by all the Fathers to confer on S. Peter, and through him on the Bishops of Rome, that supreme power over their brethren in Christ which is now claimed for them.

SECT. 1.   I. The first named of the three texts in question records our Lord's thrice repeated charge to S. Peter to "feed His sheep:"—

"Jesus saith to Simon Peter, Simon, son of Jonas, lovest thou me more than these? He saith unto Him, Yea, Lord; Thou knowest that I love Thee. He saith unto him, Feed My lambs."

1. It is natural to suppose that, after his public denial and renunciation of his blessed Master, the humbled disciple would feel many an anxious

---

[1] This Creed is printed after the Canons and Decrees of the Council of Trent, and after the Catechism of Trent in the Bull *Injunctum nobis* of Pius IV.

doubt as to his future share in the commission
which he had previously received in common with the remaining ten. One object, therefore, of this charge—introduced as it was by the repeated question, "Lovest thou Me?"—is supposed by many to have been to give an assurance to the penitent Apostle that his repentance was accepted, and that he need not fear to enter upon the office to which he had been appointed. In this view it was given to Peter only, because he only had so fallen.

i. This interpretation of the passage before us is found, more or less distinctly stated, in several early writers. Thus Gregory of Nazianzum, while arguing against the Novatians for the reception of penitents:—

"Do you reject the penitent David,—whose repentance preserved to him the gift of prophecy?—and the great Peter, because he displayed human weakness about our Saviour's passion? Yet Jesus received him, and by the threefold questioning and confession healed his threefold denial[2]."

ii. S. Ambrose offers a somewhat different explanation, but bears witness to the above as given by others:—

"Some have said that the threefold questioning about his love took place because his denial had been threefold;

[2] Orat. xxxiv. Opp. tom. i. p. 636.

that a profession of love as many times repeated might do away the fall of his threefold denial [3]."

iii. The disciple of Ambrose, greater than his master, was also among those who adopted this interpretation :—

"To Peter whom He desired to make a good Shepherd, . . . He says, Peter, lovest thou Me? Feed My sheep. This once, this a second, this a third time, till He made him sad ; and when the Lord had asked him as often as He thought fit, so that he should thrice confess Him who had thrice denied Him, and had for the third time commended to him His sheep to be fed, He says," &c.[4]

iv. S. Chrysostom :—

"*Showing that for the future he must be bold, as if his denial were forgotten,* He gives him charge of the brethren. He neither mentions the denial, nor reproaches him for the past ; but merely says, If you love Me, take charge of the brethren," &c.[5]

v. S. Cyril of Alexandria :—

" Peter had been already appointed to the sacred Apostolate with the other disciples ; . . . but since, while the plot of the Jews was in execution, he met with a fall, . . . He now heals his hurt, and exacts for his threefold

---

[3] Apol. David. i. c. ix. § 50. Opp. tom. ii. p. 148. Venet. 1781. Similarly De Obitu Theod. § 19 ; tom. vii. p. 32 :—"The threefold answer gave assurance of love, or wiped away the error of his threefold denial."

[4] In Joh. Ev. Tract. xlvii. § 2 ; tom. iii. P. ii. col. 2146. Sim. Serm. ccxcv. ; tom. v. P. ii. col. 1758, &c.

[5] In Joh. Ev. Hom. lxxxviii. ; tom. viii. p. 598.

denial a threefold confession, compensating by the one for LETTER
the other, and balancing his correction against his faults. IV.
By this threefold confession of the blessed Peter, his sin, PART I.
consisting of a threefold denial, was done away, and by SECT. I.
the words of our Lord, Feed My sheep, *a renewal*, as it
were, of the Apostolate already conferred on him is understood to take place, removing the reproach of his subsequent falls and taking from him the cowardice of human
weakness [6]."

vi. Basil, Archbishop of Seleucia :—

" To Peter, who through fear of the damsel had denied
the Lord, refraining from reproach, *He granted forgiveness*,
showing how sinners should be borne with. Peter, He
says, lovest thou Me? Thou knowest, is his answer, that
I love Thee.—Feed My sheep. Hast thou become sensible of thine infirmities? Dost thou know the slip thine
arrogance has made? Hast thou learnt from experience
not to trust to thyself? Dost thou know the measure of
natural strength? Hast thou learnt how universal the
need of grace? Grant then to others the pardon of
which thou hast been taught thine own need. That thou
mayest not lightly esteem the medicine of repentance,
of which thou hast admired the virtue in thyself,—Feed
My sheep [7]."

vii. An uncertain homilist of the fifth or sixth
century, supposed by Dupin and others to have
been Cæsarius, Bishop of Arles in France :—

" Behold Peter who had thrice denied, thrice answers

[6] Comm. in Joh. c. xxi. vv. 15—18. l. xii. Opp. tom. iv. p. 1119.
[7] Orat. xxviii. Opp. p. 152. Par. 1621.

that he loves the Lord, that love may *efface his fault*, and affection *take away the offence* [8]."

viii. And similarly our own countryman, the Venerable Bede:—

" With provident compassion the Lord for the third time asks if he loves Him, that through a thrice repeated confession He may loosen the chains which had bound him through his threefold denial [9]."

It appears, then, that according to these writers (and many others) the Apostle was at this time merely restored to a certain position from which he had fallen when he renounced his Master. Not one of them has given the least hint that this position involved a supremacy over the other Apostles. Rather they imply the very contrary by assigning *another* reason why the words in question should be spoken to him and not to the rest. It is true that all had sinned by forsaking Him at first, but the offence of Peter, as S. Cyril has expressly observed [1], exceeded that of the rest, and, therefore, required a " fuller remission,"—and that fuller remission, including a renewal of his Apostleship, was given to him in the words which you have quoted to establish his supremacy.

---

[8] Hom. Euseb. Emiss. ascript. In Vig. Petr. Biblioth. Patr. M. tom. v. p. 712. Colon. 1618.

[9] Hom. in Vig. Petr. et Paul. Opp. tom. vii. col. 108. Colon. 1688.

[1] u. s.

2. The extracts which follow will show still more distinctly that our ,Lord's charge to Peter, whether understood as a renewal of his office or not, did not, in the opinion of the writers, confer on him any other rights, or impose on him any other duties, than fell to the whole college of Apostles, and to their successors to the end of time.

i. In the year of our Lord 250, the inferior Clergy of Rome, during a vacancy of the See, addressed a letter to their brethren at Carthage on the occasion of S. Cyprian's withdrawing from persecution. In it occurs the following allusion to the passage in hand :—

" The Lord Himself, fulfilling the things that were written in the Law and the Prophets, teaches saying, I am the good Shepherd who lay down My life for My sheep, &c. To Simon also He says, Lovest thou Me? He answers, I do. He saith unto him, Feed My sheep. These words we know to have been fulfilled from the event itself; *and the other disciples did likewise.* We would, therefore, most beloved brethren, that *ye* be not found hirelings, but good *shepherds,*" &c.[2]

ii. S. Basil :—

" This truth (viz. that those who are over us in the Lord are His vicegerents) we are taught by Christ Himself, who made Peter a shepherd of the Church after Him (for He saith, Peter, Lovest thou Me more than

[2] Inter Opp. Cypr. Ep. viii. p. 16. Ed. Fell. Brem. 1690.

these? Feed My sheep), *and gave to all succeeding shep
herds* and teachers an equal authority; of which the fact
that all bind and loose as he did is a proof[3]."

iii. S. Augustine :—

"Not he alone among the disciples obtained the privilege of feeding the Lord's sheep; but when Christ speaks
to one unity is commended;—and to Peter in the first instance, because among the Apostles Peter is first[4]."
"That which was commended to Peter, that which was
enjoined him, not Peter only but also the other Apostles
heard, kept, observed, and chiefly the Apostle Paul the
companion of his death and partner of his festival[5]."

And with a more general application :—

"When it is said to him, Lovest thou Me? Feed My
sheep, it is said to all[6]." "The Lord, therefore, commended His sheep *to us*, because He commended them to
Peter[7]."

iv. Similarly S. Chrysostom discoursing with a
Bishop on the qualifications necessary for his
office :—

"It was not His intention to show how much Peter
loved Him, . . . but how much He Himself loves His
Church, and He desired that we should all learn it, that
we also may be very zealous in the *same* work. For why
did God not spare His Son and Only-begotten; but gave
up Him, whom alone He had? That He might reconcile

---

[3] Constit. Monach. c. xxii.   Opp. tom. ii. p. 718.   Par. 1618.
[4] Serm. ccxcv. § 4; tom. v. P. ii. col. 1757.
[5] Serm. ccxcvi. § 5.   Ibid. col. 1763.
[6] De Agone Christ. § 32; tom. vi. col. 439.
[7] Serm. ccxcvi. § 11; u. s. col. 1768.

to Himself those who were His enemies, and make them a 'peculiar people.' And why did He shed forth His blood? To purchase those 'sheep whom He committed to Peter and *to those after him* [8]."

v. Equally explicit is Mappinius, a Bishop of Rheims in the sixth century:—

" Although we read of this, Feed My sheep, as spoken by our Lord to S. Peter, yet does the saying belong to *all* who discharge the priestly office [9]."

vi. And S. Bede:—

": That which was said to Peter, Feed My sheep, was in truth said to them *all*. For *the other Apostles* were the *same* that Peter was, but the first place is given to Peter that the unity of the Church may be commended. They are *all* shepherds, but the flock is shown to be one, which was both then fed with unanimity by *all* the Apostles, and is since then fed by *their successors* with a common care [1]."

vii. The same doctrine is found in a tract or speech of Sylvester II. at the end of the tenth century, by which he sought to instruct the Bishops under him in the dignity and duties of their office :—

" The blessed Peter did then not only take charge of those sheep and that flock, but he received them *with us* and *we all* received them with him [2]."

[8] De Sacerd. l. ii.; tom. i. p. 454.
[9] Ep. ad Villicum, in Notis Baluz. ad Serv. Lupum, p. 425. Paris, 1654. [1] Hom. u. s.
[2] De Dign. Sacerd. c. ii. in App. ad Opp. S. Ambr.; tom. viii. p. 55. Other passages explaining this text in a manner similar to those

These writers, you must confess, in their interpretation of the text afford no countenance at all to either of your suppositions,—that all spiritual authority was centered in S. Peter, the other Apostles deriving from him whatever they possessed and exercising it under him, and that this exclusive supremacy of S. Peter is perpetuated in his successor at Rome. Or rather, I should say, their interpretation is actually incompatible with them. The *unanimous consent* of the early Fathers for many centuries witnesses distinctly *against* the meaning which you have been taught to put upon our Lord's words. It is enough, however, to have shown that there is no such consent *for* it, as that fact alone makes the adoption of your interpretation an act of heresy in any member of the Church of Rome.

II. Another of those three texts on which you build the lofty structure of Papal prerogative is thus given in the authorised version of your communion :—

"AND THE LORD SAID, SIMON, SIMON, BEHOLD SATAN HATH DESIRED TO HAVE YOU, THAT HE MAY SIFT YOU AS WHEAT ; BUT I HAVE PRAYED FOR THEE, THAT THY FAITH FAIL NOT : AND THOU, BEING ONCE CONVERTED, CONFIRM THY BRETHREN."

The argument founded on this text has certainly

given, and descending much later, may be seen in Launoy, Epp. l. ii. Ep. i ; l. viii. Ep. xv. &c.

the merit of ingenuity. A prayer that the over
confident disciple may not fail fatally in a predicted
trial, becomes a promise of infallibility in doctrine
and in morals to him and his successors for ever;
while the injunction that after his recovery he
should endeavour to support and cheer his less
ardent and less experienced brethren in their trials
is transmuted, in the alembic of controversy, into a
solemn grant of pastoral supremacy. How little
the Fathers to whom the Church of Rome has
made her blind appeal would have been prepared
for these startling inferences, I shall endeavour to
make apparent from their own writings.

i. S. Cyprian :—

" He went out into a mountain to pray, and passed the
whole night in the prayer of God, and assuredly His
prayer was for us, seeing that He was not Himself a
sinner, but bore the sins of others. Nay, so much was He
in the habit of praying for us, that we read in another
place : 'The Lord said to Peter, Behold Satan hath
desired to have you, &c., but I have prayed for thee, that
thy faith fail not.' But if He laboured and watched and
prayed for us and for our sins, how much more ought we
to give ourselves to prayers[3] ?" &c.

ii. S. Hilary, Bishop of Poitiers :—

" The Father is intreated for Peter that his faith may
not fail,—that the grief of repentance at least might not be

[3] Ep. xi. p. 25.

wanting to the weakness of his denial;—for his faith would be saved from failing by repentance [4]."

iii. S. Basil:—

"'Though all men should be offended because of Thee, yet will I never be offended.' For this cause was he given over to human fearfulness, and fell into that denial, being by his fall taught carefulness, and by the discovery of his own weakness led to spare the weak, and to know for certain that as when sinking in the sea he was raised by the right hand of Christ, so when in danger of perishing through lack of faith in the stormy sea of offence, he was preserved by the power of Christ, who also told him beforehand what should happen, saying, Simon, Simon [5]," &c.

iv. S. Ambrose:—

"Peter is winnowed (as wheat), that he may be driven to deny Christ; he falls into temptations; he spoke some things, as it were, full of chaff. . . . At last he wept and washed away his chaff, and for those temptations he obtained the intercession of Christ on his behalf. . . . He said to him, When thou art converted, strengthen thy brethren. The holy Apostle Peter was therefore converted to good corn, and was winnowed as wheat that he might be one bread with the saints of the Lord for our food. For while we read the actions of Peter, and know the precepts of Peter, he is made to us the food of life eternal and salvation [6]."

[4] De Trin. l. x. § 38; tom. i. p. 348.
[5] Hom. Div. xxii. De Humil.; tom. i. p. 550.
[6] In Ps. xliii. § 40; tom. iii. p. 161.

v. S. Chrysostom :—

" When He says, That thy faith fail not, He intimates that his faith would fail if He suffered it. But if Peter, the earnest lover of Christ, who had risked his life for Him times without number,—who was continually starting forth before the company of the Apostles, and was by his Master pronounced blessed, and received the name of Peter, because he had an unshaken and unchangeable faith,—if he would have been carried away and fallen from his confession, had Christ permitted the devil to tempt him as he desired, what other will be able to stand without His aid⁷ ?"

vi. S. Cyril of Alexandria :—

" He says that they are delivered out of the hand of the evil one, who encounter perils for God's sake ; . . . which declaring to His disciples once on a time, He said, Simon, Simon, behold Satan hath desired to have thee, &c. . . . but I have prayed for thee that thy faith fail not. . . . . For most things that concern us are secretly ordered, Christ exercising a providence and shielding the life of each one⁸."

vii. As might be expected, the passage before us was frequently cited in the Pelagian controversy, as among others by S. Jerome :—

" ' But I have prayed for thee that thy faith fail not,' &c. Without doubt, according to you (the Pelagians), it was put in the Apostle's power, had he chosen, that his

---

⁷ Hom. in Paralyt. § 2; tom. iii. p. 44.
⁸ In Joh. l. xi. c. ix.; tom. iv. p. 985.

I

faith should not fail,—on the failure of which, sin findeth its way in [9]."

viii. By S. Augustine :—

"To free-will it hath been said, My son, despise not thou the chastening of the Lord; and the Lord hath said, I have prayed for thee, Peter, that thy faith fail not. Therefore man is assisted by grace, that the command may not be given to his will unreasonably [1]."

ix. By S. Prosper :—

"The most ardent faith of Peter himself would have failed in temptations, if the Lord Himself had not intreated for him, as the Evangelist declares, saying,—But Jesus said unto Peter, Simon, Simon, &c. And that it might be more clearly proved that free-will can do nothing without grace, it is foretold to the same person to whom it had been said, Strengthen thy brethren, and, Pray that ye enter not into temptation, and who had answered, (of his free-will, forsooth), Lord, I am ready to go with Thee both into prison and to death,—that before the cock crow, he shall deny the Lord thrice,—the same thing, is it not? as that he should fail in faith [2]."

x. And by another excellent author of the same period, whose name is unknown :—

"In the Gospel according to S. Luke, it is thus brought out that God gives grace to persevere in faith: But Jesus said unto Peter, Simon, Simon [3]," &c.

---

[9] Adv. Pelag. l. ii.   Opp. tom. iv. P. ii. col. 521.
[1] De Grat. et Lib. Arb. § 9; tom. x. P. i. col. 1237.
[2] De Lib. Arb. ad Ruff. c. xi.   Opp. col. 93.   Par. 1711.
[3] De Vocat. Gent. l. i. c. xxiv. inter Opp. Prosp. col. 885.

xi. The same use was made of this text by two LETTER IV. PART I. SECT. II. African Councils held at Milevis and Carthage in the year 416, for the suppression of the Pelagian heresy; the former of which was attended by sixty-one Bishops, the latter by sixty-seven. Both argued that if man were upright, and could remain upright without the Divine aid, there would be no meaning in those words of our Blessed Lord: "I have prayed for thee that thy faith fail not[4]."

It is quite evident from these specimens of patristic interpretation, that the great teachers of the early Church referred both the prayer and the command of our Lord to S. Peter *personally*, and that they knew nothing of the allusion which you have found in them, to a supremacy of office over his brethren,—much less to the supposed privileges of his successors. Pope Agatho, who died A.D. 683, is the most ancient author in whose writings an attempt has been discovered to make this text of holy Scripture contribute to the exaltation of the see of Rome[5]. A second time, then, you must

---

[4] Mansi, tom. iv. coll. 323, 335.

[5] Ep. ad Constant. Imp. Synod. vi. Act. iv. quoted by Bellarmine, De Pontif. Rom. l. iv. c. iii.; tom. i. p. 209. Bellarmine tells his reader that there are three ways of explaining the passage:—"The first exposition is that of certain doctors of Paris, to the effect that the Lord here prayed for the universal Church, or for Peter as he was the type of the whole Church. . . . . The second is that of certain who are now living, who teach that the Lord prayed in this place for the perseverance unto the end in the grace of God of Peter only." These he rejects as false. "The third exposition is, therefore, the

confess, have you been led by misrepresentation to admit, and to propose to others an interpretation of holy Scripture that is manifestly unsupported by that *unanimous consent* of the Fathers, without which its adoption on your part involves, according to the principles of your Church, a very grievous sin.

III. The text which now remains to be considered contains a prophetical promise in favour of S. Peter,

true one; viz. that the Lord obtained two privileges for Peter; one, that he should never lose the true faith himself; . . . . the other that as Pontiff he should never be able to teach any thing against the faith, or that in his See should never be found one who would teach contrary to the true faith." The reader will recognise in the second exposition which this deceiver ascribes, as if it were a new thing, to certain of his cotemporaries, the sense in which the text was understood by every early writer whom we have quoted. A longer catena, and brought down much later, is supplied by Launoy, Epp. l. v. Ep. vi.; tom. v. P. ii. p. 71. To show that the Fathers understood our Lord's words as a promise of infallibility to the Pope, Bellarmine (u. s.) cites ten several authors. Seven of these are themselves Popes, but his quotations from the two oldest are spurious; from the third nothing at all to the purpose; while the rest, whatever they mean, are so recent (ranging from A.D. 680 to 1200) as to be of no value to his cause. Of his remaining testimonies, one is an utterly irrelevant passage from Theophylact (A.D. 1070), another is from S. Bernard (A.D. 1140) who says of the See of Rome :—"To what other See has it been said, I have prayed for thee, &c.?" and the third from a spurious addition to an Epistle of Chrysologus, which a great Roman Catholic historian and critic (Dupin, cent. v. *Petr. Chrysol.;* vol. i. p. 485) supposes to have been made to the genuine text expressly "to raise the authority of the Church of Rome." Such was the flagrant duplicity, and inaccuracy of the man who originated (Launoy, u. s. p. 93) that interpretation of our Lord's prayer for S. Peter, which is now generally received in the Church of Rome.

and a grant, or at least the promise of a grant to
him, of certain important powers. I propose to
examine the opinions of the most eminent of the
Fathers on these two subjects separately.

1. The promise runs thus:—

"I SAY UNTO THEE, THAT THOU ART PETER, AND
UPON THIS ROCK I WILL BUILD MY CHURCH; AND THE
GATES OF HELL SHALL NOT PREVAIL AGAINST IT."

Now the question is, whether the early Christians
believed that this declaration of our blessed Lord
secured to the successors of S. Peter at Rome, or
to the Church of Rome as founded by him, any
peculiar and exclusive privilege of dominion or
inerrancy.

i. Let us hear Origen:—

" Every disciple is a rock. . . . If you think that the
whole Church is built by God on that one alone (i. e. on
Peter), what will you say of John the son of thunder, or
of the other Apostles⁶?"

ii. S. Cyprian:—

" Upon one He builds His Church, and though He
gives an equal power to all the Apostles, and says, As My
Father hath sent Me, even so send I you; Receive the
Holy Ghost; Whose soever sins ye remit, &c.,—yet, that
He might manifest its unity, He settled by His authority
an origin of that unity, springing from one. The other
Apostles were indeed the same that S. Peter was,
partners, with equal shares, both in honour and power;

⁶ Comm. in Matt. tom. xii. § 10.   Opp. tom. iii. p. 525.

but the beginning proceeds from unity, that the Church may be shown to be one [7]."

Elsewhere the same writer derives the authority of all Bishops from this promise given to one of the first Bishops [8]."

iii. S. Hilary of Poitiers :—

"Upon this rock of *the confession* (of S. Peter) is the building up of the Church. . . . *This faith* is the foundation of the Church. Through this faith the gates of hell are powerless against it. This faith has the keys of the heavenly kingdom [9]."

iv. S. Epiphanius supposes the Apostle to be the rock as he was a great teacher of the faith, a primary article of which he had confessed immediately before our Lord applied that title to him :—

"He was made to us indeed a solid rock, supplying a foundation to the faith of the Lord ; upon which rock the Church has been in every way built ; in the first place, *because he confessed Christ*, the Son of the living God, and was told, Upon this rock of the sure faith will I build My Church. . . . *It is he also who gives us assurance respecting the Holy Ghost*, when he says to Ananias and his company, Why hath Satan tempted you [1]," &c.

Again, to the same purpose :—

"*To him the Father revealed His very Son*, and he is

[7] De Unit. Eccles. p. 107.   [8] Ep. xxxiii. p. 66.
[9] De Trinit. l. vi. §§ 36, 37 ; tom. i. p. 169.
[1] Adv. Hær. l. ii. t. i. cc. 7, 8.   Opp. tom. i. p. 500.

called blessed. *And he again made known His Holy Spirit.* For so it became the first of the Apostles, the solid 'rock on which the Church of God is built, and the gates of hell shall not prevail against it.' Now the gates of hell are heresies and their originators. For in every way *the faith was grounded upon him,* who received the key of heaven, who loosed on earth and bound in heaven ; *for in him are found all the subtle questions of the faith* [2]."

v. The subject is thus introduced by S. Basil in his exposition of the second vision of Isaiah :—

" The house of God on the tops of the mountains is the Church ; . . . for it is built on the foundation of the Apostles and Prophets. *One* of those mountains was Peter, upon which rock the Lord promised that He would build His Church. . . . *The soul of the blessed Peter* is called a lofty rock, because it was fixedly rooted in the faith, and was firm and unyielding against the assaults of temptations [3]."

vi. S. Ambrose :—

" This then is Peter who answered for the other Apostles,—yea, before them,—and, for that reason is called the foundation. . . . *Faith,* therefore, is the foundation of the Church ; for not of the flesh, but of the faith of Peter was it said, The gates of hell shall not prevail against it ;—but *his confession* conquered hell [4]."

Elsewhere :—

" The Rock is Christ ; . . . nor did He deny to His disciple the favour of this name, that he might be *Peter,* as

---

[2] Ancor. c. ix.; tom. ii. p. 14.   [3] Opp. tom. i. p. 869.
[4] De Incarn. Dom. cc. iv. v. §§ 33, 34; tom. vi. p. 494.

deriving from The Rock a settled constancy and firm faith. . . . Strive therefore that thou too mayest be a rock. . . . Thy faith is the rock: *faith* is the foundation of the Church. If thou art a rock, thou wilt be in the Church, for the Church is built on The Rock [5]."

vii. An uncertain author of the same age :—

" We have often said that he was called Peter by our Lord, as He says, Thou art Peter, and upon this rock will I build My Church. If therefore *Peter* is the rock on which the Church is built, he rightly heals the feet as his first miracle (an allusion to Acts iii. 7), that as he holds together the foundation of faith in the Church, so he may strengthen in the man the foundations of the other members [6]."

viii. S. Jerome :—

" As He gave light to the Apostles that they might be called the light of the world, and they received other appellations from the Lord, so to Simon who believed in *Christ* the Rock, He gave the name of Peter, and agreeably to the metaphor of a rock, it is appropriately said to him, I will build My Church on thee [7]."

Again :—

" *Christ* is The Rock, who granted to His Apostles

---

[5] In Luc. l. vi. §§ 97, 98; tom. iv. p. 143. In Ep. xliii. § 9, cl. i. (tom. vi. p. 154,) he speaks of the Flesh of Christ, i. e. His incarnation, and all that it involves, as the rock. In a hymn ascribed to this Father by Augustine (Retract. l. i. c. xxi. § 1; tom. i. col. 67), S. Peter is called "the Rock of the Church." Opp. Ambr. tom. vii. p. 45; Hymn. i. *Æterne rerum.*

[6] App. Serm. Aug. cci. tom. v. P. ii. col. 2865.

[7] Comm. in loc. Opp. tom. iv. P. i. col. 74.

that *they* should be called rocks,—Thou art Peter," &c.[8]

And elsewhere :—

" But thou sayest, ' The Church is built on Peter,' although the same thing in another place is done on *all the Apostles,* all receive the keys of the kingdom of heaven, and the strength of the Church is based on them *equally.* Nevertheless one among the twelve is chosen in order that the occasion of division may be removed by the appointment of a chief[9]."

ix. S. Augustine in his Retractations[1] tells us that in a certain place in his works he had represented S. Peter as the rock, but that subsequently he had very often expounded it of Christ Himself. The following is a specimen of his usual mode of treating the passage :—

" Upon this rock which thou hast confessed, saith He, I will build My Church. For *Christ* was the Rock, on which foundation Peter himself was also built. . . . The Church, therefore, which is founded on Christ, received from Him in Peter the keys of the kingdom of heaven, that is, the power of binding and loosing sins. For what the Church is in Christ properly, Peter is in The Rock typically; according to which typical meaning Christ is understood to be the Rock, Peter the Church[2]."

x. S. Chrysostom :—

" He built the Church on his *confession,* and so fenced

---

[8] In Amos vi. 12; tom. iii. col. 1430.
[9] Adv. Jovinian. l. ii. ; tom. iv. P. ii. col. 168.
[1] As in note [5], p. 120.
[2] In Joh. Tract. cxxiv. § 5; tom. iii. P. ii. col. 2470.

it about that perils and deaths not to be numbered cannot prevail against it [3]."

xi. To the same effect an ancient homily of unknown authorship, formerly ascribed to S. Chrysostom :—

"'Upon this Rock.' He saith not, Upon Peter; for
not upon the man, but upon *the faith* did He build His
Church. And what was the faith? Thou art the Christ,
the Son of the living God [4]."

xii. S. Cyril of Alexandria :—

"That which He called a rock, alluding to his name,
was nothing else, I think, than the unshaken and most
firm *faith* of the disciple, on which also the Church of
Christ was founded and established [5]."

Again :—

"He called him Peter, a name derived from 'petra' (a
rock); for *on him* He was going to lay the foundation of
His Church [6]."

xiii. Theodoret :—

"Our Lord permitted the first of the Apostles, whose
confession He set as a base and foundation of the Church,
to be shaken and to err; and He raised him up again,

---

[3] In S. Matt. Hom. lxxxii. § 3; tom. vii. p. 887. Sim. Hom. liv.
§ 2; p. 616.
[4] Hom. in Pentec. i. inter Opp. Chrysost.; tom. iii. p. 956. See the
Monitum prefixed.
[5] De S. Trin. Dial. iv. Opp. tom. v. P. i. p. 507. Sim. Comm.
in Esai. l. iv. Or. ii.; tom. ii. p. 593.
[6] In Joh. i. 42; tom. iv. p. 131.

giving us thus two lessons, not to trust to ourselves, and to strengthen those who are shaken [7]."

xiv. The supposed Cæsarius :—

" Unless in this name (Peter) Christ had understood strength and stability, why did He forthwith add what follows, saying, And upon this rock I will build My Church? If you do not know the meaning of *Peter*, look again at The Rock.—' But that Rock was Christ.' So then 'Peter' is from 'petra.' So 'Christian' is from 'Christ.' Let us see then what that means, And I will build My Church upon this rock. Upon this rock which thou hast just laid for a foundation of the faith, upon *this faith* which thou hast just taught, saying, Thou art the Christ, the Son of the living God,—Upon this rock and upon this faith I will build My Church. For agreeably to this view the Apostle says,—And other foundation can no man lay than is laid, which is Jesus Christ. As if he had said, There is no other foundation than that rock which Peter laid for a foundation, *when he said*, Thou art the Christ, the Son of the living God. Upon this Rock the Church of God is built [8]."

xv. Gregory the Great understands it in one place of Christ :—

" *He* is the Rock from which Peter received his name, and on which He said that He would build His Church."

But elsewhere differently [9]:—

" Persevere in the true faith and set your life firm on

---

[7] Ep. lxxvii. Opp. tom. iii. p. 945. Paris, 1642.

[8] Hom. in Nat. Petr. Euseb. Emiss. ascript. in Biblioth. P. M. tom. v. p. 712.

[9] In Psalm Pœnit. ci. v. 26. Opp. tom. iii. P. ii. col. 531. Par. 1705.

the rock of the Church, that is, on *the confession* of S. Peter the chief of the Apostles [1]."

xvi. The Venerable Bede :—

"He received the name of Peter from the Lord, because he cleaved with firm and stedfast mind to Him of whom it is written, 'And that Rock was Christ,' and, 'Upon this Rock,' that is, *upon the Lord the Saviour*, who gave to him, knowing, loving, and confessing Him faithfully, a share in His own Name,—so that he should be called Peter from the Rock (petra) upon which the Church is built, because only by the faith and love of Christ, by reception of the Sacraments of Christ, and obedience to the commands of Christ can men attain to the lot of the elect and to eternal life [2]."

xvii. A Commentator on the Apocalypse who appears to have written in the ninth century :—

"I have been blamed by a certain person because I called Peter a foundation of the Church, at that place where our Lord says, Thou art Peter, &c. If Peter is a foundation of the Church, as were the other Apostles also, as this passage (Rev. xxi. 14) plainly shows, then was the Church built on him, *as also on the rest;* but if not on him, then not on the rest, and this declaration of John is untrue. . . . . Nor are we driven from our interpretation by that saying of the Apostle, Other foundation can no man lay than that is laid, which is Jesus Christ; for Peter is not one foundation and Jesus Christ another, because Peter is a member of Christ Jesus, as He said

---

[1] Epp. l. iv. Ind. xii.   Ep. xxxviii. Ad Theodel. col. 718.
[2] Hom. in Matt. xvi. ; tom. vii. col. 112.   Colon. 1612.

to His disciples, Ye in me and I in you.   For Christ is LETTER
the foundation of *all His Apostles*, and in the same man- IV.
ner *they are the foundations* of those who have believed PART I.
through them [3]." SECT. III.

xviii. Theophylact, Bishop of Acris in Bulgaria, who wrote in the eleventh century:—

" This same *confession* which thou hast made is to be the foundation of the faithful; so that every one going to build up the house of faith will lay this confession as a foundation [4]."

[3] Berengaud. in Expos. Apoc. c. xxi. De Vis. vii. (Rev. xxi. 14); in App. ad Opp. Ambros.; tom. viii. p. 361.   In c. xvii. De Vis. v. p. 334,) he speaks of the Longobardic power in Italy, which came to an end in 774, as of a thing that had long passed away.

[4] Comm. in loc. p. 68.   Rom. 1542.   The controversial history of this text affords another shocking instance of the untruthfulness of Bellarmine, to whom the later champions of Rome are unhappily indebted so deeply both for their facts and arguments.   He asserts that " *all the Fathers* have inferred from it that Peter, *and consequently the other Pontiffs*, are incapable of error" (De Rom. Pont. l. iv. c. iii.; tom. i. p. 210); the truth being that no trace of such an inference is to be found in the remains of any one of them.   By way of sample, he refers to eight ancient authorities; but an examination of their testimony is attended by the following result.   The first passage which he produces, purporting to be from Origen (in Matt. xvi.), is either a forgery, or so disguised as to be hardly recognised in the original.   He next, without quoting the words, refers his reader to S. Chrysostom (Hom. liv. in S. Matt. xvi. 19), but the passage upon inspection proves to be entirely beside the mark, while the context is actually against him.   His third testimony, ascribed to S. Cyril (in Catena Aurea on Matt. xvi. 18), is spurious, and moreover does not speak of the successor, but of the Church of S. Peter. The fourth from Theodoret (Ep. ad Renat. Presb.) has no reference whatever to the text in question, and, further, says merely that the See of Rome had not fallen into heresy, not that it never can.   He quotes next from S. Jerome (Ep. lvii. ad Damas.), in whose language,

And here I may surely pause to claim your acknowledgment that the Church of Rome does not receive that sanction of her pretensions which you suppose from our Lord's promise to S. Peter, even if it be understood according to her own rule of interpretation. The Fathers, as we have seen, were not unanimous in their view of its meaning: some of them by the rock on which the Church is built understood *Christ;* others *faith,* of which S. Peter had just given a shining example; others, the doctrine of which he had just made confession, or the faith generally of which that

expressing his individual deference and submission to the Bishop of Rome (whose spiritual subject he was, having been baptized in that city, &c. see Launoy, Epp. l. v. Ep. v.; tom. v. P. ii. p. 65), he discovers a general principle at variance with the notorious opinions of the author, as plainly stated in other writings. His sixth testimony is furnished by an obscure triplet of S. Augustine (Psalm. c. Partem Donati), understood as the perpetual teaching of that Father (see Launoy, l. v. Ep. i. u. s. p. 17, &c.), shows that he could not himself have understood it. The next, from Gelasius (Ep. ad Anast. Imp.), calls the *confession* of S. Peter "the root of the world," not S. Peter himself, much less his successor,—and the writer is moreover speaking (as the context omitted by Bellarmine shows), not of the infallibility of the Pope, or even of S. Peter's See, but of his own zeal and care to enforce the decrees of Chalcedon against certain heretics. His last authority is Gregory I., whose meaning in one place (Epp. l. iv. Ep. xxxii. ad Maur.), the words of which he does not pretend to give, he has entirely misrepresented, and whose words in another (Ad Eulog. Ep. xl. l. vii.—from which a long extract will be given in P. ii. of this Letter), he has altered to suit his purpose. See these pretended testimonies examined at length by Launoy (Ep. vii. of l. v. u. s. p. 119, &c.), who has also in the same Epistle collected a vast number of passages from the Fathers and later writers, in proof of the novelty of the Ultramontane interpretation of the text.

doctrine is a principal part; others, S. Peter him- self, but of these a few only supposed the Church to have been built on him in an especial manner, while the remainder observing that the promise respecting binding and loosing, which formed part of our Lord's address to S. Peter, was afterwards given to all the Apostles, and that the Church is elsewhere said to be built upon all, were led to consider His declaration as nothing more than an anticipatory allusion to that joint commission which they were soon after to receive to go forth and make disciples of all nations. It should be ob- served also that many of the Fathers give different interpretations of the passage at different times. We must, therefore, consider it settled that they do not (on the principle of your Creed) furnish a conclusive testimony in favour of any particular interpretation. But there is one point on which their consent *is* unanimous. Their expositions, however various, one and all exclude the interpre- tation which the divines of modern Rome desire to thrust upon the text. Not one of the Fathers, as you must now be aware, ever supposed that our Lord in using those words intended to grant to S. Peter a prerogative of power over his co-apostles, or that the privileges which He at that moment conferred on him, whatever might be their nature, were to belong after his departure in an especial manner, either to the Bishop, or the Church of

Rome. This interpretation, therefore, must be at once abandoned by those who profess a sincere allegiance to the decrees and Creed of Trent.

But here it is worth while to observe that, even if the Fathers had been unanimous in thinking that the Church was to be built on S. Peter in some peculiar and exclusive manner, their consent in that opinion would have been of no real advantage to the cause of Rome. For those who understood the promise thus, conceived further that the work entrusted to the Apostle was to be completed by him in his own person, and was actually so completed. They do not say that the Church *is* built on Peter, but that it *was* built on him, or as Firmilian expresses it, "was once for all set firmly on the rock [5]." In explaining how this was done, they differed somewhat among themselves. The explanation of Epiphanius, already quoted, is, I believe, peculiar to him. Others saw an adequate and striking fulfilment in certain actions of the Apostle. It was S. Peter who *began* the foundation of the Church by the conversion of three thousand Israelites on the day of Pentecost; it was he who completed it, by admitting, in obedience to a vision vouchsafed to him alone, the first Gentile converts to the same fellowship in Christ. "He is called the rock," says one ancient writer, "because he was

Inter Epp. Cypr., Ep. lxxv.; p. 225.

the first to lay the foundations of the faith in the
nations [6]."   In consequence of this promise, another
tells us, "he *first* received the power of binding and
loosing, and *first* led the people to the faith by the
power of his preaching [7]."   And to the same purpose, Tertullian, arguing upon the whole of our
Lord's speech to Peter, says well and forcibly,
though in support of error:—"So the event itself
teaches.   The Church *was* built on him; that is
by him.   He *first* used the key.   What key, you
see: 'Ye men of Israel, hear these words.   Jesus
of Nazareth, a man approved of God among you,'
&c.   Finally, he also in the baptism of Christ, first
unlocked the kingdom of heaven [8]," &c.

2. The second part of the passage before us,
containing a grant, or the *promise* [9] of a grant, of

[6] App. Serm. Aug., S. cxcii. in Cath. S. Petr.; tom. v. P. ii. col.
2839.

[7] Isidor. Hispal. De Eccl. Off. l. ii. c. v.; p. 19.   Colon. 1568.

[8] De Pudic. c. xxi.; tom. iv. p. 374.   He employed this explanation to support the theory of the Montanists, that the power to remit
sin and so restore to communion had not descended to the Church
from the Apostles.   Bishop Horsley has ably maintained the same
interpretation, and without any prejudice to orthodoxy; for while he
urges with Tertullian that the promise of Christ was actually fulfilled
in the subsequent actions of S. Peter, he teaches also that it was "something quite distinct from that with which it has been generally confounded, the power of the remission and retention of sins conferred
by our Lord, after His resurrection, upon the Apostles in general,
and transmitted through them to the perpetual succession of the
priesthood."—Serm. xiii. on S. Matt. xvi. 18, 19.

[9] " Promised in the future, not given at the time."—Hieron. Comm.
in Mat. l. iii. c. xvi.; tom. iv. P. i. col. 76.

K

certain powers or privileges to the Apostle Peter, is in your version thus expressed :—

"AND I WILL GIVE TO THEE THE KEYS OF THE KINGDOM OF HEAVEN. AND WHATSOEVER THOU SHALT BIND UPON EARTH, IT SHALL BE BOUND ALSO IN HEAVEN; AND WHATSOEVER THOU SHALT LOOSE UPON EARTH, IT SHALL BE LOOSED ALSO IN HEAVEN."

There can be no question between us respecting the meaning of the second clause of this verse; for the same words were afterwards addressed by our Lord to the whole college of Apostles; but because the metaphor of the 'keys' is used in reference to S. Peter only, it has been imagined by some of your divines, that it expresses a privilege conferred upon him alone of all the Apostles, and from him descending exclusively to his successors in the see of Rome. Such however was not the interpretation put upon it by those from whom your creed would have you learn;—as the subjoined examples show.

i. Origen:—

" What, are *the keys* of the kingdom of heaven given by the Lord to Peter *only?* And shall no other of the blessed receive them? But if this promise, ' I will give thee the keys of the kingdom of heaven,' be *common to others also*, so likewise are all those things common that are recorded before and after this (i.e. in Matt. xvi. 18, 19) as spoken to Peter[1]."

ii. S. Cyprian :—

" Our Lord, . . . settling the honour of a Bishop and

[1] Comm. in Matt., as in p. 117.

the constitution of His Church, . . . says to Peter, I say unto thee, Thou art Peter, &c. And *I will give thee the keys* of the kingdom of heaven, &c. *Hence, through the several ages and successions* is carried downward the government of Bishops and the constitution of the Church; so that the Church is set up on the Bishops, and every act of the Church is under the control of those her heads [2]."

iii. S. Cyril of Jerusalem speaks as if he thought the keys a personal prerogative of this Apostle:—

" Peter was he who carried with him the keys of heaven; . . . Paul was he who had been snatched up into the third heavens, and heard unutterable words [3]," &c.

iv. S. Hilary, apostrophizing the Apostles :—

" Such great deeds, and so essentially divine, had ye seen performed by our Lord Jesus Christ the Son of God, ye holy ones and blessed, who through the merit of your faith obtained the keys of the kingdom of heaven, and acquired the right of binding and of loosing in heaven and in earth [4]."

v. S. Optatus:—

" For the promotion of unity, S. Peter, for whom it was enough after his denial to be forgiven only, both obtained a preference before the other Apostles, and received alone the keys of the kingdom of heaven, *to be imparted to the rest* [5]."

[2] Ep. xxxiii. p. 66.
[3] Catech. vi. § ix. p. 88. So Cat. xiv. § xiv. p. 201. See many similar comparisons in P. ii. of this Letter, § iii.
[4] D. Trinit. l. vi. § 33; tom. i. p. 166. Sim. in Ps. lii. § 9; tom. ii. p. 244.
[5] De Schism. Donat. l. vii. c. iii. p. 102. Antv. 1702. On this

vi. S. Pacian:— . .

" Before His passion, our Lord had said, Whatsoever things *ye* shall bind on earth shall be bound in heaven, and whatsoever things *ye* shall loose on earth shall be loosed in heaven. . . . A little before He spoke to Peter, —to one, in order that from one He might found an unity, —soon after giving *the very same* charge *in common*, yet in the same manner in which He begins to Peter, I say unto thee, That thou art Peter, and upon this rock I will build my Church, &c., and I will give to thee the keys of heaven, and whatsoever things thou shalt bind [6]," &c.

vii. S. Ambrose:—

" The Lord gave *to His Apostles* what was before part of His own judicial authority. . . . Hear Him saying, I will give thee the keys of the kingdom of heaven, that thou mayest both loose and bind. This Novatian has not heard, but the Church of God has. Peter then (received this) in his fall, we in remission ; he in impenitence, we in grace. *What is said to Peter is said to the Apostles.* We are not usurping a power (in re-admitting the penitent), but obeying a command [7]."

viii. And his friend, Gaudentius of Brescia:—

" When Christ rises, *all* the Apostles receive the keys of the heavenly kingdom in Peter ; nay, rather, they

---

passage Bossuet remarks :—" For of a truth the keys which were given to Peter (Matt. xvi.) were to be imparted to the Apostles afterwards (Matt. xviii. and John xx.) ; but they were to be imparted not by Peter, but by Christ, as is evident."—Defens. Declar. P. iii. l. viii. c. xii.; p. 90.

[6] Ad Sympron. Ep. iii. in Biblioth. Vet. Patr. ; tom. iii. p. 106.
[7] In Ps. xxxviii. § 37 ; tom. iii. p. 118.

receive the keys of the heavénly kingdom *with* Peter from the Lord Himself when He says to them, Receive the Holy Ghost; whose sins ye remit they shall be remitted; and again, Go ye and teach all nations[8]," &c.

ix. S. Jerome, as we have seen before :—

"*All* (the Apostles) receive the keys of the kingdom of heaven[9]."

x. S. Augustine :—

" These keys not one man, but the unity of the Church received.   By this then is set forth the excellency of Peter; because he represented the very universal body and unity of the Church, when it was said to him, ' I deliver to thee,' that which was delivered to *all*[1]."

xi. Leo the Great :—

" To the most blessed Peter it is said, I will give thee the keys of the kingdom of heaven, &c.   The right of this power, indeed, passed on *to the other Apostles*, and the appointment of this decree has descended to *all the heads of the Church;* but not without a reason is that committed to one which is signified to all; for this trust is given to Peter simply because the person of Peter stands for all the rulers of the Church[2]."

xii. The probable Cæsarius :—

" ' I will give thee the keys of the kingdom of heaven ;' for this, which is said principally to Peter, ought to be understood as said to *the other Apostles also ;*—and not to the Apostles only but even to Bishops and priests[3]."

---

[8] Serm. xvi. Opp. p. 185.   Patav. 1720.
[9] Adv. Jovinian. l. ii., as in p. 121.
[1] Serm. ccxcv. § 2; tom. v. P. ii. col. 1756.
[2] Serm. iv. c. iii.   Opp. tom. i. col. 18.   Ven. 1753.
[3] Hom. Euseb. Emiss. in Nat. Pet., as in p. 123.

xiii. Fulgentius, Bishop of Ruspa;—

" Remission of sins is given and received only in the Catholic Church . . . which He founded upon a rock, to which He gave the keys of the kingdom of heaven, to which He gave also the power of binding and loosing ;—as The Truth Itself truly promises to Peter, saying, Thou art Peter, &c. Whosoever is without this Church which received the keys of the kingdom of heaven is not walking in the way of heaven[4]."

xiv. S. Bede :—

" When all were questioned Peter only answered, Thou art the Christ, the Son of the Living God, and to him it is said, I will give thee the keys of the kingdom of heaven ;—as if he only received the power of binding and loosing, whereas he both made that answer *one for all*, and received this gift *with all*, as representing unity itself. And therefore one for all, because all are one[5]."

xv. Sylvester II., in the address to his suffragans before cited :—

" Woe to me . . . if I fail to unlock the bars of human ignorance with those keys of the kingdom of heaven which *all we priests* have received in the Apostle Peter[6]."

xvi. Theophylact :—

" Although the words, I will give thee, were said to Peter only, yet was the gift given to *all the Apostles.* At what time? When He said, Whose soever sins ye remit, they are remitted, for, ' I *will* give,' signifies time future[7]."

---

[4] De Rem. Pecc. l. i. c. xix. Opp. p. 374. Par. 1684. Sim. l. ii. c. xx.; p. 403.

[5] Comm. in Joh. Ev. c. xix. Opp. tom. v. col. 607.

[6] De Dign. Sacerd. c. i. App. ad Opp. Ambr.; tom. viii. p. 54.

[7] Comm. in Matt. xvi. 18; p. 68.

We have now taken the opinion of a large array of early Fathers upon each of the three texts to which you have appealed in confirmation of the Roman Catholic doctrine of Papal Supremacy, and we have not been able to find one who understood those texts as you have been taught to understand them. Obedience to the avowed principles of your own communion requires, therefore, that your appeal should be at once recalled, and the interpretation on which you based it without delay repudiated.

In conclusion, I will only point out that, while we have failed to obtain any countenance from the Fathers for the supremacy claimed by the Bishop of Rome, we do nevertheless (as we have seen in the foregoing extracts) find them *with one consent* upholding a certain specific doctrine, and mode of interpretation, with respect to the powers and duties of the chief rulers of the Church.

They do unanimously teach that, whatever personal or conventional distinctions may have had place among the Apostles of Christ, they were, as Apostles, all without exception equal,—and further, that this their equality in office and authority was by them transmitted to their successors, the duly ordained Bishops of all the Churches in every age.

LETTER IV.

PART II.

LETTER
IV.
PART II.
SECT. I.

IN many early Christian writers, though not in the earliest, we find S. Peter frequently spoken of as the first, the chief, the leader, the spokesman, the coryphæus, &c. of the Apostles. This circumstance has proved a fertile source of misconception and error; for the unlearned Roman Catholic naturally supposes that these titles are intended to express an authority over his brethren the same, both in degree and kind, as that which the modern doctrine of his supremacy assumes that he possessed. It is, how-ever, perfectly certain that such language meant no more in the mouth of S. Ambrose or S. Chry-sostom than it means when employed by any

English Churchman of the present day[1]. This is an unavoidable inference from the evidence that has been already adduced; but a brief independent proof of the assertion will perhaps appear desirable.

During our Lord's ministry on earth, the ardent temperament of S. Peter brought him ever into the foreground for praise or blame. After His ascension he was made instrumental to the foundation of the Church in a peculiar and pre-eminent manner. His subsequent successes were also remarkable, S. Paul bearing witness that God "wrought in him effectually to the Apostleship of the circumcision." These facts were not likely to be left unnoticed by the thoughtful commentators of the early Church; and accordingly, although they never ascribed to him a superiority of *power* and *function*, or rather, although they expressly denied that he possessed it, they did not hesitate to allow him- the first place, or primacy, among his coequal brethren. Thus S. Ambrose :—

"When he heard the words, But whom say ye that I am? he forthwith, not unmindful of his place, took on himself a primacy (primatum egit) ;—a primacy of con-

---

[1] Archbishop Potter, for example, cannot be suspected of any design to favour Rome, when he infers from Luke xxii. 3; xxiv. 34; Mark xiv. 37; xvi. 7; Matt. xvi. 15, &c.; John vi. 66—68, &c. that S. Peter was "the foreman of the College of Apostles, whilst our Lord lived on earth;"—and from Acts i. 15; ii. 14, 37, 38; iii. 12; iv. 8; v. 2—5, 12—15, 29; xv. 7, that "he kept the same dignity, at least for some time, after His ascension."—Discourse on Church Government, Ch. iii. § ii.

fession, to wit, not of honour; a primacy of faith, not of order. As much as to say, Now let none surpass me, now it is my part," &c. [2]

And S. Cyprian, more than a century before :—

"Nor did Peter, whom the Lord chose first, and on whom He built His Church, when Paul afterwards disputed with him concerning circumcision, improperly claim any thing for himself, or arrogantly assume,—so as to say that he held the first place (primatum) and ought rather to be obeyed by novices and his juniors [3]."

This view of S. Peter's primacy is thus developed by S. Chrysostom, a frequent panegyrist of the illustrious Apostle :—

"We must first speak of the boldness of speech of Peter, and how he was ever starting out before the other disciples. For, indeed, he received the name from his unbending and unswerving faith; for where all were asked together, he, starting out before the rest, says, Thou art the Christ, &c. . . . . And in the Mount, he only appears to speak, and when He spoke of the cross, while the others are silent, the same Apostle says, Be it far from Thee . . . And every where we see him more full of ardour than the rest, and rushing before them into danger. And when He was seen on the shore, while the rest were rowing the vessel, Peter could not bear to remain in it. And after the resurrection, when the Jews were killing, and raging, and seeking to tear them in pieces, *he first* ventured to come forward and openly declare that the crucified had been taken up, and is in heaven. But to open a door and make a beginning is

[2] De Incarn. Dom. c. iv. § 32; tom. vi. p. 493.
[3] Ep. lxxi.; p. 194.

something more than speaking with boldness when this has been done[4]." "Having effected the first entrance, and broken the front rank of the Jewish phalanx, and preached that long discourse, he made an opening for the rest of the Apostles. Though James, John, Paul, or any other, appear afterwards to do great things, yet he surpasses them all, who by his boldness of speech opened the entrance and gave them free admission[5]."

Influenced by such reasons S. Chrysostom, in passages too numerous to be cited, styles this Apostle the 'chief,' the 'foreman,' the 'tongue' or 'spokesman' of his brethren; Tertullian and Nazianzen, 'the dearest of all the disciples[6];' S. Hilary, 'the chief of the Apostolate[7];' S. Cyril of Jerusalem, 'the foreman of the Apostles, and prin-

---

[4] Comm. in Ep. ad Gal. c. ii. vv. 11, 12; tom. x. p. 813. It will be useful to let the reader see how these reflections of Chrysostom on the prompt zeal and ardour of S. Peter are handled, under another name, by the controversialists of Rome:—" All these [i. e. these instances of his activity and forwardness] are facts recorded in holy Scripture; and holy Scripture, we are assured by Protestants, is their only guide in all matters of faith. We turn then to Protestant Commentators upon these histories to see what they have to say about them, and we read that all these things come to pass, not because S. Peter had been specially commissioned to feed the flock, not because he was the rock on which the Church was built, and bore the keys of the kingdom of heaven, but because he was a very active and stirring man, 'in all deliberations nimble at propounding his advice, and in all undertakings forward to make the onset.' Can any thing be more flagrant than the wilful disrespect thus shown to the written word of God, and the preference given to opinions and prejudices of men?"—Clifton Tracts by the Brotherhood of S. Vincent of Paul; No. 42, p. 95.

[5] Hom. in Gal. ii. 11; tom. iii. p. 436.

[6] Tert. Adv. Marc. l. iv. c. xiii.; tom. i. p. 195. S. Greg. Orat. ix; tom. i. p. 157.

[7] Comm. in Matt. c. vii. § 6; tom. iii. p. 353.

cipal preacher of the Church [8];' Optatus, 'the head of all the Apostles [9];' Eusebius, 'the mighty and great one of the Apostles, for his merit, the spokesman of all the rest [1];' and S. Basil says that 'he was preferred to all the disciples, and received a higher testimony and blessing [2];'—expressions to which, although we may think some of them too rhetorical, no well-instructed Christian will make any strong objection upon the score of doctrine.

II. That they can by no possibility mean what your teachers, my dear sir, have been too eager to suppose, is further proved by the undeniable fact that the early Fathers asserted the perfect equality, as Apostles, of all the Twelve, and of all Bishops their successors. Thus in the most express terms S. Cyprian :—

"He gives an equal power after His resurrection to all the Apostles .... The other Apostles were what Peter was, endowed with an equal fellowship of honour and of power [3]." "There is one Church throughout the world distributed by Christ into many members : similarly there is one Episcopate, diffused over the united multitude of many Bishops [4]."

But though a perfect equality reigned in the glorious company of the Apostles after the day of Pentecost, yet we are told that they selected one of their number to whom the rest became canoni-

---

[8] Cat. x. c. i.; p. 136.   [9] De Schism. Don. l. ii. c. ii.; p. 31.
[1] Hist. Eccl. l. ii. c. xiv.; p. 41.   [2] De Jud. Dei; tom. ii. p. 268.
[3] De Unit. Eccles.; p. 107.   [4] Ep. lv.; p. 112.

cally inferior. Thus Eusebius, quoting from an earlier writer:—

"After the Ascension of our Saviour, Peter, James, and John, though they had been honoured by the Lord above the rest, did not lay claim to dignity, but chose James the Just to be Bishop of Jerusalem [5]."

Is it not perfectly clear from this that in the Primitive Church, James the Bishop of Jerusalem was regarded, by virtue of his office as the superior of S. Peter, no less than of the other Apostles? I need hardly point out, how well this fact tallies with the part taken by S. James in the Council held by the Apostles respecting circumcision. While others, including S. Peter, only addressed the meeting, S. James summed up and pronounced its determination [6].

In the year 341, Julius, the Bishop of Rome, wrote a strong letter of remonstrance to a Council held at Antioch, which, assuming the justice of the deposition of S. Athanasius from the see of Alexandria, had proceeded to the choice of his successor. A certain right of interference was at that time exercised by every Patriarch, when a see of the same rank became a subject of contention; but it is evident from the language of Julius as

[5] Hist. Eccl. l. ii. c. i.; p. 30; from the lost *Hypotyposes* of Clemens Al.

[6] Acts xv. 13. Comp. xii. 17; xxi. 18; Gal. i. 19; ii. 9, 12. "Peter makes a speech, but James lays down the law," says an ancient writer in Photius; Bibl. N. 275; p. 833. Aug. Vindel. 1601.

reported by the historian Sozomen, from the fact
that he wrote in his own name, and from the tone
and contents of the reply which he received, that
he exhibited already much of that "western arrogance" of which S. Basil [7], a few years later, found
reason to complain, and which has proved so disastrous to the whole Church of Christ. The substance of the reply, which proceeded from a
second Council composed of a part of those Bishops
who had been present at the former, has been preserved :—

" They professed that the Church of the Romans excited the admiration of all men, having been from the
beginning a school of Apostles and mother city of religion, although those who introduced the doctrine came
to reside in it from the East. But for all this they did
not deem it right that they should be considered his
inferiors, because they did not surpass him in the greatness or numbers of their Church, seeing that they excelled him in virtue, and in principle [8]," &c.

In asserting the abstract equality of all Bishops,
this Council seems to have gone too far, and to
have set at nought some of those conventional distinctions which had already been established by
common consent. A Synod which met at Rome,
not very long after, "thought it meet," says Athanasius, "that Julius should write to those who had

---

[7] Ep. ad Greg. Theol. x. ; tom. ii. p. 795.
[8] Sozom. l. iii. c. viii. ; p. 414. Paris, 1686.

addressed him[9]." His letter has been preserved, and it is observable that in it he does not deny that all Bishops are equal, or arrogate to himself any superiority over his brethren by divine right ; but simply contents himself with accusing his opponents of insincerity in putting forward a principle which they were not disposed to carry out in their own practice :—

"If you are really persuaded that the rank of the Bishops is equal and the same, and do not form your estimate of them from the greatness of their cities, as you declare, he who had been intrusted with a small city ought to have remained in that committed to his care, and not, despising that entrusted to him, pass over to that which was not committed to him[1]," &c.

S. Jerome, a little later, bears explicit testimony to this equality :—

"Wherever a Bishop may be, whether at Rome, or Eugubium, or Constantinople, or Rhegium, or Alexandria, or Tanæ, he has the same merit, and the same priesthood. The power of riches and the lowliness of poverty do not make a Bishop greater or less. They are all successors of the Apostles[2]."

An ancient homilist, of the Apostles :—

"They received not nations and particular cities, but were all *in common* intrusted with the whole world[3]."

[9] Ad Imp. Constant. Apol.   Opp. tom. i. p. 730.
[1] Ibid. p. 744.
[2] Ep. ci. ad Evang. (olim 85 ad Evagr.) ; tom. iv. P. ii. col. 803.
[3] Inter Opp. Chrysost. ; tom. viii. p. 115.   Ed. Savile.

Rabanus Maūrus, of the same :—

" The other Apostles received an equal share of honour and power with Peter [4]."

And Isidore of Seville, of Bishops and Apostles both :—

" The other Apostles received *an equal share* of honour and power *with Peter ;* who also being dispersed throughout the whole world, preached the Gospel,—and to whom at their decease the Bishops succeeded, who have been settled throughout the world in the seats of the Apostles [5]."

III. It is common enough to find one or more of the other Apostles made equal to S. Peter, and this is sometimes done in language as explicit and direct as could be used. Thus S. Cyril and an Alexandrian Council, in the course of an argument against Nestorius :—

" Equality of honour does not make unity of nature. Peter and John were equal in honour to one another, as Apostles and holy disciples ; nevertheless the two were not one [6]."

The casual nature of remarks like these adds greatly to their value, as no rhetorical temptation can be supposed to have suggested them, or in-

---

[4] De Instit. Cler. l. i. c. iv. in Bibl. PP. M.; tom. x. col. 567. Par. 1646.

[5] De Eccl. Off. l. ii. c. v. ; p. 19.

[6] Ep. Cyrill. et Syn. Alex. ad Nestor. Act. Conc. Ephes. c. v. Mansi. tom. iv. col. 1073.

fluenced their writer in the selection of his words. Such an exception might perhaps be taken, and not always without an appearance of reason, against those formal and elaborate comparisons which ancient authors are so fond of instituting between S. Peter and the great Apostle of the Gentiles. I do not think, however, that the objection ought ever to be allowed much weight; for it is highly improbable that writers who believed in the supremacy of S. Peter would, under any circumstances, so express themselves as to convey the idea that S. Paul was his equal in every thing. We should rather expect that the more strongly they brought out the *personal* equality or superiority of S. Paul (if that, as an advocate for Rome must plead, be the point upon which they wished to insist), the more careful would they be to make an express reservation of any privilege which they might suppose peculiar to S. Peter. But whatever may be thought of this, there are instances in which their common dignity as Apostles is expressly included in the comparison; and where this is not the case, the language of the writers is often much too precise, and their tone too sober, to afford any pretence for such a depreciation of their testimony. I shall give examples of each kind.

i. S. Hilary must certainly have considered that S. Paul had over the Gentile converts an authority

L

as complete and independent as that of S. Peter over the Jewish, when he said :—

" Peter, having the charge of those who had believed of the Jews, appeared to refrain from intercourse with those who were of the Gentiles;—but Paul, having the charge of those who had believed out of the Gentiles, did not hesitate to oppose and blame him to his face[7]."

ii. S. Ambrose is yet more explicit :—

"Nor is Paul inferior to Peter, though the one is the foundation of the Church, and the other a wise master-builder[8]," &c.

iii. An uncertain author of the same period says :—

" Both received keys of the Lord; the one of knowledge, the other of power. . . . Therefore they stand out from the whole body of the Apostles, and are distinguished by a certain prerogative peculiar to them. But which of the two is to be preferred is doubtful; for I think them equal in merit who are equal in suffering[9]," &c.

iv. Another, speaking of S. Paul :—

" He names Peter only (Gal. ii. 7), and compares him with himself, because he had received a primacy for the foundation of the Church ;—(intimating) that he was himself also chosen in a like manner, to have a primacy in

[7] Comm. in Gal. c. ii. § xxi. Spicileg. Solesm. tom. i. p. 59. Paris, 1852.

[8] De Spir. Sancto, l. ii. c. xiii. § 158; tom. vi. p. 453.

[9] Inter Hom. Maximi, in Nat. Petri et Pauli, Hom. v. Biblioth. Patr. M.; tom. v. P. i. p. 34; aliter, Augustini, de Sanct. 66; aliter Ambr. Serm. ii. in Fest. Petr. et Paul.

founding the Churches of the Gentiles; yet so as that Peter should preach to the Gentiles, if there were occasion, and Paul to the Jews.   For each is found to have done both.   But yet a full authority is discerned to have been given to Peter in preaching to the Jews; and the authority of Paul is found *complete* in preaching to the Gentiles [1]."

v. S. Chrysostom, commenting on the same expression of S. Paul:—

"He shows that he is equal to them (the Apostles) in honour; and does not compare himself with the others, but with the leader, showing that each enjoyed the same dignity [2]."

vi. Another:—

"He changed the persecutor, He changed also the fisher; although thee (Peter) first, and him afterwards; yet on both He conferred equal honour [3]."

vii. Gaudentius, Bishop of Brescia at the beginning of the fifth century:—

"I know not which I can venture to prefer to the other, since the Lord has shown them to be equal in suffering the same martyrdom [4]."

viii. Cæsarius, or the author supposed to be he:—

"I would call them equal and on a par with each other in their various and different merits.   To Peter indeed

---

[1] Comm. in Ep. ad Gal. ii. 7, in App. ad Opp. Ambr.; tom. vii. p. 254.
[2] In Gal. ii. 8; tom. x. p. 811.
[3] App. ad Serm. August.; S. cciv.; tom. v. col. 2871.
[4] Serm. de Petr. et Paul. xx.; p. 237.   Patav. 1720.

are intrusted by the Lord the keys of the kingdom of heaven, but to Paul, whether in the body or out of the body, exalted to the third throne, are the secrets of heaven laid open . . . . Paul by the keys of humility and piety penetrated to the third palace of heaven, *in all things* by his excellences *equal* to Peter; for though he was first, Paul was the very chief[5]."

ix. Elias Cretensis :—

" Peter and Paul, the greatest of Christ's disciples who, besides a power of government both in word and in deed, were enriched with the gift of healing[6]," &c.

Again, titles of honour are frequently given to S. Peter and one or more of his brethren in common, such as could hardly have been so employed by writers imbued with the modern notion of his supremacy. Tertullian, for example, speaks of them all, without distinction, as "the masters appointed for the nations[7];" S. Jerome, as "the principals of our discipline and leaders of the Christian doctrine[8];" another, as "the Vicars of Christ[9]." S. Hilary styles "James, John, and Peter the most approved of the Apostles[1]." S. Jerome says that "all were pillars, but espe-

---

[5] Hom. Euseb. Emiss. in Nat. Petr. et Paul. Biblioth. PP. M. tom. v. p. 575.

[6] Comm. in Greg. Naz. Or. i. Ed. Billii, col. 104. Colon. 1680.

[7] De Præscript. Hær. c. xx.; tom. ii. p. 18.

[8] Adv. Jovinian. l. ii.; tom. iv. P. ii. col. 168.

[9] Comment. in Ep. i. ad Cor. iii. 9, in App. ad Opp. Ambr.; tom. vii. p. 142.

[1] In Gal. ii. 9, § xviii. Spicil. Solesm. tom. i. p. 58.

cially Peter, James, and John[2]." Another calls " Peter and Andrew the chiefs of the Apostles[3]." S. Peter and S. Paul are jointly designated by Cyril of Jerusalem " the presidents of the Church[4];" by two disciples of S. Jerome, " the captains of the Christian host[5];" by Gaudentius, "the two lights of the world, the pillars of the faith, the founders of the Church[6];" by S. Chrysostom, " the pillars of the Church, the leaders of the Apostles[7];" by Maximus of Turin, "the most reverend fathers of all the Churches, by heavenly dispensation, the chiefs of all the Churches[8]," "the fathers and masters of the faith," " the pillars of the Churches[9];" by Theodoret, " the common fathers and teachers of the truth[1];" by another, probably of that age, "the doctors of the nations, the leaders of the martyrs, the chiefs of the priests[2];" by Cæsarius, "the chiefs of the Christians[3];" by Bede, "the

---

[2] In Gal. ii.   Opp. tom. iv. P. i. col. 242.

[3] Brev. in Ps. lxvii.   Append. tom. ii. Opp. S. Hieron. col. 293.

[4] Catech. vi. c. ix.; p. 88.

[5] Paul. et Eustoch. ad Marcell., inter Opp. S. Hieron.; tom. iv. P. ii. col. 550.

[6] Serm. u. s.; p. 236.

[7] κορυφαῖοι, the title which he so frequently gives to S. Peter.   De Precat. Or. ii.; tom. ii. col. 943.   Sim. c. Lud.; tom. vi. col. 319.

[8] Hom. i. in Nat. SS. Pet. et Paul.   Bibl. PP. M. tom. v. p. 31.

[9] Hom. ii. u. s.; p. 33.   Hom. iv.; ibid.

[1] Ep. ad Leon. inter Epp. Leon.; Ep. lii.; tom. i. col. 943.

[2] Serm. S. Ambr. hactenus ascr.; S. liv. § 4.   App. ad Opp. Ambr. tom. viii. p. 176.

[3] Hom. Euseb. Emiss., u. s.

chiefs of the Churches," "the princes of the whole world and teachers of the Church [4]," &c.

Once more, I beg you to observe that many epithets and designations, which, if they had been applied to S. Peter, would have been, and some which being so applied, actually have been quoted to establish his supremacy, were often assigned by ancient writers to other Apostles singly, in acknowledgement of the debt of veneration and gratitude which all Christians know to be their due. S. John, for example, is spoken of by Chrysostom, as "the pillar of all the Churches throughout the world, who hath the keys of heaven [5];" S. James, the Bishop of Jerusalem, is styled by one writer, "the Bishop of Bishops [6];" by another, "the Prince of Bishops [7];" by a third, "the Bishop of the Apostles [8];" by a fourth, "the first of the high priests [9];" by a fifth, "the chief captain of the New Jerusalem, the leader of the priests, the exarch of the Apostles, the top on the summits, of surpassing brightness among lamps, of exceeding glory among stars [1]." And so Tertullian calls S. Paul, "the teacher of the

[4] Serm. Var. Opp. tom. vii. col. 357.
[5] Hom. i. in Joh. Ev. § 1. Opp. tom. viii. p. 2.
[6] Ep. Clem. ad Jacob., an apocryphal but ancient writing, in Coteler. tom. i. p. 605.
[7] Recogn. Clem. l. i. c. lxviii. Cotel. tom. i. p. 503.
[8] Ruffini Hist. Eccles. l. i. c. i.; p. 24. Bas. 1535. Eusebius, whom he translates, has "Bishop of Jerusalem."
[9] Photii Ep. 117, ad Theodos. Mon.; p. 158. Lond. 1651.
[1] Hesych. Presb. Hieros. in Phot. Biblioth.; N. 275, p. 833.

nations in faith and truth, the builder of the Churches, the arbiter of discipline[2];" Nazianzen, "the preacher of the Gentiles, the superintendent of the Jews[3];" Vincentius, "the master of the nations, the trumpet of the Apostles, the preacher of the world[4];" Theodoret, "the best master-builder of the Churches[5];" Salvian, the "master of the faith[6];" others, "the Father of the Fathers[7]," "the lawgiver of truth, the advocate of religion[8]." Pope Gregory tells us that he was sought out, like his namesake the king of Israel, "to rule the highest place of holy Church[9]." And you will find that Chrysostom, on whose language respecting S. Peter so much is built, rises still higher in his eulogies on S. Paul, styling him "an Apostle of the world[1]," "charged with the care of cities, and peoples, and nations, nay, of the whole world[2]," "the planter of

[2] De Pudic. c. iv.; tom. iv. p. 351.
[3] Orat. i. Opp. tom. i. p. 24.
[4] Commonit. c. ix.; p. 328. Par. 1684.
[5] Epist. cxlvi. ad Johan. Œcon.; tom. iii. p. 1033.
[6] Ep. iv. Opp. p. 197. Paris, 1684.
[7] Quæst. et Resp. ad Orthod.; R. cxix. Opp. Justin. M. App. P. i. p. 492. Paris, 1742.
[8] Testim. ex S. S. inter Opp. Athan.; tom. i. p. 214.
[9] *Ad regendum culmen.* In i. Reg. l. iv. c. v. Opp. tom. ii. P. ii. col. 202. At a later period the word *culmen* was very frequently used to denote the honours of the Papal See. Examples occur in the extracts from Flodoard, &c. in Letter ix. § iii.
[1] In Ep. i. ad Cor. ix. 2; Hom. xxi.; tom. x. p. 211.
[2] In Ep. ii. ad Cor. xi. 28; Hom. xxv.; tom. x. p. 728. Sim. Or. i. in Ep. ad Rom. xvi. 3; tom. iii. p. 208.

the Church [3]," "the tongue of the world, the light
of the Churches, the foundation of the faith, the
pillar and ground of the truth [4]," who " excelled all
men who have been since men first were [5]."

IV. This proof of equality, derived from a community of titles and the ascription of equal honours,
may be extended, with the same conclusive result, to
the case of those to whom the Apostles bequeathed
their co-equal authority. For several centuries, the
Bishop of Rome had no distinctive appellation.
He was the Roman Bishop, the Bishop of the
Romans, or of Rome, and nothing more. Such is
his simple name of office,—to give some instances
for reference,—in Tertullian, in Dionysius of Corinth, in Athanasius and Eusebius, in the canons of
Nicæa and Constantinople [6]. Meanwhile, those
titles descriptive of his office, or merely honorific,
to which he now lays exclusive claim, were given
to all Bishops without exception or reserve. Thus,
by Tertullian, Ambrose, Jerome, and others, the
Bishop is styled the " chief" or " high priest," the
"first presbyter" or "priest," the "prince" or "chief

---

[3] Hom. de Fil. Zebed.; tom. i. p. 633.
[4] Or. i. in Rom. xvi. 3; tom. iii. p. 211.
[5] De Laud. S. Pauli. Or. ii.; tom. ii. p. 575.
[6] Tert. adv. Prax. c. i.; tom. ii. p. 146. De Præscript. c. xxxii.;
p. 31.—Dion. in Euseb. Hist. Eccl. l. iv. c. xxiii.; p. 117.—Athan.
Apol. ii.; tom. i. pp. 721, 739, &c.—Euseb., u. s. Sim. l. v. c. iii.;
p. 136, &c.—Conc. Nic. Can. vi. Routh. Opusc. tom. i. p. 358.—
Conc. Const. Can. iii. Routh. tom. ii. p. 375.

of the priests [7]." Sometimes we find him called by the still higher title of SUPREME PONTIFF. Paulinus thus speaks of S. Augustine; Sidonius, of some obscure Bishops in France; the Council of Agde, at the beginning of the sixth century, in a formal decree, of Bishops in general [8]. The title of POPE was similarly, for several centuries, applied without distinction to every Bishop. The Roman clergy, for example, in the middle of the third century, speak of S. Cyprian as the "blessed Pope Cyprian," and address him as "the most blessed and most glorious Pope [9]." Dionysius of Alexandria gives the title to Heraclas, his predecessor [1]; the clergy of the same city, to Alexander, a later

[7] E. g. ἀρχιερεύς; Constit. Apost. l. viii. c. x.; p. 397, &c.;—Greg. N. Or. v.; tom. i. p. 136; xix., p. 308, &c.; xx., p. 372;—Theodoret in Hierem. xxxiii. 17, and others. It is used freely by the modern Greek Church. See Orthod. Confess. Q. lxxxv., p. 139; Q. xciv., p. 151. *Summus Sacerdos;* Tertull. De Bapt. c. xvii.; tom. iv. p. 174; —Ambr. De Myst. c. ii. § 6; tom. v. p. 184; sim. the tract de Sacram. l. iii. c. i. § 4; ibid. p. 222;—Jerome, c. Lucif.; tom. iv. p. 139;— Innoc. I. Ep. xii. Mansi, tom. iii. col. 1050;—Sidonius, Epp. l. vii. Ep. ix.; p. 182. Hanov. 1617;—Quæst. V. et N. T.; Q. ci. in App. ad Opp. August.; tom. iii. col. 2941.—Pseudo-Ambr. in Eph. iv. 11, says, "In the Bishop are all the Orders; for he is the first priest, that is, the chief of the priests." App. ad Opp. Ambr. in tom. vii. p. 283.

[8] Paul. inter Epp. Aug. Cl. II. Ep. xxxii. ad Roman. § 3; *Summus Christi Pontifex.*—Sidon. Epp. l. iv. Ep. xi. p. 96; l. vii. Ep. v. p. 166; *Summus Pontifex.* The Council cited (Can. xxxv. Mansi, tom. viii. col. 330), at which Cæsarius of Arles presided, ordered that every Metropolitan should call his suffragans together to the consecration of a "Supreme Pontiff."

[9] Inter Cypr. Epp. Ep. viii.; p. 15;—Ep. xxx.; p. 61. Sim. Ep. xxii.; p. 49;—Ep. xxxi.; p. 61, &c.

[1] In Euseb. l. vii. c. vii.; p. 207.

Bishop [2]. It is ascribed to Athanasius by Ischyras, his false accuser, in a public retractation of the charges against him, by Constantine the Emperor, and Arsenius, Bishop of Hypselis [3]; to Laurentius, an unknown Bishop, by Ruffinus [4]; to another named Valerian, by Prudentius [5]; to S. Augustine and Alypius, by S. Jerome [6]; by Augustine himself, to Aurelius of Carthage [7]; by a Council of Tours in 567, to the Bishop of Vienne [8]; &c. Indeed, at this period, or a little before, it must have been the usual designation of a Bishop in France, for it is employed as such in the epistles of Sidonius, Bishop of Clermont in Auvergne towards the close of the fifth century, between eighty and a hundred times. Writers of your communion have told us that Gregory VII., in the eleventh century, was the first who attempted to restrict the application of this once general title to the Bishops of Rome [9].

[2] Ep. apud Athan. De Syn. Arim. et Seleuc.; tom. i. pp. 885, 887; —as if habitually. The Bishop of Alexandria has always borne the title in a sense of special honour; though in the Eastern Communion it has long been given, in ordinary use, to all priests. His full style is " Pope and Patriarch of the great city of Alexandria and Œcumenical Judge." Orthod. Confess. Eccles. Orient.; p. 12. Lips. 1695.

[3] Apud Athan. c. Arian. Apol. ii.; tom. i. pp. 782, 785—787.

[4] In Expos. Symb. App. ad Opp. Hieron.; tom. v. col. 127.

[5] De Coron. Hymn. xi. De S. Hippolyti Mart.; p. 160. Lugd. Bat. 1596.

[6] Inter Aug. Epp. Cl. II. Ep. xxxix.; tom. ii. P. i. col. 124;— lxviii.; col. 233;—lxxv.; col. 251, &c.

[7] U. s. Ep. xli.; col. 129;—Ep. lx.; col. 220.

[8] Conc. Turon. ii. Cann. xx. xxi. Mansi, tom. ix. coll. 800, 802.

[9] " In a Synod held at Rome (as Sirmondus on Ennodius observes)

To be the VICAR OF CHRIST on earth is a prerogative which you have been taught to ascribe exclusively to the same prelate. In ancient times, however, he shared this title as freely as any other with all to whom the Supreme Bishop and Shepherd of souls had committed any portion of His flock. Thus in the Commentary on S. Paul's Epistles formerly attributed to Ambrose:—"The Bishop represents Christ; . . . he is the Vicar of the Lord [1];" in an epistle of Pope Hormisdas to the Bishops of Spain:—" As Christ is the Head of the Church, and Bishops [2] the Vicars of Christ, evident care ought to be taken in their selection;" in a reply of the Archbishop of Sens and his suffragans to the Clergy of Paris, who had notified to him the death of their Bishop and the election of his successor:—" Being under the Good Shepherd, the Supremely Good, you desire to have a visible Vicar of Him [3];" in the laws of Charlemagne:—"They discharge by vicarial authority Christ's office in the Church [4];" in commentaries on the ritual:—" The

Gregory VII. gave command that the name of Pope should belong to one alone in the Christian world." Rigalt. in Cypr. Ep. viii. (Ed. Fell. Brem. p. 16.) Sim. Baron. ad ann. 175. But Launoy disputes the fact on the ground that no mention of such an important edict occurs in the writings of Gregory. Epp. l. vi. Ep. xiii.; tom. v. P. ii. p. 314.

[1] In 1 Cor. xi. 10. App. ad Ambr.; tom. vii. p. 173.

[2] *Sacerdotes*, Epp. xxv. § i. Mansi, tom. viii. col. 431.

[3] Inter Epp. Servati Lupi; Ep. xcix.; p. 148. Paris, 1664.

[4] Capitul. l. v. c. cccxxii. Baluz., tom. i. col. 891 ; or Mansi, tom. xv. App. v. col. 596.

consecration of a Bishop falls to the Lord's day. He is the Vicar of the Apostles, yea, even of Christ [5]." "The Bishop, because he is the Vicar of Christ, is anointed on the head [6]." "That the Bishop alone, when he salutes the people, says— The peace of the Lord;—this shows him to be the Vicar of Christ [7];" in ancient sermons:—"The Bishops of the Church are to be reverenced, as Masters, as Vicars of the Lord [8]." "Many degraded clergymen desire to minister against the will of the Lord, being prohibited by His Vicars [9];" in the decrees and epistles of numerous synods; as that of Compiègne, A.D. 833:—"It is certain that Bishops are the Vicars of Christ, and key-bearers of the kingdom of heaven [1];" of Thionville, in 845:—"Deign to seek the counsel of God . . . . from us who, albeit unworthy, are nevertheless the Vicars of Christ [2];" of Meaux, in the same year:—"We all, though unworthy, being nevertheless the Vicars of Christ and successors of His Apostles [3];" of

[5] Amalar. Fortunat. De Eccles. Off. l. ii. c. ii. Bibl. PP. M. tom. x. col. 376. The title is very frequent with this writer.

[6] Id. c. xiv. col. 387. Sim. Gerard. Camerac. in Synod. Attrebat. A.D. 525; in Spicil. Dacher. tom. i. p. 615. Paris, 1723.

[7] Johan. Rotomag. (better known as Joh. Abrincensis from his first See of Avranches) De Offic. Eccles.; col. 33. Paris, 1853.

[8] Incert. Auct. in App. ad Joh. Rotom. Serm. i.; col. 219.

[9] Id. Serm. v.; col. 232.

[1] Mansi, tom. xiv. col. 647.

[2] Baluz. Capit. Reg. Franc.; tom. ii. col. 7.

[3] Mansi, u. s. col. 815. Sim. col. 814:—"They and the other Vicars of Christ."

Kiersy, in 858:—"Respect the rulers and pastors of the Churches as Fathers and Vicars of Christ [4]." In the Greek Church this title is freely applied to Bishops to this day [5]. We are told by Launoy, one of the most learned men whom the French Church has produced, that it was at least a thousand years after Christ before the Popes of Rome " began by little and little to *call themselves* the Vicars of Christ [6]."

We find further that all Bishops, and not the Bishop of Rome only, were looked upon as the Successors or Vicars of S. Peter. Thus Hilary, speaking in irony, of the Bishops who condemned Athanasius:—"O worthy successors of Peter and Paul [7]!" Thus Gaudentius, of S. Ambrose in his presence:—"He will speak by the Holy Ghost of which he is full, . . . and, like a successor of the Apostle Peter, will be the spokesman of all the priests who stand around [8]." The preamble of certain instructions of Hincmar of Rheims to his Archdeacons begins with these words:—"The blessed Apostle Peter, whose office in the Church the Bishops discharge, and their fellow-servants under their appointment, warns them [9]," &c. So Gildas says of some British Bishops that " they occupy the

---

[4] Baluz., II. s. col. 107.
[5] Orthod. Confess. Eccl. Orient. Q. lxxxv.; p. 139.
[6] Epp. l. iii. Ep. ii.; tom. v. P. i. p. 279.
[7] Fragm. Histor. ii. § 18; tom. ii. p. 63.
[8] Serm. xvi.; p. 184:—" *cujus vice in Ecclesia funguntur Episcopi.*"
[9] Opp. tom. i. p. 738.   Paris, 1645.

seat of the Apostle Peter with unclean feet[1]."
Charlemagne the emperor:—"The blessed Peter,
whose office the Bishops bear[2]." And a Bishop of
that period, of himself:—"The blessed Peter, whose
office we unworthily do bear[3]." So Peter of Blois
to the Bishop of Bath:—"Remember that you are
the Vicar of S. Peter. To you it was once said in
him, If thou lovest Me, feed My sheep[4];" and
Peter of Celles to the Archbishop of Sens:—"In
choosing the Vicars of Peter no human interest
moves thee[5]."

To these facts we may add, that in the early
Church all Bishops, not excepting the Bishop of
Rome, were in the habit of addressing, and speaking
of, each other by titles which plainly imply equality
between those who use them. Thus "Cyprian to
his brother Cornelius greeting," is the style of the
Bishop of Carthage writing to Rome[6]. "That good
man our colleague" is his language respecting
Fabianus, its late Bishop[7]. "Our brother," "our
colleague," "our co-bishop" are the terms in which

---

[1] In Eccl. Ord. Corrept. Bibl. PP. M. tom. v. col. 407.

[2] Baluz. Capitul. Reg. Franc. l. v. c. cccxv.; tom. i. col. 888 :—
"*cujus vicem Episcopi gerunt.*" Paris, 1677. Also in Mansi, tom. xv.
App. v. col. 594.

[3] Jonas Aurelianensis de Instit. Regia, c. ii. Dacher. Spicileg.
tom. i. p. 327.

[4] Ep. clxviii. Opp. p. 233. Paris, 1667.

[5] Epp. l. vii. Ep. viii. p. 141. Paris, 1671. I am referred to most
of the examples in this paragraph by Baluzius in Not. ad Servati
Lupi Ep. lxxxiv.; p. 425.

[6] Epp. xliv. xlv. &c.   [7] Ep. ix.

he refers to his successor [8]. Declaring the satisfaction which he feels in his high character, he asks, " What priest would not express joy at the praises of his brother priest, as if they were his own [9]?" The Bishop of Rome writes back in the same style, "To Cyprian his brother," and speaks to him of others as their " co-bishops and brethren [1]." So Julius in the epistle to certain Bishops at Antioch already quoted :—" To our beloved brethren, health in the Lord [2];" while he is himself described by the Bishops in council at Sardica, as " their brother and co-bishop," " their beloved fellow-minister Julius," the same titles, word for word, which they apply to S. Athanasius and others [3]. The same Pope in an epistle to the Church of Alexandria speaks of its persecuted head as his " brother and co-bishop [4]." Damasus, but a few years later, is mentioned in a joint letter of ninety Bishops of Egypt and Libya, as " Damasus, our well beloved and fellow-minister [5]." Siricius heads an epistle :—" To our dearly beloved brethren and co-bishops in Africa [6];" Innocent I. speaks of his " brother and co-bishop of the Church of Antioch [7];"

---

[8] Ep. lv. &c.   So of Stephen, Epp. lxvii. lxxiv. &c.
[9] Ep. lx.   [1] Epp. xlix. l.
[2] Apud Athan., u. s.; p. 739.   [3] Ibid. pp. 756, 757, 761, 763.
[4] Apud Athan. Apol. ii.; tom. i. p. 770.
[5] Apud Athan. de Syn. Arim. et Seleuc., u. s.; p. 931.
[6] Siric. Ep.`iv.   Mansi, tom. iii. col. 669.
[7] Innoc. Ep. xvi.   Ibid. col. 1052.

&c.—Indeed this last form appears to have been for several centuries the ordinary style of address used by the Bishops of Rome in writing to other Bishops [8].

V. Another objection, entirely fatal to the supposition that the supremacy of Rome was known to the primitive Christians, is derived from the general prevalence in early times of the opinion that the constitution of the Church in every diocese was framed on the model of the Jewish hierarchy, or, to be more accurate, that the Mosaic dispensation was typical of the Christian, as in other respects so also, in the institution of a threefold ministry. This explains why the title of High Priest was given so often to the Bishop, and why, still more generally, deacons were known by the name of Levites [9]. The resemblance is put before us in the following manner by the very earliest of the Fathers, while exhorting the Corinthians to peace and union :—

" We ought to do in order all things that the Lord has commanded us to perform at appointed seasons ;—and He has commanded offerings and services to be performed, and that not any how and without order, but at fixed times and seasons ; and where and by whom He wills

[8] Launoy gives more than two hundred instances from forty Popes, ending with Innocent III. Epp. l. v. Ep. viii.; tom. v. P. ii. pp. 134—145.

[9] See Morinus, De Sacr. Ord. P. iii. Exerc. ix. c. iii. § 1; p. 138. Antv. 1695.

that they should be performed, He has Himself settled by His supreme will; . . . for to the High Priest have been assigned his proper services, and to the priests has their place been appointed, and on the Levites have their proper ministries been laid. The layman also has been bound by lay rules. Let every one of you, therefore, brethren, give thanks unto God in his proper station, keeping a good conscience, and observing with religious decency the appointed rule of his own service [1]."

The analogy which led S. Clement to employ this illustration is thus rigorously stated by S. Jerome :—

"That we may know that the Apostolic traditions were borrowed from the Old Testament,—that which Aaron, and his sons, and the Levites were in the Temple, the same do the Bishops, and Priests, and Deacons claim to be in the Church [2]."

I need not point out to you, that if the Bishop, as in this scheme, answers to the High Priest, there is no place left for a supreme officer such as you imagine the Pope to be. Here then, again, we have two incompatible theories, two contradictory interpretations of holy Scripture,—that of the

[1] Clem. ad Cor. Ep. i. cc. xl. xli. Patr. Apost. Jacobson. tom. i. p. 136.
[2] Ep. ci. ad Evang.; tom. iv. P. ii. col. 803. So S. Ambrose speaking to the newly baptized of those who had witnessed their vows :— "Thou sawest there the Levite, thou sawest the Priest, thou sawest the High Priest." De Myst. c. ii. § 6; tom. ii. P. i. col. 391. And the Apostolical Constitutions :—"These (the Bishops) are your High Priests; the Presbyters, your Priests; the Deacons, Readers, &c. your Levites." L. ii. c. xxv. Cotel. tom. i. p. 238. Sim. l. viii. c. xlvi. &c.

ancient Fathers, and that of your modern divines. One of them must be false, and which it is that you are bound to consider so, I again leave you to learn from the authoritative confession of your own communion.

Such then, my dear Sir, are some of the grounds on which we deny that the early Christians knew any thing of that supremacy over the Church Catholic, which you suppose to have been, in the first instance, the peculiar prerogative of S. Peter, and which you imagine further to have descended from him to his successor in the see of Rome. And here I beg you to observe that your statements would have been completely answered, if I had merely shown that the Apostles were, as Apostles, all equal. For it is clear that S. Peter could not transmit more than he received. If he were not supreme, the Pope cannot claim supremacy through him. But we have already gone beyond this. It has been shown, by other and independent testimony, both incidental and direct, that, in the primitive Church, no Bishop was supposed to possess, by *divine* right, any ecclesiastical authority whatever over any other. We have not only learnt with Cyril that, as Apostles, S. Peter and S. John were equal, but we have been taught further with Jerome that, as Bishops, the Bishops of Gubbio, of Rome, and Tan, were equal also.

VI. This surely is enough! However, to show

still more decisively the utter absence of proof, or
any thing like proof, of the Papal Supremacy, we will
proceed to inquire further into the truth of an
alleged fact, which you rightly perceive to be
essential to the argument of your divines in its
support. Assuming that the privileges of S. Peter,
whatever they might be, were to descend to his
successor, you go on to state that the Pope alone,
and no other, claims to be that successor.

In reply to this, let me remind you, in the first
place, that very many early writers believed (as we
have learnt from their own words) that whatever in
our Lord's language to S. Peter described, or otherwise regarded, his permanent commission had
equal reference to the other Apostles, and consequently, that all Bishops, being successors of the
Apostles, are, in the essentials of their office, successors equally of S. Peter: in other words, that
when our Lord said to him, I will give thee the
keys, he typified and represented the Bishops of
Hippo, or Cæsarea, as fully as he did the Bishops
of Rome.

Again, there is every reason to believe that, strictly
speaking, S. Peter was not Bishop of Rome; and,
therefore, it is not easy to understand how Pius IX.
can have succeeded to him in that capacity. The
earliest extant account of the origin of the Church
in Rome is furnished by Irenæus, who tells us that
it was "founded and established by the two most

LETTER
IV.
PART II.
SECT. VI.

glorious Apostles Peter and Paul," and that those "blessed Apostles, after having founded and organized it, committed the service of the Episcopal charge to Linus [3]." It is evident, then, that S. Peter

[3] Lib. iii. cc. ii. iii.; pp. 428, 431. His cotemporary Dionysius of Corinth writing to Soter, Bishop of Rome, who died in 172, says :— " Ye have mingled the planting of Peter and of Paul, the Romans and the Corinthians; for they having both come to our Corinth planted us and taught us alike; and having *in like manner* gone to Italy and taught *together* there, were martyred at the same time." In Euseb. l. ii. c. xxv.; p. 54. Similarly Caius the Presbyter about thirty years later :—" I am able to show you the monuments of the Apostles (Peter and Paul). If you will go to the Vatican or to the Via Ostiensis you will find the monuments of *those who founded this Church*." Ibid. Eusebius excludes S. Peter from the See of Rome by naming Linus, Anencletus and Clemens as consecutively its first occupants, and saying expressly that Clemens was " the third Bishop of the Church of the Romans." L. iii. Comp. c. iv. with cc. xiii. xv. Epiphanius says that " the Apostles Peter and Paul were also the first Bishops in Rome." Adv. Hær. l. i. t. ii. Hær. vii. c. vi; tom. i. p. 107. Theodoret speaks of the See as " *their* chair." Ad Leon. inter Leon. Epp., l. ii. col. 942. On the other hand, Cyprian calls it, " the chair of Peter;" Ep. lix.; p. 135 ; though his friend Firmilian openly ridicules the boast of Stephen that he " held the succession of Peter." Ibid. Ep. lxxv.; p. 225. (The words *locus Petri* in Ep. lv.; p. 104, are considered by Rigaltius an interpolation ; see his note.) Optatus who wrote about the year 370, at length defines the connexion strictly :—" The Episcopal chair in Rome was conferred on Peter first." L. ii. c. ii.; p. 31. At a later period, however, the Popes recurred to the original tradition, and endeavoured to turn S. Paul to account as well;—especially in their correspondence with the Greeks. The view put forth was that they derived their authority " through S. Peter . . . . to whom was joined the fellowship of the most blessed Paul, the vessel of election, the master of the truth, on whom was laid continually the care of all the Churches." Nicolai I. Ep. viii.; Mansi, tom. xv. col. 205. Hence the Apostles were often named together in official documents :—" By the authority of God, and of the blessed Apostles Peter and Paul, he is bound with the chain of anathema." Ep. xxiv.; u. s. col. 286. " He has betaken

was Bishop of Rome only as he was Bishop of any other city in which he assisted in the organization of a Church and the appointment of a chief Pastor; —and, further, that if we choose to bestow on him that title, we are also bound to give it,—and in precisely the same sense,—to his brother Apostle and fellow-labourer S. Paul.

In the third place, I beg you to remember that the Bishop of Rome is not the only Bishop who asserts his succession,—not merely to the commission, which all may do,—but even to the see of S. Peter. Your own Church must have taught you that he sat at Antioch before he came to Rome, for she has made the tradition to that effect the ground of a yearly festival which she

himself to the protection of God, and of Peter and Paul the chiefs of the Apostles (i. e. he has appealed to Rome)." Ep. xxx.; col. 297. "Rejoice that by the favour of God and of the first blessed Apostles thou art . . . . brought back to communion." Hadr. ii. Ep. xiv.; Ibid. col. 434. "Kindly receive, out of reverence for the chief Apostles, Peter and Paul, the legates of our Apostolic See." Id. in Epp. xxi. xxii.; col. 842. Nor have all traces of this notion disappeared from the more guarded phraseology of modern Popes; thus, for example, in the Bull *Auctorem fidei*, A.D. 1794, issued by Pius VI. against the Synod of Pistoja:—"If any one shall presume to attempt this (i. e. to act contrary to the decrees herein set forth), let him know that he will incur the wrath of Almighty God and of the blessed Apostles Peter and Paul." A comparatively recent school, influenced by the facts above stated, has taught that "Peter and Paul were equal in the Primacy, yea that they were partners, on a footing of equality, in the very same Primacy." See Dupin, De Ant. Disc. diss. iv. c. i. § iii.; p. 318. Two leading Jansenists, De Barcos and Ant. Arnauld, wrote in support of this doctrine.

orders to be celebrated with some splendour on the twenty-second of February.

As you cannot be ignorant of this fact, I am reduced to suppose that you imagine the Bishop of Antioch to have lost by some means the especial privileges, which, according to your hypothesis, must have been originally attached to his see as the chair of S. Peter;—but how or when this important change in his position took place, you do not offer to inform us. Your language appears to point to a lapse, or forfeiture of right, from neglect to claim. You argue, that because the Pope *only claims* to have succeeded to S. Peter, we are bound to ascribe to him, and to him only, whatever peculiar powers and privileges we suppose our Lord to have conferred upon S. Peter. But here again you are mistaken as to the fact. The eastern Patriarch has *not* forgotten, or neglected to assert his claim. He not only *is*, but *claims* to be, in the same sense in which the Bishop of Rome *formerly* claimed to be, the successor of S. Peter. "Antioch was his first see," says a learned member of the French Church, "and he was its first Bishop. This is why the Bishops of Antioch are called the successors of the chair of S. Peter [4]."

Supposing then that you had made your ground

[4] Tillemont, Mem. Eccl. *S. Pierre*, Art. xxvii.; tom. i. p. 69. Brux. 1732.

good up to this point, you would still have to show why, of two Bishops, both claiming to sit, and both acknowledged to sit, in the chair of S. Peter, one only should be allowed to plead his title to those privileges which you attribute to the first occupant of both their sees. No explanation of this mystery is to be gathered from antiquity. If the early Christians spoke with respect of Rome as founded by S.' Peter, they spoke with equal respect of Antioch as enjoying the same honourable distinction. The name of the Apostle was given, in the way of complimentary allusion, to the Bishops of both Churches equally, and they were appealed to with the same confidence by those of later origin, as witnesses to those truths which he and his brethren had in person and by word of mouth taught their first members to believe. The following example, from a homily of S. Chrysostom, is the more remarkable, because the Bishop to whom it refers was, at the time, not in communion with Rome, and therefore, if your theory be true, ought to have been regarded by all true Christians as an outcast and alien from the Church of God :—

" But since I have mentioned Peter, another Peter has come into my mind, our common father and teacher, who, being his successor in merit, has also obtained his see. For this is one privilege of our city, to have received the chief of the Apostles for its teacher from the beginning. For it was befitting that the city, which before the whole world had adorned itself with the Christian name, should have the first of the Apostles for its pastor. But though we received him for our teacher, we did not keep him to the end, but ceded him to imperial Rome,—or rather we have kept him to the end; for we kept not indeed the body of Peter, but the faith of Peter we have kept as Peter; but having the faith of Peter, we have Peter himself[5]."

Leo the Great, who was Bishop of Rome in the middle of the fifth century, seems to have carried the pretensions of his see higher than any of his predecessors; yet this ambitious, though in other respects good man, when he comes to explain the *religious* grounds on which he rests its peculiar eminence, is obliged to allow to Antioch precisely the same office and degree of authority, as a witness to the faith delivered by the same Apostle to both Churches. The extract that follows is from a letter in which he intreats the oriental Bishop to use his best endeavours to suppress and root out the Nestorian and Eutychian heresies :—

"And so, dearest brother, it behoves your charity to consider well of what Church the Lord hath willed you to be the chief pilot, and to be mindful of that doctrine of which the most blessed Peter, the chief of all the Apostles, laid the foundation,—throughout the world indeed by uniformity of preaching,—but in Antioch and Rome by a special exercise of authority[6]."

The Roman view upon this subject appears to

---

[5] Hom. in Inscript. Act. ii.; tom. iii. p. 85.
[6] Ep. cxix. ad Maxim. c. ii.; tom. i. col. 1213.

have undergone no change during the century and a half which followed the pontificate of Leo, although the authority of the Bishop of Rome had made considerable advances within that period among the Churches of the Latin tongue. Thus Gregory I., six hundred years after Christ, is found to claim for himself, as the incumbent of S. Peter's chair, no greater honour than he is willing to concede, for similar reasons, to the Bishops of Antioch and Alexandria. The following passage occurs in a letter addressed to the latter:—

" Your Holiness has spoken many things in your epistles concerning the chair of S. Peter, the chief of the Apostles, saying that he still sits therein in the person of his successors. . . . All that has been said, I have received with pleasure, because *he* has spoken to me of the chair of Peter who himself occupies the chair of Peter. And since a peculiar honour in no wise pleases me, I have rejoiced greatly, that what ye, most holy brethren, have ascribed to me, ye have also attributed to yourselves. For who can be ignorant that the holy Church was set firmly on the strength of the chief of the Apostles, whose firmness of mind gave him his name, so that he was called Peter from *petra?* To whom is said by the voice of truth, To thee will I give the keys of the kingdom, and again, And when thou art converted, strengthen thy brethren, and further, Simon, son of Jonas, lovest thou Me? Feed My sheep. Therefore, though there are many Apostles, yet, following the original chieftaincy, only the see of the chief of the Apostles,—in *three* places, of *one* Apostle,—has become powerful in authority. For he himself exalted the see in which he deigned to rest and close this present life (i.e. Rome); himself adorned the see to which he sent his disciple the Evangelist (S. Mark, i.e. Alexandria); himself established in strength the see in which, though he was to leave it, he sat seven years (i.e. Antioch). Since therefore the see is of one, and one, over which by divine authority three Bishops now preside, whatever good I hear of you, I put to my own credit. If ye hear aught good of me, impute it to your own deservings; for we are one in Him who says, That they may be all one, even as Thou, Father, art in Me, and I in Thee[7]."

Such was the attitude of Rome towards Antioch at the beginning of the seventh century. Already, however, those causes, external to religion, had been for a long time at work, which since that period have altered her relations, so strangely and unhappily, not to Antioch alone, but to every other Church throughout the world. What these were, I shall now endeavour, with God's help, to lay before you.

[7] Epp. l. vii. Ep. xl. Ad Eulog. Alex. Indict. xv.; tom. ii. col. 887. The connexion of the three Sees with each other is deduced in much the same way by Nicholas I. two centuries and a half later, in a letter to the Emperor Michael; but he joins S. Paul with S. Peter as the source of their pre-eminence:—"Per has igitur tres præcipuas ecclesias omnium ecclesiarum solicitudo beatorum Apostolorum principum Petri et Pauli proculdubio moderamen expectat." Mansi, tom. xv. col. 205.

LETTER IV.

PART III.

THE rise and progress of the Papal power are due to the operation of two distinct causes, the Apostolic origin of the Church of Rome, and the political importance of the city. The former gained for it, in common with several other Churches, the universal reverence of the Christian world, while the latter enabled its ambitious prelates to turn this feeling to better account than any other Church enjoying the same original advantage.

I. It was reasonably presumed that the faith would be preserved with greater care, and taught in greater purity, in those Churches which had been planted through the immediate agency of the

Apostles, or of their inspired companions, and from which it had been, at an earlier or later period, imparted to all the rest. Upon this principle a tradition cherished at Ephesus, at Rome, or Alexandria, was thought entitled to more confidence than one current among the later foundations of Germany or Æthiopia. So argued Irenæus within a century of the removal of the last Apostle :—

" If a dispute were to arise about any little matter, would it not behove us to have recourse to the most ancient Churches, among which the Apostles themselves went in and out, and from them obtain sure and clear information upon the point at issue [1]?"

And Tertullian writes about the same time :—

" I will lay it down as a rule, that what the Apostles preached, that is, what Christ revealed to them, ought not to be proved in any other way than through those Churches which the Apostles themselves founded, by preaching to them themselves, both in person and by letter [2]."

" If any heresies venture to claim an Apostolic origin, that they may appear to have been taught by the Apostles, because in existence in their age ; we can say, Let them then declare the origin of their Churches : let them produce the series of their Bishops, descending from the beginning, through successive tenancies, in such a manner that the first Bishop had some one of the Apostles, or Apostolic fathers, the constant associate of

[1] Lib. iii. c. iv. § 1 ; tom. i. p. 437.   Lips. 1843.
[2] De Præscr. Hær. c. xxi. ; tom. ii. p. 19.

the Apostles, for his founder and predecessor. For in LETTER IV. this way do the Apostolic Churches explain their origin, PART III. as the Church of the Smyrneans relates that Polycarp SECT. I. was put there by John; as that of the Romans, that Clement was placed in office by Peter[3]," &c.

"Run through the Apostolic Churches, in which the very chairs of the Apostles are still presiding over their own places, in which their Epistles are read in the original, thus bringing back the sound of their voices, and their face. Is Achaia nearest to thee? thou hast Corinth. If thou art not far from Macedonia, thou hast Philippi. If thou canst go into Asia, Ephesus. But if thou art placed near Italy, thou hast the Roman Church, where we (of Carthage) also have an authority for reference at hand. Happy Church, for which Apostles poured out all their doctrine with their blood; where Peter was made like unto the Lord in His passion, where Paul was crowned with the martyrdom of John (the Baptist); where the Apostle John was plunged into burning oil without injury, and then banished to the island[4]."

And to the same purpose in another treatise:—

"If it is certain that that is more true which is earlier; that earlier, which was from the beginning; and that is from the beginning, which was from the Apostles; it will surely be equally certain that that was delivered by the Apostles which has been held sacred in the Churches of the Apostles. Let us see what milk the Corinthians imbibed from Paul; according to what standard the Galatians were corrected; what the Phi-

---

[3] De Præscr. Hær. c. xxxii.; p. 31.   [4] Ibid. c. xxxvi.; p. 36.

lippians, the Thessalonians, the Ephesians read; what sound also the Romans in our neighbourhood give out, to whom both Peter and Paul bequeathed the Gospel sealed also with their blood. We have also Churches that are nurslings of John [5]."

This settled principle of deference to the authority of the Apostolic Churches naturally caused men to regard communion with them as a test of catholicity and sound faith. Thus S. Augustine in argument with Donatists:—

"If all throughout the world were such as you most groundlessly charge them with being; yet what has the chair of the Roman Church done to you, in which Peter sat, in which Anastasius now sits?—or that of Jerusalem, in which James sat, and John is now sitting,—with which we are joined in Catholic unity, and from which ye, in wicked madness, have separated yourselves [6]?"

In the same controversy, Optatus argues that his is the true Church, because he was in communion with that Roman Bishop who had succeeded, by a regular descent, to the Apostle. Peter; whereas the Donatist Bishop of Rome was but the fourth of his line, and was unable to trace his pretensions to any Apostolic source:—

"You cannot deny that you know the episcopal chair in the city of Rome was conferred on Peter first, in which chair sat Peter, the head of all the Apostles; . . .

[5] C. Marcion. l. iv. c. v; tom. i. p. 164.
[6] C. Litt. Petill. l. ii. § 118; tom. ix. col. 411.

in which one chair unity might be kept by all, that the LETTER IV. Apostles might not each claim one for himself;—so that PART III. he would be a schismatic and a sinner who against that SECT. I. one and only chair should set up another. In that one chair then sat Peter first, to whom succeeded Linus; to whom, Clemens; .... to whom, Damasus; to whom, Siricius, who is at this day our ally; with whom the whole world, in common with us, agrees in the interchange of letters of communion, and in one society of fellowship. Do you show the origin of your chair [in the same city], who wish to claim the holy Church for yourselves[7]."

Elsewhere, precisely in the same manner, he makes communion with the Apostolic Churches of Asia Minor an evidence of catholicity. The Donatists asserted in their peculiar language that with "the chair" and other essentials of the true Church, they possessed also "the Angel," meaning, according to the most probable opinion, that their Bishops had a legitimate mission. Optatus meets their boast by the following challenge:—

" Send your Angel, if you can, and let him shut out the seven Angels who are with our allies in Asia, to whose Churches John the Apostle writes;—with which you are proved to have no fellowship of communion. . . . Without the seven Churches,—whatever is beyond their pale,— is alien [from the Catholic Church]. Or if you have some one Angel derived from them, through that one you hold communion with the other Angels, and through the Angels with the Churches before mentioned, and

[7] De Schism. Donat. l. ii. cc. ii. iii.; p. 31. Conf. c. iv.; p. 33.

through the Churches with us [the Catholics of Africa, whom, however, you refuse to own [8]]."

It is probable that an appeal, or reference, of this kind was made to Rome more frequently than to any other Church at a very early period. In fact, this would be the almost inevitable result of the many and obvious external advantages which it enjoyed. It was planted, as we have seen, by the two chief Apostles, and watered by their blood; it surpassed all others in numbers and in wealth, and, being placed in the chief city of the empire, necessarily attracted to itself the thoughts and eyes of the whole Christian world. It was, moreover, the only Church in Western Christendom which was known with certainty to have been fully organized by any of the Apostles. Nothing, then, could be more natural than that S. Irenæus, who wrote in France, should, after a general appeal to all the Apostolic Churches, select Rome for particular mention, as practically the best witness to whom he could refer inquirers. Her testimony, being that of an Apostolic Church, was a sufficient warrant of Apostolic doctrine, while her greatness and importance rendered her teaching more notorious, and her position made an actual reference a matter of no difficulty to the greater part of his readers. The passage is instructive:—

[8] L. ii. c. vi.; p. 36.

"All who desire to hear truth may *in every Church* ascertain the tradition of the Apostles, which was published through the whole world;—and we are able to reckon up those who were made Bishops in the Churches by the Apostles, and their successors down to our own time, who never taught or knew any thing like the mad notions of these (heretics). . . . But *since it is too long in a volume like this to enumerate the successions of all the Churches*, we confound all who, from whatever motive, through wicked wilfulness, or from vain-glory, or through blindness and wrong opinion, hold unauthorised assemblies, by pointing to the tradition of the very great, most ancient, and universally known Church which was founded and established at Rome by the two most glorious Apostles Peter and Paul,—to that tradition which it has from the Apostles, and the faith preached unto men descending through the succession of Bishops even to our own times. For every Church (that is, the faithful every where), in which the tradition of the Apostles has been preserved throughout (by those of *any* place), must of necessity agree with this Church, on account of its pre-eminent antiquity[9]."

He then enumerates the Bishops of Rome from

---

[9] Lib. iii. c. iii. §§ 1, 2; pp. 427—430. The Latin words which I have rendered "on account of its pre-eminent antiquity" are *propter potentiorem principalitatem.* They have been usually thought to mean, "on account of its more powerful chieftancy." It is true that the Church of Rome had such a superiority as the latter rendering would express; but the whole argument of Irenæus requires that we should understand him of its antiquity and Apostolic origin. It has been shown by Stieren (in loco) that in all probability he wrote διὰ τὴν ἱκανωτέραν ἀρχαιότητα; the barbarous translator evidently employing *principalis* in several instances to express the sense of ἀρχαῖος.

N

the beginning, thus clearly showing the Apostolic source from which her doctrines were derived, and the safe channel in which they had since flowed. Shortly after, probably for the sake of friends living in the East (for he was himself a native of Asia Minor), he adds :—

"The Church at Ephesus also, which was founded by Paul, and where John dwelt until the time of Trajan, is a true witness of the Apostolical tradition."

It is perfectly clear, then, that the connexion which Rome boasted with S. Peter was not the original ground of its conventional elevation above the other Apostolic Churches. But this result of our inquiries might have been anticipated by a very little reflection. If the Primacy had been founded on considerations of a religious nature, it would rather have fallen to Jerusalem, which truly was, as it was styled, "the mother of all the Churches [1];" —a name now formally usurped by Rome ;—or else

[1] Conc. C. P. i. in Theodoret, Hist. Eccl. l. v. c. ix. p. 211. The modern Greek Church has thus expressed itself upon this subject in the Catechism of Peter Mogilas, formally approved in a Council of the four Patriarchates in the year 1643 :—" Among particular Churches, that is called the mother of the rest which was first honoured with the presence of Christ, and received eternal salvation and the remission of sins, and from which the preaching of the Gospel first went abroad over the whole world. . . . . The Church at Jerusalem then is the mother of the Churches, and the first, because from it the Gospel began to spread to the ends of the earth; though afterwards the Emperors gave the first place of honour to Old and New Rome, by reason of the Majesty of the Empire residing in them, according to the third Canon of the Second Œcumenical Council of C. P." Orthod. Confess. Eccles. Orient.; Q. lxxxiv.; pp. 134—137.

Antioch, the first great conquest of the cross, and LETTER
equally associated with the memory of S. Peter; IV.
where also the Jew and the Gentile, now to become PART III.
one in Christ, had met already on ·common ground SECT. I.
and in close civil union [2].

Again, if the first place had been conceded to
Rome, as you ˙suppose, because it was the see of
Peter, the same reason would require that Antioch,
his other see, should at least hold the second˙;
whereas Alexandria, though not founded by an
Apostle, was always put before it [3], and after a time
Constantinople was preferred to both, though a
Church of much later origin than either. The
inference is irresistible. Religious considerations
could have had no influence in determining the

[2] "Seleucus Nicanor made the Jews citizens of those cities which
he built in Asia, and in the Lower Syria, and in the Metropolis
itself, Antioch : and gave them privileges equal to those of the Mace-
donians and Greeks who were the inhabitants; insomuch that these
privileges continue to this very day." Josephus, Antiquities, b. xii.
ch. iii. § 1. Works, vol. i. p. 470.

[3] Tillemont, Mém. Eccles. *S. Pierre d'Alexandrie*, Art. i.; tom. v.
p. 186. The rank of Alexandria must have perplexed the Romans
when they claimed their primacy by descent from S. Peter. Thus
Innocent I., while flattering the Bishop of Antioch by telling him
that he owed his high position less to the magnificence of his city
than to the fact of its having been the first See of S. Peter, the place
where the Christian name arose, and the Apostles held their Council,
is obliged to put Alexandria quite out of sight, and to speak of
Antioch as if it were next to Rome ; for he argues that it would not
be inferior to Rome, but that it only had S. Peter for a time, *in transitu*,
whereas Rome fully appropriated him, and kept him to the end.
Ep. xviii. Mansi, tom. iii. col. 1055.

order of their precedency. We must seek for another ground of these distinctions, another cause of the early ascendancy of Rome.

SECT. II.   II. When we have shown that the Primitive Church was not merely ignorant of the alleged fact that the Primacy of Rome was an inheritance from S. Peter, but that it actually based it upon grounds of a totally different character, the historical refutation of her pretensions will be complete. To this task, therefore, let us at once address ourselves.

The Bishop of Rome took the first step in advance of his original position in common with several others, and with the approbation of all Christendom. Though all Bishops were esteemed equal, as such, yet, at a very early period, certain reasons of order and convenience led to the selection of a particular Bishop in every country, or civil district of the Empire, on whom the others were content to look as their superior. To him were assigned the office of convoking synods, ordaining to vacant sees within his appointed limits, communicating on matters of general interest with distant Churches, and other duties of the like kind, which must otherwise have been irregularly discharged by an unauthorized and irresponsible agency. In the greater part of Western Africa, this primacy among equals was conferred by the canons

upon the senior Bishop of the Province[4]. By the
more general arrangement, however, it was assigned to those who presided over the Churches
in the more important cities, that is, the *Metropoles,*
or mother-cities of the Empire. These were the
first distinctions of which we have any notice;
but the principle of gradation recognised by the
greater part of Christendom was fertile in development, and we soon find it applied to settle
the relative position of the Metropolitans [5] among

---

[4] "Carthage was an exception, which was not only the settled Metropolis of the Proconsular Province, but also the head of all Western Africa."—Geogr. Sacr. Afr. Opp. Optati ed. Dupin præfix. p. xxv.

[5] The name of Metropolitan was later than the thing. " Before the Nicene Council (Can. iv.) it is, I believe, no where found used in this sense." Dupin, Dissert. Histor. d. i. § i., p. 3. Sim. Bevereg. Cann. Apost. Vind. l. i. c. iv.; tom. i. p. 38. Oxon. 1848. Dupin shows, u. s. § i., p. 4, that the titles *Primate* and *Metropolitan* were at first given to the same Bishops. Afterwards, however, "the Bishops of certain principal sees arrogated the title of Primate to themselves, in which sense it often occurs in the spurious epistles of the first Popes, and in the genuine of later." The name of Archbishop " is read no where before the fourth century." Ibid. § iii., p. 5. It occurs, in fact, in three authors only within that age. It was at first given only to the more distinguished Metropolitans, as to those of Rome, Jerusalem, Carthage, &c.; but after the eighth century, to all Metropolitans, and even occasionally to others. The title of Exarch was properly given to those great Bishops who were set over a *Diocese*, i. e. a district containing several Provinces. Thus the Bishop of Cæsarea was Exarch of the Pontic Diocese, the Bishop of Ephesus, of that of Asia; each containing several Metropolitans, with their inferior Bishops. It was however sometimes applied to simple Metropolitans, the Exarch properly so called then receiving the title of Patriarch. Ibid. § iv., p. 8. This last name is first used by Socrates (l. v. c. viii., p. 217. Paris, 1686), who wrote about A. D. 440,

themselves. Thus by the end of the third century, if not before, a comprehensive system of precedency was generally established; originally, perhaps, an undesigned result of circumstance, but not the less acknowledged by the Church, and guarded by her sanctions. In determining the rank and place of a particular see, the secular basis of distinction was still deliberately retained. The political standing of the city was the avowed rule and measure of its ecclesiastical priority. Hence, because Rome was the first city of the Empire, her Bishop became of necessity the first Bishop of the Church. Thus every power or privilege now in possession of that see, beyond those which are common to it and the most humble Bishop upon earth, may be traced ultimately to the secular greatness of old heathen Rome. The Pope is Cæsar's debtor for all his means and opportunities of self-aggrandizement. The appeal to holy Scripture, as witnessing to the alleged prerogative of the successors of S. Peter, was but an afterthought, by which men sought to justify the pretensions of grasping and ambitious Pontiffs already stretched beyond the limits of their ancient Primacy.

and is applied by him to the Exarchs, or higher class of Metropolitans. After the sixth century it was in the East almost confined to the sees of Rome, Constantinople, Alexandria, Antioch, and Jerusalem. In the West it was long used with greater latitude. Dupin, u. s. § v., p. 13.

At the date of the Nicene Council, held A.D. 325, LETTER
the Bishops of Rome, Alexandria, and Antioch, the PART III.
three chief cities of the world, were the acknowledged heads of Christendom[6]. All owned their
superiority, though a few Churches, viz., those of
Cyprus, Iberia, Armenia, and Britain[7], were not
subject to any of them, or to any Metropolitan out
of their own country. Within their prescribed
limits, they all exercised great authority over their
suffragans, though their prerogatives differed con-
siderably.   You will probably be surprised to learn,
that at this period the Pope of Alexandria enjoyed
a greater power as Metropolitan than was conceded
to his rival in the West. It is evident, that practically to those within his own jurisdiction, each
Patriarch would be "the head of the whole Church."
A mere regulation of etiquette, which symbolized

[6] Valesius, Observ. Eccles. (ad calc. Hist. Socr. et Sozom.) lib. iii.
c. v.   Paris, 1686.   The Patriarch of Alexandria had this singular
prerogative, that throughout his vast obedience no Bishop (and some
have thought no priest, or deacon) could be ordained except by him,
or with his licence.   Ibid. c. ix.   The order of the three Churches,
I need hardly say, was precisely that of the cities:—"Alexandria
was the *first* city of the Empire *after* Rome " (Tillemont, u. s. *S.
Marc;* tom. ii. p. 42); while " Antioch, the Metropolis of Syria,
without dispute, deserved the place of *third* city in the habitable
earth that was under the Roman Empire, both in magnitude and
other marks of prosperity."—Josephus, Wars, b. iii. c. ii.; vol. ii.
p. 320.
[7] So the Benedictine Barnes :—" The island of Britain anciently
enjoyed the Cyprian privilege of being subject to the laws of no
Patriarch."   Cath. Rom. Pacif. § iii., p. 49.   See Is. Basier de Antiq.
Eccl. Brit. Libert.   Bruges, 1656.

no real superiority of power, would probably remain unknown to many, and even where known, would make but a faint impression on the imagination. Even S. Basil, on one occasion, employs language from which one could infer that Antioch, the seat of his own Patriarch, and ever present to his experience as the centre of supreme authority in his Church, had quite obliterated from his mind the conventional priority of the remote sees of Rome and Alexandria. The passage is the more remarkable, as it occurs in a letter which he addressed to the Bishop of the latter, entreating his assistance to heal the schism then raging at Antioch :—

" What could be more advantageous to the Churches throughout the world, than that you should begin by the pacification of Antioch? For if it so chanced that she were brought to unanimity, there would be nothing to prevent her, as a healthy head, imparting soundness to the whole body[8]."

In the year 381, the second General Council held at Constantinople provided that the Bishop of that city should, for the future, take precedence immediately after the Bishop of ancient Rome ;—and this, you must not fail to notice, it did avowedly upon the purely secular ground, that Constantinople was " New Rome[9]." The following extract from an oration of Nazianzen, its Bishop, will illustrate

[8] Ep. xlviii. ad Athan. M.; tom. ii. p. 821.
[9] Can. Conc. C. P.   Routh, Opusc. p. 375.

the motives which led the Council to this its
decision :—

"If to have confirmed and strengthened by wholesome
teaching the city which is the eye of the world, the most
powerful by land and sea, the link, as it were, uniting East
and West, in which the ends from all sides meet together,
and from which they start, as from a common emporium
of the faith,—if this be not a great action,—especially
when it was shaken on all sides by a storm of tongues,
—it would be hard to find one that is great, and deserving
of serious regard [1]."

Practically, Constantinople was already, as the
same Father has elsewhere styled it, "the first
of cities;" but the overwhelming prestige of ancient
Rome still vindicated for its Church an honorary
primacy.   During the next century, however, the
political predominance of the new capital was openly
reflected in the superior consideration of its Bishop.
A striking example occurs in a provision of the
General Council of Chalcedon, A.D. 451 :—

"If a Bishop, or clergyman, have a difference with the
Metropolitan of the same Province, let him have recourse
to the Exarch of the Diocese, or to the throne of royal
Constantinople, and have his cause tried by him [2]."

---

[1] Or. xxxii.; tom. i. p. 517.   In Or. xxvii., p. 472, he calls C. P.
absolutely "the first among cities;" but just before he had seemed
willing to allow some superiority to Rome :—"You are first immediately after the first, or not conceding even this;"—a sentence, by the
way, which Barrow by an oversight refers to Alexandria.   Treatise
on the Supremacy, p. 234.   Oxf. 1836.

[2] Can. Conc. Chalc. ix.   Routh, p. 406.   Sim. Can. xvii.

By this decree, the Bishop of Constantinople was implicitly recognised as the Primate of the whole Church, being made the judge even of causes arising within the Patriarchate of his Western brother.

Before this time, the Bishop of the most ancient and honourable of all the Churches, that of Jerusalem, was subject to the greater Metropolitan of Cæsarea, who was subordinate in his turn to the Patriarch of Antioch; such being the political relations of their respective cities. It seems, however, to have been thought improper, that merely secular considerations should entirely over-ride the religious claims of the mother Church of Christendom; and, accordingly, the Council of Chalcedon made an exception in its favour. Its Bishop was raised to the first rank, and received the three Palestines for his Patriarchate [3], though the four older Patriarchs were still permitted to take precedence of him.

In the middle of the sixth century, the Church of Constantinople was pronounced, by imperial authority, to be "the head of all other Churches [4];"

[3] Act. vii. Mansi; tom. vii. col. 180.—Some honorary distinction, without jurisdiction, had been awarded to him long before. Witness the seventh Canon of Nicæa:—"Since custom and ancient tradition hath so held that the Bishop in Ælia be honoured, let him enjoy his honours,—but without prejudice to the proper dignity of the Metropolis," i. e. of Cæsarea. Routh, p. 358.

[4] Justin. Cod. l. i. tit. ii. c. 24 (Ed. Gothofr. Genev. 1656);—a decree of Justinian. In c. 16, the Church of C. P. is called, by Leo

and such, in fact, it was, and was by most esteemed, for at that time it shared, under Justinian, the culminating fortunes of the city in which its throne was set, while Rome, though never backward in pretension, was equally depressed by the distracted and dependent state of Italy.

So early as the former half of the fifth century, we have an instance of the title of " œcumenical Bishop" being given by flattery to one of the great Patriarchs;—but it is to the Patriarch of Alexandria[5]. A century later, oriental writers began to apply the equivalent title of " œcumenical," or "universal Patriarch," to the Bishops of Rome[6] and Constantinople. In the case of Constantinople, the innovation was sanctioned by the usage of the State[7], and seems to have passed without remark until confirmed by an Ecclesiastical Synod in 588.

and Anthemius, "the mother of Our Piety and of *all* Christians of the orthodox religion." This was more than half a century before the edict of Justinian.

[5] Given by a Bishop at the second Council of Ephesus to Dioscurus, inter Acta Conc. Chalced. Mansi, tom. vi. col. 855.

[6] See an address of some Eastern monks to Agapetus, while at Constantinople, in Baronius, ad ann. 536.

[7] The usual style was, "Archbishop of Constantinople and œcumenical Patriarch;" see Novell. Constit. Justiniani, vii., p. 29; xvi., p. 66; xlii., p. 145; lv., p. 168, &c. Leonis, ii.—viii. &c. Ibid. p. 431 et seq. But it was sometimes varied, as " œcumenical Archbishop and Patriarch;" Justin. Const. lxvii., p. 186; and, "œcumenical Archbishop of Constantinople;" Leon. ix., p. 437. The present style of the Bishop of C. P. is "Archbishop of Constantinople, the New Rome, and œcumenical Patriarch." Orthod. Confess. in Præf. and pp. 10, 11.

This act, however, soon brought remonstrances from Rome, and, sadly to the prejudice of their own arrogant successors, the much-coveted title was denounced by Pelagius II. and Gregory, his successor, as "impious, antichristian, infernal, and devilish." The latter Pope, when the Bishop of Alexandria happened to address him by the title of "universal Bishop," consistently rejected it with the remark, "What is given to another above what reason asks, is so much taken from you." Similarly he argued against the title of "universal Patriarch," that if "one were called universal, the name of Patriarch itself would be taken from the rest [8]."

III. You will observe that I have given you the means of verifying the foregoing statements, by references to ancient authorities, or to writers in communion with Rome; but, that you may be able to exercise your own judgement without inconvenience upon the evidence on which they rest, I subjoin several other testimonies from ancient documents, which, unfortunately, are not within the easy reach of every one. They are selected with a view to set forth in a clear light the political basis of all metropolitan and archiepiscopal jurisdiction, and to afford authentic information respecting the early growth of Papal greatness in the West.

In the year 314, a Synod of Bishops assembled

[8] Epp. Greg. M. l. iv. epp. xxxii., xxxviii., xxxix., &c. l. vii. ep. lxix.

at Arles addressed a letter to Sylvester of Rome, LETTER IV. "their brother," directing him to take measures PART III. for the dispersion of their decrees throughout the SECT. III. Church. The reason why this office is assigned to him is thus expressly laid down:—

"It seemed good to us, that you, who hold the greater Dioceses, should be first written to, and that information should be given to all through you rather than any one else [9]."

In their first canon, the direction is repeated:—

"We ordain in the first place concerning the observance of Easter, that it be observed by us at the same day and season, and that you give notice by letter to all according to custom [1]."

At this period, the higher primacy of the greater Metropolitans was already of ancient standing, as appears from the following decree of the General Council of Nicæa, held A.D. 325:—

"Let the old customs prevail:—those in Egypt, Libya, and the Pentapolis,—so that the Bishop of Alexandria have authority over all these, since this is customary with the Bishop at Rome also. Similarly at Antioch and in the greater Provinces, let their privileges be reserved to the Churches [2]."

Among the canons published by a Synod held at Antioch, A.D. 341, and received afterwards without

---

[9] Per te potissimum: Mansi, tom. ii. col. 470.
[1] Ibid. col. 471.
[2] Can. vi.   Routh, u. s. p. 358.   Mansi, u. s. col. 670.

exception by the whole Catholic Church, is one which states in so many words the foundation of this authority : —

"It is necessary that the Bishops in every Province should know that the Bishop who presides in the *mother-city* has also charge of the whole Province ; *for the reason, that all who have business resort from all quarters to the mother-city.* For which cause it hath seemed good that he be first in honour, and that the other Bishops do nothing of importance without him, but only such things as concern their several parishes (i. e. dioceses), and the places under them, according to the ancient rule which prevailed in the time of our fathers ; . . . .. that beyond this they attempt nothing apart from the Bishop of the mother-city, and he nothing without the consent of the rest [3]."

It has been mentioned that the Church in Cyprus was not included in any Patriarchate. At the beginning of the fifth century, however, the Bishop of Antioch made a strenuous effort to bring it under his jurisdiction. Hereupon, the Cypriots appealed to the General Council of Ephesus, A.D. 431, which decided that they should retain their ancient independence. A general law was at the same time

---

[3] Can. ix. Mansi, u. s. col. 1311. The "ancient rule" here mentioned is without doubt the thirty-fourth of the so-called Apostolical Canons :—"It behoves the Bishops of every nation to know him who is first among them, and to esteem him as head, and to do nothing of importance without his consent; and each to do those things only which concern his Diocese, and the places under it. Neither let him do aught without the consent of all." Mansi, tom. i. col. 35. Bever. Cod. Eccl. Prim.; tom. i. p. xlvi.

enacted, to prevent all similar encroachments for the future:—

"And the same rule shall be observed in the case of the other Dioceses and Provinces throughout the world; so that no one of the most religious Bishops take to himself another Province which was not before and from the beginning under his authority or that of his predecessors. But if any one shall have so taken to himself and brought under him another Province, he must restore it, that the canons of the Fathers may not be transgressed, nor the pride of secular power creep in under pretence of the sacred office, and unawares we lose by little and little that liberty which Jesus Christ, the Deliverer of all, hath given us by His own blood [4]."

Since the comparative dignity of a Bishop varied with the political importance of the city in which he presided, a rule became necessary which would enable the Church to adapt herself, without delay or difficulty, to changes that might take place in civil status of the imperial cities. Such a rule was accordingly provided, in the seventeenth canon of Chalcedon, enacted in the year 451:—

"If any city has received a new constitution from imperial authority, or hereafter receive such, the order of the ecclesiastical parishes (i.e. in modern language, dioceses) shall follow the civil and public pattern [5]."

---

[4] Routh, u. s. p. 395; Mansi, tom. iv. col. 1469.

[5] Routh, p. 411; Mansi, tom. vii. col. 365; renewed *in Trullo* (Labb. A.D. 692; Harduin. A.D. 706), Can. xxxviii.; Mansi, tom. xi. col. 960. So strictly was this law observed, that when the Emperor

We are also indebted to the Fathers of Chalcedon for a clear statement of the reason which
induced the Church of those days to allow the first
place of honour to the Bishop of Rome. Perhaps
you will not now feel much surprise at finding that
the supposed prerogative of S. Peter had as yet not
entered into the consideration of the Church at
large :—

"Governed in all things by the decisions of the holy
Fathers, and acknowledging the canon just read of the
hundred and fifty most religious Bishops (viz. the third
canon, before cited, of the great Council of Constantinople,
A.D. 381), we also decide and decree the same respecting
the privileges of the most holy Church of Constantinople,
New Rome. For the Fathers properly granted those
privileges to the chair of elder Rome, *because it is the
imperial city*, and the hundred and fifty most religious
Bishops, moved by the same consideration, gave *equal*
privileges to the most holy chair of New Rome ; rightly
decreeing that the city honoured with the seat of government and a senate, and enjoying equal privileges with
elder Rome, should be raised to the same rank with her in
matters ecclesiastical, being the second after her [6]."

The point before us may be further illustrated by
an extract from a letter written by Theodoret to

decreed that a city should receive, as an honorary distinction, the
title of Metropolis, the Bishop was permitted to assume the style of
a titular Metropolitan. The Bishops of Chalcedon and Nicæa received this honour at the Council of Chalcedon ; Act. vi.; Mansi,
tom. vii. col. 177 ; Act. xiii.;—ibid. col. 313.

[6] Can. xxviii. Routh, p. 416 ; Mansi, u. s. col. 369.

Leo the Great, about two years before the Council of LETTER IV. Chalcedon met. It is a supplication for assistance; PART III. and, being written in a strain of evident flattery, SECT. III. must be supposed to make the most of the pretensions of the Roman see. The writer appears to allude to the tradition that S. Peter sat at Rome; but if he does so, it is in such a manner as to make it perfectly clear that he never imagined it to be his duty, for that reason, to acknowledge himself a subject of the Pope:—

" If Paul, the preacher of the truth, the trumpet of the Holy Ghost, betook himself to the great Peter, in order to obtain from him an answer for those at Antioch who were in doubt about the observance of the law, much more do we, in our humility and littleness, betake ourselves to your Apostolic chair, that we may receive from you a remedy for the wounds of the Churches. For on every account does the first place become you. For your chair is adorned by many advantages. Magnitude, or beauty, or a vast population, is the glory of other cities, and some which fail in these are made illustrious by spiritual gifts. But the Giver of good has given to your city an abundance of good things; *for it is itself the greatest and most famous, is at the head of the dwellers upon earth, and overflows with the multitude of its inhabitants. It has besides given birth to an imperial power now dominant, and has given its own name to those under its rule.* But faith adorns it in an especial manner; the holy Apostle is a trustworthy witness, crying, Your faith is spoken of throughout the whole world (Rom. i. 8). But if it were loaded with such

o

admirable fruits immediately after it had received the seed of the saving announcement, what words are adequate to a description of that piety which has its home in it now? It has also the tombs of Peter and Paul, the common fathers and teachers of the truth. . . . They have rendered your chair most illustrious. This is the crown of your advantages. But their God hath now again made their chair glorious by placing your holiness in it, from whom emanate rays of sound doctrine [7]."

Here, then, is a professed enumeration of all the circumstances which were calculated, in the opinion of the writer, to exalt the see of Rome; but, strange to say, we find among them no mention whatever of its Bishop's succession to the supremacy of S. Peter, on which alone the modern Roman Catholic is taught to believe its greatness to have been founded.

In the West, however, as might be expected, a few, at least, were already prepared to go a step further. There is extant a letter written in the same year by Placidia, the mother of Valentinian III., to Theodosius, in which she urges the propriety of settling the controversy then raging by reference to a Council to be held under the Apostolic see of Rome, "in which he who was worthy to receive the keys of heaven instituted the office of the high-priesthood; since it was fit to

[7] Inter Epp. Leon. M. ep. lii., col. 942; Baron. A.D. 449, Leon. Ann. x.

preserve to that mighty city, the mistress of all lands, her due honour in every thing [8]."

About four years before this, her son had published a decree by which any Bishop in his dominions who disregarded the superior authority of the see of Rome was made amenable to civil penalties. The grounds of the enactment he states to be, "the merit of S. Peter," "the dignity of the Roman state," and "the authority of the sacred Synod [9]."

From these two instances, we may infer that while the Church in Council, in assigning to the Bishop of Rome the first place among Patriarchs, was influenced solely by the unparalleled greatness of the city and her own earlier concessions, there were some already who imagined that he had in-

---

[8] Leon. Ep. lvi., col. 967; Baron. u. s. Compare this language with that addressed by Victor Maximus to Siricius sixty or seventy years earlier:—"The letters of your Holiness were both suitable to the character of a priest, and to the dignity of the most splendid city." Mansi, tom. iii. col. 671. The claim of the Bishop of that city to a primacy derived from S. Peter was as yet unknown to, or not acknowledged by, the secular prince.

[9] Leon. Ep. xi., col. 642; Baron. A.D. 445, Leon. Ann. vi. The decree was occasioned by the proceedings of Hilary of Arles, which it denounces as contrary to the "Majesty of the Empire and the reverence due to the Apostolic See." There can be no doubt that at this period the Emperors, both of the East and West, supported the extravagant pretensions of their respective Patriarchs primarily with an eye to "the Majesty of the Empire." The splendour of the see was reflected on the court, and a politic Prince found in this centralization of ecclesiastical power the ready means of moral influence over many of whose obedience and respect he was not sure through fear.

LETTER IV.
PART III.
SECT. III.
herited from S. Peter a *right* to that priority of station and those ampler powers, of which they found him in possession.

SECT. IV.
IV. The most important prerogative accorded to the see of Rome in early times was the power of entertaining the appeal of Bishops of the West, who had been condemned by a Synod of their own Province. The origin of this jurisdiction is curiously illustrative of the mode in which every substantial advantage enjoyed by Rome has been acquired and secured. In the year 347, a Council of Western Bishops assembled at Sardica had occasion to make some regulations for the settlement of disputes to which the Arian controversy had given rise. Among other canons framed with this view, we find the following, which was proposed by the celebrated Hosius, Bishop of Cordova:—

" If a Bishop in any Province have a cause against his brother and co-bishop, neither of them are to call in Bishops from another Province to take cognizance of it. But if any Bishop has been condemned in any matter, and conceive that he hath not an unsound but a good cause, so that the trial may be had over again, let us, *if it seem good* to your Charity, honour the memory of the Apostle Peter, and written notice concerning those who have tried the case be sent to *Julius*, the Bishop of Rome, so that, if it should be necessary, a fresh court may be held, through the Bishops who dwell near the Province, and he may appoint judges. But if he fail to show that the case is such as to require a fresh hearing, what has been once determined is not to be annulled, but the matter to rest as it is [1]."

You will observe, in the first place, that the powers given by this canon were conferred on a particular Pope, Julius, and not on the Bishops of Rome generally [2]; secondly, that it only authorized him, if he saw reason, to order a fresh hearing of certain causes before a local tribunal, on appeal from the parties interested [3],—and not, as his successors

---

[1] Can. iii. Mansi, tom. iii. col. 8.

[2] " It is easy to see," says an excellent divine of the French Church, " that the Canons of the Council of Sardica respecting appeals, and the power of sending legates *a latere*, were not absolute and general, but only provisory;—being intended to provide for the safety and peace of the orthodox;—forasmuch as they speak of Julius by name, and not of the Apostolic See. But *the Pope is one thing, the Apostolic See another*, as the Canonists teach," &c.—Richer, Hist. Conc. Gen. l. i. c. iii. § iv., p. 46. Colon. 1683.

[3] De Marca's notice of this canon supplies an illustration of the manner in which the most unfounded opinions maintain their ground in the Church of Rome. An independent thinker occasionally discovers an error, and finds no difficulty in approving his view to the impartial and learned; but the education of the clergy is in other hands; the correction is unheeded by the mass; and the old tradition becomes every day more firmly established, because every day adds to the number of those who, following blindly their blind leaders, are giving it their inconsiderate support. This author tells us that it had been "the universal persuasion (in his communion) that a law was found in the Canons of the Synod of Sardica concerning appeals against the sentences of Bishops, and that according to a decree of this Council such appeals were to be tried by the Supreme Pontiff." But this, he saw, was a mistake, because "only the power of granting another hearing was introduced by the Sardican Synod," and "there is a difference between an appeal and a fresh hearing;" the one "transferring the entire cognizance of the cause to a superior judge;" the other "leaving the final settlement of it to the first

affected to understánd it, to evoke any cause to Rome on his own mere motion; and, lastly, that, while Hosius referred to the Bishop of Rome's traditionary connexion with S. Peter as a ground of respect, and a reason for selecting him for this office, his language proves clearly that he was not entitled to it of right[4], that the Council might have withheld it from him, had it thought proper, or even conferred it on another. Upon this slight foundation, however, did succeeding Pontiffs contrive to build up, by slow degrees, a general appellate jurisdiction, which has been practically the chief source of the exorbitant greatness of their Church[5]. The Canons of Sardica were long quoted to justify their claim; but when that had been firmly established, they were dismissed in silence. They had done their

jurisdiction, only new judges being called to the assistance of the former." He says that he communicated this view of the matter to some learned men, who expressed their approbation of it. He suggests that the mistake arose from the use of the word 'appeal' in the canons. De Concord. Sacerd. et Imp. l. vii. c. iii. § vi.; tom. ii. p. 311. He also reminds us that the Council was only extending to the Pope a power which was acknowledged to reside in the Emperor, and which, in fact, had been often exercised by him, and that the concession was, therefore, " in quoddam velut detrimentum auctoritatis imperatoriæ." Ibid. §§ i. xv.

[4] "Hosius asks the Council to accord this honour to the memory of S. Peter; which shows very strongly that it was a right which the Pope did not possess until then." Tillemont, Hist. Eccles. *Vie de S. Athanase*, Art. l.; tom. viii. p. 47.

[5] De Marca, u. s. § vi. expressly says :—"To this Council is due the *first origin* of the power of the Supreme Pontiff with regard to canonical sentences on Bishops."

work, and thenceforth we hear only of the supremacy of S. Peter and the indefeasible inheritance
of his see of Rome [6].

The story of Apiarius, which I am about to relate, will give you some idea of the manner in which the ambitious Romans soon learnt to employ the unfortunate precedent which had been established at Sardica, and at the same time explain the state of the question arising from their attempts in the early part of the fifth century. This man was an African presbyter, who, having been degraded by his own Diocesan, the Bishop of Sicca, went to Rome, and by misrepresentation induced Zosimus to interfere in his behalf. The Pope not only restored Apiarius, but expressed himself prepared to excommunicate the Bishop of Sicca, or at least summon him to Rome for trial, if he should venture to dispute this extraordinary stretch of authority. To justify his proceedings, he appealed vaguely to the Canons of Nicæa. The puzzled Africans made one concession to these pretensions. They took the sentence of degradation off Apiarius, but refused to allow him to officiate in the diocese

---

[6] "The Canons of the Council of Sardica were never received by the Catholic Church as general laws. They were never put into the code of the Canons of the Universal Church, approved by the Council of Chalcedon. The East never received them, nor would the Bishops of Africa own them. The Popes only used them and cited them under the name of the Council of Nice to give them the greater weight and authority." Dupin, Eccl. Hist. cent. iv.; vol. i. p. 607. Sim. De Marca, l. vii. c. iii. § v.; tom. ii. p. 311.

of Sicca; while to the Pope's claim of jurisdiction, they answered that though they had read very many copies of the Canons of Nicæa, they had never read in them the decree to which he referred in his admonition [7]; and they requested him to inspect the copies at Rome, and to cause those at Alexandria and Constantinople to be examined also; promising to admit his version of the disputed canons, until the question should be settled by such investigation. They also sent to Alexandria and Constantinople themselves, and received from the Bishops of those cities certified copies of the Nicene Canons, agreeing with their own. These they immediately forwarded to Boniface, who was at that time Pope. The canons produced by Zosimus as those of Nice prove to have been the decrees of Sardica, which had never been received by the Churches of Africa, or of the East.

We hear no more of Apiarius for the next five years, at the end of which we find him again convened, and on a fresh charge, before a Council of his own Church, and the old legate of Zosimus, recommissioned by Cœlestine, again exerting himself in his defence. This time, however, the affair soon came to an end, and in a very unexpected manner. Overcome by remorse, Apiarius confessed his guilt, and nothing remained for his too

[7] Conc. Afric. Ep. ad *Bonifac.*; Zosimus having died before his legates returned. Mansi, tom. iv. col. 511.

zealous friends but to retire in confusion from the letter iv. contest which they had so unnecessarily sought. part iii. The letter addressed by the African Bishops on sect. iv. this occasion to Cœlestine is happily extant. In it they speak as follows:—

" We earnestly entreat you for the future not to admit persons coming hence to a hearing so easily, or to be willing any more to receive to communion those who have been excommunicated by us; for your Reverence will readily perceive that this point also has been settled by the Nicene Council . . . . Most wisely and justly has it provided that all matters shall be terminated in the places where they have arisen; believing that the grace of the Holy Spirit would not be wanting to each Province; . . . unless, peradventure, there is any one who believes that our God can inspire any one single person with grace to try causes justly, and refuse it to numberless Bishops assembled in Council . . . . We find it decreed in no Council of the Fathers that any should be sent from your Holiness. . . . . Whoever requests it, do not send your clergy to execute your orders, do not yield to their request, lest we appear to be bringing the arrogance, ambition, and pride of the world into the Church of Christ [s]."

About the same time the Church of Africa endeavoured to secure itself from future aggression on the part of Rome, by the enactment of several canons for the restraint of appeals. Thus in the

---

[s] Mansi, tom. iv. col. 515. The affair of Apiarius is discussed at length by Dupin, De Antiq. Discip. Eccl. diss. ii. c. ii. § iii., p. 174.

year 416, the Council of Milevis in Numidia made the following provision against foreign interference, probably in consequence of an appeal to Rome by the Pelagian Cœlestius :—

"It hath pleased the Council that if priests, deacons, or others of the lower clergy, complain of the sentences of their own Bishops, in causes which they may have had, the neighbouring Bishops shall, at their instance, with the consent of their own Bishops, hear them, and terminate all matters between them. But if they shall think good to appeal from them also, let them only appeal to African Councils, or to the Primates of their Provinces. But let not him who shall have thought good to appeal to the parts beyond sea be admitted to communion by any in Africa[9]."

When this canon was revised by the General Council of Africa in 419, the following words were introduced after the clause, " Let them only appeal to African Councils," &c.:—

"As hath also *often* been decreed respecting Bishops."

The origin and growth of the appellate jurisdiction of Rome have perhaps received a sufficient illustration from the facts already brought before you. But it may be asked whether the novel pretensions of the Pope were more respected in his own Patriarchate than they had been in

---

[9] Conc. Milev. ii. Can. xxii. Mansi, tom. iv. col. 332. Some ascribe these canons to the Council of Carthage held in 418. Respecting the clause inserted in 419, see Dupin, De Ant. Disc. diss. ii. c. i. § iv., p. 127.

Africa? We know their ultimate success in Western Europe, but from the following narrative it will appear that even there, so late as the ninth century, it needed but a firm and vigorous resistance on the part of a national Church to restrict a presuming Pontiff to the exercise of that simple function which was assigned to his predecessor by the third canon of Sardica.

In the year 871, Hincmar, Bishop of Laon in France, was deposed by a Provincial Council assembled at Douzi under his uncle and namesake, the celebrated Archbishop of Rheims. As he appealed to Rome before sentence was passed, it was recorded against him with the addition of the clause, "Saving the judgement of the Holy See." The Council sent an account of its proceedings to the Pope, Hadrian II., and requested him to confirm them, or if he saw grounds for a fresh trial, to appoint one "according to the Sardican Canons;" "or if you should resolve," it added, "to send legates from your presence, clothed with your authority, to try the case with the Bishops, the condemned, meanwhile, not being restored to his order (for so the sacred Canons of Sardica direct), we do not refuse[1]." The studied deference displayed in this epistle is in strong contrast with the independent, though respectful bearing of S. Augustine and his colleagues. Nevertheless it did

---

[1] Mansi, tom. xvi. col. 680.

not satisfy the imperious Pontiff of the ninth century. His rescript was in a strangely haughty
style :—

"We command Hincmar, Bishop of Laon, relying on
your power, to come to the threshold of the holy Apostles
and to our presence. And with him let a competent
accuser at the same time come [2]," &c.

He wrote to the king, Charles the Bald, who had
accused Hincmar of sedition before the Council in
the same words, but adding :—

"So long as we live, we will in no wise consent to his
deposition, unless he come before us himself, and the cause
of his deposition shall have been carefully sifted and determined by our inquest. After which admonition, we have
deferred giving you other commandment at present
touching the said Hincmar, beyond that of his coming to
Rome [3]."

The reply of Charles, which was composed by
Hincmar of Rheims, is clear as to the novelty of
the Pope's claim, even at that period :—

"We have wondered very much where the person who
dictated the epistle brought to us . . . found it written
that it was to be ordered by Apostolical authority that
a king,—who is the corrector of the wicked, and the
punisher of the guilty, and, according to both ecclesiastical
and mundane law, the avenger of crimes,—should send to
Rome, relying on his power, a man who has been legally
and regularly condemned for his transgressions. . . . We

[2] Mansi, tom. xv. col. 853.   [3] Mansi, tom. xv. col. 855.

kings of France, descended from a kingly race, have not
been hitherto accounted the Lords Lieutenant of Bishops,
but the Lords of the land. . . . If you will turn over the
records of your predecessors, you will certainly not find
that our predecessors ever received from yours such orders
as are contained in the letters directed to us in your name.
. . . Wherefore we entreat you, in honour of Almighty
God and reverence of the holy Apostles, to send no more
to us and the Bishops and Nobles of our realms such
letters, by which we are dishonoured, and such commands as we have up to this time received as from you,
and that you will not compel us, who desire to obey you
in those things which belong to your office (if indeed it
be your office), to treat your commands and letters, which
cannot be honoured, with contempt, and to put dishonour
on your legates [4]."

Only a fragment of the reply of the Bishops has
been preserved; but we have enough to show that
it was equally indignant and equally decided:—

" We have found some things in your epistle which
have caused us no slight astonishment, and have made
us doubt not a little whether we were to think otherwise,
or that those things were actually set down just as they
sounded to us. . . . There would have been no occasion for
us to make excuses now, if the person whom you ordered

---

[4] Hincmari Opp. tom. ii. p. 706. Probably Hincmar or the king
thought that they had gone too far in the doubt hinted by the clause,
" If indeed it be your office;" for they despatched a second letter,
a very short one, in which they entreated the Pope that no more such
orders might be sent to them, and professed a desire to obey where
obedience was rightly claimed, in the very same words as in the
other, but omitting that clause. Ibid. p. 716.

to reply to us had read in the records of our synodal acts what took place before the sentence of condemnation was pronounced against Hincmar; to wit, 'Then were read in the Council the decrees of the canons by Adalgarius, the deacon, who said as follows: The Sardican Canons have decreed, that, If any Bishop[5],'" &c.

This vigorous opposition alarmed Hadrian, who not only withdrew his injunction for a new trial at Rome, but sought to appease Charles by promising him the imperial crown on the death of Lewis II. It is curious to observe, however, that while he acknowledged that the canons required the case to be heard in France, he nevertheless endeavoured to procure the presence of the accused Bishop at Rome upon a new pretence. The precedent would have been of value :—

" Touching these matters, we dare not make any decision that may run counter to the Nicene Council and the rules of the five other Councils, or the decrees of our predecessors. . . . But because the proceedings do not appear proper and complete to our (counsellors), or suitable to the dignity of this Holy See, until he has had time to come to this most holy and Apostolic See, to which he has appealed, therefore let him come, and, when the letters which you have sent us and the Acts of the Synod, &c., have been shown to him, then, judges being chosen (but without his being restored to his order, or legates being sent *ex latere nostro*), let what has been done

[5] Mansi, tom. xvi. col. 569.

be re-enacted with our authority, and the affair canonically terminated in the Province in which it arose[6]."

I hardly need say that the French king and his Bishops did not comply with the last proposition of Hadrian. Hincmar of Laon did not go to Rome, but remained in France, and in prison, until the death of Charles; nor was he ever restored to the dignity of which he had been regularly and canonically deprived, according to the laws of his own Church and country[7].

V. You are now, my dear Sir, in possession of the principal arguments by which I have been convinced that the Bishop of Rome has no authority, *by divine right,* over any other Bishop in the whole world. It has been shown to demonstration that the Primitive Church knew nothing whatever of that *supremacy* which he now claims, and that the *primacy* which it accorded to him rested entirely on considerations of human policy, convenience, and expediency. The early Christians beheld in the foundation of the see by two illustrious Apostles a title to great respect and deference, but no evidence of transmitted rights[8]. The facts that have been

---

[6] Mansi, tom. xv. coll. 858, 859.

[7] See § xix. of the Vita Hincmari Junioris, auctore Lud. Cellotio, reprinted by Labb., tom. viii. col. 1698 (Lut. Par. 1671), and Mansi, tom. xvi. col. 721.

[8] Some Roman Catholics unable to resist the evidence of history as to the origin of the Roman Primacy, and equally unable to dispossess themselves of the persuasion that S. Peter must have a successor in

produced are undeniable.   How then will you avoid the only inference to which they lead?

his Primacy, have held that the first rank in the Church is (abstractedly) elective, and that any Bishop whom the Church might appoint to it would become, by that appointment, the successor of S. Peter. E.g.—"It is the Bishop of Rome who enjoys the Primacy. It belongs to him by *divine* right as he is the successor of S. Peter, and only by *human* as he is Bishop of Rome. S. Peter might have refrained from choosing a particular see, as in the first five years of his Pontificate; in which case, neither the Bishop of Rome, nor of Antioch, would have succeeded to S. Peter and the Primacy, but he whom the Church might have chosen. . . . It is then only because he fixed himself at Rome that the Bishop of Rome is his successor. . . . But since that which has taken place, solely through an act of man, may be changed by the authority of the Church, it follows that the Church could for just reasons assign the Primacy to another Bishop, as to the Bishop of Milan, or of Paris. . . . However, there is no appearance of any reasons ever presenting themselves strong enough to induce the Church to make this change, seeing that she has not made it up to the present time. In all probability, as long as Rome shall last, so long will her Bishop be the successor of S. Peter, and the head of the Church."—L'Etat de l'Eglise, ch. v. tom. i. p. 77. Wurtzb. 1766. This was the doctrine of Pereira. See Theologia Tentativa, Ep. Dedic.; p. 5. He quotes Dominic Soto, a name familiar to English ears:—"Whether the extreme point of dignity is *jure Divino* in the Roman Church, so that the Bishop of Rome and the Supreme Pontiff are joined in one by a Divine bond, is not so certain as some imagine" (Comm. in Sent. l. iv. p. 645); and Dominic Banhes:—"Although it is believed to be true by very Catholic and learned men, that the Roman Pontiff is *jure Divino* the successor of S. Peter, it is nevertheless not the Catholic faith, but simply a very probable opinion" (Comm. in 2m 2æ; tom. ii. p. 52); and Cardinal Cusanus (A.D. 1448), who is still more explicit:—"If by any possible contingency, the Archbishop of Treves were elected by the Church in Synod, as its President and Head, he would more properly be the successor of S. Peter in the Primacy, than the Bishop of Rome" (De Concord. Cath. l. ii. c. xxxiv.). A similar view was held by Scipio Ricci and condemned by Pius VI. as *heretical.* In his Bull it is expressed thus:—"The Roman Pontiff does not receive the power of ministry, by which he has authority in the

It may tend further, by God's help, to disabuse
your mind of prejudice against the truth which has
been proposed for your acceptance, if, in conclusion,
I present it in the words of a great writer of the
French Church. The following extract is part of
an "Abridgement," or compendious statement, "of
the discipline that was observed in the three first
ages of the Church," given by Dupin in his Library
of Ecclesiastical Authors:—

"All the Bishops were persuaded that they received
their office immediately from Jesus Christ, and that
Providence had assigned to each of them a portion of the
flock of the Heavenly Pastor to govern, in such a manner,
however, as that in an exigence, or time of necessity, they
were to relieve the wants of all Churches. They lived in
great union together, and preserved a mutual correspondence by letters, which they sent to one another.
The Bishops of *great* cities had their prerogatives in ordinations and in councils; and *as in civil matters men generally had recourse to the civil metropolis, so likewise in
ecclesiastical matters they consulted with the Bishop of the
metropolitan city.* The Churches of the *three principal
cities* of the world were looked upon as chief, and their
Bishops attributed great prerogatives to themselves.
The Church of Rome, founded by S. Peter and S. Paul,
was considered as first, and its Bishop as first amongst
all the Bishops of the world; yet they did not believe him
to be infallible, and, though they frequently consulted

universal Church as the successor of Peter, the true Vicar of
Christ, and head of the whole Church, from Christ in the person of
S. Peter, but from the Church." Prop. iii. Bullar. ad ann. 1794.

him, and his advice 'was of great consequence, yet they did not receive it blindfold and implicitly, every Bishop imagining himself to have a right to judge in ecclesiastical matters[9]."

You will observe, that the principle of metropolitical precedency, if duly carried out, would require that the Pope should lose his Primacy when Rome ceased to be the queen of the nations. If in the fourth century, Milan, or Antioch, or any other city, had been decreed by imperial authority superior to Rome for all civil purposes, there can be no doubt that the Bishop of the city so preferred would have taken precedence, in matters ecclesiastical, of the see of Rome. That no such change actually took place, though more than contemplated, as we have seen, by Justinian and others, was owing partly to the gradual manner in which the civil importance and prestige of Rome declined, and partly to the disorders of the time, which rendered united action

---

[9] Vol. i. p. 590. Contrast these representations of Dupin, the truth of which cannot be doubted by any one who has considered the evidence produced in this letter, with the doctrine now generally received in his communion; viz. that "Bishops receive all their authority, not from Christ, but from the Supreme Pontiff." Bellarm. De Rom. Pont. l. iv. cc. xxii.—xxv.; tom. i. p. 229, &c. "This fiction," says Bossuet, "falls to the ground of itself, from the fact that, having been unheard of in early times, it *began* to be brought into theology in the *thirteenth* century, after men chose for the most part to employ *philosophical reasonings*, and those of the worst kind, rather than consult the Fathers." Defens. Declar. P. iii. l. viii. c. xi., p. 88. In other words, it is a mere *rationalistic development* of speculative principles as strange to Scripture and antiquity as itself.

no longer possible; but principally, it is quite certain, to the opinion, which gained ground in Europe with the advance of ignorance and barbarism, that the prerogatives of the see of Rome were an inheritance from S. Peter. I will only add, that at the Reformation, the Church of England did not, on her own responsibility, undertake to do, what the Church Catholic of early times would certainly under the same circumstances have done; she did not offer to deprive the Bishop of Rome of Patriarchal authority within his acknowledged limits. However feeble and insignificant, as an earthly power, Rome might have become, our Reformers never sought to urge the ancient rule to a sentence of degradation against her Bishop [10]. We might have been to this day an united Church,

---

[10] Nor do the later Greeks refuse to acknowledge the Primacy of Rome. Thus Barlaam, De Papæ Principatu, says, "that the see of Rome obtained the first place many ages after Peter by the favour of the holy Fathers and the most religious Emperors," c. iv.; and that the Pope's prerogative consists in this, "that he should sit in the first place, and be called the first among brethren, and that mention of him should be made first in the mystical prayers of the divine service," c. ix. Dupin, De Ant. Disc. diss. iv. c. ii. § ii. p. 330. And Nilus, De Primatu :—" With good reason did the Fathers assign the dignity of the Primacy to the see of Old Rome, because that city was the imperial city." And again in his book De Dissens. Eccles. :—" It is not, as the Latins assert, because we wish to arrogate the Primacy to ourselves, and are not willing to stand in the second place after the first of Rome,—and for such reasons refuse to be at peace; for we do not contend with the Church of Rome about the Primacy, nor is it now a question about the second place." Dupin, u. s.

if the Popes had been willing to return to the pure Primacy enjoyed by their see in the third century, and by so doing had ceased to insist on those new terms of communion, the resolute maintenance of which was a necessity of that false position to which they had been elevated by the sinful ambition of their predecessors.

LETTER IV.

PART IV.

BEFORE we quit the subject of the Supremacy, I think it right to make a few brief remarks on one or two minor arguments, of the nature of internal evidence, which you have urged in its behalf as subsidiary to your appeal to holy Scripture.

I. I begin with what you term the "marvellous duration" of the Papal see. You are of opinion that this ought to engage the veneration and impress the imagination of all who realize it, and lead them to inquire into the recondite causes of so remarkable a fact. You read in it yourself an indication of the perpetual favour of God, and of an extraordinary Providence exerted for the protection of His Church. I need not trouble you with any consideration of the abstract value of such an argument; because it is surely sufficient to point out that the same superintending care has been extended through an equal or even greater period to several other Churches. The sees of Antioch, of Alexandria and Jerusalem, and doubtless many others of less fame but of the same Apostolic origin, have endured as long or longer in spite of many disadvantages from which their prosperous rival has been exempt. Those in particular which I have named have been oppressed, and often persecuted, during the last thousand years by an essentially hostile power; whereas the Bishop of Rome has within the same period succeeded in raising himself to a place among the sovereign princes of Europe, and in surrounding himself with the prestige of an imaginary right to govern and guide the whole Church, and of infallible aid from heaven in the discharge of that office;—attributes to which no other see has even ventured to pretend.

II. Another argument of the same nature you build on what you consider to have been the general character of the Bishops of Rome:—

" All during the first three centuries were Martyrs, amounting in number to thirty-four. Besides these forty-three more were canonized saints, and of the whole number only eleven have been very bad and seven more not good [1]."

If these statements were true, most cheerfully would I,—not indeed admit your inference,—but at least echo your exulting exclamation; "How great a glory for the Popedom!" Many I fear might go further, and, permitting their reason to be overpowered by reverence and admiration, surrender their belief at once to a claim associated with the illustrious names of so many saints and martyrs. But we have been spared this temptation. Not only is your representation without any real bearing on the exclusive pretensions of Rome; but the only imposing part of it is demonstrably a mistake.

I first remark on your admission that some of the Popes have been men of bad character. This

---

[1] M. Rohrbacher is not willing to concede so much :—" Of more than two hundred and fifty Popes, there are perhaps as many as three who have not lived better than the greater part of temporal sovereigns. . . . . During nineteen centuries, of two hundred and fifty Popes, we have found nine or ten who are accused or suspected of bad morals. Of these nine or ten, there are three at the most against whom, after a first examination, the charge has appeared to us convincing, or nearly so; one in the tenth century, another in the eleventh, and a third in the fifteenth." Hist. Univ. de l'Egl. Cath., l. 59; tom. xii. p. 441. The one guilty Pope of the fifteenth century must, I presume, be either John XXIII. (1410—1415), deposed by the Council of Constance for many grievous crimes, or the still more infamous Alexander VI. (1492—1503). The man who acquits either condemns himself. This author's mode of composing history will be exposed in Letter IX. § iii.

fact would not affect their claim to a supremacy; but it certainly does present a most distressing difficulty to those who advocate their infallibility. In what a position are you placed! Reduced to apologize for the moral conduct of a man to whom as a teacher you ascribe an absolute inerrancy in faith and morals! Why, if your doctrine of the Papacy be true, personal unholiness in a Pope must be regarded as a prodigy indeed, a portent that should shake the world with awe[2]!

SECT. III.

III. You have alleged the case of Judas; but surely the least consideration will show you- its irrelevancy. In the first place, he was not one of those whom the Father gave the Son,—of whom He "lost none,"—but being a traitor from the beginning was chosen for the traitor's work, as Pharaoh, Jeroboam and Hazael, were raised up to accomplish, by such means as their own heart should dictate, the righteous purposes of the great Go-

---

[2] Yet some cannot perceive the contradiction; e. g. Mr. W. G. Ward:—"I say that the most abominable wickedness in Popes is not inconsistent with those objects ["which, as the records of Apostolic times show, were the very purpose for which the Church was set up"]: not with the preservation of the true faith, because we hold the gift of infallibility to be no less divinely secured to the worst than to the best of Popes." *The Anglican Establishment*, &c. p. 108. London, 1850. Most, however, try, with M. Rohrbacher, to soften down the difficulty by throwing doubt upon the testimony of history against even the most infamous of the mediæval Popes. Both courses betray desperation. Oh, that they might have grace and wisdom to see the falsehood of that foregone conclusion which compels its advocates to one or the other of these incompatible extravagances!

vernor of all. Again, he was never an Apostle, in
the full sense of the word. It is true that he
helped to spread abroad the glad tidings, that "the
kingdom of heaven was *at hand;*" but ere it was
established among men, he had "gone to his own
place." He had no part in the commission to
"make disciples of all nations," nor in that gift of
"power" from above by which his brethren were
enabled to fulfil it. So that if the pretensions of
the Pope are just, it is a palpable fallacy to compare him in his sins with Judas the betrayer[3].
From your point of view, the only parallel to
wickedness in a Pope would be an equal degree
of wickedness (could such be found) in the Apostle
Peter after the day of Pentecost. Had he been
all that you imagine him to have been, and yet
become a castaway, the example would have anticipated the difficulty which you now feel when
reading of an Octavian, or a Borgia[4]. With *us,*

[3] It is most strange that one so acute as Mr. Ward should have
been able to satisfy himself with this imaginary analogy. Yet he
says of the bad Popes, and without betraying less than his usual confidence:—" I cannot but think, . . . that such an instance as that of
Judas Iscariot might prepare us for any amount of wickedness in
ecclesiastical rulers at future periods." Ibid. p. 110.

[4] Mr. Ward says:—"The Apostles claimed infallibility; but so far
were they from claiming impeccability, that S. Paul himself expresses
his need of severe self-discipline, 'lest he become a reprobate.'"
u. s. Does he really believe, then, that if S. Paul had become a
reprobate, and lived in habitual deadly sin, as some Popes have done,
he would have retained his gift of inspiration, and continued a trustworthy exponent of the faith and morals of the Gospel?

however, even the hypothetical fall of the Apostle would not supply the parallel required; because we know that the position which you assume for the Pope is very different from that which our Blessed Lord conferred upon S. Peter.

However, I do not wish to debar you from all comparison. You shall, if you desire it, have more license in this respect than your own theory consistently permits. We may presume that those Popes to whom you allude as "very bad" have all lived and sinned since the foundation of the see of Canterbury at the end of the sixth century. Now, let me ask you to name one single Bishop of Canterbury whom you are able to pronounce a "very bad" man [5]. I am convinced that honesty will here

---

[5] I am aware that all will not confess their inability to do this. I should hope, however, that the following is an extreme case :—"Q. What say you of Cranmer? A. He was the chief adviser to Henry VIII., the greatest monster that ever disgraced Christianity, in all the sacrileges and murders he committed : his name should be everlastingly execrated. The cold-blooded, perfidious, impious, blasphemous caitiff expired amidst the flames he had himself kindled. . . . . Q. Had this wicked man been a priest? A. Yes; and he had, notwithstanding his vow, one wife in Germany alive, and another in England. Q. Was Cranmer a persecutor? A. He aided Henry in all his robberies and murders. 'These horrid butcheries,' says Cobbet, 'were perpetrated under the primacy of Cranmer, and by the help of another ruffian named Thomas Cromwell, who shared with Cranmer the work of plunder, and afterwards shared in his disgraceful end.'" *Controversial Catechism* (No. 1, p. 31), by the Rev. Stephen Keenan. Tenth Thousand, publ. by Dolman. Similarly the Brothers of S. Vincent de Paul :—"There was no deed of injustice, wrong, . . . of rapine, or blood, for which King Henry did not find a ready abject tool in Cranmer." Clifton Tracts, No. 2, p. 8. I should

prevail against prejudice, and that you will confess, at the very least, that the tenants of that see have been far. less stained by vice and crime than the cotemporary series of Roman Bishops. But if so, what "glory" can accrue to the Church of Rome, or what peculiar credit to its pretensions, from the general character of its chief Pastors?

You will observe that I do not urge this comparison as an argument against the supremacy of Rome. I believe your reasoning to be unsound in principle, and therefore will not retort it on yourself. The notorious wickedness of so many Popes, though incompatible with the opinion of their infallibility, does not disprove the justice of those claims to power and jurisdiction, in support of which you allege what you consider to have been the extraordinary sanctity of the majority. I merely wish to point out, that the personal holiness of the Bishops of Rome has not been such, so unexampled and unapproachable, as to yield any inference, on your own principle, in favour of their pretensions. This is a mere question of fact, and one that we should be willing to decide without reference to its supposed bearings. Religious, as well as political theorists are under a strong temptation to

be sorry to accuse the Roman Catholics who believe and repeat these wicked statements of an avowed infidel of any thing worse than gross ignorance and credulity; but surely they are most heavily responsible for the encouragement of delusions which a glance at the more moderate of their own writers would be sufficient to dispel.

make light of sin and error in persons and institu- tions historically associated with. their particular views; but it is the duty of a Christian to look truth calmly in the face, to take facts as they are, and to measure them by no other standard than the eternal rule of right.

SECT. IV.   IV. I have noticed that considerations such as we are now discussing often exercise a very undue in- fluence on the imagination of Roman Catholics, and not the least among those who are the most highly educated.   They are much in the habit, though perhaps unconsciously, of looking for the com- mission of their Church in the lives of her saints and martyrs, the multitude of her nominal subjects, her imposing territorial extent, and other notes of a similar character.   These are practically the evidence of her pretensions with most of those who ask for any;—far more so, indeed, than the sup- posed testimony of holy Scripture and other records of sacred antiquity.   But you will agree with me, that the more importance a person attaches to this species of evidence, the more caution ought he to exercise in the admission of those allegations upon which it rests.   If he believes that to have had saints and martyrs in abundance can help to au- thenticate the claim of a particular see to the supreme government of the whole Church, let him at least see to it that he has not been cheated with an empty name.   Let him, at all events, ex-

amine the credentials which it presents. Though
they may seem satisfactory in form and matter,
they can be of no value if they are not genuine.
Bear with me then, for the sake of the truth which
we both seek, while I inquire whether your martyrology of the earlier Popes is confirmed or disowned by the authentic voice of history.

Your assertion is, that "every Pope during the
first three centuries was a martyr." Your authorities, I may assume, have been the Breviary and
Calendar of your Church, in which that title is given
to all but two who lived within the period that you
have named. The slight exception was easily
overlooked. Your authorities, however, have deceived you. Only five Popes of all to whom you
refer can be pronounced with certainty to have
suffered for the faith: viz. Telesphorus, Fabianus,
Lucius, Sixtus II., and Felix. The crown of mar-
trydom is also claimed for Anterus, on grounds of
great probability. Pontianus and Cornelius died
in exile, but by what death it is not known. For
the truth of this representation I shall appeal to a
very learned member of the Church in France, the
great historian Tillemont. Here, then, is his
account of Linus, who is said by Irenæus to have
been made Bishop of Rome by the Apostles Peter
and Paul [6] :—

---

[6] L. iii. c. iii. § 3 ; tom. i. p. 431.

"The Latin Church honours him among the martyrs in the celebration of the holy mysteries, and therefore we have reason to believe that he deserved this title by suffering for Jesus Christ; though apparently he did not suffer for him unto death, except in the disposition of his heart [7]."

Of Anacletus, his successor, the same author says:—

"We must believe that he deserves the title; but only in the same manner as S. Linus [8]."

Of S. Clement, the third Bishop, he remarks:—

"The authority of Irenæus does not permit us to declare as certain that he ended his life by martyrdom [9]."

Of Evaristus, who followed Clement:—

"The Martyrologies of Florus, Adon, and others say that he was crowned with martyrdom; which does not appear to have been known to the ancients, not even to S. Irenæus [1]."

Of Pius, who died A.D. 157:—

"The Roman Martyrology says that he was crowned with martyrdom in the persecution of Antoninus, whom we do not find to have been guilty of one [2]."

His notices of many others are very similar. You will perceive that Tillemont does not unniche your supposed martyrs with any thing like rude-

---

[7] Mém. Eccles., tom. ii. *S. Clem. R.* Art. ii. p. 70.
[8] Ibid.   [9] Ibid. Art. v. and *note* xii., p. 73.
[1] Ibid. *S. Evariste*, p. 97.   [2] Ibid. *S. Pie*, p. 131.

ness, or even willingly. He is evidently driven to his conclusion by the force of truth, while respect for the authority of his Church causes him to speak with caution, if not with hesitation. In two instances, indeed, he allows the title on grounds which, as they are stated by himself, you will, I am persuaded, deem very inconclusive. Thus of Callistus, who died A.D. 233, he says :—

"It seems credible enough that S. Callistus received the crown of martyrdom, although neither Eusebius, nor other writers of the best credit, say any thing about it. The first reason for believing it is the fact that we have the Acts of it; for though by the confession of Baronius they cannot be sustained, and though even the particulars in them which he approves . . . . appear false, yet it is rare to meet with the Acts of martyrdom of a saint, unless he were really a martyr, or at the least had suffered something for Jesus Christ. The second reason is that in the Calendar of Martyrs given by Bucherius, which is believed to have been made in the year 354, we find a Callistus down on the fourteenth of October, on which all the Martyrologies place the Festival of S. Callistus the Pope; and the Martyrologies of S. Jerome [with some later] mark on this day among the Martyrs at Rome S. Callistus, Bishop, or Pope [3]," &c.

Of Stephen, A.D. 257 :—

"There seems even to be some room for doubting whether he was really a martyr, for we may make sure that S. Augustine and Vincentius of Lerins did not know

---

[3] Tom. iii. *Note* iii. *sur Calliste,* p. 314.

it [4]." "And what seems still stronger, his martyrdom is not in the Calendar and other ancient monuments of the Roman Church given by Bucherius. . . . On the other hand, the Martyrologies of S. Jerome [and some still later monuments] put down S. Stephen, martyr at Rome, on the second of August, and some copies add the title of Bishop [5]."

These two instances will show on what slight grounds Tillemont was ready to admit the martyrdom of those Popes whom his Church styles martyrs, and therefore witness with great force to the entire absence of trustworthy evidence in the case of those whose claims to that distinction he has rejected. The truth is, that with the exception of Callistus and Stephen, and those whom I first named, the evidence of a violent death for religion is of such a nature, that historians not hampered by an obligation of respect for the Breviary seldom bestow on it even a passing allusion. It is only just to acknowledge that some learned Roman Catholics have shown a similar impartiality, though none of them, perhaps, with uniform consistency.

But here some thoughtful reader may conjecture that the word 'martyr' cannot be employed by the Church of Rome in these cases according to its modern and accepted sense; but rather as it was used in the first ages [6],—to signify one who had borne witness to the truth by suffering, whether

---

[4] Tom. iv. p. 14. *S. Etienne.*
[5] *Note* iii. *sur S. Etienne*, p. 7.
[6] Tillemont, tom. i. p. 173. *S. Jude.*

to the death or not[7]. No such charitable con-struction, however, is in this case admissible. The Breviary actually relates the *death* for Christ of several who did not so die. Thus in the service for Sept. 23, the people are told that Linus, the *first* Bishop before mentioned, was *beheaded* for his constancy in the faith; in that for Nov. 23, that S. Clement was "cast into the deep with an anchor about his neck." Again, for the Anacletus of authentic history as followed by Halloix, Valois, Cotelier, Alexandre, Dupin, Fleury, Tillemont, &c. [8] the Breviary gives us an imaginary Cletus, com-memorated April the 26th, and Anacletus, honoured July the 13th, and solemnly records of both that they were "crowned with martyrdom."

[7] This explanation is required in the case of Felix of Nola, who is not said to have died a violent death, though styled a martyr. Brev. Jan. 14. Sim. of Eusebius Vercell. Dec. 16.

[8] Tillem. tom. ii. *Note* v. *sur S. Clement*, p. 262. These fables are not confined to Popes: e.g., the Breviary gives a circumstantial account of the martyrdom of S. Timothy, Jan. 24 (see Tillem., tom. ii. p. 67 and note v. p. 255); and of Apollinaris, July 23 (Tillem., u. s. p. 47). It makes Dionysius the Areopagite, Oct. 9, the same person as Dionysius, the first Bishop of Paris, who lived two hundred years later, not forgetting to relate that he walked two miles after decapi-tation, with his head in his hands. This is the more extraordinary, because the same confusion is not found in the old Roman Martyr-ology, nor in another ancient one, several times reprinted, and therefore, I presume, much read, in the sixteenth century. See Launoy, Dispunctio Epist. Petri de Marca, c. xviii. Opp. tom. ii. P. i. p. 118. Tillemont declares the question to be so completely settled by this writer and others, that "henceforth there will be no one of any learning, and disinterested, not of their sentiment." Tom. iv. *Note* ii. *sur S. Denys*, p. 70.

V. Very painful must be the position of a good and learned man, trained to regard the sanction of his Church as an unfailing pledge of truth and right, when he becomes aware that statements like the foregoing, for which she vouches with peculiar solemnity, are thus hopelessly at variance with the truth of history. But it is a position as full of danger as of discomfort. Habitual reverence, the influence of early prejudice, above all, the fear of man, almost preclude the independent and impartial exercise of judgement in any question upon which the Church has spoken. Thus, Truth is betrayed, and Falsehood acquires strength through the connivance of those who are alone able to expose it. Even such men as Fleury, Dupin, and Tillemont succumb at times, though not habitually, to the temptation. The absence in their writings of fixed rules of historical criticism,—their fluctuating estimate of evidence,—their capricious inferences from acknowledged data,—their quick dismissal or avoidance of an unsafe subject; and, more than all, the far-fetched explanation, the startling misconstruction, the illogical reasoning, by which they sometimes strive to reconcile their Church with truth;—what are these but instances and symptoms of a subtle moral injury inflicted on men, in other respects among the best and wisest, by the inevitable working of that system which you believe to be instinct in all its parts with the Spirit of truth

and wisdom, and, *as it is*, the one appointed and LETTER IV.
infallible remedy for every evil of the soul[9]?   PART IV.
SECT. V.

I am, &c.

[9] Another distressing and very mischievous peculiarity of the Breviary is the occurrence in it of Lessons taken from writings which it ascribes to the Fathers; but which every man of learning acknowledges to be falsely attributed to them. I need hardly add that by this means an early writer is often made to lend the sanction of his name to doctrines of which he never heard. The following are examples :—(1.) Feb. 22. S. Peter's Chair at Antioch. Lessons iv—vi. purport to be from a Sermon of S. Augustine preached on this Festival. The original may be seen in the Appendix to his works, tom. v. col. 2836, Serm. cxc. (olim 15 de Sanctis). The Benedictine note says :—"It is not Augustine's, in the judgement of the Louvain editors, though read in the Roman Breviary under his name on this day . . . . This festival seems to have been unknown to the Africans in the age of Augustine, nor is it found in the Calendar of the Church of Carthage very recently published." (2.) The Sunday within the Octave of the Assumption of the B. V. (Aug. 15.) Lesson iv. is taken from an *Oratio de Laudibus Virginis* attributed to Epiphanius. Neither the style, nor the matter of this strange production belong to Epiphanius, or to his century; for which reason Petavius has excluded it from the list of his productions. He conjectures that it may be the work of another Epiphanius in the seventh or ninth century. The latter date is the more probable; for, as Rivetus observes, it appears to be "not simply a panegyric on Mary . . . . but a heap of encomiastic expressions gathered from all quarters." Special treatises in honour of the Virgin did not begin to appear until after the Council of Ephesus, A.D. 431, and Epiphanius died in 402. Oudin, tom. i. col. 534. (3.) Sept. 8. The Nativity of the B. V. Mary. Lessons iv—vi. are quoted as from S. Augustine :—"Serm. 18 de Sanctis, quæ est secunda de Annuntiatione Dominica." The same discourse also supplies three Lessons for the next day, which are repeated Dec. 9, in Fest. Concept. B. V., Die 2da. The Benedictine editors say :—"Verlinus and Vindingus reject it altogether as spurious; nor without reason in truth, though it is read in the Roman Breviary and some others under the name of Augustine . . . . To whatever day sacred to S. Mary the opening may be referred, the ancient Calendar in use in the Church of Car-

Q 2

thage at least down to the death of Augustine (who is marked in it) assuredly shows no such Festival of the Virgin." Serm. cxciv. in App. tom. v. col. 2842. (4.) Sept. 12. The fifth day within the Octave of the Nativity of the B. V. Lessons iv—vi. are said to be from a Sermon of S. Chrysostom "apud Metaphrasten." Nothing like them are to be found in the Benedictine edition of S. Chrysostom, either among the genuine or spurious writings there published. See Letters to a Seceder, p. 194. These lessons are repeated on the Fest. Patroc. B. V. (pro quibusdam locis), 2nd Sunday in November. Three other Lessons, viz. iv—vi., used July 2, Visit. B. V., are also falsely ascribed to Chrysostom upon the same authority. (5.) Oct. 14. S. Callisti Papæ et Martyris. Lessons v. vi. are attributed to S. Augustine; Serm. 44 de Sanctis. It may be seen in the Appendix to tom. v. col. 2923, numbered ccxxiii. The editors say of it:—" It has been rejected by Verlinus and Vindingus. In the Rom. Brev. it is ascribed to Augustine; but in truth the style and the method of discourse are against this." (6.) 3rd Sunday in November. Lessons iv—vi. are said to be *ex Libro S. Athanasii Episcopi ad Virgines.* This is the tract de Virginitate inter Opp. Athan.; tom. i. col. 1047. Dupin says:—"The Book of Virginity has nothing of the style of S. Athanasius, and it contains some precepts very remote from the genius and discipline of his time." *S. Athanas.;* vol. i. p. 173. "The Benedictines regard it as very doubtful on account of its inferior style, and because it is not found in the ancient collections of the works of S. Athanasius." "Bollandus thinks it excellent, but nevertheless does not believe that it is his." "Rivet and Cocus reject it absolutely, both on account of some rules of little importance in it (which proves nothing), and because the author says that those who observe its precepts will be placed in the third order of angels" (surely a sufficient disproof of the alleged authorship). Tillemont, Note lxxvii. *Sur Athan.* in *Mém. Eccl.;* tom. viii. p. 300. This author adds objections of his own, but does not speak decidedly. The reader will agree with Oudin that "it is not enough that a treatise should contain some right and orthodox doctrines for it to be ascribed to Athanasius; but that there should be found in it nothing absurd, childish, wrested aside and unworthy of a man of weight, such as many things in this treatise are." These he extracts after Rivetus and Scultetus; tom. i. col. 340. (7.) Dec. 28. Fest. H. Innoc. Lessons iv—vi. are from another Sermon falsely ascribed to S. Augustine, viz. 10 de Sanctis, now ccxx. in App. u. s. col. 2914.

LETTER V.

MY DEAR SIR,

YOU acknowledge, I observe, that the Popes have not always been content with the spiritual supremacy which you imagine to be their due; but have set up a claim to the same universal dominion over the secular interests of mankind. You believe, however, that you are not required by "Roman Catholic principles," to advocate or even to admit this extravagant enlargement of their pretensions.

I. Now it is obvious to remark that those Popes who have claimed temporal supremacy, and the advisers and abettors of those Popes, must surely have been as well acquainted with "Roman Catholic principles" as you and your friends. Whatever may be the legitimate authority of a

Pope, his competency as a witness in such matters cannot be denied by friend or foe. In the eyes of most of his adherents, however, he is much more than a witness. "It is the common opinion of Catholics" that when the Pope speaks *ex cathedrâ*, that is, when "as supreme primate of the Church he proposes any thing to be believed or held as an article of faith by all the faithful [1]," he is infallible, and what he so teaches becomes a doctrine of the Church. But it is certain that we can produce more than one assertion of temporal supremacy on the part of the Popes themselves which, judged by this rule, must be regarded as infallible. For example, in the year 1301 Boniface VIII., on occasion of a quarrel with the king of France, published a bull (*Ausculta fili*) in which he formally advanced this strange pretension, and appealed to holy Scripture in its support. He inferred from the commission given to the prophet Jeremiah to predict national revolutions and cala-

---

[1] Perrone, Prælect. Theol. Tract. de locis Theol. P. i. § ii. c. iv.; tom. ii. col. 1018. Sim. Dens, De Eccles. N. 96, Theolog. Mor. et Dogm.; tom. ii. p. 159; and others. This definition is quite arbitrary, and has been chosen with a view to exclude loose statements into which a Pope might fall on less solemn and deliberate occasions. Common sense would say that the Pope speaks *ex cathedrâ* whenever he is exercising his office of teacher. Thus Launoy :—" What is the meaning of the phrase *Pontifex ex cathedrâ?* It means *the Pope teaching*, and nothing more. Prithee, where is the oracle? Where is the mystery? When those three words are explained clearly and simply, they present nothing valuable or far-fetched." Epp. l. iii. Ep. i.; tom. v. P. i. p. 267.

mities, that "God had set him (the Pope) over the nations and the kingdoms," (not as you might suppose in order to warn them, after the example of the Prophet, of approaching change, but as the active minister of His will,) "to root out, and to pull down, and to destroy, and to throw down, to build and to plant," and he pronounced the obstinate gainsayer to his claim, "an infidel, cut off from the flock of the good Shepherd [2]." In another bull issued about the same time, he tells the king; "We will you to know that you are subject to us in spirituals and temporals . . . . Those who believe otherwise we account heretics [3]." As these measures did not produce the effect desired, he sought to enforce his doctrine by a still more elaborate and formal exposition, which accordingly appeared in the year following. The new bull (*Unam Sanctam*) did not refer especially to France, but dealt only with the general principle. It taught that there is "one holy Catholic Church," and "one chief Pastor" of this Church, and that "in it and in his power are two swords, the spiritual and the temporal;" . . . . "the latter to be drawn for the Church, the former by it; the one by the hand of the priest, the other by the hand

---

[2] Fleury, l. xc. ch. v. This interpretation of Jer. i. 10 was very common at this period.

[3] Vigor, Acta Bonif.; fol. 11, fa. 1. S. l. 1614. See Dupin, cent. xiv. c. i.; vol. ii. p. 490.

of kings and soldiers, but at the will and sufferance of the priest; that one of these should be under the other, and the temporal authority subject to the spiritual;" that "the spiritual power can create the temporal and judge it," and that resistance to this claim involves the Manichean error of two first causes which is declared to be "false and heretical." The following is the awful conclusion:—

"We declare, affirm, define and pronounce, that it is absolutely *necessary to salvation* for every human being to be subject to the Roman pontiff[4]."

It is quite impossible to plead that these declarations did not proceed *ex cathedrâ*. There is no single circumstance, required by the received theory to stamp a Papal bull with the character

---

[4] Acta Bonif. fol. 11, fa. 2. Some Gallican writers, as Bossuet, (Def. Decl. Cler. Gallic. P. i. l. iii. c. xxiv.; tom. i. p. 319. Amstel. 1745,) and Fleury, (u. s. ch. xviii.) are anxious to point out that the *words* of this declaration at the end of the Bull do not necessarily embrace both supremacies; but the question is not how little they *may* mean, but what they actually did mean in the intention of the Pope. To suppose that he did not intend them to express what it was the avowed aim of the Bull to establish is really absurd. But after all what would be gained if it could be proved that in the last clause he was thinking only of his *spiritual* supremacy? This would not nullify the declaration of his temporal supremacy in the body of the document, nor his statements to the same effect in other Bulls. Dupin (u. s. p. 492), as might be expected, is above this trifling. When Clement V. rescinded the acts of Boniface against Philip, he cautiously avoided all opposition to his *doctrine*, merely declaring with regard to this Bull, that "no prejudice was intended by it to the king and kingdom," and that they were "not more subject through it to the Church of Rome than they were before." Vigor, u. s. fol. 101. Dupin, u. s. p. 494. Modern Roman Catholics are

of infallibility, in which the documents now quoted LETTER
are defective.   The doctrine which they teach is V. SECT. I.
therefore, according to that theory, the doctrine of
the Church of Rome for ever.

II. But since the actions of men are the best in- SECT. II.
terpreters of their language, let us inquire how the
Popes have acted on the views proclaimed by
Boniface.

In the year 1080, more than two centuries
before his time, Pope Gregory VII. in full council
decreed, the second time, the deposition of Henry
IV. of Germany.   Apostrophizing the Apostles
Peter and Paul, he thus denounced the object
of his wrath:—"Trusting in the justice and
mercy of God, and of His holy mother Mary ever
virgin, and armed with your authority,—I declare
the said Henry, styled the King, together with all
his abettors, excommunicate and bound with the
bond of anathema; I take again from him, in God's
name and in yours, the government of the realms
of Germany and Italy; I deprive him of the royal
power and dignity; I forbid all Christians to obey
him as king; and I absolve all who have sworn

---

not likely to suggest that one Pope might mean to contradict the
doctrine as well as reverse the policy of another; but it may be well
to remind them that the Bull itself was renewed (without prejudice
to the declaration of Clement) by Leo X. (Bossuet, u. s. p. 320), and
that it has been inserted by later Popes in the authorized edition of
the Body of Canon Law, where it remains to this day.   See Extrav.
Commun. l. i. tit. viii. c. 1.

or shall swear allegiance to him, from the obligation of their oath . . . . So act then, I pray you, holy fathers and rulers, that all the world may know and understand that, if ye have the power of binding and loosing in heaven, ye have also that of giving and taking away, according to the merits of their holders, kingdoms, principalities, dukedoms, lordships, and all the possessions of men [5]."

Adrian IV. in the same spirit affirmed it as beyond doubt, that all islands on which Christ the Sun of righteousness had shone, belonged to the right of S. Peter and the "most holy Roman Church," and accordingly, reserving to himself an annual tribute, proceeded to confer Ireland on the king of England [6]. In 1299, Boniface VIII. in a letter to Edward I. of England, claimed the kingdom of Scotland as having belonged from ancient time and still belonging of full right to the Church of Rome. He was, however, so far more wise than Adrian, that he did not offer to set forth the original ground of its pretension [7]. In the reign of Mary, Paul IV. revived the claim to

[5] Bowden's Life of Gregory VII. b. iii. c. xvii.; from Hardouin's Concilia, tom. vi. P. i. p. 1589. The reader will observe that Gregory derives his authority not from S. Peter only, but from SS. Peter and Paul conjointly. See Note [3], p. 164.

[6] Bossuet, Defens. Decl. Cler. Gallic. P. i. l. i. § i. c. ii.; tom. i. p. 93.

[7] Fleury, l. xc. ch. ii. Rymer's Fœdera, vol. i. P. ii. p. 907. Lond. 1816.

Ireland, and affected to raise it from a lordship to the rank and style of a kingdom [8], although that had been done by an Act of Parliament some fifteen years before. The same Pope, in a dispute with the king of France, told his ambassador that "there was no man living, be he emperor or king, however great and privileged his authority, who could call himself exempt from his jurisdiction, that he had power to deprive both emperors and kings of their empires and kingdoms, without having to give account to any but God,". . . . "that if there were any privilege against his said jurisdiction, it was an abuse, bad and to be condemned, and that such must be abolished," "that it would be a great insolence and presumption and a thing but little Christian to deem otherwise," "and that there were no emperors or kings who ought not, if they were Christians, to confess that he was their master, and take and receive the law from him as disciples and inferiors [9]."

I need hardly remind you that three of our own sovereigns, John, Henry VIII. and Elizabeth, were deposed, so far as words could effect their deposition, by an exercise of the same assumed power,

[8] Minute of Privy Council, Sept. 16, 1555, published by Sir Henry Ellis in Archæologia, vol. xviii. p. 183.   Collier, P. ii. b. v. p. 380.

[9] Ribier, Lettres et Mém. d'Estat, t. ii. p. 716.   The Ambassador De Selve declined to argue the point with him for fear of the Inquisition, from which, he says, not even the character of Ambassador would have saved him.

and their subjects absolved from their allegiance. In the first-named instance the Pope, Innocent III., proceeded still further, as you will remember, and actually made a grant of the kingdom to Philip of France [1].

It should be observed however, that such acts as these have sometimes been based on a view of the supremacy, far less extravagant than that of Gregory and Boniface :——

" Bellarmine, Sylvius and others, say that the Pope has not by divine right a direct power over temporal kingdoms, but an indirect ; that is, when the spiritual power cannot be exercised freely, nor attain its end by spiritual means, then it may have recourse to temporal, according to S. Thomas (Aquinas) who teaches that princes may sometimes be deprived of their dominion, and their subjects released from their oath of fealty [2]."

III. In connexion with this subject I find you asserting that, although in " times gone by " the

---

[1] " The Pope . . . . pronounced a formal sentence that John, the king of the English, should be deposed from the throne of his kingdom, and that another who was esteemed more worthy should, through the care of the Pope, succeed. For the execution of this sentence the Lord Pope wrote to Philip, the most powerful king of the French, that he should undertake this task for the remission of all his sins, and that he and his successors should possess the kingdom of England by a perpetual right, when the king should be driven from the throne of his kingdom." Matt. Paris. Hist. Maj. ad ann. 1212; p. 232. Lond. 1640. The king, as a condition of reconciliation, gave England and Ireland to the Pope, to become a part of the " Patrimony of S. Peter," did homage for them, and agreed to pay 1000 marks yearly to the See of Rome. Rymer, vol. i. P. i. p. 112.

[2] Dens, De Eccl. N. 98, u. s., p. 164.

Popes have actually endeavoured to make good their pretensions to a temporal supremacy in this country, yet that "in *all* these cases *all* Englishmen alike have united to resist such claims and attempts." In your next communication you maintain that "until the very end of Charles II.'s reign, the (Roman) Catholics of this empire were not only liable to suffer death for their religion, but many of them actually did suffer it for no other cause [3]."

I have brought these statements together because the same answer will suffice for both. That answer, stated broadly, amounts to this:—that the sufferings to which you refer were not inflicted on the Roman Catholics for their religion, but were the punishment of their repeated treasons.

In the year 1570, Pius IV. published a bull by which he professed to take the kingdom from Elizabeth, whom all had hitherto recognised as their lawful Queen. By so doing he placed every one of her Roman Catholic subjects in the position of a traitor until he had disowned the act of his superior. The necessary effect was to divide the party into two classes; those who professed obe-

---

[3] Similarly Milner,—from whose dishonest book, the End of Controversy, too many of our Roman Catholic countrymen appear to imbibe their notions, I cannot say their knowledge, of the history and doctrines of the English Church,—asserts that they suffered "for the *mere* profession or exercise of the religion of their ancestors for almost a thousand years." Lett. xlix.; P. ii. p. 181. Lond. 1819.

dience to the bull,—the bull-papists as they were vulgarly termed,—and the loyal Roman Catholics, whose sentiments resembled those avowed by yourself. For more than half a century the country was kept in continual agitation by the treasonable practices of the "bull-papists," incited and abetted in every possible way by the emissaries of the Pope and of the King of Spain. During this period, great sufferings, we all know and acknowledge, were inflicted on Roman Catholics;—but why?—not as their descendants are too ready to assert, merely on account of their religion, but because many of them were actual traitors, and their conduct brought suspicion on many more. The death by which they suffered is of itself a sufficient proof of this. We know that by the laws of England in that age heretics were condemned to the flames; but although several persons actually underwent this penalty for their religious opinions during the reigns of Edward, Elizabeth and James, we do not find a single Roman Catholic among them. Those who suffered, suffered by the axe or halter, the common death of traitors[4]. Nor can it be denied that

---

[4] The number of Roman Catholics who suffered under the penal laws during the reign of Elizabeth is loosely stated by Milner (u. s.) to be "above two hundred." In the same page he asserts that "the persecution of her reign was far more grievous than that of her sister Mary." Yet those hangings, allowing them to be "above two hundred," were spread over a period of *thirty-three* years, while

every attempt was made to distinguish between those who acknowledged *only* the spiritual, and those who asserted the temporal supremacy of the Pope also. If the innocent sometimes suffered with the guilty, as very probably they did, it proceeded from error, and not from the intention of the ruler. As I have given elsewhere a detailed proof of these points[5], too long to be inserted here, I shall content myself at present with stating the result of my inquiries in the words of two Roman Catholic priests, who have studied the whole question with a degree of impartiality very much to their credit.

Mary crowded the accumulated horrors of nearly three hundred burnings, confessedly for religion only, into a space of less than four years. It must be remembered also that in addition to those who suffered by fire, and for heresy only, there were many disloyal and seditious favourers of the Reformation who perished on the scaffold. It is in *their* punishment, to speak generally, that we find the true parallel to the sufferings of the Roman Catholics under Elizabeth and James. Their number cannot now be ascertained, owing to the contradictory, or imperfect, accounts that have come down to us (compare, for example, Noailles, Ambass. en Angl. vol. iii. p. 124, with Speed, b. ix. p. 1116, Lond. 1632); but there is no reason to think that executions for treason were less numerous in the reign of Mary, in proportion to its duration, than in the two succeeding.

[5] Letters to a Seceder, Appendix G, p. 252. Some writers are fond of dwelling on the provocations given by a few fanatics to Mary, before the persecution became bloody : they vanish into nothing (as may be seen from the collection referred to) beside the insults, threats, and dangers to which her sister was subject from Roman Catholics throughout her reign.

My first quotation, which is from the learned Joseph Berington, refers to the reign of Elizabeth :—

"This then I infer, (and I have ample ground for the inference,) that as none of the old clergy suffered, and none of the new who roundly renounced the assumed prerogative of papal despotism, it was not for any tenet of the Catholic faith that they were exposed to persecution[6]."

To this I will merely add the title of a cotemporary pamphlet published by "sundry secular priests," only two years before the Queen's death, viz. *Important considerations which ought to move all true and sound Catholics, who are not wholly Jesuited, to acknowledge, without all equivocations, ambiguities, or shiftings, that the proceedings of her Highness's reign have been both mild and merciful[7].* The Jesuits, it will be remembered, were the chief advocates of the Pope's temporal claims, and therefore the chief instigators to rebellion.

Dr. Charles O'Conor will answer for the continuance of this policy through the succeeding reign :—

"Of all the transactions of the 17th century, that

[6] Mem. of Panzani, Introd. p. 34.
[7] Published in 1601. The most convenient reprint is that of Mr. Mendham ; London, 1831.

which, next to the Irish massacre, most injured our
ancestors and led to overwhelm their posterity by the
penal code, was the rejection of the Irish remonstrance
and King James' test of allegiance, in compliance with
the injunctions of Rome .... King James' invincible
defence of the oath of allegiance was now overwhelmed
by a *religious cry.* The works of the Jesuits Bellarmine
and Suarez against it were extolled as masterpieces of
Catholicity, and the deposing doctrines were rammed
down the throats of the English Catholics *without the
least modification,* during a period of 183 years .... Let
us be instructed by history. There is yet extant a petition to Pope Paul V., signed by eleven Priests, who
were under sentence of death in Newgate, for refusing
James' oath in 1612. Two of their companions had
already suffered death for this offence. They died in resistance to legitimate authority, and by the instigation of
a foreign power. In their petition they entreat of his
Holiness, *by all that is sacred,* to attend to their horrible
situation, and they beg of him to point out to them *clearly*
in what that oath for which they were condemned to
die, is repugnant to Catholic faith; but yet, influenced
by the courtly maxims, they declare their belief in his
unlimited power, and they conclude with a solemn protest
of blind submission to all his decrees .... Religion indig-
nantly wraps herself up in her shroud of deepest mourning
before the idol of Ecclesiastical domination, when she
observes the Roman court sacrificing to its insatiable
ambition the lives of so many heroes, who were worthy
of a better fate! perverting sacraments, which were instituted for the sanctification of souls, into engines of
worldly passions, and rendering them subservient to the

R

policy of those passions, and panders to their intrigues !
. . . . If it should be alleged that the Pope pitied . those
men who died for his worldly maxims of aggrandizement;
that he was not cruel by nature but only by policy, and
that he would have saved them if he could by money,
or at any expense short of the sacrifice of pompous pride
and uncontrollable dominion, my answer is that this
aggravates his guilt.   The horrors which hypocritical
pride and ambition create must be laid at the doors of
those hypocrites who disguise their passions with the
mask of sanctity, whilst in reality they persecute religion
and oppress truth [8]."

Let me just illustrate this extract by a brief
reference to one other group of victims to the
temporal ambition of the papacy during the same
period.   In Mr. Tierney's edition of the Church
History of Dodd are the recorded answers of
twenty-one Roman Catholics, imprisoned on suspicion of treason during the years 1614-15, to the
following question :—

" Whether, before it be defined by a general council,
a man may hold it lawful to depose or kill the king [9] ?"

[8] Letters of Columbanus, No. vi. § vi., pp. 108—119.   Ed. 1813.
"Sir John Throckmorton (a Roman Catholic) says that if in 1778 the
Catholics had had the weakness to recur to Rome, they would not
have been permitted to abjure the deposing power.   Second Letter,
Lond. 1791, p. 71; and again, App. p. 75."   Ibid. p. 110.   Yet as
much as a hundred and fifty years before, in the reign of Charles I., the
Doctors of the Sorbonne, being consulted on the lawfulness of taking
the oath proposed by James, declared under their hand and seal that
it might be done without any difficulty.   Dupin, Dissert. vii. de
Antiq. Disc. c. iii., p. 570.   [9] Vol. iv. App. No. xxxvii.

Out of the whole number, only one was found to declare that the *deposition,* only six that the *killing,* was unlawful before a council had determined the question.   One frankly declared it to be a "received opinion in the Catholic Church," and a second, "the common and approved opinion," that in some cases, *propter bonum spirituale,* it is lawful for the Pope to depose a king.   Such then was the treasonable principle—a principle on which many had already shown their readiness to act— for which those unhappy men suffered.   So little were "all Englishmen alike," prepared "to resist the claims and attempts of the Pope to exert a temporal power over England."

IV. My sole object in these remarks is to protest against a falsification of history,—not to defend any person or party from the charge of persecution.

The truth is, that, at the time of which we are speaking, no one had arrived at a just view of the duty of Toleration.   It is open to us, therefore, to compare the tendency of the doctrines held by our respective Churches to accelerate or retard its general reception ; or to point out that, while the adherents of Rome treated the Reformers in England with the utmost cruelty and violence *avowedly* on account of their *religion,* the latter, in their day of power, exhibited towards their opponents a moderation of which they were the first in that age to furnish an example, and reserved their severity for a third party, whose opinions, in many instances as hostile to social order as to revealed truth, were regarded by both with equal horror: we are also at liberty to inquire, if it be necessary, concerning any individual persecutor whether he acted in the spirit and from the motives of Galerius, or of Saul; but beyond this we are not justified in going. The truth does not permit us to assume or to say of any one, that he believed it sinful to visit misbelief with temporal pains.

But there are those among you who will demur to one part of this representation. It has been asserted that, although in fact the Reformers did not burn the favourers of Rome, it was simply from the want of power and opportunity; and that they were actually preparing to do so, when the early death of Edward reversed the position of the contending parties. Thus Dr. Lingard, with that charity which hopeth nothing, has allowed himself to say:—

" Fortunately for the professors of the ancient faith, Edward died before this code (i. e. the reformed code of ecclesiastical laws) had obtained the sanction of the legislature. By the accession of Mary the power of the sword passed from the hands of one religious party to those of the other, and within a short time Cranmer and his associates perished in the flames which they had prepared to kindle for the destruction of their opponents [1]."

[1] Vol. vii. ch. iii. p. 188. 4th ed. The Brothers of St. Vincent go a step further and assert that the sanction of the legislature had

I am willing to think that Dr. Lingard was so completely under the influence of party spirit as to believe what he has here stated. Otherwise, in a man of his research (which was considerable though it has been much overrated), the compo-

been obtained:—" Cranmer, and the rest who suffered for heresy in Mary's reign (infants and all?), had sent Anabaptists to the stake in that of Edward, and they had passed a law by which Catholics would have been condemned to the flames unless they consented to deny their faith." Clifton Tracts, No. 7, p. 13. And even this does not satisfy Dr. Newman. According to him the *burnings* actually took place. The following account of the Reformation from his pen will give many almost as much pain to read as if it were true: —" At length a change came over the land. A thousand years had well-nigh rolled (since the conversion of England), and this great people grew tired of the heavenly stranger who sojourned among them. They had had enough of blessings and absolutions—enough of the intercession of saints—enough of the grace of the sacraments —enough of the prospects of the next life. They thought it best to secure this life in the first place, because they were sure of it, and then to go on to the next, if time and means allowed. And they saw that to labour for the next world was possibly to lose this; whereas, to labour for this world, might be the way to labour for the next also. Any how, they would pursue temporal ends, and they would account any one their enemy who stood in the way of their pursuing them. It was a madness; but madmen are strong, and madmen are clever; so with the sword and the halter, and by mutilation, and *fire*, and imprisonment, they cut off, or frightened away from the land, as Israel did in the time of old, the ministers of the Most High and their ministrations: and ' altogether broke the yoke, and burst the bonds.' ' They beat one, and killed another, and another they stoned,' and at length they altogether cast out the Heir from His vineyard, and killed Him, ' that the inheritance might be theirs.' And as for the remnant of His servants whom they left, they drove them into corners and holes of the earth, and they bade them die out there; and then they rejoiced and sent gifts either to other, and made merry, because they had rid themselves of those ' who had tormented them that dwelt upon the earth.' And so they turned to enjoy this world, and to gain for themselves a name among

sition of that brief paragraph would be a crime against truth and charity too flagrant to be characterized by my pen. The sole ground of his assertion is an untenable inference from the inexact language of the draft of ecclesiastical laws prepared by Cranmer, Cox and others, understood in a manner opposed to the whole current of history, and to legislative documents of actual authority. It appears that in one part of the projected code in question the doctrines of Transubstantiation, Purgatory [2], &c. are classed with the opinions of various modern sectaries under the general name of *heresies*, while another part provides that " when all other remedies have been tried in vain," the confirmed *heretic* shall be " delivered to the civil magistrate to be punished [3]." It is assumed that, because Transubstantiation is termed a heresy, its obstinate maintainer must be a heretic in the sense of the clause just quoted, and therefore liable to capital punishment. The context, however, shows that the conclusion is not just. In the language of the re-

men, and it was given unto them according to their wish. They preferred the heathen virtues of their original nature, to the robe of grace which God had given; they fell back, with closed affections and haughty reserve, and dreariness within, upon their worldly integrity, honour, energy, prudence, and perseverance; they made the most of the natural man, and they 'received their reward.' "—*Christ on the Waters*, p. 11.

[2] Reform. Leg. Eccles. De Hær. cc. 10, 19, 21.   Comp. Epilogus, p. 22.   Oxf. 1850.

[3] Ibid. De Judic. c. 4, p. 25.

formed code, the doctrine of Impanation, a theory closely allied to the Lutheran view of the Real Presence, and the opinion that the "Sacraments are bare signs and outward tokens," and "badges of profession," are both heresies equally with the older error of Transubstantiation. The denial of original sin, the notions, that in Baptism the Holy Ghost is conveyed in and by the water, and that God will, under no circumstances, show mercy to the unbaptized [4],"—these and several other errors, of greater or less gravity, are all branded with the same common name of heresy. But if it is impossible to maintain that our Reformers were prepared to burn men for holding any one of these mistaken opinions, their language in the *Reformatio Legum* cannot be quoted as a proof that they designed that fate for the believer in Transubstantiation, or in the value of private masses. Nor is it so difficult to determine what their real sentiments upon this subject were. The sword was in their hand, as Dr. Lingard has expressed it, during the reign of Edward. Why then did they not use it as he affirms that they intended? The old ecclesiastical laws of England were not suspended, nor was the ancient provision for delivering a contumacious heretic over to the civil power either in abeyance or disuse [5]. Heretics, on the contrary, were

---

[4] See De Hær. cc. 7, 10, 17, 19.

[5] Thus Dr. Lingard:—"Though the statutes against heresy had

actually burnt. Why then did "Cranmer and his associates" not avail themselves of a power which they undoubtedly possessed, at once to avenge the cause of religion and to deliver themselves from dangerous foes? There is but one answer to the question. They did not hold that the errors in which they had themselves been reared, however grievous, were of a kind to be thus treated. If there is any evidence to the contrary, let it be brought forward. I know of none. But our proof of this assertion is not merely negative. The truth is, that even in this matter our Reformers, notwithstanding their acknowledged error, were in a degree guided by the principle which they uniformly professed of deference to holy Scripture and to the early Church. The only misbelievers delivered to the secular arm for death during the reign of Edward were Joan Bocher and Van Paris, of whom the one maintained a heresy expressly condemned by an Evangelist [6], the other was an Arian [7], and as such proscribed by the great Council of Nicæa.

---

been repealed in the first year of the King's reign, still the profession of erroneous doctrine was held to be an offence punishable by the *common law* of the land." Vol. vii. ch. i. p. 71.

[6] "She would say that our Saviour was not very man, nor had received flesh of His mother Mary, . . . and that He had a fantastical body." Latimer in Strype's Cranmer, b. ii. c. viii., p. 181. Lond. 1694. Comp. 1 Joh. iv. 3 :—"Every spirit that confesseth not that Jesus Christ is come in the flesh, is not of God; and this is that *spirit* of Antichrist."—See Burton's Bampton Lectures, L. vi. p. 168, &c.

[7] Strype, u. s.

Upon the death of Mary, though a desire to retaliate might have been expected in ordinary men to mingle with their concern for truth, the same principle prevailed, and was embodied in an Act of Parliament; so that from the first year of Elizabeth Roman Catholic error was actually excluded by implication from the category of *punishable* heresy. The Act provided that the members of the Commission Court were—

" Not in anywise to have authority and power to order, determine, or to judge any matter or cause to be heresy, but only such as have heretofore been determined, ordered, or adjudged to be heresy, by the authority of the Canonical Scriptures, or by the first four General Councils, or any of them, or by any other General Council, wherein the same was declared heresy by the express words of the said Canonical Scriptures, or such as shall hereafter be ordered, judged, and determined to be heresy by the high court of Parliament of this realm with the assent of the clergy in their Convocation [8]."

The novelty of the Roman peculiarities, if nothing else, has at least secured them from the express censure of holy Scripture, and the ban of the first four General Councils. Are you able to direct me to any subsequent Act of Parliament, or decree of Convocation, which, whether from political motives, or on mistaken religious grounds, sought to involve the Roman Catholic in the same penalties as the Arian? If not, acknowledge honestly

[8] 1 Eliz. c. i. § 36.

that whatever they may have suffered, the Reformers of the Church of England were at least guiltless of their blood.

Let me repeat that I do not deny that men were persecuted for their religious errors during the reign of Elizabeth. I merely call your attention to the fact, that her Roman Catholic subjects were not put to death for their religion but for treason. You have been trained to believe that the Reformers sanctioned a wholesale system of persecution against the first seceders to Rome, and to regard the supposed fact as a foul note against the Church. I have simply shown you that this opinion is not borne out by history. At the same time, when we consider the temper of the age, and the natural tendency of an extensive system of espionage, however necessary, we shall, I think, be justified in believing that the penal laws, though designed to guard against treason, were, from the first, often put in action by inferior agents from motives which the legislature disavowed. I am afraid too that before long, owing principally to the increased influence of the Puritans, especially in the House of Commons, and the exasperations of mutual injury, the statutes enacted in self-defence were occasionally employed by some in higher quarters as a direct engine of religious persecution [9].

[9] Our imagination and feelings are naturally much impressed by the unnecessary and shocking cruelties to which some of the sufferers were subjected in the name of justice; and many writers have en-

Before I conclude let me express a hope, that if you are not yet convinced of the unfounded nature of the charge brought against " Cranmer and his associates," you will re-examine the whole question, as it deserves, by light of *genuine* history. It may bring pain to find that we have been deceived; but the pain is for a season, and to be borne ; while the results of conscientious investigation,—a knowledge of the truth, and that habit of upright judgement which is acquired in the pursuit of it,—are at once above price, and without end.

I am, &c.

deavoured to take advantage of the indignation and horror which such tales inspire, to turn them to the prejudice of the English Reformation. Such arguments are most unjust. Those practices were not invented by the advisers of Elizabeth or James, but were bequeathed to them from an age in which the influence of Rome had been paramount. The accused were only treated like other political prisoners : a disloyal or suspected member of the Church was thrust into a dungeon as loathsome, and endured tortures as painful, as the purveyor of treason from Rome or Douay. Nor would they have received more gentle usage had they been prisoners, charged with crime against the state, in France or Spain. Rather must it be considered a note in favour of our Reformation, that ever since that period we have been advancing with far more rapidity than any country in communion with Rome, towards a truly just and merciful execution of the laws necessary for our protection, whether as individuals or as a nation.

LETTER VI.

MY DEAR SIR,

I. IN pursuing your charge of persecution against both Church and State, you are not content with enlarging on the supposed enormities of Elizabeth and James, but wish to make us responsible for the actions of Henry, a prince whose life was for many years the great, and perhaps the only, obstacle to that self-reformation of the Church of England which you so much deplore. Whatever this king may have been, he certainly was not what you call him,—a "*Protestant* persecutor." It is true that he had quarrelled with the Pope, as Louis of Bavaria, Philip the Fair of France, and many other princes had done before him, and had prohibited his subjects from all communication with the enemy of his crown and realm. It is also true that he had resumed or appropriated certain powers and pre- rogatives which various Popes had extorted from his ancestors, or from the Church, in times of weakness or of ignorance. But it is equally true that, with all his eagerness to humble the Pope, he held every Roman doctrine but that of the supremacy to the last day of his life [1]. Dr. Lingard will inform you that during his last sickness " he was constantly attended by his confessor, heard mass daily in his chamber, and received the communion under one kind [2]." In his will, he directed masses to be said for the repose of his soul. Nay, if Sanders the Jesuit is worthy of credit, he showed anxiety to be at peace with Rome before his death, and even took some steps towards a reconciliation [3].

Again, during the *last* seven years of this reign, the infamous Act of the Six Articles was in force. As this was debated and passed in Convocation as well as Parliament, the responsibility must certainly be divided between the Church and the king; but that any guilt attaches to the *reformed* Church of England on this account, Falsehood itself will hardly venture to assert. The character and objects of the Act may be inferred from the following

---

[1] " Henry had cut off the English Church from the See of Rome; but wished to retain Catholic doctrine." The Clifton Tracts, No. 40, p. 12. Sim. No. 3, p. 4.

[2] Vol. vi. ch. v. p. 363.

[3] De Schism. Angl. l. i. p. 164. Colon. 1628.

abstract of the doctrines which it sought to enforce :—

1. That in the sacrament of the altar, after the consecration, there remaineth no substance of bread and
wine, but under these forms the natural Body and Blood
of Christ are present.

2. That the communion in both kinds is not necessary
to salvation to all persons by the law of God, but that
both the flesh and blood of Christ are together in each of
the kinds.

3. That priests, after the order of priesthood, may not
marry by the law of God.

4. That vows of chastity ought to be observed by the
law of God.

5. That the use of private masses ought to be continued,
which, as it is agreeable to God's law, so men receive great
benefit thereby.

6. That auricular confession (i.e. compulsory) is expedient and necessary, and ought to be retained in the
Church [4].

The penalty for writing, preaching, or disputing
against the first of these Articles was death at the
stake;—no remission or alleviation of punishment
being permitted even on recantation. For similar
offences against the other five, the punishment on a
first conviction was imprisonment during pleasure,
with forfeiture of goods and chattels and life-interest
in all real property; on a second, death and entire

[4] 31 Hen. VIII. c. 14.   See Burnet, b. iii., p. 259.   Collier, P. ii.
b. iii., p. 168.

confiscation of all property. The year after the law was passed, its severity was slightly mitigated by the remission of the penalty of death for the second offence against the third and fourth Articles [5]; and three years afterwards its execution was rendered less easy (through the courageous exertions of Cranmer), by some regulations with regard to presentments, and a limitation of the time allowed between the commission of the offence and prosecution [6].

[5] 32 Hen. VIII. c. 25.   Collier, u. s. p. 178.

[6] 35 Hen. VIII. c. 5.   Collier, u. s. p. 201.   When this Act was first passed, " Cranmer had argued boldly in the House against it three days together," and voted against it, though desired by the king to leave the House, replying to his command, that "he thought himself bound in conscience to stay there and show his dissent." Ibid. p. 168.   No subscription to these Articles was required; in fact, they were only the definitions of offences created by an Act of Parliament; yet we find Butler, in his "Book of the Roman Catholic Church" (p. 216), asking :—" Although *Cranmer subscribed and caused his clergy to subscribe* the Six Articles, ... did he not continue to cohabit with his wife?" (A second mistake, for he sent her to Germany. Lord Herbert, Hist. p. 448.) Similarly Phillips, the biographer of Pole :—" There was no abject compliance to which he did not let himself down, to flatter the passions of Henry VIII. and to secure his own credit, &c. In consequence of this abandoned turn of mind, he subscribed to the Six famous Articles." Life of Pole, vol. ii. p. 211.   Dr. Lingard, too, calls Cranmer a "convert to the cause," on the authority of a gossiping letter of the day, the writer of which is unknown, but in opposition to the historians, and to the tenor of his subsequent actions. Vol. vi. ch. iv. p. 292.   These writers are quoted by Archdeacon Todd, in his Vindication of Cranmer, § 7, p. 85.   2nd ed. 1826.   Cranmer had serious faults and was guilty of great errors, which it is only right that an historian should state ; but he has also been most shamefully maligned, or rather let us say that few men have been more largely

II. Before we quit the reign of Henry, I wish to say a few words upon one act of cruelty and injustice, as great perhaps as any of which he was confessedly guilty. You do not mention the death of Bishop Fisher; but I cannot omit to notice it; because I believe that the Reformation in England is popularly considered among the ill-informed members of your communion to be deeply implicated in that disgraceful event. As he died ten years before the accession of Edward, this opinion is necessarily without foundation; but it is satisfactory, nevertheless, to read the following honest avowal of the truth from the pen of a zealous Roman Catholic:—

"It is a fearful and terrible example of a Catholic nation betrayed by a corrupted Catholic hierarchy. . . . .

blessed through the involuntary kindness of those who "say all manner of evil against the disciple of Christ for His sake." Sometimes the partiality of a writer displays itself in selecting him alone for blame, though Gardiner, Bonner, and others of the opposite side, were equally responsible for the course of action reprobated. E. g. Lingard charges him with hypocrisy, &c., for his part in the divorce of Katherine; but fails to point out that "though he pronounced the sentence, he was but the mouth of the rest, and that they were all in as deep as he." Strype's Life of Cranmer, b. i. ch. iv. p. 21. Burnet, b. ii. vol. i. p. 181. (In fact, he spoke for the whole Church of England, as Convocation and both the Universities had declared the first marriage unlawful.) Nor does he notice Gardiner's deliberate defence of the divorce in the tract De Verâ Obedientiâ, or the favourable mention of it in the preface to certain editions of that book, which was universally ascribed to Bonner until Dr. Maitland threw some doubt on the authorship in his Essays on the Reformation. See Nos. xvii. and xviii. Lond. 1849.

It was in a solemn convocation when England's Church-men were assembled, a reverend array of bishops, abbots, and dignitaries. . . . . Yet the fear of the tyrant, and the dread of losing a few remaining years of wealth and dignity so far prevailed, that they sacrificed the liberty of the English Church at one blow. . . . . One venerable prelate, aged in years and worn with fasting and discipline, alone protests against this sinful surrender; his remonstrance is unsupported by his colleagues, and he is speedily brought to trial and execution. His accusers are Catholics, his judges are Catholics, his jury are Catholics, his executioner is a Catholic, and the bells are ringing for High Mass in the steeples of St. Paul's, as the aged Bishop ascends the scaffold, and receives the martyr's crown. And yet how do modern Catholics ignorantly charge the death of this great and good man on the Protestant system, which was not even broached at the time. All the terrible executions of this dreadful reign were perpetrated before even the externals of the old religion were altered or its essential doctrines denied[7]."

III. Proceeding with the revision of your country's annals, you describe the son of Henry a well-disposed if not in all respects a well-instructed youth, who did not survive his sixteenth year, as a " wholesale persecutor;"—certainly a very singular emendation of the received text of history. Your great authority, a writer who is not wont to spare the favourers of the Reformation, was of a different opinion. He tells us with far more truth that,

[7] Earnest Address on the Establishment of the Hierarchy, by the late Mr. Pugin; p. 2. Dolman, 1851.

though Edward "appeared wholly taken up with that project, he seemed not inclined to shed blood on that account, and therefore no sanguinary but only penal laws were executed upon such as stood off[8]." Even to modern eyes, the Roman party suffered in this reign very little that is to be called persecution; and for that little we cannot regard the king, considering his age and circumstances, as personally responsible. In fact, the Princess Mary seems to have been the only person of importance who opposed the changes which now took place with any show of earnestness ; so that it would have been no easy matter, even for a reckless and hardened tyrant, to have found many victims for the scaffold or the stake among the supporters of the Pope or the Six Articles. As it is, but one instance of capital punishment has occurred to me after considerable research. It is recorded by Stow that two priests were " *condemned* " under Edward, (I presume to death,) "for the keeping of certain relics ;" but their offence was one which in those days would be accounted treason; for he states that among their relics was an arm with an inscription on it setting forth that it was the arm of one who had "suffered martyrdom under K. Henry VIII.[9]" Nor were the minor penalties in the

---

[8] Dodd's Church History, by Tierney ; vol. ii. p. 49.

[9] Annals, p. 594, col. 2. Lond. 1631. There was a similar case on the other side in Mary's reign. An order of Privy Council, dated May 3, 1555, directs " George Colt and Thomas Danyell, to make

hands of power inflicted on many for their fidelity to Rome or Romish doctrine. Three Bishops, Gardiner, Heath, and Day, were imprisoned for various acts of recusancy[1]. The head chaplain and three other domestics of Mary suffered a similar punishment for celebrating and hearing mass contrary to an order of the council[2]. In the king's journal, again, we find mention of one person imprisoned, and two "chidden," for the last-named offence[3]. All this was, beyond a question, religious persecution; but we must not so readily allow the same of certain other acts of this reign.

search for John Barnard and John Walshe who have used to repair to Sudbury and carrying the bones of one Pigott that was burned about them to show them to the people as relics, and persuade them to stand in their error, and upon their apprehension, &c. . . . to order them according to the laws." Archæologia, vol. xviii. p. 181. As Pigott had been put to death for religion, and there was no direct aspersion on the Sovereign in what they did, I presume that theirs was a case of pure heresy.

[1] Collier, P. ii. b. iv., pp. 230, 305, 306, 312. Archæologia, vol. xviii. pp. 135, 152; 166; 149, 150. Gardiner was treated with great mildness at first, but after a time he was "removed to a meaner lodging," not allowed to have " pen, ink, and paper to write his determinable purposes," or to " send out to any man, or to hear from any man," and "sequestered from all conference and from all means that might serve him to practise any way." This increase of rigour, however, was not owing to his adherence to any opinion concerning religion, but because " he had at all times before the judges of his cause used himself unreverently to the King's Majesty, and very slanderfully towards his Council, and specially on the day of his judgement given against him he called his judges heretics and sacramentaries." Ibid. p. 152.

[2] Dodd, vol. ii. App. xxx. pp. ccvi. ccxxii., from documents in Fox. Archæol. u. s. p. 166.

[3] March 24, 1550. In Burnet's Collection, P. ii. b. ii., p. 24.

which writers of your communion are fond of
placing in the same category.   It may with great
reason be doubted whether religious bigotry had
much share in the unjust treatment of Bonner,
whose insolent temper appears to have provoked
the enmity from which he suffered [4].   It certainly
did not suggest the deprivation of Bishop Tonstall.
He had given encouragement to the project of an
insurrection, and the opportunity was eagerly
caught at by the unprincipled Northumberland,
a secret enemy of the Reformation, to secularise
for his own benefit the lands and honours of
his see [5].   And let me remind you that the greater

[4] Collier, u. s. p. 280.

[5] Ibid. p. 324.   Northumberland's speech on the scaffold, in which
he avowed his dislike to the Reformation, is given in the Appendix
to Strype's Cranmer, No. lxxiii. from the Cotton MSS.   Church spo-
liation, not persecution, was the crying sin of Edward's reign; but it
will be news to most readers that Cranmer was a leader in that
crime.   Yet so ' say the author of the Controversial Catechism
(see p. 215 of this volume) and the Brothers of S. Vincent de
Paul:—"If it had not been for Cranmer, the Protector Somerset,
and a few other persons, who upheld the king's supremacy *in
order to gain the spoils of the abbeys, monasteries, and churches*, the
Catholics in his reign might have been spared much persecution."
Clifton Tracts, No. 40, p. 10.   There is a species of satisfaction in
seeing a bad cause supported by such means.   Its fall will be
the more sure and rapid.   *History* tells us that the desire of
Cranmer's heart was to see the Church property which Henry had
seized employed in the foundation of new bishoprics, schools of the
clergy, &c., i.e. in carrying out on a larger scale a plan which had
received the sanction of the Pope before the breach with Rome.
Burnet, P. i. b. iii.; vol. i. pp. 189, 190, 300, 301.   So in Edward's
reign, the grant of chantry lands to the king was "much opposed"
by him.   He "opposed it long," wishing to save these endowments

sufferers, and the more numerous, were among those who did not advocate either the doctrines or the pretensions of Rome. A few small congregations of Anabaptists and others were dispersed and put down by the Church Courts and a Royal Commission[6], in which you will be surprised to hear that some who favoured the cause of the Pope (such was their easy position at that period) were associated with Archbishop Cranmer[7]. Hooper was imprisoned a short time for his intemperate opposition to the use of ecclesiastical vestments[8]; one who had denied the Divinity of Christ, but recanted, was condemned to carry a faggot in public[9]; while Joan Bocher and Van Paris were

until the king were of age, being confident he was so piously disposed, that they should easily persuade him to convert them all to the bettering of the condition of the poor clergy that were now brought into extreme misery." Id. P. ii. b. i.; vol. ii. p. 47. He suffered from the spoiler himself, like every other Bishop. See stat. 37 Hen. VIII. c. 16. Strype's Cranmer, b. ii. ch. xxix., p. 281. In the latter part of Edward's reign he and Ridley "fell under great displeasure" with those who then "governed all, for opposing, as much as they could, though to no effect, the spoil of the Church goods." Ibid. b. iii. ch. xxxvi., p. 455, where the author refers to Ridley's Lamentation. It was reserved for Cobbett and his Anglo-Roman followers to discover that the Archbishop had an interest in the plunder.

[6] Strype, Mem. Eccles. Edw. VI. b. i. ch. ix., p. 68. Ed. 1721. Burnet, P. ii. b. i., p. 110.

[7] Strype, u. s. b. ii. ch. xv., p. 365. This writer says that they were "the *chief* promoters of this commission."

[8] Collier, u. s. p. 295. Archæol. u. s. p. 152.

[9] Ibid. p. 266, &c. Strype, u. s. ch. xxvi., p. 216. Life of Cranmer, b. ii. ch. viii., p. 179. Two others performed penance for similar heresies, but what penance we are not told. Ibid.

actually burned for the obstinate maintenance of undoubted heresies[1]. When you applied that phrase of sweeping condemnation to this boy king,

[1] Collier, p. 291; Strype, u. s.; Burnet, u. s. p. 112. Time has at length cleared the memory of Cranmer from the imputation under which he has long lain of having extorted from the reluctant king the warrant for the execution of Joan Bocher. The story had been suspected before, owing to the ascertained absence of Cranmer from the council which directed the issue of the writ, the silence of cotemporary writers hostile to him, and the language of the king when he refers to the subject in his private journal (May 2, 1550. Burnet, P. ii. b. ii. Records, p. 12):—"Joan Bocher, otherwise called Joan of Kent, was burnt for holding that Christ was not incarnate of the Virgin Mary;—being condemned the year before, but kept in hope of conversion;—and the 30th of April, the Bishop of London and the Bishop of Ely were to persuade her, but she withstood them, and reviled the preacher that preached at her death." It is hardly credible that this could have been written by a person who viewed the event with such horror as was asserted, and had been pained by repeated interviews with persons importuning him for an express sanction to it. But further evidence and entirely decisive has been lately produced. "It would have been contrary to constitutional custom for the king to have signed any such document." By the will of Henry, the council appointed in it were the actual governors of the kingdom during the minority of Edward. "It was not customary for him to attend the meeting of the council." When they desired that he should be consulted, "an entry was made in the council book." Such an entry actually occurs on the day on which the warrant passed, but it is in reference to another matter. The minute respecting the execution, dated April 27, 1550, runs thus:—"A warrant to the Lord Chancellor to make out a writ to the sheriff of London for the execution of Joan of Kent, condemned to be burnt for certain detestable opinions of heresy." Works of Roger Hutchinson, ed. Parker Society; Biogr. Notice by Mr. Bruce, p. v. As a further proof that Edward had no strong feeling against the punishment of death in a case of heresy, we may refer to the notice in his journal of the death of Van Paris, about a year later, April 7, 1551:—"A certain Arian of the strangers, a Dutchman, being excommunicated by the congregation of his countrymen, was, after long disputation, condemned to the fire." In Burnet, u. s. p. 24.

you referred to the sufferings of your own party only; but I am willing that you should include in the indictment every act of persecution which I have named, and any besides that may have escaped me. When all are told, how will they justify your words? Considered in themselves, those actions deserve our strongest reprobation. I avow it without reluctance; for I can do so without inconsistency, though you cannot. But surely nothing but a deep and blinding prejudice could have led you to describe them as a *wholesale* persecution, and so an argument against the English Reformation, when the same blood-stained page of history presents to you the names of Charles V., of Mary Tudor and her husband, of Catherine de Medici and her sons. If Edward shed blood in drops, they poured it forth in torrents. One Roman Catholic historian tells us that in the Netherlands alone, owing to an edict of Charles, nearly 50,000 persons were hung, beheaded, buried or burnt alive [2]! From another, we learn that according to the

---

[2] Sarpi, Hist. Conc. Trid. l. v., p. 335. According to Grotius, a very trustworthy author, more than twice this number perished :—
" After the execution of not less than a hundred thousand, from the time when they began to try whether the fire could be quenched by that blood, so great a multitude had risen up through the Low Countries, that sometimes the public executions were hindered by a sedition, whensoever the condemned person was of unusual distinction, or the tortures uncommonly dreadful." Annal. de Reb. Belg. l. i., p. 17. Amst. 1658. This proves at least that Sarpi's statement is no exaggeration.

current statement of the time, "there were slain," in the French massacre, "above forty thousand Huguenots in a few days[3]." Compare Edward then, if you would do him justice, with those Roman Catholic princes of his age, whose kingdoms were disturbed by the religious movement of the day, and you will blush to have said a single word in his dispraise. What he might have become, had he survived to encounter the opposition of a sincere and powerful Roman party it is unnecessary to conjecture. Although the tendency of the English

[3] D'Avila, Civil Wars of France, b. v. ann. 1572; p. 184. Engl. Tr. Lond. 1678. This author, who had been page to Catherine or her son, and whose family were under great obligations to the former, states that the number killed in Paris alone in two days was "above 10,000, whereof above 500 were barons, knights, and gentlemen." De Thou, whose father was implicated in the proceedings of Charles, gives a less number of the slain :—" It has been reported by many, that more than 30,000 persons were destroyed in these tumults by various kinds of death throughout the kingdom; though I believe the number was somewhat less." Hist. l. lii. c. xii. Opp. tom. iii. p. 145. Lond. 1733. D'Avila attributes to Henry II. a scheme of persecution as extensive as that of Charles, though less barbarous :—" Henry II., a religious observer of the Catholic faith, . . . with inexorable severity resolved that all who were found convict of this imputation (of heresy) should suffer death without mercy. . . . His vigilance and constancy were such, that he had reduced things to such a point as would in the end, though with much effusion of blood, have expelled all the peccant humours out of the bowels of the kingdom, if the accident (viz. of his death) which followed had not interrupted the course of his resolution." B. i.; p. 20. As it was, "those destroyed on account of their religion by sword or fire made up a notable number." Sarpi, u. s. This persecution is made the more detestable by the fact that the king bestowed the confiscated property of the convicted heretics on an infamous woman, with whom this "religious observer of the Catholic faith" lived in adultery. Sarpi, u. s. p. 314.

Reformation from the first was towards toleration, the principle has only gained upon us slowly, and by an almost imperceptible advance. Edward was probably but little, if at all, before his age in this respect; but it is important that an exaggeration of his comparative guilt, calculated to mislead, and to inflame the passions of our Roman Catholic countrymen, should not be allowed to pass without contradiction or exposure.

IV. It is not surprising that after magnifying the sufferings of your party in the reign of Edward, you should proceed to palliate the monstrous cruelties of which it was guilty during that of his successor. You confess—though somewhat faintly—that the attempt to force the faith of the nation was both "foolish and wicked;" but with the confession you mingle statements of a very different character. Thus you describe those who were "sent to the stake" as "unlearned fanatics," in imitation, I presume, of Dodd, who calls them coarsely, as better became him, "a number of illiterate wretches," and asserts that "they threw away their lives more like enthusiasts than upon any rational conviction [4]." Unlearned men and women (and children too) there were undoubtedly among them, and as might be expected some were actuated more or less by a spirit of fanaticism;

[4] Church History, P. iii. art. v.; vol. ii. p. 101.

but it is quite impossible that you could have bestowed much time upon the writings, or much reflection on the lives and actions of many who thus suffered, when you allowed yourself to adopt and repeat this unfeeling and most false statement with respect to all.

I can honestly congratulate you, however, on having arrived at a less erroneous view of Mary's reign than some of those from whom your opinions generally appear to have been borrowed. For example, the writer whom I have just named describes the persecution as a kind of necessary experiment upon the constancy of the Reformers;—the persecutors "judging that there was no other way of putting a stop to the attempt of the party than by terrifying them by some instances of *justice;* which, as it usually happens, degenerated into *something like cruelty* [5]:"—language which I am sure you cannot read without a feeling of abhorrence and disgust.

At the same time I cannot but express my sorrow that you should have been so ready to adopt the reckless untruth of Milner and some other writers, who have declared that "the persecution of Elizabeth's reign was far more grievous than that of her sister Mary [6]." The assertion is partly answered by the facts which were produced in the

---

[5] Church History, P. iii. art. v.; vol. ii. p. 101.
[6] End of Controversy, Letter xlix., p. 181.

last Letter respecting the severities under Elizabeth. The injustice of the comparison will, however, be more apparent, when I remind you of the actual events of those disastrous seven years during which her sister sat on the throne.

While the title of Mary was still disputed by the adherents of Lady Jane Gray,—"many from Norfolk came to her, and a great body of Suffolk men gathered about her who were all for the Reformation. They desired to know of her whether she would alter the religion set up in King Edward's days; to whom she gave *full assurances that she would never make any innovation or change, but be contented with the private exercise of her own religion[7].*"

This promise of the Queen was not long after urged in her favour by Lord Arundel before the Privy Council, and probably contributed not a little to induce that body to forsake the cause of her opponent[8].

The opposition to her claim had hardly ceased,

---

[7] Burnet, P. ii. b. i., p. 237. Collier, P. ii. b. v., p. 343.

[8] Bishop Godwin in Annal. l. iii.; p. 108; Lond. 1616. The Author, a cotemporary, confirms Arundel's statement about the Queen's assurance:—"Et verum id fuit." Mr. Tierney admits the fact. " It is probable, indeed, that Mary gave no *specific* promise on the subject, but this speech incontestably proves not only that her words were susceptible of a construction favourable to the wishes of the Reformers, but also that such construction was actually put on them by her partisans, in order to win the support of the people."— Dodd, vol. ii. p. 55, note[3]. Dr. Lingard, though he mentions the speech of Arundel, says not a word of the Queen's promise. Why this omission? Vol. vii. ch. ii. p. 132.

when, on the occasion of some tumults to which the fear of change had given rise in London, she commanded the Mayor and Recorder by an order of Council to declare in her name to the Common Council of the city, that "albeit her Grace's conscience was stayed in matters of religion, yet she meant graciously not to compel or constrain other men's consciences otherwise than as God should (as she trusted) put in their hearts a persuasion of the truth she was in; and this she hoped should be done through the opening of His word unto them by godly, virtuous and learned, preachers[9]." Six days only had elapsed when a proclamation appeared to prohibit all preaching "except in schools of the University" without "her Grace's special licence in writing for the same." Dissimulation had now become unnecessary, and her future intentions were accordingly intimated very clearly in this document:—

"Her Majesty being presently by the goodness of God

[9] Haynes' State Papers, Journal of Privy Council, Aug. 13, 1553, p. 168. Archæol. u. s. p. 173. A chaplain of the Queen, preaching at S. Paul's Cross, had excited the mob to violence by declaiming against the treatment of Bonner in the last reign, and other imprudencies. On this Lingard observes:—"This outrage, evidently preconcerted, injured the cause which it was designed to serve." Ibid. p. 134. There is no appearance of preconcert in the facts: there is not a shadow of reason for supposing that the outbreak was prepared, or would have happened but for the provocation given by the preacher. I notice the insinuation to the contrary, because it is one of those small touches, attracting little observation, which contribute so much to the general effect in Dr. Lingard's painting.

settled in her just possession, ... cannot now hide that religion which God and the world knoweth she hath ever professed from her infancy hitherto; which as her Majesty is minded to observe and maintain for herself by God's grace during her time, so doth her Highness much desire and would be glad the same were of all her subjects quietly and charitably entertained. And yet she doth signify to all, her Majesty's loving subjects, that of her most gracious disposition and clemency, her Highness is minded not to compel any of her subjects thereunto *until such time as* further order by common assent may be taken therein [1]."

Soon after the appearance of this inhibition, "some came from Suffolk to put the Queen in mind of her promise. This was thought insolent; and she returned them no answer but that they being members thought to rule her that was their head, but that they should learn that the members ought to obey the head and not to think to bear rule over it. One of them had spoken of her promise with more confidence than the rest; . . . so he was ordered to stand three days in the pillory as having said that which tended to the defamation of the Queen [2]."

About three months before the execution of Rogers the first martyr, the mask was finally laid aside. In certain directions to the Privy Council,

---

[1] Wilkins, vol. iv. p. 86. Collier, Records, No. lxviii., p. 81.

[2] Burnet, u. s. p. 246. I cannot find any notice of these circumstances in Dr. Lingard's History.

which the Queen " drew up" at this time " *under her own hand*," we have among other provisions the following ominous suggestions :—

" Touching punishment of heretics we think it ought to be done without rashness, not leaving in the meanwhile to do justice to such as by learning would seem to deceive the simple : and the rest so to be used that the people might well perceive them not to be condemned without just occasion, whereby they shall both understand the truth and beware to do the like ; and especially within London *I would wish none to be burnt*, without some of the council's presence, and both there and every where good sermons at the same [3]."

This revolting exhibition of duplicity and falsehood was a becoming prelude to the atrocities which followed. The persecution began in less than a month from the appearance of the proclama-

[3] In Burnet, Records, P. ii. b. ii. No. 22. Collier, P. ii. b. v. p. 371. Let me now ask the reader to decide upon the character of the following statement in a popular tract disseminated by thousands for the delusion of the people :—" The Queen kept her word rigorously that no alteration should be made in religion ' without common consent.' It was not by a bare majority, or even by a majority at all, that the old religion was restored, but with the unanimous consent of Parliament, and the joyful acquiescence of the nation. It is true that when this consent was gained, Mary used the authority she possessed by the constitution of the realm to have the laws respecting religion observed, &c. But this was no act of tyranny on her part. She did but carry out the will of the nation."—Clifton Tracts, No. 3, p. 22. The Parliament by which " the old religion was restored " was assembled under the following circumstances :—" To lessen the chance of opposition in the Commons, Mary had ordered the sheriffs to recommend to the electors those candidates who were distinguished for their attachment to the ancient faith." Lingard, Ibid. p. 176.

tion, Hooper and others being put in prison for disregarding it; but it did not break out in all its horror until after the arrival of Cardinal Pole and the formal reconciliation of the kingdom with the See of Rome. Perhaps the following statement of Bishop Coverdale, whose good faith you will not dispute, however you dislike his opinions, may help you to realize some of the lesser miseries that ensued, which, from the position that you occupy, appear to you, at present, in colours by far too faint and indistinct:—

" Some of the professors were thrown into dungeons, noisome holes, dark, loathsome, and stinking corners. Some lying in fetters and chains and loaded with so many irons that they could scarcely stir. Some tied in the stocks with their heels upwards. Some having their legs in the stocks and their necks chained to the wall with gorgets of iron. Some with both legs and hands in the stocks at once. Sometimes both hands in and both legs out. Sometimes the right hand with the left leg, or the left hand with the right leg fastened in the stocks with manacles and fetters, having neither stool nor stone to sit on to ease their woeful bodies. Some standing in Skevington's gives, which were most painful engines of iron, with their bodies doubled. Some whipped or scourged, beated with rods and buffeted with fists. Some having their hands burnt with a candle to try their patience or force them to relent. Some hunger-pined and some miserably famished and starved . . . . . Their keepers would not allow them paper, nor ink, nor book, nor light, so that the letters they writ, they writ by stealth. They oftentimes began letters, but ended them not for lack of ease, being so fettered with chains, or wanting light, or through the hasty coming of the keepers. Sometimes for lack of pens they were fain to write with the lead of the window, as for lack of ink, they used their own blood, as divers letters so writ remained then to be seen [4]."

Among the papers of Lord Burghley, who conformed and held office during the reign of Mary, was found a carefully prepared account of the numbers who suffered by fire in different parts of the country. At the foot of this document occurs these simple words of dreadful import:—

" Besides those who died of FAMINE in sundry prisons [5]."

There were in England, at the accession of Mary, about thirty thousand foreigners who had fled hither from persecution in their own countries. By an edict published early in 1554, these were commanded to withdraw from the kingdom, and many of her subjects, including several of the principal laity and clergy, about a thousand, it is said, in number, took advantage of the order to leave the kingdom in their company, willing rather to endure all the ills of poverty in a strange land than declare

[4] Ep. before the Mart. Lett. in Strype, Mem. Eccles. Q. Mary, ch. xxxi.; vol. iii. p. 229.

[5] In Strype, u. s.—Originals, No. lxxxv. and ch. lxiv. p. 474. It gives the numbers of the sufferers in each year with the places.

that to be true which they knew to be false [6]. The number of those who suffered the extreme penalty of heresy, and perished by fire, is stated, on the authority of Burghley's list, to have been two hundred and eighty-eight [7].

A few months only before the conclusion of this unhappy reign, a proclamation, signifying that any one possessing, or finding, and not at once burning

[6] Burnet, u. s. p. 250. Strada (De Bello Belgico, Dec. i. l. ii., p. 44. Mogunt. 1651.) says that "heresy was brought into Belgium in part, by the exiles and refugees from England, whom Queen Mary, in number not less than 30,000 (of those who from other quarters had passed into that island), pursuing with edicts and punishments when she purged that kingdom from heresy, expelled all at one time." He refers to F. Hier. Polinus, Hist. Angl. l. i. c. 18. The same number is given by Ribadineira, Hist. Eccles. del Scism. l. ii. c. xvii., p. 403. Emberes, 1594.

[7] Strype, u. s.—The Brothers of S. Vincent say :—"The number of victims is put at 277 ; but from this list of 'martyrs for the gospel' must be excluded the names of those who suffered for political offences or other crimes." ` Clifton Tracts, No. 7, p. 15.—The writer is not a skilful advocate. In insinuating that some of those who were burnt suffered for sedition and other crimes, he is accusing those whom he tries to defend of the further crime of employing the Church Courts and the legal penalty of heresy to avenge a civil offence ;—no venial sin, I should suppose. Happily for his clients, the insinuation is as false as it is simple. Cranmer, who had been brought in guilty of treason for supporting Lady Jane Grey, was actually pardoned that offence, and thus reserved to be made an example of for heresy. Strype's Life, b. iii. ch. v., p. 321. Two hundred and seventy-seven is the number of the martyrs whose sufferings are related by Fox (see list in Dr. Maitland's Essays on the Reformation, p. 576) ; but it is extremely improbable that he was acquainted with every single case. Dr. Lingard (vol. vii. ch. iii. p. 207) says "almost two hundred." He gives no authority. If he is right, Fox or his informants must have invented the names of more than seventy martyrs and the particulars of their sufferings,—an absurd supposition.

T

any book containing " *heresy*, sedition, and treason,"
should be "reputed and taken for a rebel, and without
delay executed for that offence, according to the
order of martial law [8]."

---

[8] Dated June 6, 1558. It is given in Strype, vol. iii. ch. lxiii.
p. 459. Some of the treasonable publications to which the proclamation referred were such as to justify very severe measures for their
suppression. They were written by Knox, Bale, Goodman, and
other Puritans, who had fled from the persecution, and were now
living at Basle or Geneva. It is a moderate account of them to say,
that they taught the most unchristian doctrines in language that
would have disgraced a heathen. Pius V., Cardinal Allen, and their
friends, certainly showed themselves masters in the art of provocation
(e. g. the Pope denounces Elizabeth as a " pretended Queen," a
" heretic and encourager of heretics," a " vassal of iniquity," who
had " restored the scandalous preachers and ministers of iniquity,"
" ordered books stuffed with downright heresy to be publicly recommended to the kingdom," " commanded her subjects to comply with
ungodly mysteries," &c. (*Bull of deposition*. Collier, P. ii. b. vi.
p. 521); while the Cardinal, in his Admonition to the Nobility and
People (Lingard, vol. viii. p. 442), charges her with "Luciferian
pride," " perjury," " filthy lust," &c., and holds her up to contempt
as " an incestuous bastard, begotten and born in sin, of an infamous
courtezan, Anne Boleyn, afterwards executed for advoutery, treason,
heresy, and incest," &c.) ;—but bitter and unscrupulous as these men
were, they were equalled, if not surpassed, by the predecessors of
Prynne and Bastwick. Nothing in fact can be more revolting than
the continuous stream of filth and venom which they poured forth on
Mary and her Bishops from their secure retreat, as reckless of any
aggravation of suffering which they might cause to their brethren in
England, as they were regardless of truth and decency. Thus Knox
laments that among so many godly and learned men " as this day by
Jezebel are exiled, none is found . . . . to dare admonish the inhabitants " of England " how abominable before God is the empire or
rule of a wicked woman, yea of a traitoress and bastard." First
Blast against the Monstrous Regiment of Women, Pref. ; in Maitland
on the Reform., p. 127. Such a man was, however, found in Goodman, who wrote a book on Obedience :—" *How superior powers ought
to be obeyed of their subjects, and wherein they may lawfully by God's*

V. Popular tradition, there can be no doubt, has LETTER VI. SECT. V. much exaggerated the share which the Queen had personally in designing and directing these atrocities. I am afraid that party zeal has led you no less to underrate it. You state, but I do not observe that you offer to prove, that the persecution was "brought about" by others in the name

word be disobeyed and resisted. Wherein also is declared the cause of all this present misery in England, and the only way to remedy the same." His principles and temper, and the remedy which he proposed, may be learnt from a very brief extract :—" If your Jezebel, though she be an unlawful governess, and ought not by God's word and your own laws to rule, would seek your peace and protection . . . then might you have some pretence to follow Jeremy's counsel; that is, to be quiet and to pray for her life, &c.; . . . . but because her doings tend all to the contrary, that is, to blaspheme God and to compel all others to do the like, *what cloke have you here to permit this wickedness ?*" p. 130; in Maitland, p. 140. It is true that these books were published after the Reformers in England had been burnt in great numbers, and this may palliate, in a degree, the guilt of their writers; but some of the party had betrayed the same spirit before blood had been shed. E. g. take the following specimens from Bale's Declaration against Bonner's Articles, published in 1554 :—" Consider, dear Christians, in these most wicked Articles of Edmond Bonner, the bloody bitesheep of London, the exceeding and horrible fury of Satan in these latter days." " This limb of the devil and working-tool of Satan, bloody Bonner, seeketh here to deprive you of faith, true doctrine," &c. Pref. in Maitl. p. 51. " I would wonder at it that this Bonner, a great doctor of both laws, sometime a king's ambassador, and now a Bishop, should appear by his own writings so beastly a buzzard and a fool so blockishly ignorant," &c., fol. 75, Maitl. p. 62. The reader must not imagine that all the English exiles sympathised with these Puritans either in their revolutionary principles or in their feelings towards those in authority. The supporters of the Prayer Book at Francfort actually accused Knox to the magistrates of that place for seditious language against Mary and her husband and father-in-law, in his " Admonition to Christians." Collier, P. ii. b. v. p. 396.

of the "poor sick Queen." It would be a sufficient reply to this assertion to point out that the persecution began before the Queen can be supposed to have been diverted from public affairs by the state of her health, and that some of the facts already quoted exhibit her as actively directing or authorising the violent suppression of the reformed doctrine. But I am disposed to enter on the question a little further. It is really of importance that we should understand how little foundation there is for some of the current opinions of Roman Catholics,—and even, in too many cases, for the deliberate statements of the writers on whom they rely. But for this consideration the degree of her guilt is not a subject upon which I should desire to argue.

Let us hear then the testimony of those who had daily opportunities of observing and conversing with this most unhappy Queen. In Rogers' Memoir of his own trial [9] occurs the following direct reference to this very point :—

" I answered that the Queen's Majesty (God save her Grace) would have done well enough, if it had not been for his counsel (i. e. the counsel of Gardiner to whom this was addressed). He said, the Queen went before him, and it was her own motion. I said without fail, I neither could nor would believe it. Then said Dr. Aldridge, the Bishop of Carlisle, that they, the Bishops, would bear him witness."

[9] Preserved in Fox, vol. iii. p. 101. Ed. 1684.

· The strength of her personal feeling against heretics and other offenders is apparent from the eagerness which she exhibited in an interview with the French Ambassador to secure and punish some of her subjects who had fled beyond seas. He tells the story thus in a despatch to his master :—

" She felt herself deeply obliged to your Majesty because it had pleased you . . . to promise to send her some prisoners her subjects who were in France,—abominable people, heretics and traitors ;—she might well call them so, she said, in regard of their crimes so vile and execrable . . . . . . And when in my answer I called the said banished men transfugees, the said lady begged me not to call them so, but abominable heretics and traitors, and worse even, if that were possible, though she was grieved to have occasion to call her subjects by such bad names. . . . . She returned to this discourse with so much vehemence and frequency that it was easy for me to see that if I had contradicted her in my reply, as I certainly might have done, she would have fallen into extreme anger[1]," &c.

VI. But you proceed to say that the persecution in Mary's reign was " protested against at once by the best of the (Roman) Catholics," and you name

[1] Noailles, vol. v. p. 352. He endeavours to account for this revengeful disposition :—" I must tell you, sir, that this princess lives continually in two great extremities of anger and suspicion, for which one must excuse her, for this reason ; that she is in a continual frenzy at not being able to enjoy the presence of her husband, or the love of her people, and is in great fear of losing her life by some of her own people, it having been discovered some time ago that one of her chaplains had undertaken to kill her," &c.

Cardinal Pole as having done so, and "the Fran-
ciscan confessor of King Philip in his sermon before
the court [2]."

I wish that you had produced some evidence of
your statement with regard to Pole. I have been
able to find none [3]. To speak plainly, I believe it
to be a mere conjecture of some careless writers of
the seventeenth century, founded on their opinion
of his character, and to be at direct variance with
the facts of history. In the first place we have his
own avowal that he believed it right in principle to
put heretics to death. In a letter written while he
was waiting at Brussels for the repeal of his
attainder to enable him to re-enter England, after
declaring that he was by nature most averse from

---

[2] Sim. Milner, End of Controversy, Letter xlix. P. iii. p. 171 ; and
several writers not of his communion, with more charity than knowledge.

[3] Heylin (Eccles. Restaur. p. 217, Lond. 1674) speaks of a difference of opinion on this subject between Gardiner and Pole. Burnet
(P. ii. b. ii. p. 298) and Collier (P. ii. b. v. p. 377) have enlarged upon
his hint,—and their statements are again extravagantly expanded by
Hume, ch. xxxvii. Ann. 1555. After all, the records contain no
allusion to a discussion which the last of these historians goes so far
as to say took place "frequently before the Queen and Council "
between these two ecclesiastics. One part of the tale in Heylin
Hume saw to be untrue, as it attributes to the Emperor advice at
direct variance with his own conduct at the time. U. s. note [b]. That
it is *altogether* untrue is amply proved by the facts respecting Pole
collected in the text. Even Phillips, his Roman Catholic biographer,
though greatly misrepresenting his connexion with the persecutions,
allows that the debate never took place :—" The author's ingenuity
has supplied the whole argument, of which I have found no trace in
history."—Life, P. ii. p. 163. Sim. Lingard, vol. vii. ch. iii. p. 190.

all cruelty, and appealing for the truth of his asser- tion to the general knowledge of his temper, he nevertheless "confesses that a person's opinions might be so pernicious, and himself so corrupt and so active and industrious in corrupting others, that he should not hesitate to say that he ought to be deprived of life and cut off from the body as a mortified member;—yet not before every gentler remedy had been tried with a view to his recovery [4]." After his arrival in England he held a Legatine Synod for the reformation of the Church. In one of the regulations proposed by him to this body, and by it accepted, we find it ordered that "all censures and punishments against heretics and their defenders, also against Ordinaries and all others to whom this duty appertains who are negligent in extirpating heresies, whether decreed by the law or man, be put in execution [5]." Heretics are defined

[4] Epp. Poli, P. iv. Ep. liii.; p. 156. Brix. 1752. This letter is dated June 20, 1554. He arrived in England Nov. 24.

[5] Wilkins' Conc.; tom. iv. p. 121. In Labb. Conc. (tom. xiv. col. 1733) a letter addressed by Pole to the Queen and nation is prefixed to the acts of this Council, which contains matter similar to that quoted in the text. Bishop Burnet has made a strange mistake here. After giving a brief abstract of the twelve decrees of the Council, he adds, having quite overlooked the clause above cited:—"By all these it may appear how well tempered this cardinal was. He never set on the clergy to persecute heretics, but to reform themselves." P. ii. b. ii.; vol. ii. p. 326. It is amusing to see how eagerly certain writers have taken advantage of this slip. Thus Phillips :—"There is no order, nor the least intimation given to the Bishops or parochial clergy to persecute others, but to amend themselves ; and I should do Dr. Burnet an injury not to acknowledge that this remark is his."

to be "all who hold and teach otherwise than the Roman Church believes and holds." This decree is better understood when we remember that the persecuting statutes directed against the Lollards had been already revived by Act of Parliament[6]. The spirit in which he was prepared to discharge this imaginary duty may be gathered from the following allusion to the martyrdom of Ridley and Latimer,— which occurs in another of his extant letters :—

" I have received a letter from Oxford, from the Reverend Father Soto, in which he tells me what has passed between himself and those two heretics who had been already condemned ;—of whom one would not even speak with him ;—with the other he did speak, but without any success ;—so that it may readily be understood that no one can save those whom God has cast off. They accordingly underwent their punishment ;—the people, it is reported, looking on without dissatisfaction, when they knew that nothing pertaining to their salvation had been left untried[7]."

It is on record that Pole's compassionate nature on two occasions got the better of his principles,

—Life of Pole, P. ii. p. 142. Similarly Milner, u. s. p. 171; and the Clifton Tracts, No. 7, p. 16. What is the reason that Dr. Lingard, who is otherwise so full on the ecclesiastical proceedings of this reign, makes no allusion to this very important synod, which sat, with prorogations, for more than a year? Its acts were published at Rome in 1562 under the title " Reformatio Angliæ ex Decretis Reginaldi Poli Cardinalis Sedis Apostolicæ Legati. Anno 1556."

[6] 5 Rich. II. stat. 2, c. v.; 2 Hen. IV. c. xv.; 2 Hen. V. stat. 1, c. vii. They were revived by 1 & 2 Ph. & M. c. vi.

[7] Epp. P. v., Ep. xx. ; p. 47.

and induced him to interfere for the preservation of several persons in the Diocese of London, who had been condemned by their Ordinary, Bonner [8]. The fact shows, however, that he was able, if he had thought proper, greatly to mitigate, and perhaps entirely to stop, the persecution. Again, if he had been, as you imagine, altogether a passive or unwilling spectator of its atrocities, he certainly would not have permitted them to extend to his own Diocese, where a trial for heresy could only proceed under the express sanction of his authority. But I find that out of fifty-one persons who suffered within it, twenty-nine were burnt while he was in actual possession of the See,—and in a period less than half the duration of the persecution [9]. Another

[8] Burnet, u. s. pp..337, 348.

[9] Burghley's List, u. s. Dr. Maitland's abstract from Fox gives the same number, twenty-nine. Essays on the Reformation, pp. 580 —582. Pole was consecrated March 22, 1556, the day after Cranmer's death, up to which period the diocese had been administered by the Dean and Chapter (Collier, u. s. pp. 354, 393); but no further executions took place within it till Jan. 1557. Most of the sufferers were burnt in companies; as at Canterbury, four, Jan. 15; seven, June 19, 1557; and five, Nov. 10, 1558; at Maidstone, seven, June 18, 1557. Maitland, u. s. In spite of these facts, Phillips, the biographer of Pole, asserts that "not one was put to death in the diocese of Canterbury after he was promoted to that see." Life, P. ii. p. 159. And Dr. Lingard:—"From that moment the persecution ceased in the diocese of Canterbury. . . . . But his moderation displeased the more zealous. . . In the last year of his life he issued a commission. . . Five persons were condemned : four months afterwards they suffered, but at a time when the Cardinal lay on his death-bed, and was probably ignorant of their fate." Vol. vii. ch. iii. p 205. He is followed by the Clifton Tracts, No. 7, p. 16. Thus falsehood spreads.

fact, almost as decisive, is pointed out by Mr. Massingberd : viz. that "in the Diocese of Lincoln the
only sufferer . . . . was committed to the flames
under a sentence, not of his own Bishop, but of
the delegates of Pole during his archiepiscopal
visitation [1]."

Nor does it appear that he ever paused or
relented in the career of cruelty. His death took
place on the 18th of November, 1558. In January
of the same year, the Convocation over which he
presided ordered the Bishops of Ely and Lincoln
"to make diligent inquiry of heretical pravity" in
the two Universities, and "to punish all offenders in
this sort;" directing them, at the same time, to
publish their commission every year, and with it
an ancient provincial Constitution of Archbishop
Arundel, enacted for the suppression of Lollardy in
the reign of Henry IV., which provided a summary
method of dealing with a suspected heretic [2]. Two
months after this, he directed his commissary-
general and others to search out obstinate heretics,

The reader will see also from the text that Pole had given up those
five persons mentioned by Lingard to be burnt four months before
his death, and while he still engaged actively in public business.

[1] Hist. of Reform., ch. xviii.; p. 392.

[2] Cardwell's Synodalia, vol. ii. p. 483. Wilkins, vol. iv. p. 166.
The Constitutions of Arundel are in Johnson's Engl. Canons, P. ii.
Ann. 1408. Wilkins, vol. iii. p. 314; &c. Dr. Lingard says in a
note, vol. vii. ch. iii. p. 205 :—"It is a mistake to suppose that inquisitors of heretical pravity were appointed by Pole in the Convocation
of 1558." How truly let the reader judge.

and on conviction, "if the atrocity of the fact required it," to deliver them to the magistrate to be burnt [3]. There is also extant a notification addressed to the Queen, in the July following, by which he certified the conviction of three men and two women accused of heresy, and handed them over "to the secular arm to receive condign punishment [4]." They were burnt at Canterbury only eight days before his own death, and seven before that of the Queen, to whose disposal this document transferred them [5].

VII. The preacher to whom you appeal with so much confidence, as another advocate of toleration and humanity, was Alphonsus a Castro, a famous Minorite, appointed afterwards by Philip to the Archbishopric of Compostella. The following facts, of which you cannot have been aware, will enable you to form a better judgement of his sincerity on the occasion to which you refer. About eight years before, he had published the first edition of a book "On the Just Punishment of Heretics," in which he inculcated at great length the duty incumbent on princes and others in authority to inflict temporal penalties, including death, for schism and misbelief. The following extracts from

---

[3] Wilkins, vol. iv. p. 173.
[4] Wilkins, u. s. p. 174. Collier, Records, No. lxxvi., vol. ii. p. 89.
[5] As appears from Fox, vol. iii. p. 750.

the preface and dedication will show the temper and design of this detestable production :—

"The principal object of this work of ours is to contend for the Catholic Church (as a son for the honour of his mother) against those who teach that heretics ought not to be punished, and to plead her cause to the best of my poor ability, that I may show that she has decreed nothing contrary to justice, or unbecoming a true mother. Of which subject, no one (that I know of) has ever treated before me. For although, against those who teach that heretics ought not to be punished, many Catholic divines and learned men have written in our age, who have proved by many and the most convincing arguments that the punishment of heretics is most just, yet that *all* those punishments which have been decreed against them by the canon and civil law are just, no one of those whom I have yet been able to see has proved[6]," &c.

The more humane sentiments of some of the

---

[6] De Justâ Hæret. Punit. Præf.   Opp. col. 1039.   Par. 1571.   A learned writer in the British Magazine, vol. xvii. p. 490, who has been followed by Mr. Massingberd, u. s. p. 399, states that Alphonsus was preparing a new edition of this work while in England, and refers, in proof, to the dedication to Philip in a second edition published at Leyden in 1556.   This is a mistake.   No edition of this work was ever dedicated to Philip, or published at Leyden.   The writing from which he quotes is a letter addressed to Philip, prefixed to the second edition of another work, Adversus Hæreses, dated Salamanca, May 20, 1566, but published at Antwerp, and it is this latter book which the author says that he was engaged in revising while in England, "serving the king in public sermons and matters touching the faith."   The edition of the work De Justâ Hæret. Punit., which appeared in 1556, was published at Lyons (Lugduni), which may account for the statement that it came out at Leyden (Lugduni Batavorum).

Reformers, he turns thus ingeniously to their disadvantage :—

"The heretics, however, dreading this infliction, that they might find a way of saving themselves, have taught, with serpent-like cunning, that the punishment of heretics is unlawful, and have called those tyrants rather than kings who punish heretics, or compel them to hold the faith by penalties and torments [7]."

But perhaps you will suggest that he may have changed his mind, and that the sermon in England was a result of his repentance. I am sorry to say that the facts of the case preclude this supposition. For he published a second edition of the book the very year after it was preached, and while the persecution was still raging here, in which no trace is visible of any change of sentiment. It was not a mere reprint of the first edition, for in it he mentions that, since that appeared, England had been reconciled to Rome, and praises Mary for "having employed all her endeavours to bring back the kingdom to the Catholic faith [8]."

It cannot be doubted, then, that the advice given by this friar to the English court was opposed to

---

[7] Ibid. Ep. Dedic. ad Car. V., col. 1035.

[8] Ibid. l. i. c. v., col. 1231. In No. 7 of the Clifton Tracts, it is asserted that a Castro "boldly denounced the measures against the Protestants as *contrary to the spirit of the Gospel*," p. 17. Similarly Lingard, vol. vii. ch. iii. p. 193. This is incredible. He might have found many arguments against the continuance of the persecution without involving himself in a direct contradiction to the *principle* of his book, which must have been well known in England.

his real principles. But if so, what could prompt him, you may ask, to this act of impious hypocrisy? A very probable conjecture has been offered in reply. Philip was at that time at variance with the Pope, and it is supposed that he was anxious to be regarded as the advocate of mild measures, in the hope of securing the alliance, or at least the neutrality, of the Reformers in the event of an open rupture[9]. The sermon is said to have produced considerable effect on the English Bishops[1], who were not in the secret, if there was one; but it produced none whatever on the court. Neither Philip nor Mary appear to have been offended by the preacher, nor, on the other hand, to have given the least heed to his remonstrances. The sermon was delivered on the 10th of February, 1555. On the 26th of March, the king and queen wrote to the justices of peace in every county, commanding them " to rebuke, to bind to good bearing, or to commit to prison," as the case might require, those who refused to conform, and to "lay special weight on the preachers and teachers of heresy, and the procurers of secret meetings for that purpose[2]." This was followed by a letter to the Bishops, dated

[9] Turner's Hist. of England, b. ii. ch. xvi.; vol. iii. p. 481, note 57. 2nd ed.

[1] Collier, u. s. p. 382.

[2] That addressed to the justices in Norfolk is preserved in the Cotton MSS. and printed by Burnet. Records, No. 19, P. ii. b. ii. p. 283.

May 24, referring to the foregoing order, and LETTER VI. SECT. VII.
expressing "no little marvel that divers of the
said disordered persons being by the justices of the
peace brought to the ordinaries, ... were either
refused to be received at their hands, or if they
were received, were neither so travailled with as
Christian charity requireth, nor yet proceeded
withal according to the order of justice." The
Bishops were accordingly admonished to "use their
good wisdom and discretion in procuring to remove
them from their errors, if it may be, or else in
proceeding against them if they should continue
obstinate, according to the order of the laws[3]."
From these facts I infer that the sermon was only
a stroke of policy on the part of Philip, who had no
intention of remitting the persecution, but found it
desirable to throw the odium attending it as much
as possible on others.

VIII. I find that Roman Catholics are apt to re- SECT. VIII.
sent with great indignation, and sometimes with
much misplaced scorn, the language of our writers
respecting the persecution of this reign. They
imagine that we exaggerate its horrors, and the
guilt of its authors; and the mistake, in conjunction

---

[3] Burnet, u. s. No. 20, p. 285, from Bonner's register. Historians
have spoken as if this order were sent only to the Bishop of London,
and that before mentioned only to the magistrates of Norfolk; but
internal evidence shows that they were both general, as might have
been expected:—"We addressed our letters to the justices of the
peace within *every* of the counties, &c." The mistake probably
originated in the headings prefixed to them in Burnet.

with many others of a similar kind, tends greatly to confirm their prejudices against the Church of England, and the primitive faith restored in her. For this reason, it seemed desirable to examine at some length one or two of the common statements which have been without consideration adopted and repeated by you. There are some other points, upon which I have touched more lightly, with regard to which, it will be enough if I call your attention to the earnest language of the best historian, as I esteem him, of your communion, Mr. Tierney:—

" To detail (the atrocities which followed the short pause consequent on the sermon of Alphonsus) would be a revolting task. The mind would shudder, the heart sicken, at the recital. Suffice it therefore to say that the persecution continued to rage until the death of Mary. At times indeed a momentary suspension of cruelty seemed to indicate the presence of a milder spirit; but the illusion was quickly dissipated; new commissions were issued; new barbarities were enacted, and a monument of infamy was erected, which even at the distance of three centuries cannot be regarded without horror [4]."

" As to the number and character of the sufferers, certain it is that no allowances can relieve the horror, no palliatives can remove the infamy, that must for ever attach to these proceedings. The amount of real victims is too great to be affected by any deductions. Were the catalogue limited to a few persons we might pause to

[4] Dodd's Church History, P. iii. Art. v.; vol. ii. p. 103, note [3]

examine the merits of each individual case; but when, LETTER
after the removal of every doubtful and objectionable VI.
name, a frightful list of not less than two hundred still SECT. VIII.
remains, we can only turn with horror from the blood-
stained page, and be thankful that such things have passed
away [5]."

If *modern* history had been always treated in this
truthful manner by the writers of your communion,
the English Reformation would have presented
itself to you under a very different aspect, and been
regarded by you in a very different spirit.   The
prominent feeling would have been simple grief;
grief, that the vicious lives, the ignorance, and
violence of those whom you believe to have held
the truth, should, by an inevitable effect, have
plunged so many good, truth-seeking, and God-
fearing men into what you deem heresy and schism,
and given their descendants reasons so strong and
many for concluding that they must have been
right.

If *ancient* history and the records of primitive
Christianity had been treated by them with equal
truthfulness and candour, all difference would have
ceased; the objects, interests, and doctrines of the
Church of Rome would long ere now have become
identical with those of the Reformed Church of
England.

I am, &c.

[5] Ibid. p. 107, note [4].

U

LETTER VII.

LETTER VII.

My dear Sir,

I come now to a question respecting persecution at once of a more general character and of more immediate interest than those which have hitherto occupied our attention.

You define persecution to be "any violence employed to force a man's conscience;" and you proceed to tell us that it is "one universal principle of Roman Catholic teaching that it is *never* right to compel men to embrace the truth." Now, I beg you to observe, that while I think it right to expose the error of this statement, I do not accuse you of knowing, or even of suspecting that it is untrue. I am too well acquainted with your sources of information not to know that your mistake may be an honest one. I give you full credit for that abhorrence of persecution which you profess, and for a sincere belief that it is reprobated in all Roman Catholic teaching. But the stronger our conviction of an opponent's truthfulness, the more deeply should we regret his error, the more anxious should be our endeavour to set him right. Earnestly, therefore, do I entreat your attention and the attention of your friends, while I show that the universal feeling of the divines of Rome neither is, *nor in consistency could be*, averse from persecution.

I. The following extracts are from a book of high authority in Ireland:—

" Unbelievers, (meaning such as are unbaptized,) not subject to a Christian prince, may be compelled not to offer hindrance to the preaching of the faith in their country. The reason is that the Church has the right and the power to preach the Gospel throughout the whole world bestowed on it by Christ (S. Matt. xxviii. 19, &c.). If, therefore, the Church is hindered in the exercise of that right, Christian princes, as defenders of the Church, may restrain those who endeavour to impede the preaching of the faith, by war or other means.

" On this ground, Alexander VI. divided India between the Spaniards and Portuguese, directly dividing between them the care and right of restraining by arms those who should oppose the preaching of the faith, &c.

" According to Suarez, Herincx, &c., a Catholic prince may compel, under pain of banishment, the unbelievers subject to him to be present at certain times at the preaching of the Gospel; because, according to the Constitution of Gregory XIII., the Jews living at Rome are obliged to be present once a week at a sermon on the subject of Christianity.

"Unbelievers who are baptized, as heretics and apostates usually are, and baptized schismatics, may be compelled, even by corporal punishments, to return to the Catholic faith and the unity of the Church. The reason is that they by baptism have become subject to the Church," &c.

An objection is then supposed:—"No one believes, except *willingly*, but the *will* cannot be forced," &c. The reply to which deserves attention, being highly characteristic of the casuistic schools of Rome:—

"The man is not forced to believe *unwilling*, but from being unwilling to become *willing*[1]."

The same author enumerates seven "external pains of heresy." I extract the chief part of his remarks on those penalties which constitute the last of these:—

"The temporal goods of heretics are *ipso jure* confiscated; nevertheless, before execution, there should be declaratory sentence on the offence from the ecclesiastical judge; because it belongs to the ecclesiastical court to take cognizance of heresy. Finally, they are deservedly visited with other corporal punishments, as exile, imprisonment, &c.

"Q. May heretics be rightly punished by death? A. S. Thomas (Aquinas) answers in the affirmative, because coiners of false money or other troublers of the state are justly punished by death: therefore, also, heretics who

[1] Dens, Theologia Mor. et dogm. de Virtut. N. 51; tom. ii. p. 79.

falsify the faith, and, as experience shows, are grievous troublers of the state. This is confirmed by the command of God in the old law, that 'false prophets should be put to death,' &c. The same is proved by the condemnation of the fourteenth article of John Huss in the Council of Constance[2]."

It is already apparent, I believe, that Roman Catholic divines do not, as you assert, *universally* teach that "it is never right to compel men to embrace the truth." I need not multiply authorities to this effect; for it is not difficult to show that on "Roman Catholic principles," the lawfulness, and, where there is a hope by that means of suppressing error, the *duty* of persecution, must be considered a *doctrine* of their Church, and one, therefore, which may not be denied or doubted by any faithful son of Rome.

II. If it were proposed to demonstrate that the lawfulness of saint-worship, or any other avowed doctrine of the Church of Rome, is really taught by her, all parties would consider it sufficient to appeal to long continued and universal practice, if such could be produced, to its repeated recognition in the public offices of the Church, and to the declarations of Popes or Councils, in whom, whether severally or jointly, all modern Roman Catholics acknowledge an infallibility in faith and morals. The same criterion, it must be granted, is applicable

---

[2] Ibid. N. 56, p. 88.

to the question of persecution.   Let us see whether the result of its employment is not the same too.

Whatever theory of the Papal office we adopt, the deliberate actions of a long series of Popes, designed for the defence or furtherance of the faith, must be regarded as a good index of the principles of that Church in which they occupy the place of chief authority.   For example, we cannot hold the Church of Rome entirely unconcerned in the injunctions of Pius V. to the commander of the troops whom he sent to assist the King of France against the Huguenots :—not to take any prisoners, but to "kill at once every heretic who fell into his hands [3];" or in the warm approbation which he bestowed upon the atrocities of the Duke of Alva, a monster who made it his boast that in the five years during which he commanded in the Netherlands, he had "taken off above eighteen thousand human beings by the hands of the executioner [4]."

---

[3] Catena, Vita del Pio V., p. 85. In Roma, 1587. Gabutius, Vita Pii, l. ii. c. ix. p. 75. Romæ, 1605. He wrote many letters to the King, the Duke of Anjou (who commanded the royal army), and others, to urge extreme measures, even declaring it a duty to be "*inexorable* to any who should presume to intercede for those most wicked wretches." Epp. Pii, l. iii. Ep. xviii., p. 168. Antv. 1640. Hearing a rumour of peace he wrote again and again most urgently to prevent it, and, when it was made, vehemently condemned it. l. iv. Ep. i.—viii. The King of France sent him the standards taken from the Huguenots in battle which he "accepted with a thankful and paternal mind" (Epp. l. iii. Ep. xvii. p. 167), and placed in S. Peter's. Catena, p. 84.

[4] Grotius, Annal. de Reb. Belg. l. ii., pp. 45, 60. Pius wrote to

The same thought forces itself upon us when we see Gregory XIII. heading a solemn procession to the church of S. Louis of France in honour of the massacre of S. Bartholomew[5]; or, hear his suc-

him :—" We thank thee in the name of the whole Church. . . . . Go on, beloved son, and by these steps, as it were, secure for thyself a way to eternal glory." Epp. l. ii. Ep. xv., p. 98. Sim. Ep. xxi., p. 110, where he refers to certain presents which he had sent to reward his achievements, and which we learn from Catena (p. 92) to have been a consecrated hat and sword. Sim. Gabut. l. ii. c. xi., p. 83.

[5] He also caused a medal to be struck, the die of which is preserved and exhibited at Rome to this day. It is figured in Bonanni's Numismata Pontificum Romanorum ; No. xxvii.; tom. i. p. 323. Romæ, 1699. That writer, who was a Jesuit, says :—" As soon as the Pope heard the news, he betook himself in solemn supplication from S. Mark's to the church of S. Louis, and by the appointment of a jubilee called on the peoples of the Christian world to commend the religion and the King of France to the Supreme Deity. He ordered the slaughter of Coligni and his companions to be painted in the hall of the Vatican by Gi. Vasari. . . . . He sends Cardinal Fl. Orsino as his legate a latere to France, to advise the king to persist boldly in his undertakings and not to spoil the cure, successfully commenced by severe remedies, through following them up with milder ones. . . . In the medal that he had struck, in which an angel armed with a sword and cross is attacking the rebels, Gregory intimated that that slaughter was not perpetrated without the aid of God and the Divine counsel." p. 336. Among the Orations of Muretus is a speech delivered by him before Gregory in the name of the French King, in which the following sentence occurs :—" O day full of joy and mirth, in which thou, most blessed Father, when this news was brought to thee, wentest on foot in the procession ordered by thee, in order to return thanks to Immortal God, and S. Louis the king, on whose very eve these things had come to pass. For what more desirable news could be brought to thee? Or we, what happier commencement of thy Pontificate could we desire than that we should see in those first months of it that fearful darkness dispersed as by the rising of the sun ?"—Or. xxii. p. 225. Ursell. 1619. I quote these authors, because some writers,

cessor, in full consistory, exult in the assassination of Henry III., and pronounce it the direct act of God [6]. Again, the Inquisition persecuted;—it lived only to persecute. Yet, of this tribunal, after centuries of trial, we find one Pope declaring, in a Bull by which he sought to enlarge its sphere of operation, that it was "the firmest bulwark of the Catholic faith [7];" another, with his dying breath, that it was "the only means to save religion [8]."

III. Such were the acts and sayings of individual Popes. Now, turn to the consideration of events for which the whole body of the Church must be allowed to be accountable. Look at the Crusades, proclaimed by the Supreme Pontiff, preached as a religious enterprise,—"for God, for the faith, and for the Church,"—by all orders of the clergy under him, and eagerly undertaken by all ranks and classes, anxious to win the absolution and indulgences blasphemously held out to the exterminators of the denounced heretic or infidel. The record of many of these expeditions of blood and rapine has been preserved. In a volume before me, compiled by a distinguished priest of your communion, I find

on no grounds whatever, have denied the facts for which they vouch.

[6] Dispaccio Veneto, 1 Sett. 1589, in Ranke, Hist. of Popes, vol. i. p. 521; Foster's Tr. Lond. 1847.

[7] Bullar. Sixti V. Ann. 1588: *Immensa æterni.*

[8] A Paramo (of Paul IV.) de Orig. et Progr. Offic. S. Inquis. lib. ii. tit. 3, cap. 2, p. 278. Matr. 1598.

authentic documents and references which commemorate no less than ninety, exclusive of more
than twenty against the Moors in Spain. The
thirteenth century witnessed six directed against
the Albigenses and other heretical Christians;
within the next, we read of three against "the
schismatical Greeks," one against certain heretics in
Novara, and several more against various states and
princes denounced as "enemies to the Church, and
infected with heresy." In the fifteenth, a holy
warfare was thrice proclaimed, with fatal effect,
against the followers of John Huss. A lull of some
duration appears to have preceded the Reformation,
but in 1530, a new *Bulla Cruciata* against "the
followers of Luther in Italy" supplied matter for
one of the most awful pages in the whole history of
the Inquisition [9]. Fifty-eight years later, a similar
proclamation encouraged the ineffectual attempt of
the Spaniards upon England [1]. The last, if I mis-

---

[9] Amort de Indulgentiis, P. i. sect. ii. Aug. Vind. 1735. The
following examples will show the inducement held forth :—" If any
one of you, having received a penance for his sins, shall die in this
expedition, we absolve him, by the merits of the saints and the
prayers of the whole Church, from the chains of his sins " (Gelas.
A. D. 1118. Amort, u. s. p. 56.) ;—" We grant remission and absolution of sins . . . . in such sort that he who has devoutly commenced
this so holy expedition and completed it, or has died in it, obtains
absolution of all his sins which he has confessed with a contrite and
humbled heart, and reaps the fruit of eternal recompense from the
Rewarder of all" (Eugen. iii. A. D. 1145. Amort, p. 58.).

[1] See Declaration of the Deposition of Elizabeth given by Mr.
Tierney. Dodd's Church History, Vol. iii., App. No. xii. p. xliv.

take not, was that which authorized the extermination of the Cevenese, at the commencement of the last century [2].

Events of this nature which gave an exciting occupation to many thousand men for many years cannot be passed over as the mistaken acts of individual Popes. They embodied the general spirit of the age, and the Bull of the Crusade did but express and direct a feeling and idea which were common to the whole Church.

It is equally clear that the proceedings of the Inquisition, though dictated and controlled by Ecclesiastics, must have been for many generations at least only too agreeable to the principles, and congenial to the temper, of all. The terror which it inspired would soon have destroyed it, had its roots been less deeply set, or less widely spread, in the public feeling and opinion. A single crime, less fearful than one of its systematised atrocities, has sufficed to alienate the affections of a nation and overthrow a dynasty. When, therefore, we read of eighty-three persons, who were condemned by this tribunal yet in its infancy, committed to the flames in the presence of a king of Navarre and a hun-

---

[2] A *Bula de la Cruzada* is still circulated in Spain, and no Indulgence is available to a Spaniard who has neglected to possess himself of it. The price is only two reals or 5½*d.*; but a fresh copy must be procured every year. See Mendham's Life of Pius V., ch. iv. p. 97; or Meyrick's Practical Working of the Church in Spain, ch. xvi. p. 308.

dred thousand of his subjects, including eighteen
Bishops, and other ecclesiastics in great number,
and find the tremendous crime regarded by Christians of that age as the offering up of a " holocaust
acceptable to God[3],"— when after a lapse of three
centuries and more we find such an event in Spain,
in Italy, in Portugal, in India, in South America
and the Netherlands,—still viewed as a *religious*
spectacle, attended with devotion[4], and called habitually an *act of faith,*—when we have realized the
habit of mind and heart, with all its bearings and
results, which could permit, in the course of three
centuries, in one kingdom alone, no less than thirty
thousand to perish at the stake, and punishments
involving the same consequences of infamy and
ruin to the families of the condemned, though less
terrible to themselves, to be inflicted within the
same period of time on upwards of three hundred
thousand more[5] ;—I say, when our imagination has
grasped the full significance of these and many kin-
dred facts as certain and as dreadful, the murderous
cruelties, for instance, of Charles V. and Alva, the

[3] Fleury, l. lxxxi. ch. xxix.
[4] Dunham's History of Spain and Portugal, vol. v. p. 86.
[5] Llorente, Inquisition in Spain, ch. xlvi.   The exact numbers are
as follows :—

Burnt in person	31,912
Burnt in effigy	17,659
Sentenced to penance with severe punishments	291,450
	341,021

horrors of S. Bartholomew, the dragonnades of Louis, the massacres in Ulster,—we cannot but feel that we are confronted by the effects—of no capricious, desultory, and partial impulse, but—of a *principle* of action, deep-seated, permanent, and all-pervading, which born, though it may have been, of the ignorant bigotry and concentrated fanaticism of the cell and cloister, had at length taken possession of every practical, and almost every religious mind, and in those terrible deeds of earnest, though misguided, zeal proclaimed its universal presence and universal power. The Church had early spoken by her schoolmen, Bishops, Popes; she was thus uttering the fixed and profound conviction of all her people.

SECT. IV.   IV. It appears then that the lawfulness, I should rather say the duty, of persecution can show on its behalf the note of *general reception* within the Church of Rome. It is in this respect in a far more favourable position than was the practice of image-worship before the second Council of Nicæa. We hear of no nation, no party in the Church, nay scarcely of an individual here and there, who ventured to deny it. The popular voice and deed bore witness to it for centuries with far more unanimity than does the present Church to the two doctrines which are now forcing their way into its Creed. In a word, it is undeniable that the collective Church has for some ages avowed the principle; and it only remains to be shown that it has received a formal recognition from the Apostolic See. If the general mind of the Church has also been deliberately proclaimed by its organic head, your own theory of ecclesiastical authority in matters of doctrine requires you to believe in the duty of persecution, as an essential article of the Christian faith.

Let me then, in the first place, enumerate some instances in which Popes have incidentally, by implication, or indirectly, yet still with the full weight of their authority, given their clear sanction to this unchristian principle.

It will not be denied that they deliberately adopted it when they established the Holy Office of the Inquisition, or that a solemn affirmation of it is of necessity implied in the bull of Sixtus V. for the remodelling of that institution. Again, the canonization of the early Inquisitors, S. Dominic and S. Peter of Vermigli, men whose business and chief merit were persecution, and, at a later period, of Josephat Koncewicz [6], is certainly to ordinary apprehensions a plain avowal, on the part of the See of Rome, of

---

[6] Archbishop of Polotzk, of the Greek Polish Church united to Rome. Having excited the hatred of the people by his severities, he was murdered July 12, 1623, and was canonized as a martyr twenty years after. The following extract from a letter of remonstrance addressed to him by Leon Sapieha, Chancellor and Grand General of Lithuania, fourteen months before his death, will show his claim to that character :—" Your Holiness assumes that you are permitted to despoil schismatics and to cut off their heads. The Gospels teach the contrary. . . . . You offer violence to consciences and you shut churches, so that Christians perish, like infidels, without worship or sacraments. You abuse the authority of the monarch without even

LETTER
VII.
SECT. IV.
admiration for the work on which their zeal was spent. Of equal significance is the fact that the only King of France who has found a place in the Roman Calendar was the devout Crusader who introduced the Holy Office into his country. Still more significant is it that the only Pope canonized since the Reformation was the zealous and stern Inquisitor Pius V. In honour of each of these a day has been set apart by various Popes, on which the people are edified by an account of their lives, and are taught to seek grace and mercy through their merits. For example, on the fourth of August, S. Dominic's day, the special lesson records that " the ability and virtue of the Saint shone out most conspicuously in the overthrow of the heretics who laboured to pervert the people of Toulouse by their pernicious errors, in which employment he spent seven years,"—while in the collect is the appropriate petition that " through his intercession the Church may never be destitute of *temporal* aids."

I feel that if such commemoration, collects, and lessons had found a place in our Book of Common Prayer, it would have been difficult,—it would

having asked permission to make use of it. When your proceedings cause disturbances, you directly write to us that it is necessary to banish the opponents of the union. God forbid that our country should be disgraced by such enormities. Whom have you converted by your severities? You have alienated the loyal Cossacks; you have converted sheep into goats; you have drawn danger on the country, and perhaps even destruction on the Catholics." Krasinski, Reformation in Poland, vol. ii. ch. ix. p. 192.

have been impossible,—to deny that the men who appointed those services both held, and by their means desired to teach others, the lawfulness of inflicting temporal penalties for an erroneous belief.

A more important piece of evidence, perhaps, is the occurrence of these startling words in the oath of obedience to the Pope taken by a Bishop immediately before his consecration :—

"Heretics and schismatics, and rebels to our said Lord (the Pope), or to his . . . . successors, I will according to my ability *persecute and assail* [7]."

The Popes who exact this oath must surely be held to decree, *ex cathedrâ*, that to be a duty which they thus solemnly impose on the head of every diocese throughout their communion.

V. It would appear, however, that there is some way of evading this conclusion. Neither the clearest *implication* of a Papal Bull, nor of the Ritual, are allowed by some to be sufficient to constitute a tenet of the Church, or article of faith. Thus, for example, although Alexander VII. in the year 1661 declared *ex cathedrâ*, that in celebrating the Festival of the Conception of the B. Virgin, "the faithful" understood that they were celebrating her exemption "from the stain of original sin [8],"— although the epithet of *holy* has long been applied

---

[7] Pontificale Romanum, De Consecr. Episc.; P. i. p. 85. Mechl. 1845.

[8] *Solicitudo omnium*. "In hoc sensu ejus conceptionis Festivitatem solenni ritu colentium."

to her conception in the Public Office for that Festival as used by the whole Church [9]; and the Breviary has long contained an " Office of the *Immaculate* Conception" for those communities which have sought and obtained permission to use it, in which the doctrine is declared with great variety of expression [1]; yet, strange to relate, it is notwithstanding forbidden to rank it among articles of faith defined by the Church, or to censure those who privately hold the contrary [2].

It is evident then from this illustration, that however clear we may have made it to ourselves that the Church of Rome does hold and teach the lawfulness or duty of persecution, the evidence hitherto adduced is not sufficient, on the singular principle which prevails in such matters, to prove that the Roman Catholic is under obligation to

[9] In Lesson vi. for 2nd day (Dec. 9) and Versicle after Lesson viii. for the 1st, 3rd, 5th, and 8th days. The present office dates from 1568. Bullar. Pii V. *Quod a Nobis.*

[1] See Breviary, Pars Hiem. p. 645. Lugd. 1816. The Encyclic of Pius IX. from Gaeta, Feb. 2, 1849, in which he speaks of his predecessor as having granted this permission to many, has led some writers to think that this office originated with Gregory XVI. The date of the Breviary to which I refer is alone sufficient to disprove this.

[2] By a bull of Sixt. IV. Ann. 1483: *Grave nimis.* It is to be found in the Corp. Jur. Can. Extrav. Comm. 1. iii. tit. xii. c. ii. One singular consequence of the indecision of the Church of Rome with regard to this doctrine is that in some authorized copies of the Litany of Loretto the words ("without stain conceived") are inserted in brackets, not to offend those who do not hold it. An instance may be seen in the Appendix to the Office of the B. V., published at Mechlin, 1844; p. 284.

receive it. I propose, therefore, to inquire further whether the doctrine has been *directly* enunciated in any decree of the Sovereign Pontiff.

I have been content to place the *Bullæ Cruciatæ* among the acts of individual Popes, and not of the See itself; because they merely preached the duty of exterminating the holders of particular heresies, and did not formally assert the general principle. These documents then we will set aside as not proceeding *ex cathedrâ*, and therefore not fulfilling the condition of inerrancy now current in your schools[3]. But there are other Bulls of various Popes, to which, unhappily, even this poor exception cannot be made. For instance, if ever Pope spoke *ex cathedrâ*, Leo X. did so, when for the instruction and warning of all Christendom he enumerated and condemned the errors of Luther. But among the propositions which he then solemnly denounced as " pestiferous, pernicious, scandalous, contrary to all charity," &c., we find the following:—

" It is contrary to the will of the Spirit that heretics should be burnt[4]."

Again, there is a solemn Constitution of Paul IV., with respect to which the common subterfuge would be equally unavailing; forasmuch as it renews against all heretics *in general*, and *for ever*, all penalties ever denounced against any :—

[3] See Note [1], p. 230.
[4] Bullar. Ann. 1520 : *Exurge Domine;* Prop. 33.

X

"After mature deliberation with our venerable brethren, the Cardinals of the Holy Roman Church, under their advice, and with their unanimous consent, by the Apostolic authority we approve and renew, all and singular the sentences of censures and penalties, of excommunication, suspension, interdict, deprivation, and any other in any wise decreed and published against heretics or schismatics by any of the Roman Pontiffs, our predecessors, or those accounted such, even in their Extravagants, or by the sacred Councils received by the Church of God, or in decrees and statutes of the holy Fathers, or in the sacred Canons and Apostolical constitutions and ordinances, and we will and decree that they be observed for ever ; and that they ought to be restored to active observance, if by chance they are not so observed, and to remain in it : also that all persons whatever who have been found out . . . to have deviated from the Catholic faith, . . . or shall hereafter deviate, &c., be they Bishops, Patriarchs, &c., Kings, Emperors, &c., do incur the aforesaid sentences, censures, and penalties [5]."

By the same decree, all heretics and fautors of heresy are deprived of every high office and dignity, which they may hold ; the Clergy are deprived of their orders, sees, parishes, &c. ; the laity of baronies, duchies, kingdoms, empires, &c., of power to make a will, and of rights of inheritance. If judges, their sentence is to be void ; if notaries, no deed of their drawing can have effect : —

[5] Bullar. Ann. 1558 : *Cum ex Apostolatús.* It was signed by the Pope and thirty-one Cardinals. Pius V. renewed it by the Bull *Inter Multiplices,* Ann. 1566. These Bulls have both been added to the Canon Law. Sept. Decret. l. v. tit. iii. cc. ix. x.

" Moreover, that seculars be left to the will of the secular power [6], to be visited with the punishments due to them ; unless on the appearance in them of signs of true repentance, . . . they shall, of the benignity and clemency of the Apostolic See, be sentenced to be thrust into some Monastery, or other Regular House, there to perform a perpetual penance, on the bread of grief and water of affliction ;—and that they ought to be held, treated, and accounted for such (i. e. for condemned heretics) by all persons of whatever condition, . . . and as such avoided, and deprived of every consolation of humanity."

When Sixtus V. remodelled the Inquisition, he imposed upon all lay powers and persons the duty of assisting and *completing* its work by the following stringent addition to his decrees :—

" We earnestly exhort in the Lord, and by the bowels of mercy of Jesus Christ and by His dreadful judgement we adjure our dearest sons in Christ, the Emperor elect and all kings, and our beloved sons the nobles and other chiefs of states, &c., to whom the power of the secular sword has been committed by God for the punishment of the wicked,—by that same Catholic faith which they have promised to defend,—so to perform each one his part, whether by aiding the aforesaid Officials, or by the punishment of offences after the sentence of the Church, (which we are confident that they will of their piety with good will do,) that under their protection such Officials may happily discharge their so great and salutary duty, to the

---

[6] The reader must not suppose from this clause that the lay heretic only was delivered to the secular power. The convicted clerk became a secular on his degradation, and *as such* was handed over to the magistrate.

glory of the Eternal King and the increase of religion [7]."

A still more complete official sanction has been given to the principle by various Popes, in the code of laws by which the decisions of their spiritual courts profess to be determined. In this collection, the whole theory and doctrine of persecution is deliberately and carefully laid down, not merely for the instruction, but for the government of the whole Church. I am aware that, according to a distinction sometimes made, the *details* of the Canon Law, though enforced by Bulls, are not matter in which infallibility is considered to have place; but it must be allowed, that if the Pope does not speak *ex cathedrá* when solemnly enunciating its *fundamental principles*, he never does so speak, and never can. But if so, how is it possible for those who hold him to be infallible, when so speaking, to relieve themselves from the obligation to receive, and, as opportunity shall offer, to carry out, those principles?

VI. For my part, I see clearly that no honest man, even though he may take a lower view of the authority from which this law derives its principal sanction, is able to deny that its doctrines, acknowledged in the mass by the whole Church of Rome, and still enforced wherever the power is equal to

---

[7] *Immensa Æterni;* Bullar. ad Ann. 1588.

the will, are in the strictest sense the teaching of the Church itself. However, there are some few who may still urge that unless a general Council has taught the same thing, the Church is not irretrievably committed to it. Let me remind you, then, to meet objections from every possible quarter, of the decrees of certain Councils, confirmed by Popes, and recognised by all as œcumenical, and therefore on *every* theory to be received by Roman Catholics as infallible exponents of the doctrine of their Church.

The Council of Constance, in 1415, condemned as heretical a proposition of John Huss, which denied the lawfulness of punishing heresy by death. This was, in effect, as Dens has already told us, a solemn affirmation of its lawfulness [8]. I need not tell you how the Council exemplified its own doctrine by making Acts of Faith of Huss and his friend Jerome.

Two centuries earlier was held the fourth Council of Lateran, also received as œcumenical in the communion of Rome. In the third Canon attributed to this assembly we read as follows:—

" We excommunicate and anathematize *every* heresy that lifts itself against this holy, orthodox, Catholic faith, which we have above expounded, condemning *universally all heretics, by whatever name they may be called.* . . . . But let the condemned be left to the secular potentates

---

[8] See p. 292.

present, or to their bailiffs, to receive the punishment due to them, those in orders being first degraded;—so that the property of those thus condemned, if they are laymen, be confiscated; if clerks, applied to the use of the Church from which they have derived their stipend. . . . . And let the secular potentates, whatever office they hold, be warned and persuaded, and, if need be, compelled, by ecclesiastical censure, to make public oath, as they would be deemed and held faithful, for the defence of the faith, that they will in good faith, and to the best of their power, labour to exterminate from the territories subject to them all heretics whatever proscribed by the Church. . . . But if the temporal lord, though required and warned by the Church, shall neglect to purge his territory from this heretical vileness, let him be excommunicated by the Metropolitan and his own provincial Bishops. And if he shall scorn to make satisfaction within the year, let this be made known to the chief Pontiff; that he may thenceforth declare his vassals released from their fealty to him, and give up his land to be seized by Catholics, who having exterminated the heretics, may possess it without opposition [9]," &c.

To show the light in which such decrees of Councils *must* necessarily be viewed by every Roman Catholic, let me once more refer you to the authoritative Creed of the Church of Rome, which binds its members to "an undoubting reception and profession of all things delivered, defined, and declared *by the sacred Canons and by the œcumenical Councils.*"

[9] Can. iii. De Hæret. in Mansi, tom. xxii. col. 986.

VII. It were sinful not to regard with pain the conclusion at which we thus arrive. For the sake of humanity, from reverence to the Christian name and profession, one would rejoice to believe that the duty of persecution is not a doctrine of the Church of Rome and her divines. But with the facts before us, we have no choice; nor is it possible to conceive that any man of average honesty, who is acquainted with them, would attempt to convince us, or to persuade himself, that we have erred. One plea, I know, is sometimes urged, so base and false, that I will not suppose any Englishman capable of alleging it in answer to these remarks. It is argued that, at all events, the Church of Rome does not persecute to the *death*, inasmuch as it was the custom of her Inquisitors, when they delivered a convicted heretic to the civil authorities, that he might be burnt, formally to bespeak their compassion for the condemned man, and to beg that they would keep him "unharmed in life and limb." It is true that the last scene of the tragedy was preluded by this fiendish piece of irony. Well may I call it so; for all present knew that those who uttered it had no thought but of his death, and would have visited with the same punishment the magistrate who ventured to take them at their word [1].

---

[1] The first Bull of Pius V., Ann. 1566, orders all men of every state and condition, under pain of excommunication and other punishments to be determined by the Pope and the Inquisitors

I am sure, my dear Sir, that you will now no longer deny the lawfulness of persecution to be an avowed doctrine of the Church of Rome. At all events, you have received a full answer to the question, which, with an indignation by no means unnatural in one ignorant of her real principles, you have put to the English public. You have heard from me why it is that so many among us believe that Church itself,—and not merely a few of its mistaken partisans,—to have been guilty of persecution, and why they fear that nothing but the want of power restrains her, in the nineteenth century, from cruelties that were still common in the last.

VIII. Before I conclude, I must observe that you have represented the feelings of your English brethren in this respect as incorrectly as the doctrine of your Church. Their sentiments are, for the most part, intolerant in the extreme, and by no means easy to be distinguished from those of acknowledged persecutors. I had intended to exhibit proofs of this startling fact in passages from several living or recent writers, who have avowed and

General, to obey every mandate of the said Inquisitors in all things concerning the Holy Office. Similarly Boniface VIII. in 1298 denounced excommunication to be followed, after a year's obstinacy, by the punishment due to heresy, against all magistrates, temporal lords, &c., who should decline to obey promptly *prout ad suum officium spectat* the order of the Inquisitors for the execution of their sentence. *This Decree is part of the Canon Law of Rome.* Sext. Dec. l. v. tit. ii. c. xviii.

gloried in their intolerance; but I shall confine
myself to one such testimony, because I am happily able to add to it the more satisfactory evidence of Roman Catholics, who have confessed, with honest shame and indignation, the prevalence of such opinions among their brethren.

In the year 1816 was published in Dublin, by subscription, an edition of the Rheims Testament, " with Annotations, &c., approved of by the Most Rev. Dr. Troy, Roman Catholic Archbishop, Dublin [2]." From this I borrow the following notes :——

Matt. xiii. 29. "*Lest perhaps.* The good must tolerate the evil when it is so strong that it cannot be redressed without danger and disturbance of the whole Church ; . . . otherwise, when ill men (*be they heretics*, or other male-factors) may be *punished or suppressed* without disturbance and hazard of the good, they may and ought, by public authority, either spiritual or temporal, to be *chastised or executed.*"

Luke xiv. 23. "*Compel them.* . . . By the two former parts of the parable, the Jews first and secondly the Gentiles, that never believed before in Christ, were invited by fair sweet means only; but by the third, such are invited as the Church of God hath power over, because they promised in baptism, and therefore are to be revoked not only by gentle means, but by *just punishment* also."

Rev. xvii. 6. "*Drunk with the blood.* . . . The Pro-

[2] See the history of this book, and of the subsequent edition in 1818, in the Preface to Mr. Mc Ghee's Complete Notes of the Douay Bible and Rhemish Testament, &c. Dublin, 1837.

testants foolishly expound it of Rome, for that *they put heretics to death* [3], *and allow of their punishment in other*

[3] Balmez (Protestantism and Catholicity compared, p. 166) has on the other hand asserted, and Dr. Wiseman has repeated the tale (Dublin Review, vol. xxviii. p. 457), that " the *Roman* Inquisition, that is to say, the tribunal which was immediately subject to the control and direction of the Popes themselves in their own city has never been known to pronounce the execution of capital punishment." " We find in all parts of Europe scaffolds prepared to punish crimes against religion ; scenes which sadden the soul were every where witnessed. Rome is an exception to the rule. Rome which it has been attempted to represent as a monster of intolerance and cruelty. . . . The Popes, armed with a tribunal of intolerance, have not spilt a drop of blood ; Protestants and Philosophers have shed torrents." Still better witnesses, if possible, to the falsehood of this assertion than the commentators of Rheims are the Benedictine authors of L'Art de Vérifier les Dates :—" Pius V. before his pontificate had been Grand Inquisitor. Become Pope, he continued to seek out those whose opinions were suspected, and many were brought and burnt *at Rome* by his orders." Chron. des Papes, p. 316. Paris, 1770. In reply to the Dublin Review, the learned Mr. Gibbings has published (Petheram : London, 1852) " A Report of the Proceedings of the Roman Inquisition against Fulgentio Manfredi " (who was burnt at Rome, July 4, 1610, after being tried in the presence of Paul V.), taken from the original MS. brought from Rome to Paris at the end of the last century. Several other instances are given in detail by Mr. Mendham in his Life of Pius V., ch. iv., pp. 114—120. London, 1832. The assertion of Balmez and the Reviewer has been adopted by Dr. Newman (Present Position of Catholics, &c., Lecture v. p. 201), who, however, adds in a note :—" I am rather surprised that this is stated so unrestrictedly, vid. Life of St. Philip Neri, vol. i. ; however the fact is substantially as stated, even though there were some exception to the rule.". The *fact* is brought forward by him " in proof of the utterly false view which Protestants take of the Inquisition and of the Holy See in connexion with it." Surely if he knew only of a few instances (exceptions to the rule, as he strangely calls them), he ought to have seen that the " view of Protestants " could not be " utterly false." That *view* is not a theory, but a belief that such and such events have taken place, and that they did take place, Dr. Newman himself does not decidedly deny.

countries ; but their blood is not called the blood of saints, any more than the blood of thieves, man-killers, and other malefactors: for the shedding of which, by order of justice, no commonwealth shall answer."

The extract which next follows is from the History of the Inquisition in Spain, by Llorente, a priest, who became its secretary in 1789, and held the office till its suppression in 1791. Experience led him to regard with horror the institution which he had served :—

"During the time that I remained in London, I heard some Catholics affirm that the Inquisition was useful in Spain, to preserve the Catholic faith, and that a similar establishment would have been useful in France. These persons were deceived, by believing that it was sufficient for people to be good Catholics not to have any fear of the Holy Office. They knew not that nine-tenths of the prisoners were deemed guilty, though true to their faith, because the ignorance or malice of the denouncers prosecuted them for points of doctrine which were not susceptible of heretical interpretation but in the judgement of an illiterate monk [4]," &c.

These passages will be sufficient to show the sentiments and principles, which some, at least, of the existing generation of English Roman Catholics derived from their parents and instructors. I propose now to give you some direct and very recent evidence on the actual state of opinion among them at the present time. This will appear from the

[4] Pref. p. xix. Eng. Tr.

following letters written in a daily journal by Mr. Chisholm Anstey, a Roman Catholic gentleman of high character and influence. I will not mar their effect by curtailment, or by any remarks of my own, but only add that they are truly valuable from a political, as well as a polemical, point of view, and deserve from every thoughtful man far more attention than, if I mistake not, they have received.

The first appeared in the "Daily News" of Nov. 8, 1852:—

"The Case of the Madiais.
"To the Editor, &c.
"SIR,

"I do not think that the liberal Roman Catholics of this country ought to be contented with the protest which Mr. Keogh, M.P., very properly put forward in his own name at the Manchester meeting against the monstrous sympathy entertained by many of the community in favour of the Grand Duke of Tuscany, and expressed so forcibly by the *Tablet*. The impression of our complicity in the persecuting tenets of other days is so general,—and, I am bound to add, supported by so probable and plausible evidence,—that a mere individual disclaimer or two would not, and ought not, to satisfy the English mind that the persecution of the Madiais is not most warmly approved by the vast majority of the English Catholics. Nothing short of a public and authoritative declaration to that effect will be sufficient,— and, if willing, Cardinal Wiseman might very easily obtain such a declaration.

"The course I propose is not without precedent. I well remember to have been present at a meeting of the

Catholic Institute in 1838, when two letters from Rome, —the one written by Dr. Wiseman himself, the other by an Irish ecclesiastic,—were communicated by the late Mr. O'Connell (to whom the latter was addressed) to the meeting, both written at the request of the then Pope, Gregory XVI., and urging him in the strongest manner to bring the case of the imprisoned Archbishop of Cologne before the notice of the English Protestant public. It was thought desirable 'to convoke in London, with the help of the English Catholics, a meeting of the Catholic as well as Protestant friends of religious liberty,' (I quote from an editorial article in the *Tablet* of a few years afterwards,) 'with a view to a public declaration in favour of the imprisoned prelate.' Some steps were taken by Mr. O'Connell and myself to carry into effect these wishes of his Holiness, but the reluctance of others to engage in a movement which appeared to them to be one of great delicacy caused the attempt to be abandoned.

" Cardinal Wiseman is now here, and in a position to carry out in the case of the Madiais of Florence the sound views which, as Dr. Wiseman, he entertained in that of Clement Augustus of Cologne, but wanted power at that time to accomplish. At all events, since the question has been raised, as the organ of a very powerful section of English Catholic opinion has decided in favour of the persecutor, it is surely very desirable that the body at large should have an opportunity afforded them of informing their Protestant countrymen, how far they approve or dissent from the doctrine of the *Tablet* and the practice of the Grand Duke.

" I am, Sir,

" Your obedient Servant,

" T. Chisholm Anstey,"

The second was published in the same journal on the 27th of January, 1853:—

"Sir,

"I have read with much interest Lord Carlisle's letter on the case of the Madiais, and I heartily concur with his lordship in the opinion, that by the conduct of the Roman Catholics of this country with reference to that case, their own sincerity as professing friends of religious equality will have to be judged.

"I regret, therefore, to say that there is likely to be but one opinion as to the utter insincerity and hollowness of all such pretences. No one who has conversed much with English Catholics, at least upon the case of the Madiais, can have failed to see that amongst them the friends of religious freedom are miserably few, and that nearly every member of the body is persuaded that, in countries professing the Roman Catholic faith, it is the bounden duty of the state to coerce heretics by temporal penalties, or, if need be, *to extirpate them by the sword.*

"A *minority* amongst us have at all times stood up to protest against these monstrous opinions, and to assert the inalienable right of man to worship God in what way his conscience tells him is the most pleasing to the Great Object of worship. But it is now, at least, a much diminished and still diminishing minority; and for some time past our orthodoxy has been publicly aspersed for belonging to it. I remember the noble but ineffectual stand made by the Rev. Mr. Macdonnell, the Catholic priest of Birmingham, in 1841, against certain doctrines openly propounded by the dean of a neighbouring Roman Catholic college, of which Dr. Wiseman was then the head, and according to which, as defended by their reverend promoter in the columns of the *Tablet*, ' *it is false to hold that any Church but the true Church is entitled to toleration, and the conduct of those political Catholics is very much to be censured, who, instead of accepting in silence the concessions of the legislature, and waiting until a convenient season for the assertion of their true principles, have had the deplorable weakness to applaud the detestable principle on which the concessions were made by Parliament,—the principle, namely, of religious equality.*'

" I firmly believe, Sir, that opinion has marched, and that in 1853 it will be even less safe for men like Mr. Macdonnell to attack the opinions in question than it was in 1841.

" In my first letter on this very subject I laid before you a curious instance of the readiness with which the Court of Rome for Roman Catholic ends raises the cry of ' religious liberty,' and calls on Protestants to join in it. I allude to the case of the Archbishop of Cologne, and to the part taken by Dr. Wiseman in 1838, with the sanction of Gregory XVI., in endeavouring to get up a meeting of the friends of civil and religious liberty in London,—Catholic and Protestant,—to protest against that prelate's imprisonment.

" Why does not Cardinal Wiseman in 1853 do that for the Madiais of Florence which in 1838 he wished Mr. O'Connell to do for Clement Augustus of Cologne? The answer is obvious. The prelate was a Roman Catholic, the lay prisoners are Protestants.

" Under these circumstances, Sir, Lord Carlisle will see how hopeless it is to expect a Roman Catholic demonstration against the contemptible and cruel bigotry of the Tuscan despot. Were we to attempt it, we should not be able to fill a meeting, and our speeches would be delivered to bare walls. On the other hand, we are excluded from the Protestant gatherings which are being held by the narrow and sectarian spirit of the conveners. We are *not* 'friends and supporters of the Protestant Alliance.' We have therefore no right to intrude upon assemblies of persons meeting under that title in Exeter Hall.

> " I am, Sir,
>
> " Your obedient Servant,
>
> " T. CHISHOLM ANSTEY."

" The Temple, Jan. 25."

Such, then, are some of my reasons for believing that all Roman Catholics *must*, if they would be consistent, hold, and that English Roman Catholics in particular *do*, for the most part, hold the lawfulness, and, where considerations of expediency do not intervene, the duty of employing violence to compel men to adopt their peculiar creed, or to punish them for their desertion of it.

> I am, &c.

LETTER VIII.

PART I.

I. ON THE RISE AND PROGRESS OF FALSE DOCTRINE WITHIN THE LATIN CHURCH. II. MANY THINGS NOW HELD NECESSARY WHICH ARE NOT EXPRESSED OR IMPLIED IN HOLY SCRIPTURE. III. THE THEORY OF DEVELOPMENTS AS HELD AND EXPLAINED BY VARIOUS WRITERS FROM THE FOURTEENTH TO THE SEVENTEENTH CENTURY INCLUSIVE. IV. SIMILAR EXAMPLES FROM THE MODERN ENGLISH SCHOOL.

MY DEAR SIR,

PROCEEDING with your explanation of "Roman Catholic principles" you give us to understand that, according to those principles, "the Pope can neither invent, nor innovate;" that "the rule for him, as for all, is, Let there be nothing new,—nothing enforced but what was once delivered as the deposit of the faith."

I am not surprised at this statement. I believe that, until very lately, few Roman Catholics had any suspicion of the momentous changes which have gradually taken place,—and are at this time proceeding,—in the faith and worship of their Church. It is probable, however, that before long the teaching and confessions of the Developmentists will have led you to understand your position a

Y

little better; and that, at all events, we shall not have so frequent occasion to correct assertions respecting the antiquity and unchangeableness of your peculiar doctrines.

SECT. I. I. The true state of the case may be explained in a very few words. From the fourth century downwards, various practices and opinions, which were unknown to the Apostles and the earlier Church, have been, and still are, from time to time establishing themselves over the greater part of Christendom. A vigilant and learned clergy might have checked them in their beginnings without difficulty; but, unfortunately, during the several periods at which they arose, sound learning was an impossibility. The convulsions of the expiring Empire at first, and subsequently the rude and violent habits of its barbarian conquerors, not only discouraged the pursuit of knowledge and the cultivation of every peaceful art, but, to a great extent, deprived the Christian student of access to the wisdom and experience of former ages. The natural result was that the popular tendencies to innovation too often found encouragement from those whose duty it was to restrain them; and who, under happier circumstances, would, we may, hope, have been prepared to meet them with an enlightened and conscientious opposition. No part of the Church was exempt from these evils; but in no part were the corruptions so numerous, or so completely sanctioned by

authority, as in the western Patriarchate. Some
centuries before the Reformation, many of these
novel doctrines and ordinances had been enforced
by the Church of Rome as necessary to salvation,
and their rejection visited by all the penalties of
heresy. Soon after that event, the Council of
Trent, and Pius IV. who embodied the chief conclusions of the Council in the Confession known by
his name, placed the greater part of them, to the
number of eleven, on precisely the same footing
with the articles of the Apostles' Creed. Two
other novelties of the same kind have been long on
the anvil,—the doctrines of Papal infallibility, and
of the Immaculate Conception of the Blessed
Virgin;—but they are now so generally received,
and so agreeable to the Court of Rome, that we
have reason to fear that they will both, ere long,
have become articles of faith. The present Pope
has already taken the first step towards a "solemn
judgement" in favour of the latter, as may be seen
in his encyclical of Feb. 2, 1849, dated from Gaeta.
Should he effect his apparent purpose, it will
become as much heresy to believe that the Blessed
Virgin was conceived in sin, like every other human
being, her Divine Son alone excepted, as it is now
to deny the Divinity of Christ, or the existence of a
Purgatory.

Before that revival of sound learning which
followed the invention of printing, it was morally

impossible for any man, however studious and devout, to form a just estimate of the changes which had taken place in the teaching and the worship of the Christian Church. It must be confessed, too, that the advocates of superstition had a strong argument, and therefore a considerable excuse, for many years later, in the supposed authority of several books, then held in general esteem, and confidently ascribed to eminent Fathers, though in reality composed long after the corruption of the primitive faith. But we are in a different position now. The spuriousness of those writings is no longer a matter of dispute; and the learned Roman Catholic is well aware that in the Creed of his Church are articles of faith which were so far from being held essential in the primitive Church, that they were *not even known* as private speculations for several centuries after Christ. What then is to be done? Two courses are open :—either to confess at once, fearlessly and honestly, that the Church of Rome has erred, and to labour, as God shall make a way, to bring about her reformation,—or to embrace the explanation that has been lately offered, of a *design* on the part of God that Christian doctrine should be progressive, and should receive from age to age those very additions and increments which Rome, as a fact, has ingrafted on the original deposit of the faith. In the present state of things, the former of these courses demands great courage, faith in the divine strength of truth, and a conversation above reproach in those who venture to adopt it. Their number, it may be feared, will not be great. May God make it otherwise! On the other hand, there is much to tempt a Roman Catholic, made anxious and perplexed by the discovery of his position, to seek refuge in the theory of Development. It is true that it is a mere conjecture, "an expedient" devised to meet "a difficulty," that not a shadow of evidence can be produced on its behalf from Scripture or antiquity:—but then, it promises repose from anxious thoughts; it justifies the prejudices of education, so hard to be renounced; it relieves men from the duty, certainly painful and perhaps dangerous, of "contending for the once-delivered faith;" and allows, or rather encourages them to resign themselves to the stream of popular feeling and belief, in calm persuasion of the necessary truth of that which is generally thought true, and to look forward to the time when an opinion which is now perchance a novelty,—and may by some be thought a heresy,—will have received the stamp of Apostolic sanction, and assumed its destined place in the front rank of Christian verities.

II. The truth of these observations I now proceed to prove by the cumulative testimony of many divines of your communion, from the fourteenth century downward. From the early period at which the series begins, you will see that the notion of a gradual growth of Christian doctrine did not originate with Dr. Newman and his school, but that men of learning within the Church of Rome have long been more or less conscious of the novelty of her peculiarities, and have endeavoured to satisfy their minds by a very similar explanation.

I shall first cite a few *general* statements, which avow or imply the variable character of the Roman faith, and then produce similar proof with respect to some particular doctrines. In the first place, then, it is acknowledged that several things which you esteem vital are not taught in the writings of the Apostles; as (for example) by Melchior Canus:—

"Many things belong to the doctrine and faith of Christians, which are not contained either plainly or obscurely in holy Scripture [1]."

And Dominic Banhes:—

"Not all things that belong to the Catholic faith are contained in the Canonical Books, either clearly or obscurely [2]." "All things necessary to salvation have not been committed to the sacred Scriptures [3]."

---

[1] De Loc. Theol. l. iii. c. 3. Opp. tom. i. p. 198. Matrit. 1785. He says that this has been proved by Innocent III. in his treatise De Celebr. Missæ; cap. *Cum Marthæ*.

[2] In 2ᵐ 2ᵃ S. Thomæ, Q. i. Art. x. concl. ii., col. 519. Ven. 1587.

[3] Ibid. Concl. v., col. 542. The prevalence of this opinion is so notorious, as hardly to require proof; but see other authorities, with opposite statements from the Fathers, in Note [1], p. 9.

III. Such being the case, it becomes necessary to plead either a continuous tradition, or a power of adding to the faith once delivered. The word *development* is preferred now; but it will be seen by some of the following examples, that what are now called *developments* were at an early period more accurately termed *additions*.

Thus Augustinus Triumphus de Ancona, an eminent writer at the beginning of the fourteenth century :—

" It is expedient that the Pope exercise his power in adding articles (to the Creed), in explaining and illustrating it, or in recasting it at times, on account of rising heresies. Therefore it is in the same way expedient, that he should sometimes so exercise it, that matters of faith be put out of sight, and not explained, lest the simple fall into error [4]."

Such writers did not always avow thus plainly that they admitted a variable standard of belief. Some only taught that the Pope was the supreme teacher and final judge of doctrine, without at the same time asserting his inerrancy, the only protection that could in that case be provided against continual change. The following passage from the elder Torquemada, who flourished in the fifteenth century, will serve as an example :—

" It is easy to understand that it belongs to the authority of the Roman Pontiff, as to the general chief

---

[4] De Potest. Eccl. lix. 3, fol. 208. Colon. 1478.

master and teacher of the whole world, to determine those things which are matters of faith, and by consequence to put forth a symbol of the faith, to interpret the meanings of holy Scripture, and to approve or condemn the sayings of the several doctors relating to the faith. . . . . Since the Roman Pontiff is the first and greatest of the Prelates in the Church, it will belong to him chiefly to be the measure, and rule, and knowledge of things to be believed, and of all things which are necessary to direct the faithful to life eternal. . . . . Hence the Apostolic See is called by the holy Fathers, *the mistress and mother of the faith*[5]."

Cardinal Cusanus, who was the Pope's legate in Bohemia in the middle of the fifteenth century, endeavoured to reconcile the people of that country to the innovation of Communion in one kind by the following argument :—

" Let not this disturb you, that different modes of administration of sacrifices, and even of sacraments, are found to have existed at different times, the truth remaining the same, and that the Scriptures have been accommodated to the times and variously understood, so as to be explained at one period according to the rite then universally current, and again their meaning changed when the mode of administration was altered.   For Christ, to whom the Father has given a kingdom in heaven and earth, governing in both, dispenses the mysteries of men and angels in a wonderful order,

---

[5] Joh. de Turrecremata, Summa de Eccl. l. ii. c. 107, fol. 248. Venet. 1561. The title " Mistress of the Faith " is claimed for the Church of Rome in the Bull against Luther. Bullar. Leon. X. Ann. 1520. *Exurge Domine*.

according to the variety of times, and, either by secret
inspiration or clearer illustration, suggests the things
suitable to each period. . . . . Wherefore, if the Church's
interpretation of the same evangelical precept shall be
different in the present day to what it was formerly,
nevertheless the sense now current, being inspired for
the government of the Church, as suitable to the time,
ought to be received as the way of salvation. . . . . And
this is no change dependent on a less authority than that
of Christ who gave the precept, because the Church
which is the body of Christ, and is nourished by His Spirit,
does nothing but what Christ wills ; and so that change
of interpretation depends on the inspiring will of Christ,
who now wills to such effect, even as the precept itself
was formerly put in practice in a different manner,
according to the requirements of that time ; and for this
reason, this power of binding and loosing is not less in the
Church than in Christ [6]."

Again :—

"Nor is it surprising if the practice of the Church
interprets Scripture at one time in one manner, and at
another in another. For the understanding of it goes
along with the practice ; for that mode of understanding
it which concurs with the practice, is the 'spirit that
giveth life.' . . . . For the Scriptures follow the Church,
which is the earlier of the two, and on account of which
Scripture (is given), and not conversely [7]."

[6] Ep. ii., ad Bohem. i. Opp. tom. ii. pp. 833—835. Basil. 1565.
[7] Ep. vii., ad Boh. vi.; pp. 857, 858. How *necessary* this theory was
to the theology of Cusanus may be judged from the fact that, while
he upheld the authority of the Pope as he found it, he repudiated
the basis on which others place it :—" We know that Peter received
from Christ no more power than the other Apostles ;" for nothing, he

Eggeling of Brunswick, and Biel, his more famous editor, were equally aware that serious innovations had taken place, and naturally fell into a similar mode of accounting for them :—

" Without doubt, the Church having the Spirit of Christ her spouse, and being therefore infallible, assigns every thing to its proper time, as it is expedient, being moved and illuminated by the Spirit of God, who knows the times that the Father hath put in His own power [8]."

The same apology for change in doctrine occurred to Bishop Fisher, the pious victim of the tyrant Henry. In reply to the assertion of his opponent, that " though differing from the present Church, he agreed altogether with the primitive," he argues :—

" What, then, are there two Churches? or is the present not taught and ruled by the *same* Spirit as was the primitive? Far from it! Both suppositions are untrue. For it is written, My dove is one. To which also Christ sent His Spirit to teach it the whole truth, and to abide with it for ever. And although according to the change of times diverse things have been delivered to the faithful, yet one and the same Spirit has delivered them as it seemed to Him that it would be more profitable to the Church [9]."

argued, " was said to Peter, that was not also said to the rest ; ... and therefore we say rightly that all the Apostles were equal in power to Peter." De Concord. Cath. l. ii. c. xiii. p. 727.

[8] Biel de Canone Missæ. Lect. lvii., fol. 139. Lugd. 1542.

[9] Assert. Lutheri Confut., Prol. ad Lect. Opp. p. 273. Wirceb. 1597.

" No one can doubt that there are many things both
out of the Gospels and the other Scriptures more
thoroughly sifted and more clearly understood by later
wits than they have been of old. And this either because
by the ancients the ice was not yet broken through, and
that the time as yet had not sufficed for an exact investigation of that whole sea of Scripture, or because in the
very wide field of Scripture it will always be possible to
glean some yet untouched ears, even after the most careful reapers. For there are still in the Gospels many passages sufficiently obscure, which I doubt not will become
much clearer to posterity. For why should we despair
of that when the Gospel was given us that we might
understand it to the last tittle? Since, therefore, the
love of Christ to His Church continues no less strong now
than it was before, and His power likewise has hitherto
suffered no diminution, and since the Holy Spirit, whose
gifts flow as unceasingly and in the same abundance as in
the beginning, will be for ever the guardian and keeper of
the same Church, who can doubt but that the minds of
our descendants will be enlightened to the clear knowledge of those things which still remain unknown in the
Gospel [1]."

He is endeavouring by this explanation to account
for the absence of primitive testimony to the Roman
doctrines of Purgatory and Indulgences.

A party of Divines at the Council of Trent
expressed their direct approbation of the theory :—

" It was well said by Cardinal Cusanus, a man of surpassing learning and integrity, that the interpretation of

---

[1] Ibid. Art. xviii., col. 496.

the Scriptures should be adapted to the time, and that they should be expounded according to the accustomed manner; that so it did not appear strange if the custom of the Church interpreted the same passage of Scripture differently at different times. Nor ought the last Council of Lateran to be taken in any other sense, when it decided that Scripture is to be explained according to the Doctors of the Church, or as long custom has approved. So that new expositions are not to be forbidden, except when they are at variance with the sense of the age [2]."

In the year 1557, Paul IV. addressed a Council of Divines assembled to advise with him on a question respecting marriage in these remarkable words :—

" I beg you not to stop at the doings and example of my predecessors, which I desire to follow only so far as the authority of Scripture and the reasonings of Divines shall lead you so to do. . . . I doubt not but that I and my predecessors have sometimes been permitted to err, not only in the matter before us, but also in many other kinds of things, and yet we are not in any wise to be condemned. For God so governs the Church, that for a certain time He hides from it many things which afterwards He reveals [3]." " Who knows then whether God may not intend that things concerning the indissoluble bond of marriage, which are unknown to the rest, shall be now brought into open light through us ? "

The doctrine here served ·a double purpose ; it furnished the Pope with an excuse for past errors,

[2] Hist. Conc. Trid. Sarpi, l. ii. p. 124.   Aug. Trin. 1620.
[3] In Epp. Launoii, l. iii. Ep. i. ; tom. v. P. i. p. 264.

and gave him at the same time much of the con- fidence which a belief in his own infallibility would have inspired.

To the objection that the present Church cannot decree the Divine authority of books, respecting which the Council of Laodicea, "assembled in the Holy Ghost," was at the least "in doubt," Alphonsus a Castro makes the following reply:—

" The weakness of the inference is proved by the progressive advance which a man makes in knowledge, which is such that he now knows for certain many things of which he was once either doubtful or altogether ignorant. Why may not the same thing be said of the Church in its members? Will the Church be always in the same state, so as never to make any progress? Not so. For as it advances in virtue and goodness, *so does it also in knowledge and doctrine*, God enlightening it ever more daily. For this reason the Church is compared in the Canticles to the morning dawn, ' Who is she that looketh forth as the morning?' But the dawn grows brighter, beams more gloriously, as time goes on. So, too, if we will bring the Church back from the goal to her place of starting, how little was the light in the beginning of the infant Church! whether you carry it back to the days of just Abel, or to the death of Christ when it arose new in the heavens. For then that hidden mystery was known to very few, and those to whom it was given to know it (I except the Apostles), *did not know it so fully and perfectly as their successors*. For the dawn expands, and the sun rises and pours out on our eyes more copious rays of his light. Whence it comes to pass that we know many things now of which the first Fathers were either doubtful or. quite ignorant [4]."

Elsewhere, defending the modern Indulgences, the same author declares:—

" There are many things known to later writers of which the ancient were utterly ignorant. . . . . Whence I doubt not but there are many things, of which we at present know nothing, that will be clearly and evidently discovered by our posterity [5]."

Salmeron, a celebrated author among the Jesuits, often expresses the same opinion with great boldness; as for example:—

" There is then in the Church a consent to the whole doctrine of the faith, *which, however, admits of addition in essentials*, though not of contradiction:—but in things accidental and adventitious even change [6]."

Baronius, your great historian:—

" In the interpretation of the Scriptures, the Catholic Church does not always and in all things follow the most holy Fathers, whom, on account of their lofty erudition, we deservedly name the doctors of the Church, how clear soever it may be that they were imbued with the power of the Holy Spirit above other men [7]."

This doctrine has been found by Estius and others in the writings of Gregory the Great; though it is certain that his meaning was not what

[4] Adv. Hæres. l. i. fol. 3, fa. 2.   Colon. 1549.

[5] L. viii., fol. 184, fa. 2.

[6] In Epist. ad Rom. P. iii. Disp. vi. Opp. tom. xiii. p. 208. Colon. 1604.

[7] A.D. 34, § ccix.; tom. i. p. 188.   Luc. 1738.

they suppose. I quote the author whom I have named, a very eminent divine of your communion, because he appears to see no impropriety in the opinion which he erroneously ascribes to Gregory :—

" He thus concludes respecting the Apostles (Hom. xvi. in Ezek.) :—' They therefore knew more of divine science than the Prophets ; because what the latter saw by the Spirit alone, the former saw also with the eyes of the body.' But of the whole course of the Church's existence, he adds :—' By how much nearer the world draws to an end, so much the more widely is the entrance to heavenly knowledge opened to us.' And very like to this is what we read in the same author (Lib. ix. Moral. cap. 8) :— 'As the end of the world presses on, heavenly knowledge makes progress, and grows more abundantly with time.' And a little after :—' Whatever was hid in the beginning of the holy Church, the end is daily bringing to light.' Though S. Thomas (Aquinas) appears to differ from this opinion of Gregory (2. 2. 9. 1. art. 7, ad 4,) attributing a fuller knowledge of mysteries to those who were nearer to Christ, e.g. to John the Baptist, as the last of the Prophets, and to the Apostles, as the first preachers of the Gospel[8]."

· [8] In Lib. Sent. Comm. l. iii. Dist. xxv. § 3; vol. ii. p. 79. Par. 1638. Gregory lived under an impression that the day of judgement was actually impending in his time ; and in one of his works (Dial. iv.) has put together a number of superstitious tales of dreams, apparitions, &c., which he believed to be revelations from above designed to prepare men for that event. " He observes that many things have been discovered a little while ago, which were unknown in antiquity, concerning the state of souls after death ; the reason which he gives for it is this, *that at the end of the world drawing near, the transactions of the other begin to be discovered.*" Dupin, Cent. vi. *S. Gregory ;*

About the same time, Gretser, the Jesuit:—

"The rule does not say that that is an Apostolical tradition which the universal Church has always and at all times believed, but that which the whole Church embraces and believes at the present time; for it may so happen that in the past ages the matter was not fully opened up and perfectly discussed [9]."

A little later, Petavius, another learned Jesuit, in a formal system of divinity, endeavoured to convince the world that the Church did not rightly hold the doctrine of the Holy Trinity, until the fourth century after Christ [1]. His motive in advancing this opinion was probably the same as that of certain modern writers in reproducing it,—a desire to supply his Church with a precedent for adding to the Creed articles of faith unknown in previous ages. His representation was, however, virtually retracted.

In the original draft of the famous *Exposition de la Foi* of Bossuet, the imperfection of the ante-Nicene theology was asserted as expressly as by Petavius himself:—

"For Monsieur Daillé, he thinks fit to confine himself

---

vol. i. p. 581. He cannot, therefore, be quoted as having held a general theory of development, or any thing approaching to it.

[9] Defens. Bellarm. De Verbo Dei, l. iv. c. ix. Opp. tom. viii. p. 895. Ratisb. 1736. The primitive rule, *Quod semper, quod ubique, quod ab omnibus*, is here expressly rejected.

[1] Theol. Dogm.; De Trin. l. i. c. iii. § 1. For the retractation, see tom. ii. Præf. c. i. § xii., c. vi. §§ i. ii.

to the first three centuries, in which it is certain that the Church, more exercised in suffering than in writing, has left many things to be cleared afterwards, both in its doctrine and in its practice [2]."

The work of Bossuet was entrusted for correction to some Doctors of the Sorbonne, the Divines of which were always strong assertors of the immutability of the traditions of the Church, and the result was that the above passage was, with many others, suppressed.

IV. The series shall conclude with two examples from the revived English school of Developmentists. You will thus be enabled to trace the identity, under various forms of expression, of an ingenious and subtle hypothesis, by which observant members of the Church of Rome have laboured during the last four hundred years to explain and justify those changes in her doctrine and practice, which they found themselves unable to deny, and wanted faith and courage to condemn. The following extract is from a writer, who, when he penned it, was still a member of the Church of England, though tending rapidly towards your communion. His view, according to his own statement, might be expressed by the position, that doctrines " not only may be, but " actually have been " ruled by the Church as part of

---

[2] Wake's Exposition of the Faith of the Church of England : a *Collection of Passages*, &c., annexed to Preface. No. 3.

Z

the necessary faith, which were not held *even implicitly* by the early Fathers :"—

"Viewing, then, the Church collective starting after the Apostle's death on her aggressive course, we find her, as might have been expected, fully possessed of, and energizing · in, these doctrines, which are the cardinal points of faith : e.g. the Trinity, the Incarnation, the Eucharistic Presence. . . . . On these subjects, then, the task which remains for her is, to bring before her own notice one particular after another of her complex and mysterious consciousness, to regard it steadily and distinctly, to project it, as it were, from the moral on the intellectual faculty, to express in accurate language the result of such projection, and to follow out the result so obtained into those intellectual consequences which necessarily flow from it. . . . . The science of *these* doctrines (and it is a science which has been in fact growing, we may say, almost to the present day, nay, which is still pregnant with an indefinite number of unexplored inferences) will consist entirely of *analytical and deducible* propositions. . . . .

" Still, though the foundations of the faith were fully realized from the first, *other* principles there were, no doubt, and very far from unimportant ones, which were deposited, as it were, in germ within the bosom of the Church, that her internal action might gradually nurture them, or external circumstances hasten their appearance on the surface. And *on these subjects* the Church herself does form *synthetical* judgments, by dint of moral action and meditation. In other doctrines, again, the spiritual experience which she accumulates from age to age forms a most important part of the premisses to be taken into

account; here, then, also part of the premisses are synthetical. And it should be pointed out distinctly, that
when this theory of 'development' is maintained, it is
not necessary, in order to account for it, to allege, as the
cause of such maintenance, the necessities of some immediate object, or undue sympathy with some external
system. If developments had not existed in Christianity,
it would have been necessary to suppose that God works
a continual miracle to separate off Christian from all other
religious and moral truth. It is of the very nature of
moral belief, that the same principles shall appear, in each
successive age, *in a new aspect, or a more advanced growth,
or more harmonious proportions* [3]."

When Dr. Newman entered the Church of
Rome, the grounds on which he thought the step
might be defended were given to the world in an
Essay on the Development of Christian Doctrine.
The object of this work is thus stated by him-
self:—

" The following Essay is directed towards a solution of
the difficulty which has been stated,—the difficulty which
lies in the way of using the testimony of our most natural
informant concerning the doctrine and worship of Christianity, viz. the history of eighteen hundred years. The
view on which it is written has at all times, perhaps, been
implicitly adopted by theologians, and, I believe, has
recently been illustrated by several distinguished writers
of the Continent, such as De Maistre and Möhler: viz.

---

[3] Ideal of a Christian Church, by W. G. Ward, p. 549. The above
passage was reprinted in this work by Mr. Ward from an article
which he contributed to the British Critic.

that the increase and expansion of the Christian creed and ritual, and the variations which have attended the process in the case of individual writers and Churches, are the necessary attendants on any philosophy or polity which takes possession of the intellect and heart, and has any wide or extended dominion; that from the nature of the human mind, time is necessary for the full comprehension and perfection of great ideas; and that the highest and most wonderful truths, though communicated to the world once for all by inspired teachers, could not be comprehended all at once by the recipients, but, as received and transmitted by minds not inspired and through media which were human, have required only the longer time and deeper thought for their full elucidation. This may be called the Theory of Developments [4]."

[4] Essay, Introd. p. 27.   2nd edit.

LETTER VIII.

PART II.

I PROPOSE now to take, one by one, some of the peculiar doctrines and practices of the Church of Rome, and to show, from the confession of your own writers, and from the language of the Fathers, that they are not of the antiquity that you suppose; and, consequently, that the divines whom I have already quoted were by no means engaged in a superfluous task, when they attempted to show that, even if unprimitive, they might nevertheless be right. I shall first call your attention to two errors, the one in doctrine, the other in practice, connected with the Sacrament of the Lord's Supper.

I. OF TRANSUBSTANTIATION.

I. The Church of England, following the teaching of Holy Scripture and of the Primitive Church, maintains the real presence of Christ in the holy Eucharist, without presuming to define the manner of that presence. The Church of Rome, on the contrary, not only imposes on her children a definition of the mode in which He is present, but denounces a curse against all who deny it :—

" If any one shall say, that in the most holy Sacrament of the Eucharist, the substance of bread and wine remains together with the Body and Blood of our Lord Jesus Christ, and shall deny that wonderful and singular change of the whole substance of the bread into the Body, and of the whole substance of the wine into the Blood,—the appearances of bread and wine alone being left,—which change the Catholic Church most fitly terms transubstantiation, let him be Anathema [1]."

She teaches further, under the same penalty, that :—

" In the Sacrament of the most holy Eucharist are contained, truly, really, and substantially, the Body and Blood, together with the soul and Divinity of our Lord Jesus Christ,—and so whole Christ [2]."

Or more fully, in the Catechism of Trent :—

" It ought to be explained by Pastors, that not only the true Body of Christ, and whatever appertains to the true nature of a body, as bones and sinews, but that whole Christ is also contained in this sacrament. It should be taught, then, that ' Christ ' is the name of God and man, that is, of One Person, in Whom the Divine and

---

[1] Sess. xiii. De Euch. Sacr. Can. ii.
[2] Ibid. Can. i.

human natures have been united. Wherefore it includes either substance, His Divinity and His entire human nature, consisting of the soul and all the parts of the body and the blood also. For since in heaven complete humanity has been united to Divinity in one person and hypostasis, it is unlawful to imagine that the Body, which is in the Sacrament, has been separated from the same Divinity [3]."

Another statement for which the Church of Rome has made herself responsible is that, " in the Eucharist, the accidents (of the bread and wine) subsist together without a subject :"—

" The species of bread and wine subsist together in this Sacrament without any subject. For since . . . the Body and Blood of the Lord are truly in the Sacrament, so that no substance of bread and wine is any longer there; forasmuch as those accidents cannot inhere in the Body and Blood of Christ, it remains that, in a manner above the whole order of nature, they support themselves without dependence on any other thing [4]."

Before we proceed to show that the teaching of these extracts is at variance with that of the early Church, it is necessary to point out distinctly the sense in which they are to be understood.

It has been thought doubtful by some English writers, whether the Church of Rome necessarily understands, by the transubstantiation of the bread and wine, that physical and material change of the

---

[3] Cat. Trid. P. ii. De Euch. Sacr. c. xxxi.
[4] Ibid. c. xliv.

consecrated elements, which is so clearly taught by
the overwhelming majority of your divines, and
popularly believed among you.   The doubt is built
on a distinction made between *matter* and *substance*.
Thus, Mr. Robert Wilberforce :—

"By *matter* is meant that of which the senses take
note ; by *substance* an abstract notion which the intellect
obtains by disregarding those accidents by which one
individual of a class is distinguished from others [5]."

They conceive, therefore, that when the Church
of Rome asserts, and the Church of England denies,
the doctrine of Transubstantiation, they are speaking
of two different things :—

"The word *substance*, in the twenty-eighth Article,
seems intended to express that which is material in the
consecrated elements; the *sacramentum*, namely, or
outward and visible sign. . . . . The meaning of the word
substance, as understood by the schoolmen, was wholly
different.   The Aristotelian philosophy, on which their
expressions were moulded, divided all objects into the
accidental part, which was an object to the senses, and
the substantial, which was an object only to the mind.
By *substance*, therefore, in the holy Eucharist, they understood not the *sacramentum*, but the *res sacramenti*.   This
more subtle sense of the word *substance*, which had
become familiar in theology, was employed by the Council
of Trent [6]," &c.

It should be observed here, in the first place, that

[5] Doctrine of the Incarnation, Note on ch. x. ; p. 446.   Ed. 4.
[6] Doctrine of the Holy Eucharist, ch. v. ; p. 108.   Ed. 3.

there is no reason whatever to doubt the meaning
of the twenty-eighth Article.   The word *substance*
as there used not only "seems," but certainly *is*
"intended to express that which is material in the
consecrated elements."   And this is capable of a
very simple proof. Our present Articles were "published under the superintendence of Bishop Jewel,"
who also "made several minute corrections" in
them, and "put the finishing hand to them [7]."   The
sense in which he employed that word is, therefore,
the sense to be assigned to it in these formularies.
Now it so happens that a very precise definition of
the term in question is found in his writings :—

"In every natural thing two things are specially to be
considered : the Substance and the Accident. . . . . For
example, the *material* thing that feedeth us, and is changed
into the blood, and nourishment of our bodies, is called
the *substance* of the bread ; the whiteness, the roundness,
the thickness, the sweetness, and other the like that are
perceived outwardly by our senses are called accidents [8]."

And again :—

"It is well known that *materia* evermore is *substantia*
and never otherwise [9]."

To the same purpose Bishop Ridley, whose assistance is "generally said" to have been used in the
first compilation of the Articles [1] :—

---

[7] Short's Church History, ch. x. App. C. § 485 ; p. 326.   Ed. 2.
[8] Defence of the Apology, c. 13, div. 1 ; P. ii. ; p. 231.   London,
1609.
[9] Ibid. p. 255.   [1] Short, § 482 ; p. 322.

"Origen [2], speaking of the sacrament of the Lord's Supper, doth mean and teach that the material substance thereof is received and digested, as the material substance of other bread and meats is;—which could not be if there were no material substance of bread at all, as the fantastical opinion of Transubstantiation doth put [3]."

The Church of England, then, in denying Transubstantiation, must mean beyond all question to deny a change of *matter into matter*, as the effect of the consecration in the Lord's Supper.

But we are told that the Church of Rome does not assert this; that in *her* formularies *substance* is not equivalent to *matter*, and consequently that while she denies that the *substance* of the bread remains after consecration, she does not deny that the *matter* is still left.

One objection to this opinion occurs *in limine*. A mere "abstract notion," at which the intellect arrives by a purely intellectual process, a simple conception of the mind, without objective reality, does not fall within the legitimate province of true theology at all. To affirm that such an "abstract notion" of bread is changed into the similar "abstract notion" of Christ's Body, is to deal with words and

---

[2] In S. Matt. tom. xi. § i.   Opp. tom. iii. p. 500.

[3] Treatise against Transubstantiation, in Enchir. Theol. vol. i. p. 154.   The Reformers continually represent the Roman doctrine as teaching a "*corporal*" or "carnal presence," the presence of Christ's "*natural and organical Body*," &c.   See, e. g. Catech. Noell., Ibid. vol. ii. p. 230; Protestatio Ridleii, Ibid. vol. i. p. 85; Cranmer in Foxe, vol. iii. p. 38; &c.

thoughts, and not with things. To make an assent to this proposition a term of Christian communion is at once an outrage to common sense and a crime against religion.

It will hardly be suggested that Mr. Wilberforce, while defining "substance" to be an "abstract notion," has in reality understood by it something more. The doctrine of the objective existence of a "substance," in the metaphysical sense of the word, if now held by any, is a mere relic of the exploded system of Realism, and involves a principle which he has himself distinctly classed among the "erroneous" opinions of "the schoolmen [4]."

But what are the *positive* grounds, on which it is alleged that the Council of Trent excluded the notion of matter from its definition of substance, when it employed this latter term in its determinations respecting the holy Eucharist? They are not stated by Mr. Wilberforce, and I am not able to supply the omission. On the contrary, I find every reason to believe that, in affirming a change of *substance*, the Council meant to affirm a change of *matter*, whether those terms are co-extensive in signification or not [5]; and, therefore,

[4] Incarnation, ch. iii. § 1.
[5] I express myself thus, because I believe that, while all parties knew perfectly well what the Roman view of the Real Presence was, the word *substance* was not employed at this period, any more than it is now, to express always precisely the same notion. Thus *matter*, as may be seen in the text, was sometimes identical with *substance*,

that the Church of Rome does plainly teach the
"material presence" of Christ's Body after the consecration,—the very thing which "the Church of
England in denying transubstantiation" is said to
"mean apparently to deny [6]."

In the first place, it is not conceivable that the
compilers of our Articles, learned and thoughtful as
they undeniably were; trained, too, as they had
been, in the philosophy and divinity of the schools;
and versed in all the controversies of their day,
should, in a question of such moment, have played
at cross purposes with the divines of Rome, from
ignorance of the proper meaning of a scholastic
term, which was "familiar," by the hypothesis, to
every student of theology.

There is direct proof, however, that the question
at issue was really understood perfectly by both
parties, and that they were engaged, the one in

sometimes a part of it. Again at the Council of Trent, while the
Dominicans include the matter of the bread in their notion of its substance, the Franciscans seem to imply that *their* substance is immaterial; for they say that bulk, when by a miracle it occupies no
space, has put on the nature of substance. See p. 353. The narrative
of Sarpi implies, however, that the language of the schools was not
very well understood at Trent:—"The Elector of Cologne, who, with
John Gropper, was a constant listener to their debates, is reported to
have said that, ... with regard to their positive statements of doctrine, it seemed to him not very likely that they sufficiently understood the subject about which they talked so confidently, but rather
that they were following the form and custom of the schools," l. iv.;
p. 265. If they did not *understand* the words which they employed,
they could have used them at all times correctly.

[6] Incarnation, Note u. s.; p. 450.

attacking, the other in defending, identically the
same doctrine. There are no traces, to give one example, of any ambiguity in the controversy between
Jewel and Harding ;—whose joint evidence will, I
presume, be accepted as conclusive on this point.
On the contrary, the transubstantiation of which
Harding speaks is clearly said by him to involve an
actual change of the material parts of the bread
and wine. Thus, when the Bishop quotes Origen
as saying that " the bread which is sanctified by the
word of God, *as touching the material substance
thereof*, goeth into the belly," his opponent accuses
him of mistranslation, with a view to persuade the
ignorant that " the *matter and substance* of very
bread remain." He gives his own version of the
disputed clause :—" *according to that material which
it hath*," and meets the argument of Jewel by asserting that Origen meant by " *that material* the accidents or qualities remaining after consecration,"
and " not the *matter* of bread itself, *which is one
part of a perfect substance* [7]."

It must be supposed, too, that the Fathers at
Trent made it their business to declare the doctrine
which prevailed at that period in the Church which
they professed to represent ;—and it is impossible
to deny that general opinion was then altogether in
favour of the theory of a *material* change.

[7] Defence, P. ii., u. s.; p. 254. This point might be proved also
from the disputations of Philpot, Ridley, Cranmer, &c., in Foxe, vol. iii.
An abstract is given by Collier, P. ii. b. v. ; pp. 355—359, 367—369.

And what were they understood to teach by the great leaders of thought in your communion, when their decrees were put forth ?

The Catechism of Trent has taught us that the "accidents" of the bread and wine are left after the consecration "without a subject." Now we are informed by Bellarmine, that "according to the better philosophers, the matter is the subject of the accidents." The inference is unavoidable, that, unless the compilers of this Catechism were ignorant of the better philosophy, they certainly meant to teach that the *matter* of the bread and wine passes away, when the transubstantiation takes place.

The same great authority, whose works, we are told, stand at Rome in the place of all tradition [8], argues that to hold that the matter of the bread remains is to contradict the doctrine of the Council of Trent, that "the *whole* substance of the bread is changed into the Body of the Lord [9]." It is therefore certain that he considered the matter of the bread to be the same as its substance, or else to be a part of it.

How deliberately this doctrine, that "the matter of the bread does not remain," has been adopted by your teachers may be understood from the fact that they do not think such a destruction of the original

---

[8] Bossuet, in Biogr. Univ. at *Bellarmine*.

[9] De Sacr. Euch. l. iii. c. xiii. ; Disp. tom. iii. p. 152.

matter necessary in every miraculous change. LETTER
Bellarmine, for example, allows that in the change VIII.
of water into wine at Cana, of Moses' rod into a PART II.
serpent, &c., "it is probable that the first matter ART. I.
remained *in utroque termino*," but adds, that "in SECT. I.
this change, (i.e. in that which he supposes in the
Eucharist,) it is certain that it does not remain [1]."

Such, then, has been the teaching of Roman
Catholic divines during the last three centuries;
and such, therefore, we must suppose to be the
teaching of their Church, as settled by the Council
to which we are referred by Mr. Wilberforce.

In the absence of all evidence to the contrary,
the considerations already adduced appear to me
decisive; but, in reality, they are superfluous. The
meaning of the Tridentine Fathers is made known
to us by the historical record of their deliberations.
It appears that a long and abstruse discussion
respecting the *mode* of transubstantiation arose in
their thirteenth Session between the Franciscans
and Dominicans. These parties differed widely

[1] Ibid. c. xviii.; p. 155. He shows at length why the "matter " of
the bread cannot remain in answer to Durandus, who held that it
does (c. xiii.; p. 152). As the property of nourishing, &c., is not
lost, this change of the matter leads to a difficulty which is sur-
mounted by conjecturing the *substitution* of other matter where it
becomes necessary :—" If there be a corruption of the species as in
nourishing man, in burning, &c., then matter is required, but this is
substituted by God in that very instant of time in which those species
cease to exist, and in which a something else is generated, and this
without a miracle," &c. Ibid. c. xxiv., p. 162. Sim. Liebermann,
Instit. Theol. l. vi. P. iii. Art. ii.; tom. ii. p. 500. Mogunt. 1853.

from each other upon this point; but they agreed, as their language shows, in believing that, after the consecration, the material part of the bread is no longer on the altar, and that its place there is occupied by the material Body of Christ :—

" The Dominicans would have it that Christ is said to be in the Eucharist, not as coming into the Eucharist from some other place in which He was before, but because the substance of bread is converted into the Body of Christ, which is done in that place in which the bread was, without His going to that place; the whole substance of the bread being transmuted into the whole substance of the body, [that is to say [2],] *the matter of the bread into the matter of the body, and the form into the form,* &c. . . . . .

" But the Franciscans would have it that . . . . God has so ordained, that where the Body of Christ is, there the substance of another thing remains not, but ceases to be ; yet not so as to pass into nothing, because the substance of Christ succeeds it ;—and that this is truly called transubstantiation, not because the one substance is made out of the other, as the Dominicans assert, but because the one succeeds the other. For that the mode of Christ's presence in heaven does not differ from the mode of His presence in the Sacrament as to substance, but *only* in respect of bulk; that in heaven the size of His Body takes up the space corresponding to it in dimensions, but that in the Sacrament it has a substantial existence, and occupies no space. That either mode, therefore, is true,

---

[2] The clause in brackets is interposed by Dupin, who gives these arguments at length. It shows clearly in what sense he understood the word *substance.* Cent. xvi. *Council of Trent, Sess.* xiii. ; vol. iii. p. 475.

real, and substantial, and even natural, with regard to the LETTER
substance, but that in respect of bulk, the mode of its VIII.
PART II.
being in heaven is natural, *and in the Sacrament, mira-* ART. I.
SECT. I.
culous: and that they differ in this respect only,—that in
heaven, bulk has the effect of bulk, whereas in the Sacrament, it puts on the nature of substance [3]."

It is evident, then, that the doctrine of a material
change was held by both of the parties who, upon
questions respecting this Sacrament, divided the
Council between them. The Dominicans said
expressly, that " the matter of the bread is changed
into the matter of Christ's Body;" while their
opponents, too eager to dispute on other points,
showed no desire to contest this; but, on the contrary, proposed themselves an explanation of the
mystery which necessarily involves the same principle. For they implied that the Body of Christ in
the Sacrament has bulk as well as substance, and
bulk has no existence, except as a property of

[3] Sarpi, Hist. Conc. Trid. Sess. xiii. l. iv.; p. 265. Pallavicino
complains bitterly of Sarpi for having recorded these disputes; because their publication might give men the impression that there had
been difference of opinion about the points actually defined. He is
therefore careful to explain, with Sarpi, that the Council did not
touch the subject of those disputes, but framed its definitions in
accordance with the views of both parties. Dell' Hist. del Conc. di
Trento, l. xii. c. i., P. ii. p. 266; c. vi., p. 291. In Roma, 1664.
The same author, in explaining the propriety of the term " transubstantiation," asserted by the Council (see p. 342), states the notion
which it was chosen to express in a manner much to our purpose :—
" The one substance is changed into the other, the whole into the
whole, without any common matter remaining, without precedent
alteration, and in an instant," c. vii., p. 295.

A a

matter [4]. One of the difficulties, from which the interpretation now proposed is free, they sought to avoid, by suggesting that bulk is in this instance deprived by a special miracle of its natural relation to space.

Now we are told by the historian that the decrees of the Council were purposely expressed in such terms, as "to satisfy both parties, and to be easily adapted to the sense of each." The opinions, therefore, upon which there was no question between them, and, among these, the opinion of a material change in the sacred elements, were accepted and approved by the Council, and are accordingly the authorized doctrine of the present Church of Rome.

Moreover, the denial of this doctrine was condemned, and, therefore, the doctrine itself affirmed,

---

[4] So that, whatever they meant by 'substance,' they must have believed the Body of Christ to be materially present. But if they really understood the schoolmen (see Note [5], p. 347), they certainly comprehended *matter* in *substance ;* for these taught, that "in things composed of matter and form," *essence,* or *substance* (substantia quidditatis rei = οὐσία = essentia), "signifies not form simply, nor matter simply, but a something composed of *matter* and common form." Aquinas, Summa Theol. P. i. Q. xxix. A. ii. ad 3[m], p. 59. Colon. 1604. By saying, then, that in the Sacrament the bulk of Christ's Body "puts on the condition of substance," the Franciscans would mean to assert with Aquinas, that "the dimensive quantity of His Body is there *per modum substantiæ*" (P. iii. Q. lxxvi. A. iv. ad 2[m], p. 169) ; or as it was quaintly expressed by Cranmer's opponents at Oxford :—" Corpus quantum, sed non per modum quanti " (Collier, P. ii. b. v., p. 368) ;—a proposition which with them could not possibly imply that *substance* meant something immaterial.

by the Church of Rome, more than a century before the framing of the decrees of Trent. This was done when the following propositions, attributed to Wycliffe, were denounced by the Council of Constance as heretical and impious:—

" 1. The substance of the material bread, and similarly the substance of the material wine, remain in the Sacrament of the Altar. 2. The accidents of bread do not remain without a subject in the said Sacrament. 3. Christ is not in the said Sacrament identically and really, in *proper bodily* presence[5]."

This is of course decisive, though we take "substance" in the philosophical sense. From "the substance of *material* bread" it is impossible to exclude the substance of the matter of which that bread is composed. We are here taught, then, that this matter, in its substance, or essential part, does not remain after consecration, but is superseded by a proper bodily presence, identical and real, of Christ.

The great Lateran Council in 1215 was the first

[5] Sess. viii. Mansi, tom. xxvii. col. 632. With the remark in the text on the language of the first proposition compare Aquinas, P. i. Q. lxxxv. A. i. p. 160:—"Res materiales non possunt intelligi sine materia." By condemning the second, the Church of Rome affirms that the accidents of the bread are left without their subject, i. e. its matter (see p. 350). Now it is taught by Roman Catholic divines, that "by virtue of real concomitancy the whole dimensive quantity of Christ's Body, and all the accidents thereof, are in this Sacrament" (Aquinas, P. iii. Q. lxxvi. A. iv. concl., p. 169); but no corresponding theory is put forth to explain that the accidents of this Body subsist with a subject. The inference is, that the *matter*, which is their subject, is supposed to be present with them.

to express the supposed effect of the consecration'
by the term "transubstantiation." As its decree
was drawn up by Innocent III., and adopted without
debate, we must have recourse to the works of
that Pope, to ascertain the sense in which its
language is to be understood. The following sentence from his Treatise on the Mass is clear to the
point before us, and, as it appears to me, entirely
satisfactory :—

"The *matter* of the bread and wine is changed into the
substance of the Flesh and Blood ;—nor is any thing added
to the Body, but transubstantiated into the Body [6]."

Even so early as the middle of the eleventh
century, the Western Church had been committed,
as far as a Pope and Roman Council could commit
it, to a very gross expression of this material theory.
I allude to the following declaration, which was
extorted by Nicholas II., in 1059, from Berengarius,
who had written in favour of the more ancient
doctrine [7] :—

[6] Myst. Lib. Missæ, l. iv. c. vii.   Opp. tom. i. p. 378.   Colon. 1575.
[7] " I have said that Humbert is a champion of the truth, because
he says that the most holy bread of the altar is the body of Christ ;—
who however himself,—wherein he is an enemy of the truth,—denies
that the bread remains after the consecration of the altar." Berengarius de Sacrâ Cœnâ, p. 31.   Ed. Vischers, Berlin, 1834.   " By the
consecration of the altar the bread and wine become sacraments of
religion,—not that they cease to be what they were, but that they are
what they were, and are changed to something else." Bereng. p. 123.
He claimed to teach the ancient and catholic doctrine :—" You consider me a heretic because I am not ignorant of the incorruptibility
of Christ's Body, because I avow a belief that the bread, an object of
sense, is made a sacrament by the consecration of the altar, is the

"I agree with the holy Roman Church . . . that the bread and wine which are placed on the altar are, after consecration, not only a sacrament, but even the true Body and Blood of our Lord Jesus Christ; and that these are sensibly, and not merely sacramentally, but in truth handled and broken by the hands of the priest, and ground by the teeth of the faithful[8]."

Language like this may sometimes be explained away as a mere flourish of rhetoric, or the unguarded effusion of devout feeling[9]; but in a studied confession of faith, propounded by a Pope in council as a test of orthodoxy, no explanation of the kind would be admissible. Here every thing is deliberate, every word must be understood to the letter.

It is quite clear, then, that the Church of Rome

Body of Christ;—but without this heresy no one ever was, is, or will be, a catholic," p. 34. He constantly quotes the chief Latin Fathers as witnessing to his view.

[8] Bowden's Life of Gregory VII., b. iii. ch. xvi.; vol. ii. p. 243. A hundred and thirteen Bishops were present at this Council. Besides attending to the affair of Berengarius, it enacted thirteen Canons and published a constitution respecting the election of Popes. The Church of Rome, therefore, was fully represented by it. Landon's Manual of Councils, p. 538.

[9] It may be well to give an instance or two of the effect of this belief on the authorized language of devotion. E. g. "The sight, the feeling, and the taste are here deceived" (from the hymn *Adoro te devote*, Garden of the Soul, p. 168; ed. 1839). "Under the familiar forms of bread and wine Thou permittest Thyself to be seen and touched and tasted" (Litany of the Sacrament, Ibid. p. 388). He could not Himself be "seen, touched, and tasted," if the seeming bread were not the actual matter of His Body, but the mere "substance" of philosophy; nor would the senses be "deceived" if the matter of the bread remained after consecration; for in that case the impression conveyed to them would correspond to the real nature of the object.

does not accept the apology which has been offered on her behalf.   Her doctrine, beyond further question, is that the very matter of the bread and wine passes away in consecration, and that the very matter of Christ's Body and Blood is thenceforth in its place [1].

[1] A recent controversy within the Anglo-Roman communion puts the intrinsic grossness of Transubstantiation in a very strong light. A well-known Irish priest, named Cahill, had taken upon himself to explain the doctrine of Transubstantiation in a letter addressed to a Dissenting Minister:—"Transubstantiation, though a stupendous, mysterious fact, and beyond the power of men, is yet, Sir, a very common occurrence with God; and indeed may be called one of the most general laws of nature. . . . . He created man by changing 'the slime of the earth' into the flesh and bones of Adam in His first official act of transubstantiation. . . . . Christ changed water into wine at the wedding in Cana. . . . . The bread and wine which you and all men may have eaten on this day has been changed into flesh and blood. . . . . The universal crop of wood, and grasses and flowers, and vegetables, and human and animal food, which the earth annually produces, is an actual evidence of Transubstantiation by the word of God the Father on the productive energy of the entire earth.   The hat on your head, the silk in your cravat, &c. &c., even the paper of your spurious Bible, &c. are such evidences of Transubstantiation, that one can scarcely conceive how you could read that very Bible without being burned with scalding shame at the stark staring nonsense and incongruous maniasm you have written to me on the subject."   In Rambler, New Ser., vol. i. p. 171. · These illustrations are condemned in the Magazine from which I quote (said to be written by converts to the Roman Communion), as "most profane and irreverent," p. 172, and "equivalent to an assertion that no real transubstantiation takes place in the consecrated elements," that word having been adopted "to express the annihilation of one substance and the substitution of another," &c., p. 173.   In a word, Dr. Cahill does not appear to have specified that, in his illustrations, the original matter remains *in utroque termino*, while, in the Eucharist, the first matter is destroyed and another substituted for it.   Had he done this, they might have passed.   He could not have been blamed for illustrating one instance of physical, corporeal, and material change by

II. Such, then, being the doctrine of the Church of Rome, the case for England, and against her, may be thus stated:—that, whereas in the writers of the first six centuries, we cannot find a single passage, which, when fairly viewed in the context, or compared with other statements of the same author, does not harmonize with the English doctrine of the Real Presence, there are very many which no ingenuity has been able to reconcile with the Roman Catholic. Here, then, you have one instance in which the Church of Rome has exercised that authority, which has been claimed for her, as " mistress of the faith," by adding a new and a most important article to the primitive Creed. I shall subjoin several testimonies in proof, some of them extending beyond the period which I have named, and must then leave you to choose between the ancient doctrine of your Church and its mediæval development.

others of the same kind, if he had not (perhaps in inadvertence rather than ignorance) implied that they took place in a similar manner. At all events the Reviewer should have felt that such illustrations cannot fail to occur to a believer in Transubstantiation, and have known that Dr. Cahill was not the first to put them upon paper. E. g. the famous Salmeron :—" Man by virtue of natural heat turns food into flesh and blood, and into bones, sinews, humours, nails, hairs; grass is changed into the fleeces of sheep, hard stones in the stomach of doves into flesh; iron is digested by the ostrich and becomes flesh; an egg is changed into the wonderful peacock, a little acorn into the mighty oak, the watery juice of the vine into wine; bees turn whatever they eat on the flowers into wax and honey; water is changed by the force of cold into frost and ice. If, therefore, art and nature can do so much, what may not God?" Comm. in Ev. tom. ix. Tr. xvi. p. 110.

i. S. Clemens of Alexandria :—

"Be sure He partook Himself of *wine*, ... for He blessed the wine when He said, Take drink, this is My Blood,—*the blood of the vine* [2]."

ii. Tertullian, arguing against Marcion, who denied the reality of Christ's body :—

"He made the bread which He took and distributed to His disciples His Body, saying, This is My Body, i.e. a *figure* of My Body. But it would not be a figure, if His Body were not real [3]."

iii. The same argument is thus urged by another against the followers of Marcion and Valentinus :—

"If, as they assert, He was without flesh and without blood, of what flesh, or of what body, or of what blood was it that He gave *images*, (namely, the bread and the cup,) when He charged His disciples to make a memorial of Him with them [4]."

[2] Pædag. l. ii. c. 2, p. 158. Colon. 1688.
[3] C. Marcion. l. iv. c. 40 ; vol. i. p. 403.
[4] Dial. c. Marcion. § iv.; p. 116. Ed. Basle, 1674. Picus, the translator of this dialogue, attempted to nullify its witness by rendering the word εἰκόνας (images) by "sacraments." The passage next quoted in the text presenting the same difficulty, Sextus Senensis conjectured that it was corrupted by heretics; Cardinal Perron and Genebrard, by Erasmus!—Wetstein, Notes, u. s. col. 71. The word εἰκὼν is similarly used by Eusebius, as after; by the Council of C. P. A.D. 754, in Act. vi. Conc. Nic. ii. (Mansi, tom. xiii. col. 263) ; &c. The modern answer to the argument from the use of this and similar words, as *type*, *resemblance*, *figure*, &c., begs the whole question. The Fathers, it is said, believed in Transubstantiation, and their language ought to be understood accordingly. The sense that will accommodate it to that theory, however forced, unnatural, or even absurd it may appear, is therefore necessarily ·the true one. "Since it is certain," says Liebermann, "that they . . . were altogether persuaded that the Body of Christ is substantially contained in the Eucharist, it must be clear that *such* a figure is understood by them as includes the

iv. Origen :—

" It is not the matter of bread, but the word spoken over it, which profits him who eats it in a manner not unworthy of the Lord. And this I say of the *typical* and *symbolical* body [5]."

v. The Fathers at Nicæa :—

" Let us not fix our thoughts unworthily on the bread and the cup set before us, but, lifting up our mind, let us by faith deem that, on that holy table, is lying the Lamb of God, that taketh away the sin of the world [6]," &c.

vi. Eusebius :—

" We have received a charge, according to the laws of the New Testament, to celebrate the memorial of this sacrifice upon a table, by means of *symbols* of His Body and of His saving Blood."

" He delivered to His disciples the *symbols* of His Divine dispensation, commanding them to make the *image* of His own Body [7]."

vii. S. Cyril of Jerusalem :—

·" Those who taste are commanded to taste, not bread, but the *sign* of the Body and Blood of Christ [8]."

thing itself." Instit. Theol. l. vi. P. iii. Art. i.; tom. ii. p. 489. Quite as singular, and equally defiant of every sound principle of reasoning, is the attempt of Bellarmine and others to meet the same difficulty. They require it to be granted that a thing may properly and naturally be called a sign, or figure, or resemblance, of *itself*. " That true Body itself, as it is in the Eucharist, is a type and symbol of itself, as it was on the cross, and as it now is in heaven." Bellarm. de Sacr. Euch. l. ii. c. viii.; tom. iii. p. 122.

[5] Comm. in Matt. tom. xi. § i. Opp. tom. iii. p. 500.
[6] Hist. Conc. Nic. Gelasio Cyz. ascr. c. xxx. Mansi, tom. ii. col. 888.
[7] Demonstr. Evang. l. i. cap. ult., and l. viii. c. i. in fine.
[8] Catech. Myst. v. § xvii.; p. 300.

This writer speaks strongly of a change :—" Know and be fully assured of this, that the seeming bread is not bread, even if it appear so to the taste, but the Body of Christ [9]," &c. ; but his explanation overthrows the doctrine of Rome ; for he institutes a comparison between the sanctification of the elements in the Lord's Supper and that which was imparted to the consecrated oil, with which the newly baptized were at that time anointed :—

" Take care that you do not look upon that as mere oil. For as the bread of the Eucharist after the invocation of the Holy Ghost is no longer simple bread, but the Body of Christ, so also the sacred oil is no longer bare oil, or, so to speak, common after the invocation, but the gift of Christ [1]," &c.

Again he says :—

" He once changed water into wine, . . . and is He not worthy of credit, when He changes wine into blood ? "

But this is closely followed by the words :—

" Wherefore let us with all confidence partake *as* of the Body and Blood of Christ ; for in a *figure* of bread His Body is given thee, in a *figure* of wine His Blood [2]."

viii. A similar contrast presents itself in the writings of S. Gregory of Nyssa :—

" As this holy altar, at which we are standing, is in its

[9] Ibid. iv. § iii. ; p. 294.
[1] Catech. Myst. iii. § iii. ; p. 290.
[2] Cat. Myst. iv. § i. ; p. 292. Grodecius, the Roman Catholic translator of S. Cyril, and Bellarmine, u. s. omit the word ' *as* ' (ὡς) after ' partake.' Ἐν τύπῳ, *in a figure*, they render by *sub specie*. The Benedictines correctly give ' *tanquam* ' and ' *in figura*.'

nature common stone, ... but after its consecration to the service of God . . . . is a holy table, an undefiled altar; . . . . as the bread, again, is up to a time common bread, but when the mystery has made it a sacrifice, is both called, and is, the Body of Christ; . . . and the same power of the word makes the priest reverend and honourable, . . . and one, who but lately was one of the multitude and of the vulgar, becomes all at once a ruler, &c., and this without any change of body or of form; . . . so by analogy of considerations, the water, though it is nothing but water, renews man to the inward regeneration [3]."

It is perfectly clear from this, that the brother of the great Basil knew no more of a transubstantiation of bread and wine, than he did of a transubstantiation of stone, or of water, or of the candidate for holy orders, and yet elsewhere he does not scruple to employ language, which, if Transubstantiation had been the doctrine of the day, would certainly have appeared to his hearers intended to express it :—

"That which is the property of all flesh confessedly belonged to the flesh of Christ : viz. that even that Body was supported by bread ; but the Body was changed to the Divine dignity by the indwelling of God the Word. For that Body was virtually bread, but was sanctified by the indwelling of the Word, who tabernacled in the flesh. By the same virtue, then, whereby the bread that had undergone change in that Body was raised to a Divine power, does the like now also take place (in the holy Eucharist).[4]"

[3] Orat. in Bapt. Christi. Opp. tom. iii. pp. 369—371. Par. 1638.
[4] Orat. Catech. cxxxvii. ; p. 70. Monach. 1835. This passage, if taken to the letter, implies Transubstantiation ; but then it implies

ix. S. Macarius :—

" The great and righteous, kings and prophets, knew that the Saviour was coming, but His sufferings, His crucifixion, &c., or the offering of bread and wine in the Church, as a *type* of His flesh and blood, or that the partakers of the visible bread spiritually eat the flesh of the Lord, &c., these things they knew not [5]."

x. The author of the treatise on the Sacraments, ascribed to S. Ambrose :—

" The priest says : Make this oblation imputed to us, effectual, reasonable, acceptable ; which thing is a figure of the Body and Blood of our Lord Jesus Christ [6]."

also the " error of Durandus," that the same matter exists under either form (see pp. 351, 378),—an opinion which Roman Catholic divines reject. It is therefore useless as a testimony to their doctrine, even without the elucidation of which it admits from other writings of the author. The same remark holds of S. Cyril's comparison of the water turned to wine.

[5] Hom. xxvii. De Dign. Christiani; p. 372. Francof. 1594. His word is ἀντίτυπον, used also by Cyril Hieros. (as above, Myst. v. § xvii.) ; by Greg. Naz. (in Gorgon. Or. xi.; tom. i. p. 187) ; Theodoret (Dial. ii. ; tom. iv. p. 84. Lutet. 1642) ; &c. Bellarmine appears to see much less difficulty in the use of this word than of *figure, type,* &c. In reply to an objection from its occurrence in the Liturgy of S. Basil, he says :—" The Body itself and the Blood of the Lord, as they are under those species, are signs of the same Body and Blood, as they were on the cross ; for the Eucharist represents the Passion of Christ; and perhaps Basil and other Fathers do not call the Eucharist a figure, or type [which, however, many do], but an antitype, for the reason that not all figures are called antitypes, but only those which differ scarcely at all from the truth." He adds an illustration which I feel some difficulty in transcribing :—" It would be a similar case, if a king, at the end of a very serious war, were to desire that the war itself should be represented on the stage for the amusement of the people, and the very same person who had really fought were to represent himself on the stage ; for he would himself be truly the antitype of himself." De Sacr. Euch. l. ii. c. xv. ; tom. iii. p. 128.

[6] " Sacerdos dicit :—Fac nobis, inquit, hanc oblationem adscrip-

"That bread is bread before the words of sacramental
blessing; but when the consecration has been added, from
tam, ratam, rationabilem, acceptabilem, quod figura est Corporis et
Sanguinis Domini nostri Jesu Christi." L. iv. c. v. § 21; tom. v.
p. 231. In the Canon of the Mass, as it now stands, we read :—
"Quam oblationem tu, Deus, ·in omnibus, quæsumus, benedictam,
ascriptam, ratam, rationabilem, acceptabilemque facere digneris."
The sense of the ancient form of consecration appears to have been
ruined by the omission of *nobis* and the intrusion of *benedictam*.
The common traditional rendering of *ascriptam* is *approved*. Berington and Kirk (Faith of Catholics; p. 197. Lond. 1830) give
admitted. Neither of these meanings could it have been intended
to express. In the version given for the benefit of the laity in the
Key of Heaven (p. 111; 17th ed.), the passage is made intelligible
by a very unjustifiable expedient; the important word *rationabilem*
(comp. Rom. xii. 1) being passed over without notice :—" Which oblation do thou, O God, vouchsafe in all respects to bless, *approve*,
ratify, and accept." Critics are not agreed about the authorship of
the treatise *De Sacramentis;* but since it is, in the part from which I
have quoted, only an enlargement on the piece *De Mysteriis* (see
Dupin, Cent. iv. *S. Ambrose*, vol. i. p. 284), certainly written by
S. Ambrose, its teaching at least shows the sense in which that
Father was understood by his early readers. In his brief tract (a
highly oratorical address to the newly baptized) he dwells, in very
strong language, on the change which the consecration of the bread
implies, and Roman Catholic writers have claimed his testimony as
wholly on their side; but when the author *De Sacramentis* follows,
and "explains the change which is made in the sacrament more
largely" (Dupin), we find that the change intended is something very
different from a transubstantiation. We have seen, then, in the case
of S. Cyril and S. Gregory of Nyssa, the literal meaning of passages
modified by the context, or by the teaching of the author in another
portion of his writings; and now in the case of S. Ambrose (supposing
the work *De Sacramentis* not to be his), by the interpretation which his
disciples evidently put upon his words. It is, however, right to point
out that, even when we have no such means of correcting the first apparent meaning of an ancient writer, the Roman Catholic divine cannot
condemn us, if, to reduce it to the true standard of the early Church,
we make an abatement for the extravagances of devout fervour, or
even of popular oratory. For he is himself obliged to have recourse
to the same explanation to bring the very free expressions of certain

bread it becomes the flesh of Christ. . . . How can that which is bread become the Body of Christ? By consecration. : . . If there was so great power in the word of the Lord, that those things began to be which before were not, how much more effectual is it to cause that things *remain what they were*, and be changed into something else [7]? . . . . Thou thyself wast, . . . but wast an old creature;—after thou wast consecrated, thou didst begin to be a new creature [8]."

The first part of this second extract has been quoted by Bellarmine and others as a testimony to the Roman doctrine; because it speaks of the change

Fathers into accordance even with the literal dogmatism of his own Church; as, for example, when Tertullian says,—" The flesh feeds on the Body and Blood of Christ " (De Resurr. Carn. c. viii.; tom. iii. p. 176), or Chrysostom,—" He gives Himself to thee,—not for thee to see only, but also to touch and to eat and to receive within " (Hom. lxxxii. in S. Matt.);—" not to behold only, but to touch, and eat, and to fix the teeth in His flesh " (Hom. xlvi. in S. Joh. quoted in Faith of Catholics, p. 235). Compare, e. g., Harding writing against Jewel :—" It is not now a mortal and corruptible body wherein we may fasten our teeth." In Defence of the Apology, P. ii.; p. 261 ; ed. 1609. It is of Chrysostom that Bishop Taylor has said that "his rhetoric hath cast him on the Roman side, but it also bears him beyond it; and his divinity and sober opinion have fixed him on ours " (Real Presence, sect. xii. 27),—and the remark may be applied to others. It should be added that Romish language, employed in popular discourses by writers whose deliberate statements are found to tell on the other side, is in reality a strong argument against the antiquity of the doctrine, even as a private opinion, which it appears to Roman Catholics to have been intended to teach. For they would certainly have been more guarded in their expressions, if there had been reason to suppose that they would encourage any of their hearers or readers in a view, which they did not hold themselves.

[7] When this passage was urged by Berengarius in the eleventh century, his opponent could only meet it by asserting that it was not to be found in the writings of Ambrose. See Berengar. de S. Cœnâ, p. 140.

[8] De Sacram. l. iv. c. iv. §§ 14, 16 ; pp. 228—230.

of the unconsecrated element into the sacramental Body of Christ. The context, however, shows that the writer did not intend to express any such theory. For, in the first place, he says that the bread remains what it was, though it has become also the Body of Christ; and, secondly, he illustrates the effect of the consecration by that of Baptism; so that, unless we suppose him to have held that the substance of the human soul is, in Baptism, converted into the Holy Ghost, we have no ground to infer that he believed the eucharistic bread to be substantially converted by the consecration into " whole Christ."

xi. S. Jerome:—

" For a *type* of His Blood, He did not offer water, but wine [9]."

xii. S. John Chrysostom:—

" Before the bread is consecrated, we call it bread; but when the Divine grace, through the act of the priest, has consecrated it, it has been freed from the name of bread, and is counted worthy of the name of the Lord's Body; though the nature of bread has remained in it [1]."

---

[9] Adv. Jovinian. l. ii.; tom. iv. P. ii. col. 198.

[1] Ad Cæsarium. Opp. tom. iii. p. 987. This passage has a curious history. It was first quoted by Peter Martyr, who had copied the Epistle from a Latin MS. in the library of the Dominicans at Florence, his native city. His copy was deposited with Cranmer, but disappeared at the destruction of the Archbishop's library in the reign of Mary,—and in the absence of such evidence as it would have afforded, Cardinal Perron and others accused Martyr of having forged the testimony which he ascribed to S. Chrysostom. More than a century after his death another copy of the Epistle was made from

xiii. S. Augustine :—

" The Lord did not scruple to say, This is My Body, when He delivered the *sign* of His Body [2]."

" That feast in which He commended and delivered to His disciples a *figure* of His Body and Blood [3]."

And again, supposing our Lord to speak :—

" Understand spiritually what I have said. Ye are *not* to eat this Body, which ye see, and to drink the Blood, which My crucifiers will shed. I have commended a certain *Sacrament* to you : spiritually understood, it will quicken you [4]."

And once more, explaining how infants, having the Sacrament of faith, may be said to have faith :—

the same MS. by Emery Bigot, and printed (with considerable fragments of the original Greek found in Anastasius, Nicephorus, and
John Damascene) in his edition of S. Chrysostom's Life by Palladius
(Paris, 1680). But before the volume was published, the Epistle
(occupying pp. 236—244) and a part of the preface which referred
to it were torn out by an order from the King, obtained by certain Doctors of the Sorbonne. This attempt at suppression was followed by the usual result. In 1685, Stephen Lemoyne published the
Latin version in his *Varia Sacra* (Lugd. Bat.), and in the following
year Archbishop Wake, who had obtained a set of the leaves torn
from the volume of Bigot, printed an exact copy of his edition in
England in the Appendix to his " Defence of the Exposition of the
Doctrine of the Church of England." (In Gibson's Preservative,
tit. ix.; vol. iii. London, 1738.) The next year, 1687, saw a third
edition, also from the suppressed impression of Bigot, published at
Utrecht, by James Basnage; and a fourth, also " with the Greek
fragments in the margin, at Rotterdam, by Achers." In 1689 ap-
peared a fifth by Hardouin. See Wake, u. s.; Dupin, Cent. iv. in
S. John Chrys. vol. i. p. 317; Cave, Hist. Litt. p. 204. Genev. 1705;
Routh, Opusc.; ed. 2, p. 479; or the Monitum prefixed in the Ed.
Ben., u. s. p. 889.

[2] Contra Adimant. c. xii. § 3 ; tom. viii. P. i. col. 224.

[3] Enarr. in Ps. iii. § 1 ; tom. iv. P. ii. col. 9.

[4] In Ps. xcviii. § ix., u. s. col. 1521.

" If the Sacraments had not a certain resemblance to those things of which they are Sacraments, they would not be Sacraments at all.   But from this *resemblance*, they generally receive even the names of the things themselves. If, therefore, the Sacrament of the Body of Christ is, *in a certain manner*, the Body of Christ, and the Sacrament of the Blood of Christ is the Blood of Christ, so the Sacrament of faith is faith [5]."

xiv. Theodoret :—

" In the delivery of the mysteries, He called the bread, body, and the mixture (of wine and water), blood. . . . . But according to nature, the body would be called body, and the blood, blood. . . . . Our Lord, however, by an interchange, gave the name of the *symbol* to the body, and the name of body to the symbol. . . . . For He who spoke of the natural body as corn and bread, and again called Himself the vine, honoured the visible symbols by the title of the Body and Blood, not changing their nature, but adding grace to nature [6]."

xv. Gelasius I., who died A.D. 496 :—

" The Sacraments which we take of the Body and Blood of Christ are a divine thing, by reason of which, and by means of which same, we are made partakers of the Divine nature ; and yet *the substance, or nature of the bread and wine, does not cease to be.*   And truly an *image* and a *similitude* of the Body and Blood of Christ are celebrated in the actions of the mysteries [7]."

[5] Ad Bonifac. Epp. cl. ii. Ep. xcviii. § 9 ; tom. ii. col. 400.
[6] Dial. i. Opp. tom. iv. pp. 17, 18.   Sim. Dial. ii., pp. 84, 85 ;— and Comm. in Ps. cix. 4 ; tom. i. p. 852.
[7] C. Eutychen, Biblioth. Patr. M. tom. v. P. iii. p. 671.   Earlier Roman Catholic critics, as Baronius, Bellarmine, &c., "doubted,"

xvi. Procopius of Gaza, who lived in the sixth century, compiled a commentary on several parts of holy Scripture from the works of various early expositors. From him, therefore, we may learn how the Greek Fathers, who wrote before him, usually expressed themselves on this mysterious subject:—

" He gave an *image*, or *figure*, or *type*, of His Body to the disciples, no longer permitting and accepting the bloody sacrifices of the law[8]."

xvii. Facundus of Hermiana, an African Bishop in the middle of the sixth century,—to illustrate an expression which had been blamed:—

" The Sacrament of the Body and Blood of Christ, which is in the consecrated bread and cup, we call His Body and Blood; not because the bread is *properly* His Body, and the cup His Blood, but because they contain in them the mystery (sacrament) of His Body and Blood. Hence, too, the Lord Himself called the blessed bread and cup, which He gave to His disciples, His Body and Blood. Wherefore, as Christ's faithful people, receiving the Sacrament of His Body and Blood, are rightly said to receive His Body and Blood, so Christ Himself, when He had received the Sacrament of the adoption of sons, might be rightly said to have received the adoption of sons[9]."

says Dupin, " whether this treatise belonged to the Pope " of that name; but the grounds on which this author (Cent. v. *Gelas.* I.; vol. i. p. 520), Labbæus (De Script. Eccles. tom. i. p. 342.   Par. 1660), and others ascribe it to him are decisive against them.

[8] In Octateuch. Gen. lix.; p. 206, in Vers. Claud. Thrasybuli, 1560. The Greek has not been printed, though according to Cave an edition was prepared for the press by Godfrey Oelschläger.   Hist. Litt. p. 327.   Genev. 1705.

[9] Pro Trib. Cap. l. ix. c. v.; p. 404.   Paris, 1629.

xviii. To the next extract, from Rhabanus Mau- rus, Archbishop of Mentz, who died A.D. 856, I beg your particular attention. It shows in a lively manner the astonishment of a devout and learned divine of the ninth century, when he discovered that some of his cotemporaries understood the rhetorical language of earlier writers in its most literal sense, and were thus led to confound the Sacrament of Christ's Body with His Body itself. The work of Paschasius Radbertus, the first who wrote in favour of this view, had fallen into his hands, and it is to this that he refers :—

" I confess that what I have found in this book under the name of S. Ambrose is a thing entirely new to me : namely, that this flesh of Christ is no other than that which was born of Mary, and suffered on the cross, and rose from the tomb. . . . . . I fairly confess that I never heard this before, and I have wondered much that S. Ambrose should have said it, and I wonder too, much more, that the author of this volume should have stated it therein [1]."

[1] Ep. iii. ad Ægilum. Opp. tom. vi. col. 1513. Paris, 1852. S. Ambrose (de Myst. c. ix. § 53; tom. v. p. 197) says :—" This Body which we make is from the Virgin. Why do you look for a natural process in the case of Christ's Body (in the Eucharist), where the Lord Jesus Himself was born of a Virgin in a manner preternatural ? " Such language, though innocuous to the well-instructed Christian of the fourth century, could not fail to be a source of error in the ninth. See end of Note [6], p. 366. Paschasius wrote after the year 831. Nearly a century and a half before this, an opinion in advance of that which he propounded, had incidentally dropped from an Eastern monk in the heat of controversy. Anastasius Sinaita, A.D. 685, in his Hodegus (c. xxiii. Biblioth. PP. tom. ix. p. 855), as

The impression, which the novelty of this doctrine made on the mind of Rhabanus, is shown by his recurring to it in a Penitential, that he issued not long after;—a document the subject of which has no necessary or direct connexion with it:—

"Certain persons of late, not thinking aright concerning the Sacrament of our Lord's Body and Blood, have asserted that this is the very Body and Blood of the Lord, which was born of the Virgin Mary, and in which the Lord Himself suffered on the cross, and rose from the tomb;—which error we have opposed to the best of our ability in an epistle to the Abbot Ægilus, setting forth that which ought truly to be believed concerning that Body [2]."

quoted by Mr. Wilberforce (Eucharist, ch. v.; p. 107), supposes that the sacramental Body of Christ, being identical with His natural Body, is necessarily incorruptible, and argues on that assumption. Mr. Wilberforce says that he is the only "ancient writer whose words at all sanction the error of the Capernaites." P. 106. If so, he is the only writer for seven hundred years whose language sanctions the doctrine of Rome, when rightly understood. The Capernaites thought of a literal eating of the Flesh of our Lord, in which they agree with Anastasius and with Rome. The comparison cannot take in the question of its corruptibility, on which he erred also; for of this there is no mention in the Gospel narrative. Some of the followers of Paschasius also insisted on the incorruptibility of the consecrated elements. Thus Guitmond, Archbishop of Aversa, 1080, maintained that,—"Though the consecrated bread seems to be corrupted to the apprehension of corrupted men, yet in reality it is not changed at all; and that it does not appear altered, unless as a punishment of the infidelity and negligence of men; that it cannot be gnawn by mice and other vermin; and if at any time it appear to be so, it is only to punish the negligence, or to try the faith of men. Nor will he admit that the fire can consume these mysteries, and he says, that with veneration they commit it to this most pure element, to be carried up into heaven," &c. Dupin, Cent. xi. *Guitmond;* tom. ii. p. 203.

[2] Pœnitentiale, c. xxxiii.; tom. iv. col. 493.

xix. The next testimony which I select may be considered that of the Church of England in the tenth century. The following extract is from a homily of Ælfric, appointed to be read in the churches before the Communion on Easter-day:—

" Much is betwixt the Body, Christ suffered in, and the Body, that is hallowed to housel. The Body truly, that Christ suffered in, was born of the flesh of Mary, with blood and with bone, with skin and with sinews, in human limbs, with a reasonable soul living ; and His ghostly Body, which we call the housel, is gathered of many corns, without blood and bone, without limb, without soul ; and therefore nothing is to be understood therein bodily, but all is ghostly to be understood. . . . . This mystery is a pledge and a *figure:* Christ's Body is truth itself. This pledge we do keep mystically, until that we be come to the truth itself; and then is this pledge ended[3]."

"The like matter also was delivered to the Clergy by the Bishops at their Synods, out of two other writings of the same Ælfric[4]:"—

" That housel is Christ's Body, not bodily, but spiritually ; not the Body which He suffered in, but the Body of which He spake, when He blessed bread and wine to housel, the night before His suffering[5]."

" The Lord, which hallowed housel before His suffering, and saith that the bread was His own Body, and that the wine was truly His Blood, halloweth daily by the hands of the priest bread to His Body, and wine to His Blood,

---

[3] App. to the Book of Ratramn, pp. 62, 63. Oxf. 1838.
[4] Ussher, Answer to a Jesuit, p. 79. Dubl. 1624. Sim. Cosin, Hist. Transubst. c. v. § xxxvi. Works, vol. iv. p. 88. Oxf. 1851.
[5] Ussher, p. 79.

LETTER
VIII.
PART II.
ART. I.
SECT. II.

in spiritual mystery, as we read in books. And yet, notwithstanding, that lively bread is not bodily so, nor the selfsame Body that Christ suffered in, nor that holy wine is the Saviour's Blood which was shed for us, in bodily thing, but in spiritual understanding[6]."

xx. You are aware that Berengarius, in the middle of the eleventh century, was the first person condemned by the Church of Rome, for denying that the Body of Christ upon the altar is in very substance the same Body which hung upon the cross. You are not perhaps equally aware that one of the Popes, before whom he recanted this opinion, was himself known to hold it, though induced by fear of a powerful faction to consent to the persecution of his friend. The following address of Gregory VII. to Berengarius will probably exhibit that generally resolute Pontiff in a very unexpected light:—

"I do not at all doubt your correct Scriptural views touching the sacrifice of Christ; nevertheless, because I am wont in things that disturb me to have recourse to the Blessed Mary, some days ago I charged a certain religious, my friend, to give himself to fasting and prayer, and so obtain from the Blessed Mary to reveal to me, through him, what position I should take up in the matter which I had in hand concerning the sacrifice of Christ,—in which I might remain immoveable. The monk . . . . was told by the Blessed Virgin, that nothing must be thought, nothing told, respecting the sacrifice of Christ, but what the genuine Scriptures contain, contrary to which Berengarius held nothing. This I have desired to make known

---

[6] Ussher, u. s. p. 80.

to you, that you may have stronger confidence in us, and more cheerful hope [7]."

III. From the brief extracts which follow, you will find that many of your own divines, even while understating the case against the modern doctrine, have been compelled to acknowledge that it has little or no foundation in Scripture and antiquity.

Thus Dùns Scotus, as quoted by Bellarmine:—

" There is no place of Scripture so express as evidently to compel us to admit transubstantiation without the declaration of the Church [8]."

And William of Occham:—

"Although it is expressly delivered in the Canonical Scripture that the Body of Christ is to be offered to the faithful under the species of bread, yet that the substance of bread is really converted or transubstantiated into the Body of Christ is not found expressly stated in the Canon of the Bible, but is believed to have been revealed by God to the Fathers, or proved, by a diligent and skilful investigation, from Scriptural testimonies [9]."

Again:—

" That the substance of the bread does not remain is not expressed there (in the New Testament). Whence there were in old times divers opinions concerning this matter [1]."

[7] Mansi, tom. xix. col. 766. Bowden, vol. ii. p. 246. " Behold," says one of Gregory's opponents, " behold a true Pontiff and priest who is in doubt whether that which is received at the Lord's table be the true Body and Blood of Christ." Egilberti Archiep. Trevir. Epist. adv. Greg. VII., quoted by Bowden from Eccardi Corp. Hist. Medii Ævi, tom. ii. p. 170.

[8] Bellarm., u. s., l. iii. c. xxiii.; p. 160, B.

[9] Access. ad Tract. de Sacr. Alt. c. iii.; sig. E iii. Paris, 1513.

[1] Ibid. c. v.; sig. EV.

The liturgical commentary under the name of Biel:—

"Although it is expressly delivered in Scripture that the Body of Christ is truly contained under the species of bread, and received by the faithful, yet how the Body of Christ is there, whether by the conversion of any thing into Him, or whether without such conversion the Body of Christ begins to be with the bread, the substance and accidents of the bread remaining,—this is not found expressly in the Canon of the Bible. Whence there were in old time divers opinions about it [2]."

Cardinal Caietan:—

"The words of the Lord (This is My Body) have been understood by the Church in their literal sense. . . . . I say, *by the Church*, because from the Gospel there does not appear any thing of force to oblige us to understand these words literally. We obtain, then, from the truth of our Lord's words in their literal sense, that the Body of Christ is truly in the Eucharist. . . . . But the other truth, which the Gospel has not explained expressly, namely, the (substantial) conversion of the bread into the Body of Christ, we have received from the Church [3]."

Alphonsus a Castro:—

"Of the transubstantiation of the bread into the Body of Christ there is rare mention in ancient authors [4]."

A party of English Jesuits, towards the end of

---

[2] Biel de Canone Missæ, Lect. xl.; fol. 85. Lugd. 1542.

[3] In Thom. Aquin. P. iii. Q. lxxv. Art. i.; fol. 301. Bonon. 1528. The clause ["I say by the Church . . . . literally"] has been expunged from later editions, as Venet. 1596 and Rom. 1773.

[4] Adv. Hæres. l. viii.; fol. 184, fa. 2.

Elizabeth's reign, appear to have come still nearer to the truth, being accused by the secular priests of "the heretical and most dangerous assertion, that the ancient Fathers did not even touch the subject of Transubstantiation [5]."

The Spanish Jesuit Salmeron :—

" Some writers have thought that this article can [not] be proved against heretics out of Scripture alone, or by reasonings alone, but only by the definition of Councils, and the tradition of the Fathers ; for it would be easy to answer the passage of Scripture quoted, and the reasons. So that it seems right to stand more on the tradition of the Fathers, than on them,—which tradition, without doubt, as Scotus has remarked, (in iv. Dist. ii. Q. 3,) would not have obliged posterity to believe a thing so hard,—nor would they have so constantly affirmed it,— had it not been received from Christ Himself, and handed down through the pillars of the Church [6]."

The Benedictine Barnes :—

" Both the Scriptures and Fathers, which teach a change (μετουσίαν), may be explained sufficiently of that wonderful and supernatural change of the bread, through the presence of the Body of Christ being added to it, without supposing that the substantial bread ceases to be [7]."

IV. The word "transubstantiation" was intro-

[5] Watson's Decachordon, Quodl. ii. Art. iv.; p. 31. S. l. 1602; or A Sparing Discovery of our English Jesuits, p. 13. S. l. (Francfort) 1601. They made the declaration from hostility to the priests, whose office they thought to lower by it.

[6] Comm. in verba, *Hoc est Corpus Meum*, Tract. xvi. tom. ix. p. 110.

[7] Cath.-Rom. Pacif. § v. Paralip. c.; p. 90.

duced, as I have already stated, by Innocent III., and adopted from him by the Church of Rome so early as the year 1215; but the doctrine which it expresses was not fully developed and defined before the thirteenth Session of Trent, in 1551. We need not be surprised, therefore, if we find Innocent himself falling far short of the dogmatic fulness, precision, and confidence, which mark the most recent standard of Roman orthodoxy:—

"The matter of the bread and wine is changed into the substance of the Flesh and Blood;—nor is any thing added to the Body, but transubstantiated into the Body." "But whether the parts pass into the parts, whether the whole into the whole, whether the one altogether into the other altogether, He knows who effects it. . . . . We are ordered to believe; we are forbidden to discuss. If, however, an inquirer be very urgent, I would grant,—without prejudice to the faith,—that the whole bread together is changed into the whole Body together, so as that no part of the bread passes into any part of the Body. But I think,—without prejudice to the majesty of the faith,—that where the consecrated bread is, the whole Body exists under the whole species [8]."

We find the same liberty of thought permitted throughout the fourteenth century. Witness the bold speculations of the Resolute Doctor:—

"What then shall be said to the question proposed concerning the conversion of the substance of bread into the Body of Christ? Saving a better judgement, it may

[8] Myst. Lib. Missæ, l. iv. cc. vii. viii. Opp. tom. i. p. 378.

be thought that, if in that Sacrament a conversion of bread into the Body of Christ takes place, it is in this way:—that, the form of the bread being corrupted, *its matter is under the form of Christ's Body*, suddenly and by the Divine power, as the matter of food becomes under the form of the animal fed, by the power of nature. . . . . It may therefore be held with probability, according to this mode, that the conversion of the substance of bread into the Body of Christ is miraculous as to the manner of its being done, but not as to the thing done itself; because by the power of nature a similar conversion takes place of food into the nature of an animal, but not in the same manner; and that power of matter by which it is capable of being changed, or of becoming under the form of another thing, is the same in either case [9]."

William of Occham, who lived into the middle of the fourteenth century, tells us that in his time there were "three several opinions respecting the change of the bread into the Body of Christ:"—

" One asserts that that substance which was bread at first is afterwards the flesh of Christ. The second holds that the substance of bread and wine ceases to be there, and that their accidents only are left, to wit, their taste, colour, weight, and the like. The third holds that *the*

[9] Durandus in Sent. l. iv. Dist. xi. Q. iii.; fol. cccxlii. fa. 2. Paris, 1515. The reader will observe the use of ' matter ' as synonymous with substance, when the change is spoken of. Sim. Occham, in Note [2], p. 380, and D'Ailly in the text, p. 381. See p. 351. Bellarmine employs a chapter in refuting this "error of Durandus," that the matter of the bread remains under another form. He declares " his opinion heretical, though he ought not to be called a heretic himself, because he was ready to acquiesce in the judgement of the Church." De Sacr. l. iii. c. xiii.; tom. iii. p. 152.

substance of the bread and wine remains, and that the Body of Christ is in the same place under the same appearance [1]."

The advocates of these three opinions all used the term "transubstantiation," though it was strictly applicable to the first only, and not at all to the third. Occham himself favoured the second, which he believed to be "the determination of the Roman Church" at that time. The assertors of the third maintained, he tells us, "that it was no article of faith to believe that the bread by the transubstantiation ceases to exist," and he does not contradict them [2].

Petrus de Alliaco, a Cardinal present at the Council of Constance [3] : —

"Though Catholics have agreed in this, that the Body of Christ is truly and essentially in the Sacrament under the species of bread and wine, or where the species appear, nevertheless, ... about the manner in which this is effected, there have been diverse opinions. The first was that the substance of the bread becomes the Body of Christ; and some of those who held this said that,

---

[1] Access. ad Tract. de Sacr. Alt. c. v. ; sig. EV.

[2] Centiloquium ; Concl. xxxix.; sig. BB. Lugd. 1495. Here as also in Comm. in Sent., lib. iv. Q. vi. ; sig. Sviii. (in the same volume), he explains the three opinions given in the text more formally and fully. In the latter book he adds a fourth, given also by D'Ailly,— "that the substance of the bread is reduced to a matter either self-subsisting, or taking another form,—and that, whether in the same or another (place),—and in this case the body of Christ coexists with it in matter and accidents." Ibid.

[3] See p. 354.

although the bread becomes the Body of Christ, it is not to be granted that that substance is ever the flesh of Christ. But others said that that which before consecration was bread, is after it the Body of Christ. But neither from this does it follow that the bread *is* the flesh of Christ; for, as they say, the substance of the bread, after it has become the flesh of Christ, is not the substance of bread, but the substance of flesh. . . . . A second opinion was, that the substance of the bread does not remain bread, nor yet simply ceases to be, but is reduced to a matter subsisting alone, or receiving another form. . . . . A third proposition was, that the substance of the bread remains, and this may be conceived in two ways:—one, according to which it remains in the same place in which the Body of Christ begins to be, and so the substance of the bread would be said to pass into the substance of the Body; because where the one is, the other begins to be:—another, according to which, the substance of the bread would suddenly withdraw from its first place to another place, and the accidents would remain in the same place without a subject, and the Body of Christ would there coexist with them. . . . The fourth opinion and the more common is that the substance of the bread does not remain, but simply ceases to be. . . . And though it does not evidently follow from Scripture that it is so, nor even (so far as I see) from the determination of the Church, nevertheless, because it is more agreeable to it and to the common opinion of the saints and doctors, therefore I hold it [4]."

Ferus, an eminent commentator on holy Scripture, three years before whose death the doctrine of the Eucharist was finally defined at Trent:—

[4] In Sent. lib. iv. Q. vi. Litt. E, F ; sig. B vi. S. l. 1500.

" That you may understand this *metaphor* of eating, observe [5]," &c. " His Body is eaten in a twofold manner, spiritually and sacramentally. What it is to eat the Body of Christ spiritually, that is to say, when it is offered in the Word, He has Himself declared, when He says, ' Whoso cometh to me shall not hunger; and whoso believeth,' &c. Spiritually to eat the Body of Christ, therefore, is to believe from the heart. . . . . . Secondly, Christ is offered to us in a Sacrament; which is done in order to remind us of the promises by this outward sign, and to assure us by this bodily eating that Christ has been truly given to us with all that He hath. For He who gave His Body, what would He not give [6] ? "

" As it is certain that the Body of Christ is there, what is the use of disputing whether the substance of the bread remains or not [7] ? "

" The Sacrament of the Eucharist is that bread, or *species* of bread, united to the word of Christ saying, ' Take,' &c. This Sacrament is truly the sign of a sacred thing; for it signifies, yea, it contains the Body of Christ [8]. "

It is probable that the word ' transubstantiation ' itself, once adopted, exercised a considerable influence in preparing the minds of men for the general reception of the doctrine in its present form. For though it had been variously used, from the time of Innocent downwards, to denote every conceivable mode of the real presence, it could only be applied with any propriety to the change of one substance into another, or to the substitu-

---

[5] In Matt. xxvii.; p. 408. Lugd. 1562.
[6] Ibid. p. 409.   [7] p. 411.   [8] p. 413.

tion of one for another. Accordingly these two theories alone appear to have been put forward at the Council of Trent. Since that period the latter explanation of the mystery appears to have been almost forgotten,—a result due, I think, in no small measure to the circumstance that the word more naturally conveys the idea of an actual change of the bread into the Body. Could the thirteenth Session of Trent be acted over again in our day, it is probable that the theory of *productive* conversion [9], as it was termed, would be found without an advocate [1].

[9] So called because it is effected "by the annihilation of one, and the production or creation of another substance." The mode now generally held is called the *adductive*, because, according to it, " the Body of Christ does not then simply begin to be, but begins to be under the species of bread; not that the Body itself, being assumed, descends from heaven, but that the bread and wine are changed into the Body and Blood." Liebermann, u. s. c. i. Art. ii. ; p. 495. The latter explanation was that of the Thomists, and therefore of the Dominicans; the former of the Scotists and Franciscans.

[1] Since the Council of Trent there has been very little opposition to its doctrine from those who have remained in the communion of Rome. Take, however, one instance in Barnes :—" The assertion of a transubstantiation, or change of the substantial bread, though it be the more common opinion, is nevertheless not the faith of the Church " (Cath.-Rom. Pacif., u. s.); another in De Marca, the famous Archbishop of Paris :—" It is necessary for the full explication of the Sacrament to observe diligently that there are two parts of this mystery, the one that may be looked upon,—sensible, visible, and offered to the senses of man,—which may be distinguished from the other by the appellation of bread ; the other an object of mental perception, and open to faith alone, which is the spiritual Body of Christ, so joined, in an invisible manner, with the other part, that there results one undivided Eucharist of the Body and Blood of Christ." (De Sacr. Euch. ; p. 34. Paris, 1682.) " It was rightly ob-

II. COMMUNION IN ONE KIND.

I. On the denial of the cup to the laity in the holy Communion it is not necessary to say much; because the Council of Constance, in the very decree by which your present custom was finally established, acknowledged that it enjoined a departure from the ancient rule :—

"Although in the Primitive Church this Sacrament was received under both kinds, yet has this custom been introduced, ... that it should be taken by the officiating priests under both kinds, and by the laity under the kind of bread only. . . . Wherefore, since this custom has been introduced by the Church and the holy Fathers on reasonable grounds, and has been very long observed, it is to be esteemed a law [2]," &c.

Salmeron will tell you at what period this custom of half-communion was introduced :—

" It is certain that the present Church, and that which preceded it *by three or two centuries*, has been wont to communicate the laity under one kind in many Churches, as S. Thomas (Aquinas) teaches, on John, in these words:

served by Gelasius, that the Sacraments of the Body and Blood of Christ are a divine thing, because the bread and wine pass into the Divine substance through the operation of the Holy Ghost, namely, into the spiritual Body of Christ;—but that, in another respect, the substance and nature of the bread and wine do not cease,—but that those elements remain in their own proper nature." (Ibid. p. 61.) In this treatise, written with the professed design of explaining the Roman doctrine, I have not observed any use of the word " transubstantiation."

[2] Sess. xiii. Mansi, tom. xxvii. col. 727.

—'According to the ancient custom of the Church all
partook of the Blood as of the Body, which custom is
still kept up in some Churches [3]."

Salmeron died in 1585, Thomas Aquinas in
1274. The practice appears to have begun in some
Churches so early as the eleventh century, but not
to have been generally imposed before the fourteenth. The intermediate period presented a singular spectacle of diversity in custom. Thus, for
example, in England we have a constitution of
Archbishop Peckham, dated 1281, in which communion in both kinds is said to be permitted to
the celebrant only "in such small churches [4]," by
which it is implied that in the larger it was allowed
to others; while a canon enacted at Exeter six
years later directs that the laity be taught by the
priest, before they communicate, that under the
species of bread they receive that which hung for
their salvation on the cross, and in the cup that
which was shed from the Body of Christ [5]."

The early Church of Rome was not only innocent

---

[3] D. Thom. in Joh. vi. Lect. 7, sub init. tom. xiv. Salm. tom. ix.
Tract. 35.

[4] Johnson's English Canons, P. ii. p. 274. Oxf. 1851. Lynde-
wood, Provinc. l. i. c. ii. *Altissimus;* fol. 7. Ed. 1525. The same
canon implies the practice (said by Johnson to have been continued
by "the Romish priests" down to "the reigns of King Charles and
James II.") of giving unconsecrated wine to the people, of which they
were to be taught that it was "not the Sacrament, but mere wine to
be drunk for the more easy swallowing of the Sacrament which they
have taken."

[5] Wilkins' Conc. vol. ii. p. 133.

C C

of this "dismemberment of one and the same Sacrament," but actually condemned it through Pope Gelasius as a "huge sacrilege." If he thought such language applicable to a voluntary abstinence from the cup on the part of a mistaken communicant, what would he have said of its denial to the whole Church, in despite of loud complaints, remonstrance, and intreaty [6]?

SECT. II.

II. The crime of Rome in this strange act of mingled tyranny and presumption is aggravated by the fact that several of her own writers teach that reception in both kinds is essential to the completeness of the Sacrament as a significative rite; and, what is of more importance, that, while in partaking of the Body we receive all that is necessary to life, the cup conveys a further gift of spiritual comfort and refreshment. This statement requires no further explanation than one or two examples will supply.

Hugo de Sancto Victore :—

" He willed both to be received, that our body and our soul together may be glorified with Him. . . . For He is the ransom of body and soul, which would not be represented were He received in one kind only, because though both are received under either kind, yet both are not signified in either. But the species of bread signifies the Body, and the species of wine the Blood of Christ in respect of

---

[6] Gratian, P. iii. dist. ii. c. xii. *Comperimus autem.* This was about the year 494.

the resurrection, and participation in both kinds at once signifies the redemption of the body and soul of the partaker [7]."

Albertus Magnus :—

" The practice of the faithful and the unity of the mystical body are not completely represented and expressed except under the twofold sign ; . . . and therefore, by the nature of the Sacrament, both ought to be had, . . . and those united in one institution and one sign [8]."

John de Lugo :—

" Francis Blanco, Archbishop of Compostella, who was present at the Council of Trent, (to whom Henriquez refers, lib. viii. de Euch., without giving his name,) has said that this was the unanimous opinion of the Fathers present, [that the several species convey grace separately,] but that they were unwilling to define it at an unseasonable time, lest occasion should be given to the heretics to make an outcry ;—with which agree the words of the Council itself [9], where it is cautiously said that ' as regards the benefit received, they are defrauded of no grace *necessary to salvation*, who receive one kind only.' It did not say absolutely, ' of no grace,' but ' of no grace *necessary to salvation*.' . . . In addition to which we have the authority of Clement VI., who in a Bull addressed to the King of France, granted him communion in both kinds, and the Pope adds that he grants this '*for the greater increase of grace ;*'—

[7] In Spec. Eccl. c. vii. Opp. tom. iii. p. 247. Mogunt. 1617. This writer explains that in the proposition that the Body and Blood of Christ are both received under one kind, we are to understand " that body of Christ which is the Church." Ibid.

[8] De Sent. l. iv. dist. viii. art. xiii. ; sig. ff vi. Bas. 1506.

[9] Sess. xxi. De Commun. c. iii.

c c 2

for the reason that both kinds give more grace than each severally [1]."

One of the divines who maintained this opinion at Trent is related to have argued for the withholding of the cup from the laity on the ground that, "as the priest has a higher dignity and a double share of authority, it is befitting that he should receive double grace [2]."

Vasquez :—

"The opinion of those has always appeared to me the more probable, who say that greater fruit of grace is acquired from both species of this Sacrament, than from one only [3]."

[1] De Sacr. Euch. Disp. xii. § iii. N. 68 ; p. 418. Lugd. 1644. Henriquez himself taught that "a new degree of grace is not conferred *ex operato* by the drinking of the Blood " (Theol. Moral. l. viii. c. xliv. § v. ; p. 475. Mogunt. 1613) ; but he says :—" Suarez with reason confesses that this whole controversy is within the limits of mere scholastic opinion " (Ibid. N. 67), and that Soto, Tapper, and others say that it is " a problem " (u. s.). Lugo's author had probably forgotten something of what took place at Trent, when he said that the divines present were unanimous on this point. Pallavicino's account is that,—" Some said that less is received by those who communicate under one kind than by those who communicate under both,"—among whom he names Melchior Canus,—but that "more were of the contrary opinion." L. xii. c. ii. ; P. ii. p. 270.—Sarpi says that " *many* believed that, though more of the Sacrament was not received, more of grace was." L. iv. ; p. 263.

[2] Pallav. l. xii. c. ii. ; P. ii. p. 270.

[3] Comm. in Part. iii. Q. lxxx. Disp. ccxv. c. ii ; tom. iii. p. 351. Lugd. 1631. He quotes, as holding this opinion, Alexander of Hales n 4, Q. ii. Memb. 2, art. 4, § 3, Gaspar Casalius, lib. 2, de Cœnâ, Arboreus in cap. vi. Joh., and Ruardus (Tapper), Art. 15, § *Respondeo utramque speciem.* Caietan held it, but for a very puerile reason not worth mentioning, though he was not without followers. Ibid.

" The Fathers at the Council of Trent . . . . made it their object to define that the whole entire Body of Christ is contained under each kind, and that a *true* Sacrament is therefore found in each. They did not say a *complete*, but a *true ;* for although there is a true sign of the sacred thing sanctifying us under each kind, there is not a complete spiritual banquet [4]."

" Lastly, we grant that according to this our opinion, the laity, to whom one species is denied, are defrauded of some grace indeed,—yet not of any necessary to salvation ; —and that the Council did not mean to deny this [5]."

Cassander accounts for the universal adherence to communion in both kinds " for more than a thousand years after Christ," by the influence of such views :—

" Both because they believed that in the Sacrament of the Blood a certain peculiar virtue and grace is signified by this symbol of wine, and also for mystical reasons [5]," &c.

[4] Ibid. c. iii. ; p. 354.   [5] Ibid.
[6] Consult. Art. xxii. ; p. 181.   Lugd. 1608.

LETTER VIII.

PART III.

I. PURGATORY.

THE following is the candid confession of Bishop Fisher:—

"No orthodox person now doubts whether there be a Purgatory, of which, however, among the ancients, there was no mention, or the very rarest. Nay, to this day, the Greeks do not believe in Purgatory. Let who will read the commentaries of the ancient Greeks, and he will find no discourse, as I think,—or the most infrequent,—of Purgatory. Nor did the Latins all at once, but by degrees, conceive the truth of this matter [1]."

Alphonsus a Castro:—

"Of Purgatory there is almost no mention in ancient writers, especially among the Greeks [2]."

[1] Assert. Luth. Confut. Art. xviii.; col. 496.
[2] Ib. l. viii.; fol. 184, fa. 2.

The Benedictine Barnes:—

" Punishment in Purgatory is a matter of human opinion, which cannot be satisfactorily deduced either from Scripture, the Fathers, or from Councils:—nay, (with deference to better judgements,) the opposite opinion was more agreeable to them [3]."

Dr. Newman:—

"*As time went on*, the doctrine of Purgatory was *opened* upon the apprehension of the Church, as a portion or form of penance for sins committed after Baptism [4]."

II. INDULGENCES.

I. Durandus, the Schoolman :—

"Of Indulgences little can be said with certainty, because Scripture does not speak expressly about them [5]."

S. Antoninus, Archbishop of Florence, in the fifteenth century:—

" We have nothing express in holy Scripture concerning Indulgences; . . . nor even out of the sayings of the Old Doctors, but out of those of the modern (only) [6]."

Eggeling and Biel :—

" Before the time of S. Gregory, there was little or no use of Indulgences; but now their use is multiplied [7]," &c.

The following extract from Bishop Fisher is in

---

[3] Barnes, Cath.-Rom. Pacif. § 9, Paralip. c ; p. 130.
[4] Essay on Development, ch. viii. sec. i. 2; p. 417.
[5] In Sent. l. iv. Dist. xx. Q. 3; fol. cccc. fa. 2.   Paris, 1515.
[6] Summa, P. i. tit. x. c. iii.   Procem. tom. i. sig. p2.   Bas. 1511.
[7] De Can. Miss. Lect. lvii. ; fol. 139.

continuation of the passage respecting Purgatory just quoted :—

" In the Primitive Church, the belief in Purgatory, or in Indulgences, was not so necessary as it is now. For their charity was so ardent, that every Christian was ready to die for Christ; crimes were rare, and, when they did occur, were punished by great severity of the canons. But now a great part of the people would rather put off their Christianity than endure the rigour of the canons; so that it has not been without an admirable dispensation of the Holy Spirit, that belief in Purgatory and the use of Indulgences has been generally received by the orthodox. As long as there was no anxiety about Purgatory, no one sought after Indulgences; for on that depends the whole value of Indulgences. If you take away Purgatory, where will be the good of Indulgences? For we shall not need them if there be no Purgatory. Seeing therefore that Purgatory was once unknown, that afterwards it was believed by some gradually, partly from revelations, partly from Scripture, and so at length the belief in it was generally and in the fullest manner received by the orthodox Church, we shall very easily understand something of the history of Indulgences, that there was no use of them in the infancy of the Church. Indulgences began after men had trembled somewhile at the torments of Purgatory. For it seems likely that the holy Fathers considered then more carefully by what means they might save their flocks from these torments, and especially such penitents as from their age had not time for the fulfilment of canonical penance. . . . From this source, if I mistake not, did Indulgences arise."

Part of the above passage from Bishop Fisher is

quoted by Polydore Vergil, in his Treatise on the *Discoverers of Things*, as explaining the origin of Indulgences. His remark on it is worthy of notice :—

" So far my author. But these things, considering their vast importance, you perhaps expected to hear from the mouth of God, as being so more certain [8]."

Alphonsus a Castro :—

" Of all the things which we discuss in this work, there is not one which the sacred Scriptures have delivered with less clearness, and about which ancient writers have said less [9]."

Suarez :—

" It ought not to move any one, that among the old Doctors of the Church, Greek and Latin, Augustine, Chrysostom, &c., no express mention of Indulgences is found. . . . Perhaps they do not make express and special mention of the mode of remitting punishment by Indulgences, because it was not necessary in order either to recommend or to defend the faith ; the heretical calumniators of Indulgences not having then arisen [1]."

Barnes :—

" It remains therefore to be said, that, *if we consult the ancients*, . . . Indulgences are nothing more than remission of public punishments, by which the discipline of the Church ought to be satisfied, notwithstanding that

[8] L. viii. c. i. ; p. 475. Amst. 1671.
[9] Adv. Hær. l. viii. ; fol. 184, fa. 2.
[1] In D. Thom. P. iii. Disp. xlix. § 2, n. 14; tom. iv. p. 625. Mogunt. 1616.

writers of a later age, after the rigour of the ancient canons and practice became relaxed, have understood them otherwise ².”

² Catholico-Romanus Pacificus, § ix. Paralip. a; p. 124. It is a common practice with Roman Catholics, writing for the English public, to put altogether out of sight the connexion between Purgatory and the modern Indulgences. The most open falsehood, with this object in view, which has come under my notice, occurs in Gother's Papist Misrepresented and Represented :—" Indulgences are *nothing else but* a mitigation, or relaxation, upon just causes, of *Canonical Penances*, which are or may be enjoined by the Pastors of the Church on penitent sinners according to their several degrees of demerits." In Gibson's Preservative, tit. ix., Rome truly represented, § viii., p. 285. When Bossuet (Exposition de la Foi, § 8) made a similar representation to the French Protestants, it was remarked by Wake that " he would find more in his own Church than in ours to oppose his doctrine." Exposition, &c., P. i. Art. viii., in Gibson, u. s. p. 26. In fact, as Milner tells us, " it has been condemned by Leo X. (*Exsurge, Domine*) and Pius VI." (*Auctorem Fidei.*) End of Controv. Lett. xliii.; p. 101. The misrepresentation, however, must have been thought useful, for it has been often reproduced, at least in part. Milner himself misleads his reader on this subject almost as grossly as Gother. While he explains, with great show of fulness and method, that an Indulgence is the remission of "the temporary punishment to be endured by penitent sinners " after the eternal has been forgiven, he carefully avoids dropping the least hint from which we could gather that any portion of that temporary punishment is to be endured in purgatory; and, as if to divert inquiry into a totally different channel, proceeds at once to find a parallel for *his* Indulgences in the commutations for public penance allowed by an English canon of 1640. Ibid. Dr. Lingard's account of Indulgences is equally deceptive. His narrative is so constructed, that an ill-informed person must necessarily rise from its perusal with an impression that the shameless questors of the sixteenth century have been the only authorities for their bearing upon Purgatory,—if indeed those worthies were not misrepresented by the Reformers. After stating that in early times " austerities *enjoined by the canons* " for flagrant sins were " occasionally mitigated by the *indulgence* of the Bishops," he tells us that Urban II. offered the first crusaders a *Plenary Indulgence ;* that is, he enacted that all who, having confessed

II. Indulgences, as the author whom I have last quoted rightly informs us, were originally only re-

their sins with true repentance of heart, might engage in the expedition, should be exempted from the *canonical penances* to which they were otherwise liable." He does *not* tell us, however, that Urban added :—" But for those who shall depart this life there (on the expedition) in true repentance, let them not doubt that they will have the indulgence of their sins, and the fruit of an eternal reward." Amort, de Indulg. P. i. sect. ii. N. iii. See also Note 9, p. 297. "Two centuries later," continues Dr. Lingard, " in the Council of Lyons, the same indulgence was extended to those who, unable to join the crusade in person, should by voluntary donations contribute to its success." Here is a great mistake. This Council was held in 1305 (Amort, u. s. N. xl.); but an equal indulgence was extended to contributors by Innocent III. in 1199, more than a century before; and a less privilege,—pardon of their sins according to the discretion of their Bishops, by Cœlestine still earlier; and these may not be the first examples. Ibid. Nn. xiv. xv. "From that period," says our historian, " Indulgences began to be multiplied. As often as money was required for any object really or apparently connected with the interests of religion, they were offered to the people. . . . But abuses of two kinds grew out of the practice. 1. The money was frequently diverted from its original destination, and found its way into the private coffers of the Pontiff, or into the treasuries of the secular prince. 2. The office of collecting the contributions was committed to inferior agents called questors, whose interest it was, as they received a percentage on the amount, to exaggerate the advantages of the Indulgences, and to impose on the simplicity and credulity of the people," &c. After mentioning the Indulgence published by Julius II. and Leo X. to raise money for the erection of S. Peter's, he proceeds :— " The brethren of Tetzel (i. e. the questors of that tax) rapidly spread themselves over Saxony : some not content with their sermons from the pulpit, offered Indulgences in the streets and markets, in taverns and private houses ; they even taught, *if we may credit the interested declamation of their adversary*, that every contributor, if he paid on his own, infallibly *opened to himself the gates of heaven ;* if on account of the dead, instantly *liberated a soul from the prison of Purgatory.*" Vol. vi. ch. ii. pp. 89—91. The last sentence really contains the *only* mention of the supposed *post mortem* benefits of an Indulgence, upon which Dr. Lingard has ventured in a professed account of their laxations or remissions of canonical penance; but in the fourteenth century, the Popes began to profess themselves able by means of them to save the living from the future pains of Purgatory, and, before the end of the fifteenth, they claimed the additional power of delivering souls already subject to those sufferings.

There is extant a "Summary Account of a Bull of Indulgences," granted in the year 1477 by Sixtus IV., to raise money for the repair of the Cathedral of Saintes in Saintogne, in which occurs the following important remark with regard to the last-named pretence:—

"The third principal grace also granted by our most holy Lord, is a plenary remission for souls in Purgatory, —which grace though it cause many to wonder, chiefly because it is not read to have been granted for a long time, nevertheless if the Doctors of Theology be consulted, . . . those who are led to wonder and doubt, . . . at least ought to believe, according to that which is contained in the Bull, that the Pope has power to give plenary remission to the souls in Purgatory [3]."

nature, rise, and growth. Phenomena like this require an explanation ; and I fear that we can find one only in the widely-spread influence of those detestable maxims of casuistry which, long taught and practised, have now at length, in the canonized teaching of Liguori, received the deliberate and formal sanction of the Roman Church itself.   See Note [7], p. 97.

[3] This document is printed in Mendham's Venal Indulgences. See p. 26.   The author is supposed to have been Raymond Perault, an author of some note, made a Cardinal by Alexander VI. (p. 8.)   He was Bishop of Saintes.   The Bull of Sixtus is given with the Com-

The novelty of the claim at this period is further established by the following entry in the cotemporary annals of the Abbot Trithemius:—

"A.D. 1490. In this year, Pope Innocent VIII. held private counsel with his cardinals, to which he invited by letter the ambassadors of nearly all the kings and princes of Europe, many of whom having assembled with him, he laid the matter before them, and begged their counsel. His proposal was, that an expedition of all the forces of Christendom should move against the Turks; and because large sums of money would be wanted to effect his design, he hit upon the following expedient. He sent into the whole of Germany the plenary indulgences of a Jubilee, not only for the living but even for the dead, which, because they were rare up to this time, became a subject of debate with very many. The proposition discussed was in sum this:—That the Pope, in the plenitude of his power, is not only able to remit the penalty otherwise due to sins to persons now living, being contrite and confessed, but even to remit the punishment of all souls now in Purgatory, in such wise as to be able, if he please, completely to empty Purgatory itself. This *novel* assertion found some to attack and some to maintain it, who wrote various treatises on either side, according to their views,

ment, pp. 12—48. He published another some months later, in which he complains of having been misunderstood, and declares that he had "granted that full Indulgence for souls in Purgatory *per modum suffragii*, not that the faithful people of Christ might be withheld from pious and good works through the said Indulgence, but that it might promote the health of souls *in modum suffragii*, and that that Indulgence might profit in the same manner, as if devout prayers and pious alms were said and offered for the health of the same souls." It seems that some had inferred from his first bull that "it was no longer necessary to pray for souls," &c. Amort, P. ii. sect. v. § iii.

with more caution however than freedom, lest by chance they should incur proscription themselves [4]."

The earliest assertion of this power, addressed to the whole Church, and thus, according to the current definition, proceeding *ex cathedrâ*, and therefore stamped *infallible*, or at least the earliest now extant, occurs in the Jubilee Bull of the infamous Alexander VI., A.D. 1500 [5].

---

[4] Annal. Hirsaug. tom. ii. p. 535.   S. Gall. 1690.

[5] Amort de Indulgentiis, P. i. sect. iii. N. xix.   Lest the reader should imagine that Indulgences have been of late years, from wiser management, less ruinous to the spiritual well-being of the multitude than they were formerly, or that the better class of Roman Catholic divines, since the more learned days of Thiers and Fleury, have become insensible to their evil, I beg to call his attention to the courageous remonstrance of the excellent Hirscher, "the Fenelon of the nineteenth century." After lamenting the mischief done by the present system of the confessional, the abuse of death-bed sacraments, and "the whole business of Masses for the dead," and avowing the "indignation" which is excited in him, "when he sees the people losing sight of the earnest work of life and abandoning themselves to a false security, and when he knows that they are encouraged in these fatal delusions by the personal interests of their Pastors," he proceeds to the subject before us in the following terms:—"A further practical and deeply-seated evil, to which the attention of the Church must be directed, is the idea entertained by the popular mind concerning Indulgences. Say what you will, there it remains : the people understand by indulgence, the remission of sins. Explain to them that not the sins, but only the penalties of sin, are affected by Indulgences ; very well, it is the penalty, and not the guilt of sin, which the people regard as the important thing; and whatever frees them from the punishment of sin, frees them, so far as they care about it, from sin itself. The penalty is what they are afraid of. The Indulgence, therefore, is the thing for them ; it bears the highest value in their estimate ; and conversion,—earnest conversion,—the true conversion, with its efforts towards a progressive moral purification,— this looks but mean in comparison, when they suppose they can easily

III. THE ROMAN DOCTRINE OF JUSTIFICATION.

I shall on this more abstruse point merely call your attention to the avowal of Dr. Newman :—

relieve themselves of all the consequences of sin by another way. To this it is answered, that Indulgences, so far from doing any damage to the repentance of the sinner, on the contrary rather encourage repentance, inasmuch as to acquire a Plenary Indulgence, a worthy partaking of the sacraments of penance and of the altar is always exacted as the condition. But on the other hand, I reply, that nevertheless, repentance is still no gainer, seeing that the reception of the sacrament of penance, amounting to nothing more than a performance, at a set time, of a formal confession, is far from synonymous, in the popular apprehension, with the undertaking of a thorough reform. Besides, the Indulgence is never conceded as consequent to the sacrament of confession, but always as connected with some specified work, so that in any case these works occupy the foreground, while the sacrament is cast into the shade. It is true that the sacrament must be worthily received, no doubt; but that gets a man no Indulgence ; the Indulgence is wholly dependent on something else. So it is; and hence may be imagined how gross and deeply pernicious is such a manifest corruption of the institution in question. But this is not all. Hence it follows, in the opinion of the common folk, that larger Indulgences may be had in certain places, or on certain feasts, and accordingly these places and festivals are sought out and observed by innumerable swarms of the populace. Here again no account is made of the sacrament; the Indulgence appears to depend entirely on the place and the day. And when on these festivals, and in such places, the most splendid festivities are celebrated, and graces are poured forth in streams, how is the poor man of the commonalty to suppose that all this is nothing, and helps him not at all, without repentance and reformation? If so, what is the use of all this pomp? In that case, better stay at home and bewail one's guilt in the secret chamber : it would help one more! Yes, indeed, to remain in the house, and in honest silence to labour for moral perfection, that were far better. In fact the greater the glorification of Indulgences, and the more pompous the solemnities connected with them, so much the more will it be impossible for the masses to imagine that no greater benefits are thereby imparted, or

"It is certain that the doctrine of Justification defined at Trent was in some sense new [6]."

IV. IMAGE WORSHIP.

I. There is a well-known letter of S. Epiphanius to John, Bishop of Jerusalem, in which he relates of himself, that entering a certain Church in Palestine, he found on a curtain hanging over the door a representation of our Lord or some saint; whereupon "seeing in the Church of Christ the image of a man, contrary to the authority of Scripture, he tore it, and gave orders to the churchwardens to bury some dead body in the curtain." Now I beg to call your attention to some remarks of Dupin on this narrative:—

"It is very probable that the use of images, which had been *very rare* in the first three ages of the Church, was not yet established in Palestine and Cyprus, and that S. Epiphanius, who was a plain, zealous man, thought it was dangerous to introduce it, and that he also spoke in too rigid a manner against this custom; . . . though it be true as appears from the testimony of S. Gregory Nyssen, in his panegyric upon Theodorus, and in his treatise on the Divinity of the Son and the Holy Ghost, that from that time there were pictures in some churches which represented the *histories* of Scripture and of the *actions* of saints and martyrs; yet it cannot be said that this custom was general, and it must be confessed that that even here they may not be partakers of them by the performance of no very severe obligations." State of the Church, p. 210.

[6] Development, ch. ii. sec. i. 2; p. 96.

S. Epiphanius disapproved it, though without reason, and that he was mistaken in saying it did not agree with the holy Scripture [7]."

You will observe then that at this period, even *historical* pictures (such as are allowed in English churches) were "very rare," and that their introduction was viewed with great jealousy.

In the fifth century pictures began to be worshipped by some of those semi-converts from paganism, whom the stricter discipline of the first three centuries would not have admitted within the fold. The Church, however, refused to tolerate the abuse. Thus S. Augustine tells us:—

"I know that many are worshippers of tombs and pictures. . . . Now I warn you to cease at length to speak evil of the Catholic Church in blaming the practices of men, whom she herself condemns, and whom she daily labours to correct as bad sons [8]."

At the end of the sixth century or beginning of the next, Serenus, Bishop of Marseilles, finding that the people actually worshipped the pictures in the Church, caused them to be pulled down and destroyed. This led to a correspondence between him and his Patriarch, Gregory the Great, in the course of which the latter writes as follows:—

" We praise you, because you were zealous, that nothing made by man's hand should be worshipped ; but we must

[7] Cent. iv. *S. Epiphanius ;* vol. i. p. 296.
[8] De Mor. Eccl. l. i. §§ 75, 76 ; tom. i. P. ii. col. 1153..

point out that it was not right to break those representations. For a picture is used in the churches to the end
that those who are ignorant of letters may at least, by
seeing them on the walls, read what they are not able to
read in books [9]." " Explain, then, to your people, that it
was not the sight itself of the history, hanging up, represented by the picture, which offended you, but that
worship had been unduly shown to them. . . . And if any
one shall wish to make such representations, by no means
forbid it; but by all manner of means forbid their being
worshipped [1]."

I need hardly point out to you the inconsistency
of this language with the decree of Trent respecting the religious use of images :—

" *The honour which is shown to them* is referred to the
prototypes which they represent ; so that through the
images, *which we kiss, and before which we uncover the
head and fall down*, we adore Christ and worship the
saints, whose resemblance they bear [2]."

II. I shall now add the confession of some of
your divines that such practices were not sanctioned
by the primitive Churches.

Polydore Vergil :—

" Not only did men not of our religion condemn the
worship of images, but, as Jerome bears witness, almost
all the ancient holy Fathers condemned it for fear of
idolatry, than which no crime can be more execrable [3]."

---

[9] Epp. l. ix. Ind. ii. Ep. cv. Opp. tom. ii. col. 1006.
[1] L. xi. Ind. iv. Ep. xiii.; col. 1101.
[2] Sess. xxv. De Invoc. &c.
[3] De Invent. Rer. l. vi. c. xiii. ; p. 419.

Banhes:—

" He would be a heretic, who should assert, with the Iconomachs, that the Church errs in the veneration and worship of images. Therefore our conclusion (that to condemn any universal custom of the Church savours of heresy) is to be understood of certain other customs, which have been introduced *since the time of the Apostles* [4]."

Cassander :—

" As to the images of the saints, it is certain that, when the Gospel was first preached, there was for some time no use of images among Christians, especially in the Churches [5]."

Petavius :—

" It is clear that in this our controversy about images, account must be had of the example and practice of the later rather than of the earlier Church. For while the superstition of the Gentiles was still borne along with full sails, it appeared better that many things, which were either not unprofitable in themselves, or even beneficial, should in those first times of the Church be suppressed or omitted ; . . . as that the images of Christ and the saints might not be taken by the rude and ignorant for the idols to which they had been used [6]."

Dr. Newman is very explicit upon this point :—

" The introduction of images was still later [than the fifth century], and met with more opposition in the west than in the east [7]."

[4] In 2ᵐ 2ᵈᵃ S. Thom. Q. i. Art. x.; p. 238.
[5] Consult. Art. xxi. de Imag.; p. 163.
[6] Dogm. Theol. tom. iv. P. ii. l. 15, c. 13, § 3, p. 582.
[7] Ch. vi. sec. ii.; p. 362.

In the context he speaks of the practices connected with their use, as "developments" of the
eighth century.

ARTICLE V.   V. WORSHIP OF SAINTS AND ANGELS.

SECT. I.   I. This practice is very frequently condemned by
implication in early writers, when they insist on
God as the only object of worship, or on Christ as
the only Mediator. It is also inconsistent with
their common argument for the Divinity of Christ
from the fact that He was and had been worshipped. Sometimes, however, they are led to use
language expressly and directly opposed to it. For
a reason which you will see presently I shall select
no instance earlier than the fourth century.

S. Epiphanius :—

" Neither is Elias to be worshipped, though he is still
among the living; nor is John to be worshipped, though
by prayer he rendered his death wonderful, or rather
received that grace from God,—nor is Thecla, nor is any
one of the saints worshipped[8]."

S Chrysostom, speaking of S. Paul's habit of
praying for his disciples :—

" Who then will pray for us now that Paul has departed? These followers of Paul[9]!"

S. Augustine :—

" Let not our religion be the worship of dead men:

[8] Adv. Hær. l. iii. tom. ii. Hær. lxxix. § v. Opp. tom. i. p. 1062.
[9] In Ep. ad Rom. xvi. 24; Hom. xxxii.; tom. ix. p. 834.

because, if they lived piously, they are not in a condition
to seek such honours ; but they desire *Him* to be worshipped by us, through whose illumination they rejoice
that we have a share in their merit. They are to be
honoured, therefore, by being imitated, not adored out of
religion [1]."

The same author discusses the question, whether
the dead know what passes on earth, in a manner
that has caused great perplexity to Roman Catholic
writers :—

" It must be confessed that the dead do not know what
is done here, while it is being done, but hear of it afterwards from those who die and go to them hence ; not all
things indeed, but such as they are permitted to tell, who
also are permitted to remember those things ;—and such
as it is right for those to whom they tell them to hear.
The dead may also hear something from angels who are
present at things done here. . . . The spirits of the dead
may also know some things done here, which it is necessary they should know, . . . not only past or present, but
even future,—by revelation of the Spirit of God [2]."

It is often pleaded by your divines that the many
strong condemnations of angel-worship, met with in
ancient writers, refer only to the invocation of evil
angels. The following passages, as you will see,
can by no possibility allude to any but the good.

S. Athanasius thus argues for the true Godhead
of Christ from that prayer of S. Paul, 1 Thess.

---

[1] De Vera Relig. § 108; tom. i. P. ii. col. 1263.
[2] De Curâ pro Mort. § 18; u. s. coll. 882, 883.

iii. 11:—" Now God himself and our Father, and our Lord Jesus Christ, direct our way unto you."—

" No one would pray that he might receive aught from the Father and the angels, or from any of the other creatures,—nor would any one say, God and the angels grant thee,—but from the Father and the Son [3]."

S. Augustine, supposing a heathen to justify his idolatry by saying:—" We do not worship evil demons; we worship the angels, as you call them, —the powers of the great God, and agents of the great God," replies to him thus:—

" Would that you did worship them; you would soon learn from them not to do so. Hear the teaching of an angel. He was instructing a certain disciple of Christ, and showing him many wonders (in the Revelation of John). But he was greatly terrified by a certain miraculous sight presented to him, and threw himself at the feet of the angel; and that angel, seeking only his Lord's glory, said, Arise, what doest thou? Worship Him. For I am thy fellow-servant and of thy brethren [4]."

II. Such passages as these tell the more strongly against your present practice, because it is certain that it may be traced, *in its germ*, up to the century in which they were written. They prove clearly that it was then only in its infancy. Indeed, some of your divines have made no scruple of avowing that it receives no countenance from Scripture, or from the example of the earlier Church.

---

[3] C. Arian. Or. iv.; tom. i. p. 464.
[4] Enarr. in Ps. xcvi. § 12; tom. iv. P. ii. col. 1497.

Thus Dominic Banhes:—

" The sacred writings do not teach, even in effect and by implication, that prayers are to be made to the saints, that their images are to be worshipped, &c. . . . Therefore it is sufficiently clear that many things belong to the Catholic faith, which have no place in the sacred page [5]."

Cardinal Perron:—

" There is neither precept nor formal example of it in the Scripture; . . . but that which is not formally and expressly commanded in Scripture is, as regards this matter, commanded by analogy [6]," &c.

Salmeron :—

" To the objection, that it has not been expressly set forth in the New Testament, and that the Primitive Church did not use this invocation, we must say that it has been so set forth abundantly,—if not in writing, at least in living tradition and custom, which has the force of law. Nor was it needful that they should be more expressly set forth; because it behoved that Christ should establish and explain the Scriptures composed and published in the Primitive Church, Who, by secret suggestions of the Spirit, carried the saints along with Him ;—and it would be a hard thing to enjoin it on the Jews, and an occasion

---

[5] In 2ᵐ 2ᵃ S. Thom. Q. i. Art. x. Concl. ii.; col. 521. With the practices here named, which are actually condemned in holy Scripture, this author, by a strange confusion, classes, as also belonging to the faith, though not taught in Scripture, the observance of saints' days, and the rule against iteration of Confirmation and Orders,—a practice and rule not only essentially different in their nature, but agreeable to Scripture, if not found in it, and actually taught by the full authority of the early Church.

[6] C. Le Roy de Bretagne, l. iv. ch. xii.; p. 980. Paris, 1620.

would thereby be given to the Gentiles of thinking that many gods had been given them, in the stead of the multitude of gods whom they left. And this as to the Scriptures; for as to the doctrine taught by word of mouth, there is no doubt that the Apostles delivered it to the Churches [7]."

.And Dr. Newman :—

" The treatment of the Arian and Monophysite errors ... became the natural *introduction* to the *cultus Sanctorum* [8]."

Again, respecting the higher worship which at a still later period began to be offered to the Blessed Virgin :—

" There was one other subject on which the Arian controversy had a more intimate, though not an immediate influence. . . . The controversy opened a question which it did not settle. It discovered a new sphere, if we may so speak, in the realms of light, to which the Church had *not yet* assigned an inhabitant. . . . The Nicene Council recognised the eventful principle, that, while we believe and profess any thing to be a creature, such a being is really no God to us, though honoured by us with whatever high titles and with whatever homage. Arius and Asterius did all but confess that Christ was the Almighty: they said much more than St. Bernard or St. Alphonso have since said of St. Mary, yet they left Him a creature, and were found wanting. . . . I speak of the Arians, who taught that our Lord's substance was created; and concerning them it is true that St. Athanasius' condemnation of their theology is a vindication of the medieval [9]."

---

[7] In 1 Tim. ii. Disp. viii. § *Postremo :* Comment. tom. xv. p. 473.
[8] Ch. viii. sec. i. ; p. 400. [9] Ib. 404—406.

How "St. Bernard and St. Alphonso" are justified in their worship of the Virgin, because the Arians were inconsistent enough to worship Christ, and yet deny His proper Divinity, is not very easy to understand. I quote the passage, however, not for its logic, but for the testimony which it bears to the late rise of a particular error. If Dr. Newman is right, the Mariolatry of modern Rome was a thing unknown to the Church of the first four centuries, to the Church of Irenæus, of Athanasius, and Augustine.

LETTER VIII.

PART IV.

LETTER
VIII.
PART IV.

In the present division, I propose to offer some testimonies with respect to two doctrines which are very generally received by members of the Church of Rome, but are not yet to be considered articles of faith, because they have not been defined, either by the Pope himself, speaking *ex cathedrá,* or by any Council received as œcumenical. We will begin with the more important and more notorious of these novelties,——the doctrine of Papal Infallibility.

ARTICLE I.

I. THE INFALLIBILITY OF THE POPE.

As it has been already shown that the supremacy claimed by the Bishop of Rome has no foundation either in Scripture or antiquity, a disproof of his pretension to infallibility may, from one point of view, appear superfluous. I notice it, however, because the history of this extravagance exhibits the process of development still incomplete, and will thus serve to diversify the illustration which has been given of the ever-changing character of the faith of Rome. Five hundred years ago it had not entered into the mind of man; but now, while it is still no more than an *opinion*, how few who wish, or dare, to resist its progress, or speak of it as truth, and as the interests of truth require!

If we can show that many Popes have, for themselves or predecessors, expressly or by necessary implication, disclaimed this attribute, we are surely precluded from ascribing it to them:—unless indeed some valid reason can be given why, while they are preserved from other error, they should be permitted to fall into an heretical denial of their own infallibility. Some instances of such disclaimer I proceed, therefore, to set before you.

i. In the year 547, Vigilius, Bishop of Rome, published a document, styled *Judicatum*, in which he condemned three writings, the authors of which, in their zeal against the Eutychian heresy, had laid themselves open to the suspicion of Nestorianism. He did this, although their profession of belief in the twofold nature and single personality of Christ had so far satisfied the Council of Chalcedon, as to restrain it from proceeding to their excommunication. One result was that the Bishops of Africa and Illyria separated from his communion. However, not long after, he withdrew his *Judicatum ;* and, when the Emperor, in 551, published an edict against the writings which it condemned, now become famous as *The Three Chapters,* he declared all who should receive it excommunicated. This was followed by a solemn Constitution, issued in 553, in which he " ordained and decreed, that from that time forth, it should not be lawful for any person in holy orders . . . to write, speak, or teach any thing touching those Three Chapters contrary to that which, by the present Constitution, he had taught and decreed." Concerning one of these Chapters, the Epistle of Ibas, he says :—

" We pronounce, declare, and define, by this our present Constitution, that the said Epistle . . . is truly orthodox, and will, therefore, by no means condemn it ourselves, nor suffer it to be condemned by others."

The Second Council of Constantinople, which is received as œcumenical by the Church of Rome, was at this time sitting, and the matter necessarily came before it for adjudication. After deliberating on the Constitution of Vigilius, it made a decree in direct opposition to it, "anathematizing the Three Chapters, and.all who received or defended them, or had written, or were writing, in their favour [1]," &c.

The next year, the Pope again changed his mind, and announced the fact in a letter addressed to the

[1] Conc. v. C. P. cc. xii.—xiv. Mansi, tom. ix. col. 384.

Patriarch of Constantinople, and again in a second LETTER VIII. general Constitution as formal as his first. In both PART iv. of these documents he says:— ART. I.

" We anathematize and condemn the aforesaid Three Chapters. . . . Whatsoever things have been put forth, either in my name, or in the name of any one, for the defence of the afore-mentioned Chapters, yea, wheresoever they have been found, by the authority of our present most full Constitution, we do make void [2]."

Here then we behold a Pope deliberately revoking his own solemn judgement upon a question of heresy, and pronouncing *ex cathedrâ*, (for he spoke to the whole Church,) certain writings to contain blasphemy, which, but a year previously, he had, with the same solemnity and form, declared to be " truly orthodox." Could he more plainly and emphatically disavow a belief in his own inerrancy? Or can we, in the face of such facts, persuade ourselves that he did not err?

ii. Now let us hear what another Pope thought of all this about thirty years later. The following extract is from a letter of Pelagius II. to some Bishops in Italy, who refused to receive the decree of the Council, but chose to adhere to the first Constitution of Vigilius:—

---

[2] Mansi, u. s. coll. 418, 488. The palinode addressed to the Bishop of Constantinople is most absurdly entitled in this collection—" The Decretal Letter of Vigilius for the confirmation of the Fifth Œcumenical Synod."—Col. 413. Thus does delusion keep its ground.

" You say that, in the beginning of the affair, even the Apostolic See through Pope Vigilius, and all the chiefs of the Latin Provinces, strenuously resisted the condemnation of the Three Chapters. . . . Let your brotherhood call to mind the deed of Peter. . . . He long resisted the reception of the Gentiles to the faith by holy Church without circumcision, . . . who, nevertheless, after a time, . . . when he saw certain loading the Gentiles, who were coming over to the Church, with the burden of the observance of circumcision, said, Why do ye tempt God, by laying on the necks of the disciples a yoke, which neither our fathers nor we have been able to bear ?   Ought then Peter, the prince of the Apostles, dearly beloved brethren, when he thus taught things at variance with his former teaching, to have been answered in this manner :—' We cannot listen to what you say, because you preached differently before ?'   If, therefore, in the matter of the Three Chapters, one thing was said when the truth was being sought, and another when the truth was found, why is this change of opinion made a subject of accusation against this see, which is humbly reverenced in its founder by the whole Church[3]?"

iii. About the year 715, was compiled a volume, known as the " Day Book of the Popes of Rome," and containing the various official forms which they employed on occasions of ecclesiastical business. Among these we find a solemn profession of faith, in which it was customary for the newly-appointed Pope to declare publicly his attachment to the received doctrine of the Church.   In the words of

---

[3] Mansi, tom. ix. col. 440.

this formula, every Pope condemned and anathe-
matized "the authors of the new heretical doctrine,
(i.e. the Monothelite heresy,) viz. Sergius, Pyrrhus,
Paul and Peter of Constantinople, together with
Honorius, who bestowed encouragement on their
wicked assertions, &c.   Now this Honorius was
Bishop of Rome from 625 to 638, and had been
expressly condemned as a Monothelite by the
Sixth General Council [4].

The new Pope was required also to declare in
the same confession of faith :—

" We also put under the ban of a severe anathema any
one, whether *ourselves,* or another, who may ever venture
upon any novelty contrary to this evangelical tradition,
and the integrity of the orthodox faith and Christian
religion [5]," &c.

iv. Urban II. about the year 1090 :—   . .

" Where the Lord, or His Apostles, and the holy
Fathers following them, have plainly defined any thing
by way of sentence, there the Roman Pontiff ought not
to make a new law, but rather to maintain with his life
and blood that which has been preached.   For if he were
to attempt (which heaven forbid) to destroy that which
the Apostles and Prophets have taught, he would be
proved not to be giving sentence, but rather to be erring.
But far be this from those who have always excellently
guarded the Church of God against the wiles of wolves [6]."

---

[4] Dupin, Cent. viii. *Conc. C. P. iii.;* vol. ii. p. 15.
[5] Liber Diurnus, tit. ix.; p. 43.   Paris, 1680.   In Routh's Opusc.
p. 508.   [6] Gratian, P. ii. Caus. xxv. Q. vi. *Sunt quidam.*

v. Innocent III. shall be our next witness, a man little apt to disclaim a prerogative, or resign a privilege, to which he thought himself entitled:—

"So highly necessary is (a right) faith to me, that whereas with respect to other sins I should have God for my judge, only for a sin against the faith could I be judged by the Church[7]."

vi. Clement IV.:—

"Our predecessors have granted to monasteries privileges contrary to the law of God and of man[8]."

vii. The following declaration is taken from the will of Gregory XI.:—

"Also we will, say, and protest, of our certain knowledge, that if in consistory, or in councils, or in sermons, or in public or private conferences, ... we have given utterance to any erroneous sayings contrary to the Catholic faith, ... whether by knowingly attaching ourselves to the opinions of any persons that are contrary to the Catholic faith, which we do not believe (that we have done), or even by doing so in ignorance,—or by showing favour to any who spoke against the Catholic religion,— those things we do, expressly and specifically, recal, execrate, and desire to account as not said[9]."

viii. Before the canonization of a saint the Popes were formerly wont to make a solemn protestation of their good intention, in order to provide against any future discovery of error in their decision. We

---

[7] In Consecr. Pont. M. Serm. ii.   Opp. tom. i. p. 188.
[8] In Launoy, Epp. l. iii. Ep. i.; tom. v. P. i. p. 263.
[9] In Spicil. D'Acher.; tom. iii. p. 738.

are told that the following form was employed by many :—

" Before we proceed to the declaration, we publicly protest before you, who are here present, that by this act of canonization we do not intend to do any thing, which may be against the faith, or the Catholic Church, or the honour of God [1]."

ix. Adrian VI., while Professor of Divinity at Louvaine, taught the fallibility of the Roman Pontiff in very clear and express terms :—

" If by the Roman Church is understood its head, to wit, the Pope, it is certain that he can err, even in those things which touch the faith, by the assertion of heresy in a definition or decretal. For several Roman Pontiffs have been heretics."

Among others he instances John XXII., who publicly taught, declared, and commanded to be held by all, that " purified souls have not their robe ; that is, the clear and direct vision of God, before the final judgement," a doctrine which he solemnly recanted on his death bed [2]. He concludes by saying that his object, in making these statements, is to " refute that impossibility of erring, which others assert [3]."

As Adrian was not yet Pope, his teaching upon

---

[1] Sacr. Cærim., by Chr. Marcellus, Archbishop of Corfu, l. i. sect. vi. c. iii. ; fol. 52, fa. 2.   Ven. 1582.

[2] Fleury, l. xciv. c. xxxviii.

[3] De Minist. Sacram. Art. iii., in Launoy, Epp. l. iv. Ep. iv. ; p. 481.

this point is less destructive than it would have been a few years later; but it is nevertheless well worthy of your attention, as it will enable you to see the full significance of his confession, quoted in my first Letter, respecting the fearful evils to which the errors of former Popes had given rise[4]."

x. The avowal of Paul IV. has been already cited :—

" I do not doubt but that I and my predecessors have sometimes been permitted to err, not only in the matter before us (a question respecting Marriage), but also in many other kinds of things[5]."

xi. The next passage, which I shall cite, occurs in the collection of Gratian. It is not originally from a Pontifical author; but as the book, in which it occurs, has been " revised, corrected, and expurgated " by the Pope's order, and is solemnly approved and commended to the whole Church by a Papal bull, it certainly must be allowed to be of very great authority :—

" His faults (the Pope's) no mortal presumes to reprehend ; for being to judge all, he is to be judged by none ; unless he be found astray from the faith[6]."

I shall conclude the notice of this doctrine by an extract from Fleury, which will inform you at what

---

[4] See p. 27.
[5] In Epp. Laun. l. iii. Ep. i.; u. s. p. 264. See p. 332.
[6] Decr. P. i. Dist. xl. c. vi. *Si Papa.* See the bull of Greg. XIII. prefixed to the editions since 1580.

period the speculative licence of the schools and LETTER
the impious flattery of the Roman court began to VIII.
ascribe "infallibility in faith and morals" to the PART IV.
ART. I.
successors of Liberius and Octavian:—

"James Fournier, Cardinal of S. Prisca, afterwards
Pope under the name of Benedict XII., writing against
the Fratricelli, said :—'They pretend that Nicholas III.
has determined that their poverty was that of Jesus
Christ and the Apostles. . . . And they say that, in questions of faith and morals, what has once been decided by
one Pope cannot be recalled by another. I answer that
it is false ;'—and he brings for proof the examples of
S. Peter reproved by S. Paul, and the opposition of
S. Cyprian to the decision of the Pope S. Stephen, before
a general council had determined the question of the baptism of heretics. Such were the sentiments of this Cardinal, raised afterwards to the holy See for his merit ;—
and the opinion of the infallibility of the Pope was not
introduced into the schools for more than *a hundred years
after*[7]."

II. THE IMMACULATE CONCEPTION OF THE BLESSED
VIRGIN.

Article II.

This is another doctrine in the same stage of
development as the foregoing, being generally received, but not yet imposed as necessary to be
believed. It was utterly unknown to the primitive
Church, and is manifestly at variance with the
whole tone and tenour of its theology. Petavius
the Jesuit, who was disposed to admit the truth of

[7] Liv. xciii. ch. xv. Benedict XII. died in 1342.

it, has collected many passages bearing on the subject, but not one has he produced from any author,
whose antiquity deserves respect, which does not
directly contradict, or otherwise quite clearly mili-
tate against, this modern fiction [8]. Its falsehood is
of course implièd, whenever a writer asserts that
our Blessed Lord alone was conceived without sin;
but it has so happened, through the good Providence of God, that some have *expressly named*
His mother, as subject to the universal law of our
fallen nature. Petavius quotes to this effect from
S. Augustine, Fulgentius, Ferrandus, Peter Da-
mian, Anselm of Canterbury, and Rupert of Duytz.
I give an instance from Anselm, a man of deserved
weight in his day, and representing a comparatively
recent period :—

"Although the conception itself of that same Man
(Jesus) was pure; ... nevertheless the Virgin, from
whom He was taken, was conceived in iniquities, and in
sins did her mother conceive her, and was born with original sin; because she too sinned in Adam, in whom all
have sinned [9]."

Anselm himself, however, with Hugo Victorinus
and Peter Lombard, supposed her to have been
sanctified and freed from every stain of sin, either

---

[8] See Theolog. Dogm. l. xiv. c. ii. In c. i. he shows that Origen
and Tertullian, Basil, Chrysostom, Cyril Alex., Amphilochius, Pro-
clus, Maximus Taur., Theophylact, Eutbymius, and Anselm have
spoken of the Virgin as guilty of actual transgression.

[9] Cur Deus homo ? l. ii. c. xvi. Opp. tom. iii. p. 60. Colon. 1612.

before the conception of her Son, or in the instant of its taking place.

An opinion in advance of this, but still, when viewed in its doctrinal bearings and consequences, entirely distinct from that now generally received, was held by S. Bernard, Bonaventura, Durandus, Thomas Aquinas, and others. While they denied the sinless conception of the Blessed Virgin, they imagined that an especial and extraordinary sanctification was granted to her before her birth,—a privilege which they supposed her to share with Jeremiah and John the Baptist [1].

Popular superstition had, however, outstripped, as usual, the speculative conclusions of the schools. While divines were disputing, a festival in honour of the conception of the Virgin was introduced and grew rapidly into general observance. It was first held in Normandy, in 1070, at the instance of William, the first Norman king of England, and is said to have been the consequence of a vow made by the Abbot of Ramsey, when in danger of shipwreck on a voyage undertaken by the king's command. In 1072, a "confraternity of the Conception of our Lady" was established at Rouen [2].

The festival was afterwards introduced into England by Anselm, himself a Norman, who became

[1] Petavius, u. s.
[2] Notice Historique de l'Académie des Palinodes par A. G. Ballin. Rouen, Périaux, 1834.

Archbishop of Canterbury in 1093.   As he could have no doctrinal grounds for its celebration, he was probably influenced by a desire to conciliate the king, by undertaking the patronage of an observance, which had originated with his father.   The following extract from a letter addressed to Anselm is interesting, as it exhibits the commencement of a furious battle of parties within the Church of Rome, which has raged, with more or less violence, from that time to the present :—

"Seeing that your anxious diligence has in different parts of the world inflamed many to a fervent love of the blessed and glorious Mary, Mother of God, who conceived and brought forth from the chaste bowels of perpetual virginity the Lord Christ, the Creator of heaven and earth, and through your care her joyful Conception is celebrated in many places, which of old, in the days of the ancient (Lat. *referes*; lege *veteres*) Fathers, the Christian religion was not wont to celebrate;—owing to which, when we were observing the festivity of that day, certain persons, going away after Satan, said that it was a ridiculous thing, because down to our own time it had been unheard of by all ages, and, persisting in their envy and the gall of their malice, went to two bishops, viz. Roger and Bernard, who happened to be then in the neighbourhood, and, talking to them about the novelty of the solemnity, provoked their minds to indignation, who, saying that this festival had been forbidden, affirmed in Council that that tradition ought to be broken and not kept [3];" &c.

[3] Epp. Osberti de Clara, Ep. viii.   Epp. Herb. de Losinga, &c., p. 124. Brux. 1846. A curious parallel to this early dispute respect-

The observance, however, does not seem to have made much progress, even in France, for seventy years or more; for when the Canons of Lyons introduced it in their Cathedral about the year 1145, they were rebuked by S. Bernard, quite as much for the novelty of the festival, as for the doctrinal error which it implied :—

"I am astonished that some of you should have chosen at this time to forego the excellent character (for consistency that your body has acquired), by the introduction of a new festival, unknown to the ritual of the Church, not approved by reason, not commended to us by ancient tradition. Are we more learned, or more devout, than the Fathers? It is dangerous for us to venture on that

ing the Conception occurs in the history of the persecution of the late Bishop Baines. One cause of the offence given by him was that he had censured the practice of making dedications of books to the Immaculate Conception, "a doctrine not belonging to the code of defined dogmas, and which Catholics, therefore, may without censure reject." He was summoned to Rome, and there compelled to subscribe a declaration that he approved, and always had "approved, whatever the Church or its organ, the holy See, approves." See Cathol. Mag., No. lxviii.; p. 164, &c.; or Letters to a Seceder, p. 178. Hirscher probably refers principally to this doctrine when he speaks of "the longings of many to be freed from the tyranny of certain matters of theological opinion, which are in full force, or struggling for dominion." He says, with Bishop Baines, that, "in all questions upon which the Church has not dogmatically fixed her decisions, every believer may freely, and without in the least ceasing to be a faithful Catholic, follow that opinion which appears to him to be the truth;" but he adds, in accordance with this Bishop's experience, that, while "this holds good in theory, practically one will not unfrequently experience a milder censure for embracing a heresy, than for the slightest deviation from such theological notions as happen to be dominant." State of the Church, p. 197.

which their prudence in such matters has passed by. Nor is this of a nature that the diligence of the Fathers could have passed over, unless it ought to be passed over [4]."

It would have been a happy thing for the Church, if this good and noble man had been equally zealous for every incommunicable prerogative of the Divine Son of Mary!

By the middle of the fifteenth century, if not before, the celebration of the festival had become general, and the Council of Basle only expressed the prevailing opinion, when, in 1439, it declared the doctrine, which is logically involved in it, to be " agreeable to the Catholic faith, to right reason and Sacred Writ [5]." Thirty-seven years later, Sixtus IV. appointed a Mass and canonical Office for the festival, in which the conception was spoken of as immaculate, and granted Indulgences to those who should observe it [6]. In 1483, he forbad the open

---

[4] Ep. clxxiv., ad Canonn. Lugd. col. 1537. S. Bernard argues in this Epistle that the festival has no meaning, unless it is understood to imply that the conception was holy, i. e. free from original sin. This difficulty has pressed upon many, and several solutions have been attempted. Caietan said that " the festival was not celebrated as that of the Virgin's conception, but of her sanctification in her mother's womb; but because the Church is ignorant of the time and day of her sanctification, it celebrates a festival on the day of her conception." Maldonatus and others say that the solemnity does not commemorate any sanctification of the Virgin, but is merely an office of thanksgiving for the benefits which we derive from the conception. See Richer, Hist. Conc. Gen. l. iii. c. v. § xvi.; p. 143.

[5] Sess. xxxvi. Mansi, tom. xxx. col. 182.

[6] Amort de Indulg., P. i. sect. vii. ad ann. 1476; *Cum præcelsa.* The Office was appended to the bull. It contained a collect in which

denial of the doctrine under pain of excommunication, awarding the same penalty, however, to
those who should denounce its rejection as heresy.
In 1661, Alexander VII. declared that " the faithful," in observing the festival, had respect to the supposed exemption of the Blessed Virgin from " the stain of original sin," while Benedict XIII., Gregory XVI., and Pius IX. have allowed the phrase " Immaculate Conception," the first in the title to the Office, the two latter in the preface of the Mass, in Churches where the clergy have desired it [7]. It only remains now that the doctrine should be formally declared an article of faith and necessary to salvation. You are probably aware that both Pius and his predecessor have been strongly importuned to take this final step, and that its propriety has been for the last five years the subject of earnest consultation in the Vatican. The appointment of a committee of divines to consider the question in all its bearings, and to report to the Pope accordingly, was notified to the Roman Catholic world in an Encyclic dated from Gaeta, Feb. 2, 1849.

CONCLUSION.

I am sure, my dear Sir, that, after a candid consideration of the facts adduced in this letter, you will

the conception is termed " immaculate," and the Virgin is said to have been " preserved from all stain." See Richer, u. s. § xiv. ; p. 140.

[7] See p. 303, where some facts relating to this subject have been anticipated for the sake of illustration.

be ready to admit that the rule of your Church is not as you have been led to suppose :—"Let there be nothing new,—nothing enforced, but what was once delivered as the deposit of the faith." However reluctantly, you must at last subscribe to the confession of Bishop Fisher, and acknowledge that, "according to the change of times diverse things have been," as a matter of fact, "delivered to the faithful [8]."

I have already explained, that Roman Catholics, who become aware of the unprimitive character of many doctrines and observances of their Church, but are resolved, nevertheless, not to renounce them, frequently endeavour to extricate themselves from the difficulties in which the discovery involves them, by having recourse to the theory of developments. This happy expedient at once enables them to dispense with the sanction of antiquity to the present system of their Church, and secures an equal licence for every future change. As you may naturally be disposed to consider my statement the invidious representation of an enemy, and to receive it with distrust, I desire, before we quit the subject, to repeat what I have said in the words of Dr. Newman, the most able, as well as the most prominent, expositor of the defensive tactics of his party :—

"It is undoubtedly an hypothesis to account for a difficulty. . . . It is an expedient to enable us to solve what has

---

[8] See p. 330.

now become a necessary and an anxious problem. . . . The
state of things is not as it was, when an appeal lay to the supposed works of the Areopagite, or to the primitive Decretals, or to St. Dionysius' Answers to Paul, or to the Cœna
Domini of St. Cyprian [some of those spurious writings to
which I referred, as bearing a fallacious testimony to certain peculiarities of Rome]. The assailants of dogmatic
truth have got the start of its adherents of whatever
creed. . . . An argument is needed, unless Christianity is
to abandon the province of argument ; and those who
find fault with the explanation here offered of its historical
phenomena will find it their duty to provide one of their
own [9]."

Happily the interests of Christianity are not, as
Dr. Newman assumes, identical with those of Ro-
manism ; nor is the duty of which he speaks incumbent on any one who, with the Church of England,
is content to believe and worship as the first saints
and martyrs believed and worshipped. But,—let
me ask in all seriousness,—will it not be incumbent
upon *you*, unless (which may God grant !) you cease
to be an alien from that Church ? The imaginary
stronghold of an invariable tradition is now confessed to be untenable. Another line of defence
must be adopted, another shelter from the assaults
of infidelity must be discovered. The substitute accepted by Dr. Newman and his followers can never,
I feel sure, approve itself to one who writes in the
tone and spirit which pervade your letters. The rock

---

[9] Essay on Development; Introd. ; pp. 27—29.

on which you stood has crumbled beneath your feet; but you will not, therefore, leap on a bank of quicksand. One other choice remains. If you would not be engulfed in a sea of doubts, or drift into the fatal shallows of indifference, strike out for the firm land that looms before you, in the primitive Creed and Apostolical constitution of the hitherto despised Church of your own native land.

I am, &c.

LETTER IX.

MY DEAR SIR,

I FIND but little in your reply to my earlier letters that requires particular notice. Most of your observations have been already answered,— and not perhaps the less effectually, because incidentally,—in some of my more recent communications. There still remain, however, two or three points of some interest and importance, on which I think it right to offer a few remarks, before we close a painful, but, as I trust, not an unfriendly correspondence.

But let me first express my satisfaction, at having found an opponent so ready to acknowledge and reciprocate the kind feelings, which it has been throughout my study to preserve. Some acquaintance with the periodicals and controversialists of your communion enables me to appreciate your Christian courtesy and gentleness. But if in this I have endeavoured to be your follower, you will not, I am sure, infer that I esteem your errors of small importance. If I have sometimes spoken of a corruption of doctrine, or a falsification of history without severity, it is not because they fail to excite sorrow or indignation in my mind. I regard the authors of that crime with horror, but I do not, believe me, desire to make you responsible for it. You, my dear Sir, with the great bulk of our Roman Catholic countrymen, have been deceived by writers whom you naturally respect, and whose accuracy you have no means of testing. There is one circumstance, however, which ought, I think, to have put you on your guard,—a providential warning which you are not free to overlook. Surely the *temper* almost invariably displayed by those writers, on whose authority you have relied, ought to have excited some feeling of mistrust [1]. Truth, self-assured, is calm, peaceable, and loving. But when men are uncertain of their grounds, or in their heart suspect the cause, for which, nevertheless, they are determined to contend, they are tempted to seek a false assurance in passion and excitement. The progress of self-deception is then sure and rapid. The power of reasoning and spirit of honest inquiry are soon lost in vehemence of feeling and the desire of victory. Any just doubts, the clues to truth, with

---

[1] I am unwilling,—nor is it necessary,—to do more than refer to some passages already cited for a different purpose. See pp. 218 (note), 245 (note), 314 (text).

which they may have entered on the controversy, have quickly disappeared. They have acquired confidence, and are at ease, in their position; for they no longer understand the difficulties by which they were once harassed; and they imagine them-selves to have investigated and proved, whereas they have but followed their own fancies and de-sires, and dogmatized and boasted.

I turn now to the yet untouched portion of your reply.

I. The first subject to which I find it desirable SECT. I. to revert is the bull Unigenitus. You think it incumbent on you to defend its condemnation of Quesnel's exhortations to the general study of holy Scripture [2]. You say :—

" I can at once perceive that they may be rightly con-demned, in one sense at least; for instance, the first pro-position quoted,—'The reading of Scripture is for all.' This is not a complete sentence. It may mean *useful* for all, or *easy* for all, or *necessary* for all; and in this last sense, at least, it is untrue; for the illiterate can go to heaven, though they cannot read."

Now, my dear Sir, I am quite content to put it to yourself, to say whether, on calm reflection, you really do think, that the Pope condemned that pro-position, simply because it does not contain a formal and express exception of those who cannot read, &c. Your apology supposes him to have been a mere

[2] See p. 63.

captious word-catcher, exercising his ingenuity on a very inappropriate subject; whereas you must upon consideration acknowledge that he believed himself to be condemning, not an "imperfect sentence," but a *principle*. To apply such epithets as *impious, blasphemous, heretical,* &c. to the expression of a general truth, merely because it does not name some particular exceptions, which every one understands and allows, would (give me leave to say) be absolute rant and nonsense. What the Pope really did condemn, when he denounced the proposition, you will be better able to judge, when I put before you the passage from which it was extracted by the compilers of the bull:—

" When we read (as in Acts viii. 28) of *holy Scripture* in the hands even of a man of business and finance,—this shows that it *is for all* the world."

The author explained his meaning by parallel passages from Gregory IX., who said :—" Ignorance of Scripture gives rise to errors: it is useful and beneficial to all to read it, or hear it read ;" from Thomas Aquinas :—" Scripture, which is meant generally for all the world, naturally describes spiritual things under the image of sensible ;" and by referring to a Homily of S. Chrysostom, in which that great Father labours to " incite all, even the most simple, to read the holy Scriptures [3]."

You notice another of the condemned propositions

---

[3] La Constitution *Unigenitus*, avec des Remarques, &c. ; p. cvii.

cited by me, and you say of it :—"To interdict the reading of Scripture is not always reprehensible." I quite agree with you : for instance, it may be necessary to take the sacred volume out of the hands of a person whose mind is affected, or likely to become so. But what is this to your purpose? The proposition in question refers to a *general* prohibition :—

" To forbid to Christians the reading of holy Scripture, and especially of the Gospel, is to forbid the use of light to the sons of light, and cause them to suffer a kind of excommunication."

No, my dear Sir, I will never believe that you, or any other serious English Christian, will, with a due knowledge of the facts, attempt to justify the condemnation of these pious and simple remarks of the devout Quesnel. His book may possibly, as you assert, contain some errors. But why do you plead this? Condemn his errors, if you will; but do not ask us,—do not force yourself,—to believe that a pious truth has become an impious falsehood, merely because a Bishop of Rome, in the eighteenth century, thought proper to proscribe it. The first duty of every man is to his own conscience.

II. The next question, which you have revived between us, has reference to the misinterpretation of a very different document from that which we have been now discussing.

You asserted in your first letter that " the

F f

Church never was corrupt." To this I replied by quoting from Bellarmine and others grievous complaints of her corruption at different periods[4]. You now explain that, when you employed that language, you only meant to assert that the Church had never ceased to be "holy;"—a truth to which all who believe their baptismal Creed will readily assent. But then you intimate, that, whereas the "Creed calls her holy, the Reformation declared her to be corrupt;"—thereby implying that the Reformation denied her to be holy, in the same sense in which the Creed affirms her to be so.

It may by some be thought unnecessary to offer any remark upon so palpable an error. I have reason to fear, however, that it has deceived many. Ignorant persons are taught that the Reformation was a denial of the holiness of the Church, as it is asserted in the Creed, and are then invited to join the only communion which, as they are told, allows them still to hold that article of faith. But what if, after all, the interpretation of the word "holy," on which this argument is built, should not be recognised by your Church itself? Yet so it is. The Catechism of Trent, in its exposition of the Creed, assigns the following three reasons for its declaring that the Church is "holy:"—

(1.) "Because it is consecrated or dedicated to God. (2.) Because it is united as a body with its *holy* Head,

---

[4] See Lett. I. sect. vi.; pp. 22—32.

the Lord Christ, the source of all *holiness*, &c.   (3.) Because the Church alone has the lawful worship of sacrifice, and the saving use of the sacraments, by which, as effectual instruments of Divine grace, God produces true *holiness*[5]," &c.

We find, then, that Rome herself, by the interpretation which she has put upon this doctrine, defends our Reformers from the charge, which you have too hastily brought against them, of contradicting it by implication.   But though she has wrested from your hand a weapon of some service, as you have been led to think, against the reformed Church of England, I persuade myself that you will soon learn to view its loss without regret.   To suppose yourself required to believe, that "the Church never was corrupt," is a most dangerous error, and snare.   It will tempt you, either to shut your eyes to the most glaring facts of history, or to distrust the Creed,—nay, holy Scripture too,—which, as you understand them, have been so abundantly refuted by the event.   There can be little doubt, that such false views of Christian obligation do often lead weak minds into an untruthful habit, and prepare the way for others to scepticism and apostasy.

Would that every snare, which besets a thoughtful Roman Catholic, could be swept from your path as easily as this!

III. To one other mistake, or rather to a con-

[5] P. i. Art. ix. § xvii.

nected series of mistakes, I think it right to ask your attention before I conclude. I do so; because it is desirable that all should be made aware of the worthless character of the authority, to which you have unfortunately trusted.

In your anxiety to prove that the Church of Rome did not fall into that state of corruption which is commonly supposed to have disgraced it in the tenth century, you assert that Baronius was misled in his estimate of that "iron age" by Liudprand [6], "a mere partisan who wrote purposely to blacken the Popes, and actually entitled his book Revenge." For this you allege the authority of the Abbé Rohrbacher, the Ultramontane author of the Histoire Universelle de l'Église Catholique [7].

---

[6] The name is variously spelt by the authors whom I quote; but for the sake of uniformity, as well as correctness, I shall write it every where as it appears in the last and best edition of his works by Pertz, Monumenta Germaniæ Historica, tom. v. pp. 264—363. A very impartial estimate of the character and authority of this writer is given by Koepke, De Vitâ et Scriptis Liudprandi Commentatio Historica. Berol. 1842. He has carefully compared his statements with those of others, both Greek and Latin, and concludes that, in spite of many mistakes (from which, however, no writer of that period is free), and many exaggerations from the vehemence of his likes and dislikes, he is not to be accused of fabrication, or any other act of wilful dishonesty.

[7] M. Rohrbacher asserts that Liudprand is, and has been, the *only* original witness against the Popes of the early part of the tenth century. "The accuser and sole witness, if witness he can be called, is named Liudprand. . . . Those who afterwards repeat the accusation are but echoes and copyists of the first." L. 59; tome 12, p. 437. This is utterly unwarrantable. It is true that Liudprand is *our* earliest authority for a few facts; but what right have we to assume that even

Having some experience in such matters, I gene- rally go to the fountain-head at once. If you will do the same, and examine Liudprand for yourself, you will find yourself constrained to acknowledge the truth of the following statements.

1. He did not "write purposely to blacken the Popes." He is the author of three several works: one, the *Antapodosis*, a Commentary on "the actions of the Emperors and Kings of Europe;" another, the History of Otho the Great; and a third, in which he gives an account of his embassy to the Court of Constantinople. Such being the subjects of his writings, the Popes are not often mentioned

those few were not recorded by other writers of the tenth century, now no longer extant? That Sigebert, Amalric, &c., are not mere copyists of Liudprand is clear, as will be seen, from the additional circumstances which they record, and some slight discrepancies between his statements and theirs; while it is otherwise probable, from what we know of the very great number of mediæval writers whose works have perished, that they, or those whom they followed, had early sources of information to which we are denied access. One fact will show how great this probability is. In the Catalogue of Eccle-'siastical Writers in the fifteenth century given by Trithemius (who completed it in 1494), no less than ninety-eight are mentioned whose works have disappeared since then. The names are extracted by Dupin, vol. iii. p. 79. Authors older by five centuries, who had to pass through the darkest period of ignorance and violence, are not likely to have fared better. It should be remembered also, that, if it could be proved, that this author was mistaken with regard to Sergius and John X., the only result would be, that those two Popes would be so far cleared. The character of others, whom he does not mention, and of the age at large, would remain as dark as ever. The contrary impression, however, is produced when a principal witness against it is first exhibited as the *only* witness on that side, and then declared unworthy of credit.

in them, and when they are so, it is, of course, incidentally only, as they happen to come in contact
with the Princes, whose actions he is relating.   Out
of twenty-seven Popes, who lived during the period
traversed by the historian, he has occasion to name
seven only.   I will give all the instances, to show
clearly the incidental manner in which he is led to
speak of them.   In giving an account of the Emperor Arnulph in his Antapodosis, he has occasion
to speak of Formosus :—" At this time Formosus,
the most religious Pope, was grievously harassed by
the Romans, by whose invitation (i. e. the Pope's)
it was that Arnulph had come to Rome[8]," &c.
Concluding his mention of this Pope, he adds, as if
he considered it a digression :—" But leaving this
matter, let us return to the order of our narrative[9]."
The war with the Saracens leads in the same manner to the history of John X., who opposed them
with great vigour and success[1].   His murder, and
the elevation of John XI., are narrated in connexion
with the actions of Wido, whose wife Marozia is
said to have been the mother of the latter by Sergius III.[2]   Sergius himself is thrice named, once
when the barbarous usage of the body of Formosus
is related, and twice without comment, as the father
of John XI.[3]   The brief history of Otho, or rather

---

[8] L. i. c. 28.   Pertz, tom. v. p. 282.
[1] L. ii. cc. 47—54 ; pp. 297, 298.
[3] U. s. and l. ii. c. 48; p. 297.

[9] Ibid. c. 31 ; p. 283.
[2] L. iii. c. 43; p. 312.

of Otho's proceedings in Italy, is necessarily almost LETTER IX. SECT. III. taken up with the affair of John XII. and Leo VIII., one of whom was deposed, and the other appointed, by that Emperor[4]. In the "Embassy" Liudprand mentions that, while he was at Constantinople, a letter was brought to the Emperor from John XIII., the superscription of which gave great offence[5]. It is evident, then, that our author did not write for the sake of the Popes at all, and, therefore, could not have written for the express purpose of defaming them.

2. But further, if he recounts the bad actions of some Popes, he is not backward in praising others. Thus he ascribes to Formosus "true religion and a knowledge of the divine doctrines," and relates a miracle to attest his sanctity[6]. He frequently styles Leo VIII. "the venerable," and speaks of him as "a lamb among wolves[7];" nor is he led by party spirit to say a word against the character of his rival Benedict, whom, I observe, M. Rohrbacher chooses to regard as the true Pope[8]. It is something to the purpose, also, that he zealously maintains the superiority of the Pope over the Patriarch of Constantinople, arguing that Rome was not to be despised by the Greeks, because Constantine had

[4] Pertz, u. s. pp. 341—346.
[5] C. 47. Pertz, u. s. p. 357.
[6] Antapodosis, l. i. cc. 29. 31 ; p. 282.
[7] Hist. Ott. c. 17 ; p. 345.
[8] Hist. l. 61 ; tome 13, p. 133.

left it, but to be more honoured, "because the Apostles and holy doctors, Peter and Paul, had come to it [9]."

3. When to your statement that Liudprand wrote " purposely to blacken the Popes," you add, " and actually entitled his book Revenge," you must mean that he called it by that name, because he hoped, by writing it, to revenge himself upon the Popes. You have here incautiously, though, I must say, with every excuse, gone a little beyond your authority. M. Rohrbacher says :—

" As to the spirit that animates him, he shows that to us plainly enough, when he explains the title of *Antidosis*, or Revenge, which he gives to his Third Book, as being chosen because he therein takes his revenge on those who have injured him or his family [1]."

This writer, however, has told but half the truth, and by this means has strangely blinded and misled his unsuspecting readers. By *Antapodosis* Liud-

[9] Legatio, c. 62 ; p. 361.
[1] L. 59 ; tome 12, p. 438. M. Rohrbacher exemplifies the partiality of Liudprand :—" All the ladies of the opposite party are prostitutes, all their husbands tyrants. On the other hand, Hugh, King of Provence, afterwards of Italy, is a philosophical and religious prince, the friend of good people, though he had a herd of concubines ; and the proof of it is that this king had a great regard for Liudprand, then one of his pages, because he sang better than any of his companions." U. s. p. 439. The reader will be surprised after this to find Liudprand expressing himself thus with regard to Hugh : —" Though he was illustrious by so many virtues, nevertheless he befouled them by licentiousness." Antapodosis, l. iii. c. 19. Pertz, tom. v. p. 306. Again speaking of his expulsion from Rome, he says :—" It is clear that this was so ordered by Divine providence, that what King Hugh had so basely acquired by crime, he was not able by any manner of means to keep." Ibid. c. 45 ; p. 313.

prand did not mean revenge, but, more generally, *retribution,* a return of good for good, or evil for evil, according to the radical signification of the word. His reason for the choice of this singular title he thus explains in a short preface to the Third Book :—

" The object of this work is to point out, set forth and proclaim, the deeds [not of the Popes, observe, but] of this Berengarius, who is now, not reigning, but tyrannizing, in Italy, and of his wife Willa, a second Jezebel, &c. . . . To them then let the present page be Antapodosis, i. e. a retribution, while for my misfortunes I shall expose their impiety to the present generation and to posterity. Nor will it be less Antapodosis to (certain) most holy and fortunate individuals for the benefits which they have conferred on me. Truly, of those who have been, or are to be mentioned, *not one, or scarcely one is found, that impious Berengarius alone excepted,* for whose favours my parents or myself would not express the warmest gratitude [2]."

The proper inference from all this is that Liudprand, so far from having a design to defame the Popes who were his contemporaries, actually regarded them as his friends, and the friends of his family. It is worthy of note also that John XII., the most infamous of them all, and the one of whom he speaks most, was the enemy of his enemy Berengarius [3], and that his language affords actual evidence of his being on friendly terms with the family of

---

[2] Antap. l. iii. c. 1 ; Pertz, u. s., p. 303. The older editions give *Antidosis,* as in Rohrbacher.

[3] Hist. Ott. c. 1 ; Pertz, u. s., p. 340.

LETTER IX. SECT. III.

this Pope; for, after mentioning that he did not receive the holy Communion when dying, he adds: —"as I have very often heard under attestation from his relations and friends who were present[4]." I leave the verdict to yourself.

4. You represent again, (and here also you do but echo M. Rohrbacher,) that the statements of Liudprand are disproved by the opposite testimony of Flodoard, who, as you both assert, lived *nearer* to the time of some of those Popes, of whom the former has transmitted such a bad report. In this too you are deceived. Flodoard was born in 894 and died in 966[5]. The precise dates of the birth and death of Liudprand are not known; but it is certain that he was of mature age in 948; for he was sent in that year on an embassy to Constantinople; and before that he had long been secretary to Beren-

---

[4] Ibid. c. 19; p. 346. I observe that M. Rohrbacher is bold enough to insinuate, though not to assert, that Liudprand is alone in his witness against this Pope also:—"We think the authority of Liudprand too light, to regard it as certain that John XII. actually committed the crimes, with which he reproaches him." L. 61; tome 13, p. 130. The fact is, that in this case Liudprand has done little more than transcribe public documents. The charges against the Pope rest on the authority of a cotemporary Council, consisting of forty Bishops, fifteen Cardinals, and others, and of the Emperor Otho, who acted against him with evident reluctance, and treated him with great moderation. Mansi, tom. xviii. col. 465. See the proceedings of this Council discussed, and many testimonies (beginning with the continuator of Regino, "a cotemporary of the events," and Adam of Bremen, who lived in the next century) adduced by Launoy, Epp. l. iv. Ep. i.; tom. v. P. i. p. 430, *et seq.*

[5] Dupin, Cent. x. *Flodoard;* vol. ii. p. 178.

garius[6]. He appears to have been alive in 970. It is probable, then, that he was a few years younger than Flodoard; but it is also possible that he was older. In a word, they were cotemporaries. The work of Flodoard, which M. Rohrbacher opposes to the authority of Liudprand, is The Lives of the Popes (from S. Peter to Leo VII., who died in 939). The European history of Liudprand ranges from 862 to 950. The actions of Otho, which he records, belong to 960 and the four following years. His second embassy, of which the account remains, took place in 968. He mentions one bad Pope, viz. John XII., of whom Flodoard gives no account; and in the work which brings him before us, we find Liudprand personally engaged in the proceedings which he describes. In this case then, at least, a more competent witness could not be found. But even with regard to the earlier Popes of the same period, his opportunities of information must have been much greater than any within the reach of Flodoard. He was for some years deacon of the Church of Pavia, and afterwards Bishop of Cremona. He mixed much in public affairs, and was present at the Council by which John XII. was condemned. Flodoard, on the other hand, only paid a short visit to Italy in 936. He was born in France, and became a canon of Rheims. When he visited Rome, he received great attention and many presents from

[6] Dupin, u. s. *Liudprand;* p. 169.

Leo VII. [7], so that, if his favourable language of that Pope and his predecessors be, as M. Rohrbacher ostentatiously reiterates, perfectly impartial, he must be allowed to have overcome a temptation, which few persons in his age could have withstood. His Lives of the Popes, I should observe, are written in verse, a form of composition which does not prepare us to expect a strict adherence to the letter of history.

5. You say of Sergius III. and John X. that, whereas Baronius and others, deceived by Liudprand, have represented them as " monsters," M. Rohrbacher has proved them to have been " remarkably good." You do not mistake your author's meaning: let us see whether you have formed a correct estimate of his fidelity and judgement.

Liudprand accuses Sergius of an inhuman outrage on the dead body of Formosus, one of his predecessors. Flodoard and others ascribe a *similar* crime to Stephen VI. M. Rohrbacher assumes that Liudprand is altogether wrong, and on account of this " gross blunder " refuses to trust to his testimony in any thing. Let us investigate this matter.

We have three accounts of the affair in question, proceeding from the generation which witnessed its occurrence. The one which I shall quote first does not mention either Stephen or Sergius as impli-

[7] Muratori, Rerum Italicarum Scriptores, tom. iii. P. ii. col. 324. Mediol. 1723.

cated in the crime, but charges it generally upon the *proceres* of Rome, as if it were the act of the party then dominant in that city. The unknown writer says that he had " lately heard from his brethren . . . that the body of Formosus, already nine months buried, had been dragged by the feet out of its grave, . . . seated in a Council, . . . judged, . . . deposed, . . . and that one hand had been cut off and cast into the Tiber [8]."

6. By Auxilius, an actual sufferer in the persecution of those who had been ordained by Formosus, we are told that Stephen VI., his immediate successor but one, caused the body of that Pope to be " dragged out of its tomb into a Council, where stripping him of his original dress, *they* clothed him in a lay habit, and after cutting off with a knife two fingers of the right hand, buried him in a certain tomb of strangers, *and not long after they cast him into the river Tiber* [9]."

[8] Invectiva in Romam pro Formoso, printed by the Blanchini in the Prolegomena to their Edition of Anastasius; tom. iv. pp. lxx. lxxi. Romæ, 1735. This tract furnishes a curious illustration of the difficulties which beset a chronicler in those days. It was written in the Pontificate of John X., at least eighteen years after the disinterment of Formosus, and yet the writer says that he had only heard of that event lately.

[9] De Sacr. Ordinat. c. xxx. Biblioth. PP. Max. tom. xvii. p. 21. Morinus has also printed it in his Comment. de Ord. P. ii. p. 307. It is in the form of a dialogue, and is intitled Infensor et Defensor. There is another tract by Auxilius, given also by Morinus, and in the Biblioth., which is a collection of authorities for the validity of the orders conferred by Formosus; and a third published by Mabillon, Vetera Analecta, tom. iv. p. 610. Paris, 1685.

7. From these accounts we learn, that others were considered as deeply involved, as Stephen, in the proceedings which they describe, and also that there were *two* several exhumations of the remains of Formosus. Now it occurred to me, at this point of the inquiry, that possibly, while Stephen was chiefly responsible for the first outrage described by Auxilius, Sergius might have been the principal actor in the second. A little further examination proved the conjecture to be right. On the death of Stephen, Sergius, then Cardinal Presbyter, was a candidate for the Papacy, but the opposite faction prevailed, and John IX. was elected. Under this Pope a synod met at Rome, to annul the proceedings against Formosus, and those who had been ordained by him. In the first chapter of its decrees we are told, that "the body of the venerable Pope Formosus had been dragged from its violated grave along the ground, and being brought, as it were, to judgement, had been presumptuously judged and condemned." *This* crime is ascribed to Stephen and a Council under him [1]. But we learn afterwards, from the eighth and ninth chapters, that "*Sergius*, Benedictus, and Marinus, presbyters of the holy Roman Church, and Leo, Paschalis, and John, deacons," had been excommunicated, because, "dragging the body, they were not afraid to fling it into the Tiber [2]."

---

[1] Mansi, tom. xviii. col. 223.

[2] Mansi, u. s. col. 225. "Sergium, Benedictum, &c., juste et

It appears then, that, not long after Stephen had
caused the body to be re-interred, it was torn from its second resting-place by Sergius and his fellows, and by *them* cast into the Tiber. The act of Stephen, however barbarous, was judicial, and pretended to some of the usual forms of justice; while that of Sergius was altogether irregular and tumultuary, and done in the undisguised wantonness of party malice. Now it is worthy of notice, that all later writers, who at all enter into particulars, and among them Liudprand, though they may have made mistakes in details, have, with surprising uniformity, observed this distinction. When they speak of Stephen ill-treating the remains of Formosus, they describe a judicial process; and when of Sergius, an act of lawless violence [3]. Thus Flo-

canonice damnatos, et a gremio sanctæ Dei Ecclesiæ sequestratos,— si aliquis homo . . . illos inter ecclesiasticos viros . . . habere voluerit, . . . sciat se fore anathemate percussum. . . . Violatores namque seu corruptores sacri tumuli ejusdem domni Formosi Papæ, qui, sub fœdere conspirationis ad capiendum thesaurum, corpus illius trahentes in flumen Tiberim jactare non timuerunt, divina auctoritate, synodalique nostro consultu, nisi resipuerint, sint (qu. sunt) a sanctæ Dei Ecclesiæ liminibus separati." It is incredible that they should have expected to find any thing valuable buried with Formosus, after the usage to which his remains had been subject from Stephen. I presume, therefore, that the charge of treasure-seeking was merely a fiction of party malice. Besides, if gain had been their object, why not content themselves with searching the tomb? Some other motive must have led them to cast the body into the Tiber. To this other motive the whole transaction is imputed by every other authority. This Council burnt the acts of the former under Stephen.

[3] It may be worth while to give the proof of this. A very ancient Chronicle, which ends in 926, says:—" Pope Stephen cast Formosus

doard says of the former :—"He inflicts cruelties on the living, more dreadful things on the buried.

out of his grave, and placed him in the Apostolic seat, and *appointed a deacon to answer for him,* and took off his Apostolic habit, and dragged him through the basilica,, and blood flowed from his mouth; —and he was thrown into the river." Pertz, tom. i. p. 53. The Annals of Fulda, ad ann. 896 :—Stephen "ordered his predecessor, Formosus, to wit, after being cast out of his tomb in an unheard-of manner, *and deposed, through an advocate answering for him,* to be buried without the usual burial-ground of the Apostolics." Ibid. p. 412. Sigebert of Gemblours :—"It is read that he (and not Sergius) clothed the body of Formosus, after having dragged it out of the grave *into a council,* and stripped it of the Papal habit, in a lay dress, and after cutting off two fingers of his right hand, caused it (or them ?) to be cast into the Tiber." Chronicon, in Pertz, tom. viii. p. 344. Amalric Augerii, Chaplain to Urban V., A.D. 1362 :—"Stephen *assembled his Council,* and celebrated it in the city of Rome, and then caused the body of Pope Formosus, without his Papal habit, yea in a lay dress, to be placed before him, and afterwards had two (Lat. *suos,* lege *duos*) fingers cut off his right hand, and after that ordered his hand to be cast into the river Tiber." Murat. Rer. Ital. Script. tom. iii. P. ii. col. 317. Platina, Librarian to Sixtus IV., A.D. 1475 :—"Martin the writer (about 1320) says that Stephen raged with such fury that, *holding a Council,* he committed the body of Formosus, after it was dragged from its grave, stripped of the Pontifical habit, and clothed in a secular, to the burial-place of the laity ; —having, however, cut off two fingers of his right hand,—those, to wit, which priests use in consecration,—and cast them into the Tiber." Vitæ Pontif. N. 116; p. 126. Colon. 1562. Stella, who wrote in 1505, speaking also of Stephen :—"*Holding a Council,* he caused the body of Formosus to be dragged out of its grave, stripped of the Pontifical vestments, and clothed in a secular habit, and afterwards two fingers of his right hand to be cut off and cast into the Tiber ;—and lastly, ordered the rest of his body to be buried in the burial-place of laymen," p. 122. S. l. 1601.

The extracts which follow speak of Sergius. Sigebert :—"He ordered Formosus, after being dragged out of his grave and placed, robed in a sacerdotal habit, in the Pontifical chair, to be beheaded, and, three fingers having, besides been cut off, to be cast into the Tiber." Pertz, tom. viii. p. 345. Amalric :—"He caused Pope

... He collects an ill-omened *Council*, ... and *casts off and deposes* his predecessor and patron [4];" and Liudprand of Sergius, that he ordered Formosus to be dragged out of his grave, placed him on the pontifical chair, clothed in sacerdotal vestments, addressed reproaches to him, caused him to be

Formosus to be dragged out of his grave, and, being placed on a certain seat, clothed in a Pontifical and sacerdotal habit, to be publicly beheaded in the presence of all, and afterwards had him cast into the river Tiber." Murat., u. s. col. 321.   An anonymous Chronicler :—
" This Pope Formosus did Pope Sergius his successor ... cause to be disinterred, and set in the Apostolic chair clothed in his Pontificals, and he ordered him to be beheaded on the Apostolic chair, and, three of his fingers having been cut off, to be cast, stripped of the Pontifical ornaments, into the Tiber." In Compilat. Chronol. apud Scriptor. Rer. German. p. 730.   Francof. 1613.   Platina :—" He inflicts capital punishment on his corpse, dragged out of the grave, as if he were alive, and casts the body itself into the Tiber, as unworthy of burial and of the honour of man." No. 123 ; p. 128.   Stella, p. 126, uses almost the same words as Platina.
If the Acts of the Council under John IX. had been lost, the uniformity with which these writers distinguish the modes of proceeding of Stephen and Sergius, would have made it, in spite of discrepancies and errors in detail, in the highest degree probable that both had been guilty of similar outrages.   As it is, we do not require their testimony.   I may observe, however, that a comparison of their relations reveals a fact, not before noticed, which must have contributed greatly to confuse the early traditions respecting these two Popes.   It appears that Stephen caused the fingers, which were cut off, to be *cast into the Tiber*,—into which same river, " the rest of the body " was (" not long after," as Auxilius says, and as we might infer from the Acts of the Council,) also ignominiously flung by a party of which Sergius was the leader.   The popular mind would not long continue able to discriminate between actions which approximated to each other at so many points.

[4] In Muratori, Rer. Ital. Script. ; tom. iii. P. ii. col. 318.

G g

stripped again, to lose his head, and three fingers, and finally to be cast into the Tiber [5].

Whether these details, given by Liudprand, are all true, it is impossible to say; but that Sergius and his party, and not Stephen, caused the body to be disinterred a second time, and cast into the Tiber, is certain from the words of the Council held under John IX. The only errors, therefore, with which we are in a position to charge him, are that he has placed Sergius too near to Formosus [6], and supposed that he was already Pope at the time when he committed that outrage.

8. But M. Rohrbacher has aggravated the mistakes of Liudprand by two mis-statements of his own. He speaks of that writer, as saying that Sergius " gave Formosus an advocate to answer in his name [7];"—a very serious misrepresentation, as it imposes a *judicial* character on the proceedings of

---

[5] Antapodosis, l. i. c. 30.   Pertz, tom. v. p. 282.

[6] Errors of this kind are very common in the mediæval writers. E. g. The Annals of Fulda make Stephen succeed immediately to Formosus, the name of Boniface being inserted by a later hand. Pertz, tom. i. p. 412.   The Chronicle of Benedict, written between 998 and 1001, gives a series of five Popes in the following order:— Sergius III., Lando, Formosus, John X., John XI.; whereas they should stand with several others thus:—Formosus, *Boniface VI., Stephen VI., Romanus, Theodore II., John IX., Benedict IV., Leo V., Christopher*, Sergius III., *Anastasius III.*, Lando, John X., *Leo VI., Stephen VII.*, John XI. Tom. v. p. 714.   Such a mistake, then, ought not to detract much from our comparative estimate of Liudprand's general accuracy.

[7] Hist. Eccles. l. 59; tome 12, p. 468.

Sergius, and thus gives a greater air of probability to M. Rohrbacher's opinion that he is only relating the act of Stephen under another name. Again he declares, *thrice over*, that Liudprand has " even made Sergius succeed immediately to Formosus[8]," whereas he says distinctly :—" The Pope appointed after the death of Formosus is expelled, and Sergius is made Pope by Adalbert[9]." This error is not so important as the former; but it is any thing but creditable to an historian engaged at the very time in denouncing the " gross blunders " of another.

9. M. Rohrbacher appeals to the silence of Flodoard as a convincing proof of the innocence of Sergius. It is by no means clear to me that Flodoard is silent. I observe that he hints at some severities exercised by that Pope against more than one of his predecessors :—" He strikes the usurpers[1]."

[8] Tome 12, pp. 468, 507, 508.
[9] Antapodosis, l. i. c. 30.   Pertz, tom. v. p. 282.
[1] I will give here all that he says about this Pope :—

> " Sergius inde redit, dudum qui lectus ad arcem
>   Culminis, exilio tulerat rapiente repulsam :
>   Quo profugus latuit *septem volventibus annis.*
>   Hinc *populi* remeans *precibus ; sacratur* honore
>   Pridem assignato, quo nomine Tertius exit
>   Antistes : Petri eximiâ quo *sede recepto*
>   Præsule *gaudet* ovans annis septem amplius orbis (qu. *urbis*).
>   Ipse favens cleri censura in culmine rapto
>   *Falce* ferit pervasores."
>   Muratori, Rer. It. Scr. tom. iii. P. ii. col. 324.

The words in Italics appear to have been suggested to Flodoard by the Epitaph on Sergius, which he must have seen, when he visited Rome about twenty-five years after his death.   See Note [5], p. 461.

G g 2

One of these was, of course, Christopher, whom he dethroned and imprisoned; but where do we find another, if not in Formosus?

10. It is certain, then, that Sergius was deeply implicated, during the pontificate of Stephen, in a barbarous outrage on the remains of Formosus. Have we any reason to think that he was penitent for the crime when Pope? One of his acts then was to honour the tomb of Stephen with an epitaph, in which he thus commemorates his similar deeds:— " He first beat back the filthinesses of the proud Formosus, who invaded the honours of the Apostolic See [2]." The man who could write of such an event in this spirit, ten years after it had taken place, was not far from being the wretch described by Baronius.

11. I have also met with two letters of Sergius, both of which betray the same bitterness against the

---

[2] I transcribe the whole Epitaph :—

" Hoc Stephani Papæ clauduntur membra locello ;
   Sextus dictus erat ordine quippe Patrum.
Hic primum repulit Formosi spurca superbi,
   Culmina qui invasit Sedis Apostolicæ.
Concilium instituit, præsedit Pastor et ipsi
   Leges satis fessis * (loc. corr.) jure dedit famulis.
Cumque pater multum certaret dogmate sancto,
   Captus, et a Sede pulsus ad ima, fuit.
Carceris intereà vinclis constrictus, et uno
   Strangulatus nervo, exuit et hominem.
Post decimumque regens Sedem eum transtulit annum
   Sergius huc Papa, funera sacra colens."
               In Baron. ad Ann. 900.

memory of his injured predecessor. In one of them
he tells the Bishop of Hamburg, how grieved he is
at the wrongs, which he and his Church had suffered
with " the unjust consent " of Formosus :—

" For what more wrongful than for Churches to be deprived of the honours justly assigned to them ? What more
unjust than to violate and break through privileges, &c. ?
Whatever, therefore, has been rashly perpetrated against
thee with the unjust consent of Formosus, . . . we revoke
under anathema, and altogether make void [3]."

In the other, addressed to a French Bishop,
named Amelius, he says :—

" Since the whole world is witness to the condemnation of Formosus, the invader of the holy Apostolic
See, we have been astonished at your letters, which named
him among priests. Therefore, if it is unknown to thee,
and has not been told to thee, know by these Apostolic
letters that Formosus has been condemned. . . . He has
been condemned for evermore [4]."

It appears, then, that Sergius, as Pope, was still
identified with the party of Stephen, whose bar-
barity he had so well seconded in a lower station ;
and, such being the case, ought we to refuse all
credit to an author, who,—in an age in which
written records, if in existence, were extremely
difficult of access,—appears, after a lapse of forty
years, to have confounded them together, in one or
two particulars ?

[3] Mansi, tom. xviii. col. 251.
[4] Bouquet, Rer. Gallic. Script. tom. ix. p. 213.

12. But I observe that M. Rohrbacher is not always so incredulous. He adopts one statement of Liudprand respecting Sergius, which is even rejected by Muratori, from whom he professes to have learnt the value of that writer's authority. He tells us that when Formosus was made Pope, "Sergius, the Cardinal Deacon, appears to have at least divided the votes[5]." This was rather to the credit of his hero, and therefore more easy to be believed.

13. Another circumstance, less honourable to him, is of course false. Liudprand mentions incidentally that Sergius was the father of John XI.[6] by Marozia, and Muratori confesses:—"It may be that he says the truth[7];" but here the Abbé again ventures to quit his guide:—

"A *cotemporary* author, the anonymous chronicler of Salerno, says that John XI. was the son of the Patrician Alberic; Leo of Ostia, who wrote in the following century, asserts similarly that John X. [XI.] was the son of Alberic and Marozia. . . . Behold what these *cotemporary* authors, as well as many others, say of the birth of John XI. Liudprand makes him the son of Sergius III.

---

[5] L. 59 ; tome 12, p. 455. Liudprand and the Abbé are undoubtedly wrong here. See Pagi (Crit in Baron. ad ann. 898; tom. iii. p. 770. Colon. 1705), or Muratori (Annali d'Italia, ann. 891 ; vol. viii. p. 165. Milano, 1819).

[6] Antapodosis, l. ii. c. 48; l. iii. c. 43. Pertz, tom. v. pp. 297, 312.

[7] Annali, u. s. ann. 911 ; p. 291. Yet with reference to this very subject, M. Rohrbacher says:—" We believe with Muratori and Kertz that these anecdotes of Liudprand are nothing but tales which well examined destroy each other." L. 60 ; tom. 13, p. 8.

Happily Liudprand is alone in his knowledge of this fact, and we know what confidence he deserves[8]."

Let us see what confidence M. Rohrbacher himself deserves. In the first place the chronicler of Salerno was not, as he asserts, a cotemporary of Sergius, or even of John XI. Muratori, who has printed his work, shows, after Pellegrino, from internal evidence, that it could not have been written before A.D. 980, seventy years after the death of Sergius, and more than forty after that of John[9]. In the next place the writer in question, in the passage to which the Abbé refers, is not speaking of John XI., but of a very different person, viz. John XII., who became Pope some thirty years later. He is describing an unprovoked attack, which the latter made upon the Princes of Capua and Benevento :—

" At this time Pope John was over the holy See of Rome, the son of the whilom Patrician Alberic. While he was a young man, and given to such vices, he gave orders to get an army together from all quarters, and hired to assist him, not only the Roman army, but also the Tuscans and Spoletines[1]," &c.

I believe that M. Rohrbacher never saw this passage in the original, but was misled by Muratori, who, in his account of John XI., says that

[8] L. 60 ; tome 13, p. 8.
[9] Rer. Ital. Script. tom. ii. P. ii. p. 165.
[1] Pertz, tom. v. p. 553.   Murat., u. s. col. 280.

the chronicler of Salerno calls him the son of Alberic[2]. This was, however, a piece of carelessness on the part of that learned man; for when he comes to describe the actions of John XII., he quotes largely from the passage before _us, and refers the whole narrative to him[3]. If M. Rohrbacher had read his author, he could hardly have failed to observe that the action related in the context of " Pope John " could not possibly belong to John XI., who, as he tells us himself, was utterly destitute of temporal authority[4].

14. The second witness, produced by M. Rohrbacher, is Leo of Ostia, to whom, though he does not acknowledge the obligation, he appears also to have been introduced by Muratori. You observe that he styles him a *cotemporary* too, though allowing that he wrote in the next century, that is, *at least* ninety years after the death of Sergius; whereas Liudprand was not a cotemporary, though actually born before that event. I am afraid, however, that this inconsistency is not the worst feature of the

[2] Annali, u. s. ann. 911; p. 292.

[3] Ann. 959; p. 511. Muratori has made more than one mistake about this passage; for in a note to the Chronicler of Salerno, Script., u. s. col. 280, he says by way of explaining it: Nempe X., Papa; while the index (col. 1136), doubling the blunder, refers it to the same Pope, and to his war against the Saracens. However, the error in the note was probably a misprint; for the parentage of John X. is quite unknown, and the Alberic of Liudprand, to whom he alludes as the father of the Pope intended, was, according to Liudprand himself (Legatio, c. 50. Pertz, tom. v. p. 358), the father of John XII.

[4] L. 60; tome 13, p. 9.

case. The Abbé tells you, while professing to make a great point of dates, that Leo of Ostia wrote in the next, that is, in the eleventh, century. Will you think this a fair statement, when you learn that he wrote at the very end of that century, if not at the beginning of the twelfth? Yet so it is. The probable date assigned by the critics is 1100 [5],—that is, not less than two hundred years after the birth of John XI., of whose legitimacy M. Rohrbacher represents him a trustworthy, because a *cotemporary*, witness.

But let us examine the supposed testimony of Leo :—

" At that time, the aforesaid Pope Agapetus II. being dead, John XI., a Roman by nation, the son of Alberic the consul of the Romans, succeeds him in the pontificate [6]."

It is perfectly certain that there is a mistake here in the numerical designation of the Pope mentioned ;—a venial error, precisely similar to that of M. Rohrbacher, or his printer, in the passage which I have quoted from him. It was John XII., and not John XI., who succeeded Agapetus II., and it was John XII. who, as all history tells us, was the son of Alberic. We are told by Flo-

[5] He was alive in 1115. Dupin, Cent. xii. ; vol. ii. p. 374. Cave, Hist. Litt. Sæc. xii. ; p. 557.
[6] Chron. S. Monast. Casin. l. i. c. lxi.; p. 205. Lut. Par. 1668. This edition, with notes, &c., is reprinted verbatim in Murat. Rer. Ital. Script. tom. iv.

doard, M. Rohrbacher's boasted authority, in two several works, that John XI. was the *brother* of Alberic, and the son of Marozia[7]. The same writer in his verses on the Popes speaks of Marozia, whom he there represents as the mother of John and Alberic, as an unchaste woman,—a fact with which M. Rohrbacher has not thought proper to acquaint us. Liudprand confirms these statements, and only adds to our information, that he was the son of Sergius by this adulteress.

A further deduction, if it be possible, must be made from the value of the testimony attributed to Leo of Ostia. *It was not written by him*, but is a manifest interpolation, "This clause," says the learned Abbot of Casino, who, in the seventeenth century, edited the ancient Chronicles of his house, "this clause neither owns Leo for its author, nor is it inserted in the right place." He ascribes it to

---

[7] Hist. Eccl. Rem. l. iv. c. xxiv.; in Biblioth. PP. Max. tom. xvii. p. 606. Chron. Rem. ad 933; in Du Chesne, Hist. Franc. Script. tom. ii. p. 600. Paris, 1636; or Pertz, tom. v. p. 381. The following is the account which he gives of this John in his poetical Lives of the Popes:—

"Nato Patriciæ hinc cedunt pia jura Johanni:
Undecimus Petri hoc qui nomine sede levatur,
Vi vacuus, splendore carens, modo sacra ministrans.
Fratre a Patricio juris moderamine rapto,
Qui matrem incestam rerum fastigia mæcho
Tradere conantem, Decimum sub claustra Johannem
Quæ dederat, claustris vigili et custode subegit.
Artoldus noster sub quo sacra pallia sumit,
Papaque obit, nomen geminum fere nactus in annum."
        Murat. Script. Ital. tom. iii. P. ii. col. 324.

Peter the Deacon, the continuator of Leo, a Roman by birth, whom he supposes to have been anxious to find a place in the book for the name of his countryman [8]. The passage is thus brought down to the middle of the twelfth century.

But M. Rohrbacher is not contented with the interpolation of Peter. He must improve it with a little insertion of his own. He has made it affirm that John XI. was the son of Alberic *and Marozia.* The latter name would certainly have gone some way to identify the John mentioned with John XI.; but unfortunately for our historian, not a trace of it is to be found in his authority [9].

And now that we have seen what the spurious Leo does not say, let us see what the genuine does. It really appears almost incredible, but it is nevertheless a fact that this same Leo, who has been vaunted as a witness for the innocence of Sergius, actually comes forward to condemn him. Only

---

[8] Note in loco. The passage is accordingly placed in the margin by Wattenbach, who has recently edited Leo for Pertz, tom. ix. p. 623. De Nuce used only two MSS.; one in Roman characters, containing only the Chronicle of Leo; the other in Longobardic, which had the additions of Peter the Deacon. The clause in question (see *monitum ad Lectorem* prefixed) was found in the latter only. Wattenbach, who has had access to many, has met with it in no other. The Chronicle of Peter ends with the year 1138. He was born in 1110. Cave, Sæc. xii. p. 579.

[9] He adds that "many *others,*" beside Leo and the Salernite, have spoken of John XI. as the son of Alberic, or of Alberic and Marozia; —a dream in a dream. L. 60; tome 13, p. 8.

four or five pages before the interpolation which we have been discussing, we read:—

"Adalbert was Abbot . . . in the times of Pope Stephen the Seventh and of Pope John the Eleventh, *who was the son of Pope Sergius*[1]."

So much for the defence of Sergius. Now for the evidence of good in him. M. Rohrbacher assures us that "during the seven years of his pontificate he was considered by the Christian world as a Pontiff worthy of its most profound veneration[2]." For the truth of this he appeals, as he informs us, from the prejudiced Liudprand to "the impartial testimony of three *cotemporary* witnesses." These are the poetical Flodoard, who might be five or six years older than the Bishop of Cremona,—the epitaph placed over the tomb of Sergius, as veracious, it is to be hoped, as epitaphs proverbially are,—and John the Deacon, an author who, according to him, "lived at the same time[3]" with Sergius, but, ac-

---

[1] Chron. Casin. c. liv.; p. 196. Pertz, tom. ix. p. 619.

[2] L. 59; tome 12, p. 509. "Not only irreproachable, but full of faith, of piety, and of zeal." Ibid. p. 508.

[3] M. Rohrbacher iterates and reiterates this statement, according to his usual custom. I find it no less than five times within fourteen pages (see tome 12, pp. 507—509, 520). But what is the truth? John the Deacon dedicated his book, De Ecclesia Lateranensi, to Alexander III., who sat from 1159 to 1181. It is printed by Mabillon in his Musæum Italicum, tom. ii. App. Ord. Rom., p. 560. Lut. Par. 1724. The learned Abbé has probably confounded him with John Hymonides, also a Roman Deacon, and better known as an author. This latter certainly "lived at the same time" with Sergius,

cording to his own account of the matter, at least two centuries and a half later!

15. Of these Flodoard, after mentioning his return to Rome at the intreaty of the people, merely says, in his hyperbolical strain, that the glad world (or city?) rejoiced in his præsulate more than seven years [4]. He says nothing of his personal qualities, nor can they be inferred from his statement that he was recalled by the people. He belonged to the national party in Rome, and his return would of course be eagerly desired, and joyfully hailed, by all connected with it.

16. The epitaph, to which we are referred by M. Rohrbacher, relates the exile of Sergius, and his return at the popular instance, and tells us in his praise that " the shepherd loved all his flocks at the same time ;"—an intimation, perhaps, of correspondence with foreign Churches. Surely, an epitaph could hardly say less in favour of the Pope, whom it professed to honour [5].

but unfortunately died in the pontificate of John VIII., at least twenty-five years before Sergius became Pope. See Mabillon, u. s. tom. i. P. ii. p. 78.

[4] See Note [1], p. 451.

[5] I give it at length, printing in Italics the expressions which appear to have been adopted by Flodoard :—

"Limina quisquis adis Petri metuenda beati,
    Cerne pii Sergii, excubiasque (Murat. *exuvias*) Petri
Culmen Apostolicæ Sedis, is jure paterno
    Electus tenuit, ut Theodorus obiit.
Pellitur Urbe pater, pervadit sacra Johannes,
    Romuleosque greges dissipat ipse lupus.   [Exulerat

Nor must we fail to notice the more than suspicious resemblance in the language of Flodoard to that of the epitaph. It is clear, on comparing them, that the French monk had the epitaph before him when he wrote, and that it supplied him both with facts and phrases. These two authorities, therefore, must be considered one. When Flodoard tells us that Sergius returned "at the prayers of the people," the epitaph is again speaking, and *in the very same words.*

But let me ask, what right our historian can have to employ the testimony of this epitaph in favour of Sergius, while he neglects its witness against John IX.? If it calls the one a faithful shepherd, it represents the other as a "wolf, scattering the flock." These statements come to us on the same authority, and must stand or fall together.

> Exulerat patria *septem volventibus annis :*
> Post *populi* multis Urbe redit *precibus,*
> Suscipitur Papa, *sacratur, sede recepta,*
> *Gaudet ;* amat pastor agmina cuncta simul.
> Hic invasores sanctorum *falce* subegit
> Romanæ Ecclesiæ, judiciisque Patrum."
>
> In Baron. ad Ann. 701.

We can infer nothing from the epithet *pious* in this record. It is employed in the epitaph on Christopher, whom Sergius expelled :— " Hic *pia* Christophori requiescunt membra sepulti;" and Stephen VI., in the acts of the Council which condemned his treatment of Formosus, is called by John IX. "our predecessor of *pious* memory." Mansi, tom. xviii. col. 223. Baronius strangely refers the epitaph on Sergius to the first Pope of that name ;—a mistake only to be accounted for, by supposing that he knew nothing of the life of Sergius III., when he wrote the history of the eighth century. That it retained its place in his last edition is *un*accountable.

Similarly, the epitaph on Stephen vilifies Formosus[6]; but this does not deter M. Rohrbacher from
describing him as a "good Pope," and possessed of
"many virtues[7]." Who can avoid seeing that his
respect for these fallacious memorials depends not
on their own merits, but on the nature of the
testimony, which they yield?

17. In John the Deacon we read simply, that the
Church of the Lateran was in ruins until the time
"when our Lord Sergius, the Presbyter, was recalled, and elected out of exile, and consecrated
it[8]," &c. He does not even say, as M. Rohrbacher
declares that he says[9], that Sergius was recalled *by
the prayers of the people.*

Such then are the three testimonies (or rather
two; for Flodoard and the epitaph can hardly be
considered independent), which M. Rohrbacher has
opposed to the general voice of history, supported
by the witness of Sergius himself, yet speaking and
breathing malice in his epistles, and in his inscription over the tomb of Stephen. Such is the
authority, for he pretends to no other, upon which
the monster of Baronius is not merely cleared from
infamy, but actually pronounced a model of piety
and virtue.

18. But we have not done with Sergius yet. His

[6] See Note [2], p. 452.
[7] L. 59; tome 12, p. 455.
[8] C. xvii. Mabill., u. s. tom. ii. p. 575.
[9] L. 59; tome 12, p. 507.

advocate reads a whole volume of panegyric in the simple statement of his epitaph, and of Flodoard, who appears to have copied it, that he returned " at the prayers of the people." Now there is an early version of this matter extant, with which M. Rohrbacher has not favoured his readers, though he could not have been ignorant of it, as it is quoted by Baronius. To its antiquity he can make no exception, as its author was a cotemporary of Leo of Ostia, and died nearly sixty years before John the Deacon wrote. We are informed, then, by Sigebert of Gemblours, that Sergius, " with the aid of the Francs, seized the usurper Christopher, and thrust him into prison, that he entered Rome *secretly*, *invaded* the Papacy, and drove the Romans by *threats and terrors* to regard all the ordinations of Formosus as invalid [1]." Our author's favourite plea, that Liudprand is the source of every bad tale against Sergius and his æra, cannot avail here ; for that author says not a word of any secret entry into Rome, or of the imprisonment of Christopher, or of any compulsion of the people by threats and terrors. Sigebert says, moreover, that he *invaded* the Papacy, whereas Liudprand evidently considered him duly appointed [2].

[1] Sigeb. Chron. in Biblioth. PP. tom. vii. col. 1464. Paris, 1589. Pertz, tom. viii. p. 345.

[2] His words are :—" Dum in eo esset, ut Sergius Apostolorum vicarius ordinari debuisset, ea, quæ Formosi favebat partibus, pars Sergium, non mediocri cum tumultu et injuria, ab altari expulit, et

19. The manner in which our historian has treated another, and much earlier, witness against Sergius, is yet more remarkable. I have already mentioned the Council at Rome under John IX. Now we find this assembly denouncing an anathema against any who should recognise the orders of Sergius, Benedict, and others; and the reason, which it assigns for this severity, is the excommunication of those who had violated the grave of Formosus, and cast his body into the Tiber. The necessary inference from this is, that Sergius, &c. (whom the same decree speaks of as already condemned, and cast out of the Church) were excommunicated, *because* they had outraged the grave and the remains of Formosus. M. Rohrbacher, however, does not permit his readers to understand the Council thus. The following is his paraphrase of the decree to which I refer:—

" If any one regard as ecclesiastics, Sergius, Benedict, and Marinus, formerly priests of the Roman Church, or Leo, Paschalis, and John, formerly Deacons, who have been canonically condemned, and expelled from the bosom of the Church, or pretend to restore them to their rank without our consent, he shall be anathema, as a violator of the Canons. *We also declare* separated from the Church those who have violated the sacred grave of Formosus, to

Formosum Papam constituit. . . . Formoso defuncto, . . . iis, qui post Formosi necem constitutus est, expellitur, Sergiusque Papa per Adalbertum constituitur." Antapodosis, l. i. cc. 29, 30. Pertz, tom. v. p. 282.

H h

obtain treasure from it, and dared to drag his body into the Tiber, unless they repent [3]."

The reason why Sergius and his friends were excommunicated is here concealed, and their crime transferred to another party, whose names do not appear. Whether M. Rohrbacher did not understand his authority, or has been tempted to pervert it in his zeal for Sergius, is a question which I will leave for others to decide.

20. His defence of John X. will detain us but a short time.

Liudprand says that John, while Deacon of the Church of Ravenna, being often sent to Rome by his Bishop, formed there a criminal connexion with Theodora (the sister of Marozia), and through her interest was promoted, first to the See of Ravenna, and shortly after to that of Rome [4]. There is no-

---

[3] Liv. 59; tome 12, p. 473. The Acts say (in brief) :—" Si aliquis illos inter ecclesiasticos viros habere voluerit, sciat se fore anathemate percussum. Violatores *namque* sacri tumuli Formosi sint (sunt) a sanctæ Dei Ecclesiæ liminibus separati." The passage is given more fully in Note [2], p. 446.

[4] Antapodosis, l. ii. c. 48; p. 297. A corrupt manuscript (5[a]; Pertz, p. 272), from which the *editio princeps* was printed by Badius Ascensius and Johannes Parvus in 1514, had the following reading in this chapter :—" Theodora, ut testatur sua, meretrix satis impudentissima," &c. This was altered on conjecture by Guil. Parvus (Petit) the editor into—" Theodora, ut testatur vita meretrix ejus impudentissima," &c. Hereupon Muratori (Annali, Ann. 914; vol. viii. p. 302), misreading his author, asserts that " Liudprand himself declared that he had received his knowledge (of the facts which he relates) from the *Life* of Theodora, *ut testatur ejus Vita*," which Life he supposes to have been one of those Scandalous Chronicles, or

thing improbable in the story itself, and as Liudprand was an inhabitant of Italy, and of man's
estate at the death of John, an historian ought not
to be taxed with excessive credulity for having
repeated it after him. Nay, there is much that
tends to confirm the statement of Liudprand in the
circumstances under which John is known to have
been elected; for they make it certain that some
unusual interest must have been exerted on his behalf. He was translated to the See of Rome only
three years after the death of Sergius, during whose
Pontificate, as we have already seen, the Church
was still violently agitated by the disturbances to
which the translation of Formosus had given rise.
Yet we hear of no opposition at the time to the
equally uncanonical appointment of John, or condemnation of it after his death;—a circumstance
that is perfectly unaccountable, unless he had the
support of Theodora's family and party, then paramount at Rome. Again, the mere attachment of
that family to an Archbishop of the distant city of

Secret Histories, by which unprincipled writers have sought in every
age to gratify the malice of the vulgar wicked against the objects of
their envy. M. Rohrbacher follows Muratori (though without naming
him) :—" He derives these anecdotes from a Life of Theodora; that is
to say, from a romance, or libel spread among the people," &c.
L. 59; tom. 12, p. 521. The whole thing is a dream; the genuine
reading, restored by Pertz from a MS. of the tenth century, revised
by Liudprand himself (see p. 269), being :—" Theodora, *ut testatus
sum*, meretrix satis impudentissima." The effect of this restoration
is observed by Koepke, p. 89.

Ravenna,—especially if he were a man of character, —is in itself a remarkable thing, and requires some explanation. These difficulties are at once solved by the information which Liudprand gives us; and as no other solution is even offered, I do ́not see that we can do otherwise than accept his [5]. Nor

[5] I must remark here upon a very singular circumstance in M. Rohrbacher's management of this affair. Liudprand (Antapodosis, l. ii. c. 48; Pertz, tom. v. p. 297) tells us that Theodora, a woman of infamous character, had two daughters, Marozia and Theodora, worse than herself. He then gives some account of Marozia, which finished, he proceeds to speak of the connexion between Theodora and John. He does not say distinctly whether he means the mother or daughter, but the order of the narrative implies that he is speaking of the younger. Accordingly Fleury says, that he was "elected through the interest of Theodora *the younger*, the *sister* of Marozia" (l. liv. ch. xlix.), and then gives an account of the whole affair from Liudprand. M. Rohrbacher, however, while he professes to follow Fleury, supplants the daughter by the mother :—" Liudprand, that narrator of scandalous anecdotes, recounts that Theodora, the *mother* of Marozia, . . . governed Rome, as its absolute mistress. To make use here, however, of the words of Fleury, . . . 'This John was a clerk of Ravenna, whom Peter, Archbishop of that city, often sent to Rome on business with the Pope. He was handsome ; Theodora became amorous of him,'" &c. L. 59 ; tom. 12, p. 520. Now what can be the reason that M. Rohrbacher, while "using the words of Fleury," has chosen to deviate from that writer's interpretation of Liudprand upon this sole point,—and that, without vouchsafing to give his readers the slightest intimation of his having done so ? By representing that Liudprand accused John of a criminal connexion with the *mother* of Marozia, instead of her *younger sister*, he is importing a grave improbability into the narrative of that historian, and wounding his credit seriously with a reflecting reader. It is clear, both from Liudprand and others, that Sergius was not a young man when he became Pope. It may be presumed then, if Liudprand's story of his connexion with Marozia be true, that *she* was not very young either at that time. Her mother, then, must at least have passed the middle term of life, when John, then in his prime, as every thing related of

is the narrative of this author inconsistent with any thing that is recorded of John, after he became Pope. The qualities that he displayed in that capacity, which were those of a politic chief and spirited soldier, are by no means inconsistent with the character of licentiousness attributed to him by his cotemporary.

21. One part of Liudprand's story is certainly inaccurate. John became Archbishop of Ravenna nine years before he was removed to Rome; and this circumstance might suggest that he and Theodora could not have met till then. But the inference is neutralized by the fact, that he had been expelled from Ravenna. Their connexion may have commenced during his exile, and not in the manner described by Liudprand. I believe that this writer is the only cotemporary author, who distinctly ascribes his elevation to such a cause; but, contrary to the insinuations of M. Rohrbacher, we are informed by two other authorities that he obtained the see in a discreditable and irregular manner. One of these is the writer of the cotemporary Invective against Rome, already quoted:—

him implies, was made Bishop of Rome. Under these circumstances, it is very difficult to believe the tale which M. Rohrbacher ascribes to Liudprand; viz. that these two persons lived in criminal intercourse with each other. But there is nothing improbable in the assertion which Fleury (and with good reason) supposes him to make. It is natural enough to find John on the same terms with Theodora, the daughter, that Sergius, an older man, had been some years before with Marozia, her elder sister.

" This John, contrary to all authority of the Canons, presumed to invade the Church of Bologna. . . . Likewise after his consecration he unworthily performed the solemnities of Masses by the Pontifical rite, and went through unlawful consecrations. Leaving this, *he usurped, by nefarious attempts*, the holy Roman and Apostolic Church; and now he wishes to loose and bind at his pleasure; and, like that Lucifer who sought to place his seat in the North, and lifting himself on high, boasted that he would be like God, he desires to excommunicate the Catholic and Universal Church, and seeks to anathematize men more just and holy than himself[6]."

22. The other testimony, to which I refer, is contained in the following entry, made soon after the death of John, in the " Chronicle of S. Benedict," an ancient register of passing events kept in the Italian monastery of Mount Casino :—

" John, Archbishop of the Church of Ravenna, *being invited by the chiefs of Rome*, acting contrary to the provisions of the Canons, invaded the Roman Church, and presided in it sixteen years, at the end of which he was deposed by them in his lifetime, through the secret, but just, judgement of God[7]."

Those chiefs of Rome, be it remembered, would be the party of Theodora.

23. M. Rohrbacher does not notice the two last-

[6] In Proleg. ad Anast. Opp.; tom. iv. p. lxxiv. Liudprand says that he was chosen to Bologna, but transferred to Ravenna before he was consecrated. Antapodosis, l. ii. c. 48. Pertz, tom. v. p. 297.

[7] In Pertz, tom. v. p. 199. I have been directed to these two important testimonies by Koepke, p. 91.

cited authorities; but to the statements of Liudprand he opposes the testimony of two cotemporary
versemakers,—Flodoard, and the author of a Panegyric on the Emperor Berengarius. Of the former
he says:—

"Flodoard, a cotemporary and impartial author, says
that John X., having governed *with wisdom* the Church
of Ravenna, was called to govern the principal Church,
the Church of Rome; that he shone there a little more
than fourteen years, by his zeal to adorn this Church,
and by the peace which he caused to reign there[8]."

Here is another instance of our historian's un-
faithfulness. The *wisdom* with which John governed
at Ravenna is simply a discovery of his own. Flodoard says nothing about it; nor is there a single
word, to justify the interpolation, in any of the
ancient writers whom I have examined. And
beyond the phrase, for which we are indebted to the
ingenuity of the Abbé himself, what is there in the
vague generalities of Flodoard, as above quoted,
that contradicts the character of John as gathered

---

[8] L. 59; tom. 12, p. 520. I transcribe the words of Flodoard:—

"Surgit abhinc Decimus scandens sacra jura Johannes.
Rexerat ille Ravennatem moderamine plebem.
Inde petitus ad hanc Romanam percolit arcem;
Bis septem qua prænituit paulo amplius annis.
Pontifici hic nostro legat segmenta Seulfo;
Munificisque sacram decorans ornatibus aulam,
Pace nitet; dum Patricia deceptus iniqua
Carcere conjicitur, claustrisque arctatur opacis.
Spiritus at sævis retineri non valet antris:
Emicat immo æthræ decreta sedilia scandens."
                Murat. Rer. It. Scr. tom. iii. P. ii. col. 324.

from the account of Liudprand?   He *did* shine as
Pope, by the remarkable victory which his sagacity
and courage obtained over the Saracens, and by the
peace that resulted from it; but how does this
prove him to have been a moral and religious man,
—or rather, I should say, a wise and holy Bishop?
Unfortunately too for M. Rohrbacher's interpretation of the poetical Flodoard, the tone in which he
speaks of him in prose, and the facts which he
relates of him, are more suitable to the Pope described by Liudprand, than to the saintly hero of
our historian.   Thus he has occasion to refer to him
several times, in connexion with the elevation of a
boy only five years old to the Archiepiscopal see of
Rheims, an appointment which this " remarkably
good " Pope confirmed [9]; and again as follows:—
" Meanwhile the envoy of Count Heribert returns
from Rome with an account of the imprisonment of
Pope John by Wido, the brother of King Hugo,
*because of a quarrel that had sprung up between
them* [1];" and in recording the events of the following
year:—" Pope John, being deprived of his chief-

[9] Hist. Eccl. Rem. l. iv. c. xx.   Biblioth. PP. Man. tom. xvii.
p. 605. M. Rohrbacher is very amusing here :—" This condescension
of the Pope John X. is without doubt very extraordinary.   What
could be his motives?   As we have recognised in him up to this time
a superior genius, we may imagine for him motives that were not
contemptible.   For example, as Count Heribert held King Charles in
prison, let us suppose that the Pope only granted him his unwonted
request, on condition that he should give the king his liberty, and
even re-establish him on the throne."   L. 60; tom. 13, p. 4.

[1] Chron. Eccl. Rem. ad ann. 928, in Du Chesne, tom. ii. p. 598.
Sim. Hist. Eccl. Rem. l. iv. c. xxi., u. s. p. 606.

taincy by a certain powerful woman named Marozia, is kept in prison, and dies, as some affirm, by violence; as more, however, from the effect of grief[2]." It must be apparent to every one, that Flodoard knew nothing of those high qualities, which M. Rohrbacher ascribes to John, when he penned these brief notices,—in his prose writings the only notices,—of his conduct and fate.

24. The writer of the Panegyric on Berengarius is said by M. Rohrbacher to be of " unsuspected " authority[3]; from which the reader would naturally infer that his impartiality is beyond a question. That he is not justified in giving this impression of his author's character must, however, be the conclusion of all, who are aware that he wrote that poem, a piece of fulsome and extravagant flattery, during the life of Berengarius, and that his hero and the Pope were in close alliance, and under great obligations to each other.   John had renewed the coronation of the Emperor, which one of his predecessors had declared null, and, in return for this favour, Berengarius had assisted him in the war against the Saracens[4].   Is it then likely that the poet, describing the coronation of his imperial patron, would venture to speak without commendation of the Pope, who, under such circumstances, had placed the much coveted crown upon his head ?

[2] Chron. u. s., ad ann. 929.   [3] L. 59 ; tom. 12, p. 520.
[4] Rohrbacher, u. s. p. 522.

And after all, what is it that he says of John? He speaks indeed of his sagacity, which no˙one disputes; but of his moral and religious character, he says not one single word. The Pope is introduced, calling Berengarius to the imperial dignity:—

"The chief pastor in the city at that time was John, greatly illustrious by his office, and full of wisdom, and long deservedly reserved for such a work [5]."

The whole of the truth respecting Sergius and John, it is, of course, impossible for us to ascertain. My object has not been to convict them; but to enable you to see what qualifications your favourite historian has brought to his task. The matter upon which I have commented does not occupy above a dozen pages of his voluminous work; but within that narrow compass, we have observed many instances of rash and partial judgement, many of gross exaggeration, and many of palpable misrepresentation and misstatement. The part which has been subjected to our scrutiny was not selected for the purpose, but came before us quite fortuitously. Such being the case, I feel justified in asking you to withdraw all confidence from the representations of M. Rohrbacher, until you have convinced your-

---

[5] "Summus erat pastor tunc temporis Urbe Johannes,
Officio affatim clarus, sophiaque repletus,
Atque diu talem merito servatus ad usum."

L. iv.   Pertz, tom. vi. p. 208.

This last book is entirely occupied with the visit of Berengarius to Rome on the occasion mentioned.

self, by actual investigation, that those specimens of his production, which we have now examined, are an exception to its general character. The task may be tedious; but it is without other difficulty. The result I can foretell. You will find every portion of his history of the same texture, and of the same value.

IV. But you referred me to that person's supposed vindication of John and Sergius, as some answer to a remark upon the general state of the Western Church in the tenth century. It may perhaps occur to you now, that, although M. Rohrbacher's defence of the Popes cannot be sustained, the Church at large may, notwithstanding, have been free from the gross ignorance, and vile corruptions in discipline and morals, which Baronius and others have laid to its charge. If so, the suggestion may be at once refuted by an appeal to the still extant testimony of some few writers of the age, to whose authority no exception, that I am aware, has been, or can be, made [6].

[6] There is one peculiarity about Liudprand's principal work which may be mentioned here. It contains several stories of revolting indecency. M. Rohrbacher urges that this ought to discredit his authority as an historian (l. 59 ; tom. 12, p. 438, &c.),—an argument to which he endeavours to give weight by asserting that "they have no relation to his history;" whereas, in truth, however unnecessary to be told, they have (I believe, *all*) a very close connexion with events of importance to the personages of whom he writes. But what must have been the deep and general corruption of an age, which could allow an eminent ecclesiastic, one of the principal public characters of his day, and soon to become a bishop, to compose, and dedicate to

Among the remains of Atto, Bishop of Vercelli from 945 to 960, are eleven epistles, the greater part of which were written on occasions, which could only have arisen at a period, when the principles and practice of Christianity were to a very great extent lost sight of, even by those who were its authorized guardians and teachers. The first is to a Bishop, who refused obedience to his sovereign. The second and third are against certain in his diocese, who forsook the Churches, and addicted themselves to "unlawful arts" of divination, &c. The fourth is against others, who, on a plea of principle, chose to make Friday a day of idleness and feasting. The ninth and tenth are to his Clergy, and refer to the habits of incontinence which prevailed among them. The excuse for concubinage, which he had received from some, will not increase your reverence for those who offered it :—"They say, 'If we were not supported by the hands of these women, we should soon perish with hunger or nakedness,'—which," says the Bishop, "we know to be false." The eleventh is addressed to his brother Bishops, and refers to the practice of Princes in demanding hostages from them, on the prospect of war, as a security for their loyalty. He enters at length on the duties of Bishops towards

an actual bishop, whom he styles his "most holy father," "reverend and full of all sanctity " (l. i. c. 1; l. iii. c. 1), a book of which he evidently considers those obscene narratives one of the most interesting features ?

their secular Prince, and also towards the hostages, whose lives they place in his power. The following few words reveal a hideous picture :—

" We have heard and seen *many* who, after giving hostages, have violated their pledge ; but *some* who have kept faith till death, even without having given hostages. . . . How could they expose others to peril on their account, who are bound to expose themselves for them [7] ? "

In a tract on the Afflictions of the Church, he complains bitterly of the Simoniacal Ordinations so common in that age, and of the impiety of the secular princes, who conferred Bishoprics on their unworthy favourites and relations, sometimes even on mere children.   He describes with indignation the farce of the preliminary election in this last case :—

" Having no merits to recommend them, they are praised for their chastity only ;—and how can he be called chaste, who has not yet arrived at the age of passion ?   A little boy is set in the midst.   The people are asked what his character is.   Not willingly, however, but against their feelings, do they bear testimony to him.   Why do they superfluously seek praise for him, when his uselessness is seen by all ?   The wishes of all are asked, which they are afraid to declare publicly. Of those, however, which, extorted by fear, they do avow, the very persons who ask them do not canvass for the expression.   Most laugh ; some as if they were pleased at the child's honour, others, however, in mockery of the visible and open juggle [8]."

[7] D'Acher. Spicil. tom. i. p. 442.   [8] Ibid., p. 423.

Evidence still more decisive is found in the remains of Rathierus, who was Bishop of Verona and Liège in the middle of the same century:—

" Whence has arisen that general contempt of the present age for the Canons,—nay, for the Gospels, and *all* the precepts of the Lord? That men suppose that it will not profit them to observe the lesser, who are conscious that they have despised the greater? For on this principle, what advantage does it bring, if a man abstain from keeping hounds for his amusement, while he has harlots for his lust? If he refuse to take arms for the defence of himself and others, while he ceases not to commit crime to his own destruction and that of many? If he refrain from striking the faithful who sin with his fist, or with a stick (which also is forbidden by the Canons), while he is slaying them with the scourge of his false absolution, his gifts, or at all events, his blessing, or by an example of the worst actions [9]?"

" When the laity see us often read (of the terrors of the Lord, in church), and laugh, and so obstinately and boldly stand out against them, and show ourselves hardened in avowed rebellion against God, can it seem strange to any one, if *they* do not care for them? . . . Whence they hold our excommunications and absolutions cheap; because, as far as they can understand, they know that we are excommunicated ourselves by the holy Canons, and they understand that no one, who is himself bound, can bind or loose another at his will [1]."

" All the sons of the Church perceiving this (i.e. the corruption of the Clergy, &c.), also themselves put a slight value on all the things contained in the Scriptures, resting

[9] Volum. Perpend. P. i. in D'Acher. Spicil.; tom. i. p. 350.
[1] Ibid., p. 353.

on the example of such, and trusting to the mercy of God beyond His promises, and casting His righteousness behind them. And thus all men every where are serving their lusts and death-bringing inclinations. . . . And if any one should ask why the *Italians* despise the Canon law, and have the Clergy in low esteem, beyond other nations who have been born again in Baptism, the reason has been told:—because . . . the continual wine-bibbing, and more careless living of their teachers, makes them more prone to vice. In which respect, fashion and the example of the greater have now long carried them to such shamelessness, that only by their smooth chin and bare crown, and a slight difference of dress, and from their officiating in Church,—with no small carelessness, making it rather their object to please the world than God,—can you distinguish between them and the laity. Hence the latter despise them in comparison of themselves, and have them in execration [2]."

Rathierus was reproached with lowering himself by seeing personally to the distribution of the corn, wine, and money, which were due to the Subdeacons and other inferior Clergy in his diocese. He replied, that certainly, he *might* do it by his Priests and Deacons, if he could find any who were to be trusted. He says, at the same time, that the lower orders did not complain of the fraud which had been practised on them by the higher; partly, because it gave them an excuse for idleness, and partly, because they looked forward to the time, when they themselves might take the same advantage of others.

[2] Ibid. P. ii., p. 354.

One evil attending the abuse of ecclesiastical patronage he points out pretty plainly:—

" Suppose one of our noble youths sent to the schools, which now-a-days, I trow, is done more as a road to a Bishopric than from a desire to become the soldier of the Lord. . . . He falls into disgraceful licentiousness. After this, he is at length, *without examination*, advanced to the priesthood, though he has become not so much a bigamist as a polygamist [3]."

He gives two extraordinary proofs of the deplorable ignorance of his Clergy:—

" Making inquiry into their faith, I found that very many of them did not even know the Creed, which is believed to have been composed by the Apostles [4]."

He accordingly gave them the three Creeds to learn by heart, and repeat to him at his next visitation [5]. The second instance is yet more surprising:—

" The day before yesterday, some of our people told us that the priests of the diocese of Vicenza, our neighbours, are of opinion that God is corporeal;—being led thereto by that which is read in Scripture: ' The *eyes* of the Lord are over the righteous [6],' &c. . . . And when I was not a little moved by this, I found, O horror, that the same misbelief had taken such hold of the flock committed to me, that when, by way of trial, I preached before the people, and proved by testimonies from Scripture that God is a Spirit, . . . incorporeal, invisible, intangible, imponderable, some even of our priests, alas! murmured and said:

---

[3] Ibid. P. i., p. 352.   [4] Itinerarium, p. 381.
[5] Ibid. and Synod. ad Presbyt., p. 376.
[6] De Quadriges. Serm. i. § xxix., p. 388.

' What shall we do now? Hitherto we have seemed to LETTER know something of God. Now it appears to us that God IX. SECT. IV. is absolutely nothing at all, if He has no head, no eyes, no ears [7],' " &c.

The errors and vices of men, who lived and sinned CONCLUSION. nine hundred years ago, may appear to be a matter of little importance now to any but themselves. Yet when the character of a bygone age in any degree involves that of a religious system, which puts forth an exclusive claim to be the means ordained by God for the recovery of lost mankind, it becomes the duty of every one, who knows the truth, to come forward and maintain it against the perversions of unscrupulous and blind partisans. That a period of grievous darkness and corruption,— especially if the centre (and, as most now hold, the infallible centre) of all authority, in questions of morality and doctrine, is itself compromised,—must offer an overwhelming difficulty to the inquiring Roman Catholic, is obvious upon the least reflection ; and that the pressure of the difficulty has been most deeply felt may be inferred from the extraordinary efforts, which have been made of late, to induce us to reverse the unanimous verdict of our forefathers upon many periods and passages of ecclesiastical history. Those efforts, I am sorry to find, have been attended with some success, or you would not have challenged me, with so much confidence, to a

[7] Ibid. § xxx.

reconsideration of the evidence against the Popes of the tenth century. I am conscious that in my remarks on this subject, and indeed upon some others, in former Letters, I have occasionally betrayed my conviction, that the misstatements of certain authors cannot have been always the involuntary effect of ignorance, or inadvertence, or of the innocent prejudices of education. It is right, therefore, that I should once more assure you that I do not confound you, and those who, like you, have unwittingly drawn their opinions from unreliable sources, with the deliberate falsifiers of history. I trust that I have never even appeared to forget the distinction, and that nothing, either in the tone, or spirit, in which I have written, has tended to create a prejudice against the facts, which it has been my part to set before you. There are some who will blame me for too little warmth, and for the neglect of many exciting topics. I shall be content, if I have not violated charity, and given unnecessary pain. I am aware, also, that much more might have been said upon those subjects which have been discussed. I do not pretend, or wish, to supersede inquiry on your part. My object has been rather to point out by what methods, and in what spirit, it ought to be pursued. Let it suffice, then, if I have shown where the truth may be, and where it cannot be found. A clue, at least, has been put into your hands. Use it, in God's name; and, with His blessing, it will extricate you from the maze, in which, not wholly LETTER
IX.
CONCL. blind, if I infer truly, to the embarrassments of your position, you are now wandering and lost.   Dare to know all, and you will soon know it.   Your eyes will be opened, as you gaze fearlessly on the troubled vision of the past, and it will be given you to behold that creed and polity, which you now deem in every part divine, originating, so far as they are peculiar to Rome, in the superstitions of a period, of which the bold neglect of every law of God was as conspicuous a feature as the perversion of His Gospel.   As you proceed to trace their growth, you will observe error after error acquiring shape and gathering strength, under the shelter of political and personal interests, from the incentives of ambition, of party spirit, and of avarice; and you will see their final triumph over "the faith once delivered," through means of an appeal, commenced in fraud, and continued in ignorance, to the supposititious authority of Saints and Fathers, to falsified Councils and forged Decretals, to things which have had no existence, and events which have never taken place.

I am, &c.

THE END.

GILBERT AND RIVINGTON, PRINTERS, ST. JOHN'S SQUARE, LONDON.

Lightning Source UK Ltd.
Milton Keynes UK
UKOW06f2326170316

270434UK00014B/328/P